SPEECH IN ACTION

Karl F. Robinson

Charlotte Lee

Scott, Foresman and Company

SPEECH IN ACTION

Karl F. Robinson
Presidential Professor and Co-ordinator of
Graduate Studies in Speech and Drama
California State College at Hayward
Hayward, California

Charlotte Lee
Professor of Interpretation
Northwestern University
Evanston, Illinois

CONSULTANTS

Margaret A. Nielsen
Speech and Drama Director
North High School
Omaha, Nebraska

William R. Haushalter
Assistant Professor of Education
Western Michigan University
Kalamazoo, Michigan

Wanda Mitchell
Chairman, Speech Arts Department
Evanston Township High School
Evanston, Illinois

Robert J. Phillips
Chairman, Department of Language Arts
Thornton Fractional Township High School
Lansing, Illinois

Goddard W. Winterbottom
Former Director of Theater
Briarcliff College
Briarcliff Manor, New York

Table of Contents

Part I

Part II

PART I

CHAPTER 1

SPEECH
IN
YOUR
WORLD

When Demosthenes was asked what was the first part of oratory,

he answered, "Action"; and which was second, he replied, "Action";

and which was the third, he still answered, "Action."

Language is our chief means of communication. Whether we try to convey a simple want such as "I'm hungry," or a profound religious, philosophical, or scientific idea, we have to use language. There is always a purpose to communication. We are trying to convey something to somebody else—our ideas, our aims, our wants, our values, our very personalities. We are trying to influence, inform, entertain, inspire, persuade, or move someone to action.

We speak more often than we write because speech is fast, immediate, recordable, and almost limitless in its impact on people and the world around us. In an age of electronic devices that instantly transmit speech to all parts of the world, the spoken word is the main means of communication in our time. It enters all levels of our lives.

The result of effective speech is action. There is a speaker and a listener, and the result of the speech is action. David Lloyd George said, "The finest eloquence is that which gets things done; the worst is that which delays them." If your purpose is to entertain, the result is laughter. If your purpose is to instruct, the result should be that the audience can act with greater knowledge in the future. A child makes known his wants to his parents, and his needs are fulfilled. The President on a nation-wide hookup tries to persuade the nation to adopt his farm policy, so that he will receive legislative support. In all cases action of some kind is the result of effective speech.

All of us learned certain basic speech skills from our parents. But this was only a beginning. From the first day of school your teachers have been correcting and perfecting your oral communication methods. Speech skills must be learned. Mastery of these skills gives you powerful tools to help achieve your purposes. It provides you with the means to influence the actions of others and the environment in which you live.

It is important to realize that all you know and are—your intelligence, sincerity, honesty, sense of humor, your most serious ideas—are revealed in your speech. What kind of person you are in the eyes of others depends on how effectively you communicate. Test yourself:

Is your speaking governed by clear, definite purposes?
By speaking, can you secure the action you wish from others?
Do you have the speech skills to handle the situations you face?
Does your speech sound like that of an educated person?
Can you, by oral communication, make friends easily and get along with all types of people?
Can you make your knowledge function in human relationships by the effectiveness of your speech skills?
Do you have confidence and security in all speaking situations?
Are you a courteous and interested listener?

If your answers are often a "No" or an uncertain "Yes," you are beginning to realize that effective speech is essential to your development as a person. You are aware of the extent your speech is *you*—that it is a vital part of your personality.

Consider for a moment the impression people make on you when you first meet them. You admire a young woman. Her face and figure are striking, her dress in the best taste. Yet the whole illusion disappears when she says, "Hey, Mame, whenner we gonna eat?" A scientist, re-

Members of the Peace Corps in many parts of the world use speech to further mutual understanding.

nowned for his research in nuclear physics, appears before your science club, but he rarely glances at the audience as he reads monotonously and timidly from a sheaf of notes. His knowledge is not transferred to you. A poet, whose work you enjoy, comes to your town to read his own poetry. He does it so badly that you lose all interest in his work.

These examples show that your judgment of a person is never complete until he speaks. It includes not only what he says, but how he says it—his voice, his diction, and his manner. Aristotle, the great classic writer and teacher of speech, pointed out that a speaker's personality reveals his intelligence, character, and good will.

Have you considered how you sound? Your thinking—that is, your inner speech—is revealed when you speak. In fact, many things are revealed when you speak before an audience—including some you may not be aware of expressing. Your speech is you!

Effective speaking and listening are important social assets—the means of strengthening your human relationships. Smoothness and glibness of tongue are not what you strive for—people quickly detect a phony. If your whole manner of speaking is friendly, if you are honest, direct, and sincere, your listeners will react by becoming your friends.

People will like you because of the quality and depth of your ideas. Some of your talk will be light and humorous. It should be; there is a

4

time and a place for it. But today you are challenged by serious problems. You will try to solve some of them. Educational programs are accelerated; you are learning more each day. You can make yourself worth listening to by acting on your knowledge. You can earn respect for your ideas, and for yourself as a person, by availing yourself of these opportunities.

YOUR SUCCESS IN LIFE DEPENDS ON EFFECTIVE SPEECH AND LISTENING

The success of democracy rests on the ability of each citizen to participate in government. The responsibility of a good citizen goes beyond going to the polls once a year. He discusses vital issues, informs and influences others regarding his views, and sees that action is taken by the appropriate governmental bodies. The American Civil Liberties Union has stated that liberty is always unfinished business. To be denied freedom of speech is an intolerable violation of the rights of free men. To be denied the opportunity to learn to speak and listen effectively is equally intolerable. Failure to learn such skills means failure in discharging the obligations of a citizen, and such failures impair the efficiency of democracy. Therefore, as an individual citizen, you have the responsibility to learn to speak and listen effectively, in order to participate competently in your government. You learn to speak so your listeners will act together to achieve a good purpose.

Not long ago a large Middle Western high school made a survey of its graduates over a ten-year period. Among the questions asked was "What, that you have found essential to your success, did your high school fail to provide?" Over 90 per cent of the alumni, most of whom had entered business and the professions, answered, "High school did not provide adequate training in speaking."

In another study, 1088 persons were interviewed regarding the importance of speech training. These included students, unskilled laborers, housewives, secretaries, technicians, accountants, sales clerks, managers, teachers, and professional men. Of these, 75 per cent said that skillful use of speech was important or essential to their work. At the executive level 90 per cent indicated that speech was especially important to them. Work in speech skills plays a major rôle in most business and industrial training programs for administrative personnel.

5

Successful teamwork is a matter of good communications.

This is only a small portion of the mounting evidence that oral communication is essential for leadership in business, industry, and the professions. If you cannot persuade people to act, you will never attain leadership or success.

Because teaching depends on the ability to use all speech skills, speech proficiency is required in most teacher-training programs. The usual requisites include tests in personal speech habits, and the development of oral reading, speaking, discussion, and interviewing skills. These are basic skills, but other, more specialized, skills are needed for success. The purpose of these speech skills is to inform.

Theological seminaries of all faiths stress speech skills as basic tools in the ministry. Certainly congregations the country over welcome this effort to ensure an effective preaching ministry. Here the purpose of the speech is to inspire, to inform, and to persuade.

For years, courses in informative and argumentative speaking have been part of prelegal training. Courtroom work and public appearances demand that the speaker be able to convince the judge or jury.

Effective speech is a means to better community living. You may be asked to serve on a committee or take part in the affairs of local government. Good speech helps you assume your share of the work of your community with greater confidence, ease, and efficiency.

It is not necessary to wait until you are an adult to use skills in speech. Most school leaders have reasonable competence in speech in addition to their talents in other fields. Consider your student council, class officers, club leaders, and outstanding debaters. All of these influence the student body, in part because they speak effectively and listen well. Often the only difference between the leader and the follower is the ability of the one to make his ideas known and respected through speech.

Finally, speech can add a new dimension to your life. You have seen and heard shows on TV or radio, but do you know what goes on before the production? During this course you will take part in rehearsals and learn some mechanics of TV and radio production. Producing or acting in plays may be particularly appealing to you and give you a lifelong interest. At the very least you will become an educated and sympathetic member of the audience. Class discussions and debates will present topics and issues of contemporary importance. Through them you can learn to find your place in the community and in the nation. You will learn to enjoy great literature because you have heard it properly interpreted. These and other activities give you new and varied experiences that can provide rewarding and lasting interests.

Training in speaking and listening offered in this course meets some fundamental needs in your education; it (1) improves your personal speech habits, (2) develops attitudes of confidence and security toward all types of oral communications situations, (3) provides the essential information and theory you need to know about speech skills, (4) helps you master the performance of the *basic* skills of speaking, listening, and reading aloud, (5) assists you to become more proficient in the specialized forms of discussion, parliamentary procedure, debate, and drama, (6) acquaints you with the areas of radio and television.

This text and your speech course offer the means to develop a natural, effective manner of speech, appropriate to the different situations you meet. The skills you achieve are permanent; no one can take them away from you; they are yours for your lifetime.

CHAPTER 2

ESSENTIALS
OF
SPEAKING

*Half the world is composed of people who have
something to say and can't, and the other half who have
nothing to say and keep on saying it.*

—ROBERT FROST

The study of speaking techniques is no recent fad in education. Speech is man's oldest and most important communication tool, and training in speech dates from man's earliest civilizations. The Egyptians mention it as essential in the education of their leaders. Greek and Roman writings on speech are the foundations for what we teach today.

In Greece, Plato, Aristotle, Corax, and Tisias wrote about speech skills (rhetoric) hundreds of years before Christ. Speech training was a necessary part of the education that prepared Greek men for a place in the democracy of the Athenians. In their lives, speaking had significant, practical purposes. Men had to be able to present their own cases in the courts of the day, and juries composed of other citizens voted on the basis of a man's skill in pleading his case. A citizen participated in political discussions and appeared at public ceremonials to speak in praise or blame of the leaders of the state. He knew that success in meeting his obligations, in getting the actions he wanted, depended upon his proficiency in speaking. Therefore, it was imperative for him to learn speech skills, or rhetoric.

Aristotle defined rhetoric as "the discovery of the available means of persuasion." About 322 B.C. he wrote *Rhetoric,* a book in which he analyzed the speaker, the audience, and the speech. Both Aristotle and Plato, his teacher, were interested in *oral,* not written, communication, and were concerned with the truth and ethical standards of its teaching and practice. They believed that a speaker must have integrity and base his argument on a thorough knowledge of the facts. He should never distort the truth or use verbal trickery to prove his point.

Aristotle and Plato opposed the "practical" teachers of the day, known as Sophists, whose school of speech had been started earlier (460 B.C.) by Corax and Tisias. These men were not interested in conscientious attention to truth or ethics. They taught tactics that would win an argument, whether they were based on knowledge and truth or not. They developed techniques of bombast, glibness, and mental blitzkrieg—what is called a "snow job" in today's slang.

The techniques of the Sophists are sometimes used in political debate, law, and sales promotion. We have the same arguments today about ethics in persuasion and public speaking that existed two thousand years ago; and we have among our teachers Platos and Aristotles, as well as Sophists.

In Rome the two great names in speech were Cicero (106-43 B.C.) and Quintilian (35-95 A.D.). Cicero, a consul of Rome, was a renowned political orator and writer. His skill as a speaker had a profound effect on Roman political action during his lifetime. His works *On Oratory* and *The Orator* are still studied in colleges. Quintilian was the first great writer on the teaching of speech. In training students, he emphasized the development of personal qualities and stressed individual work as an aid to improvement. "An orator," said Quintilian, "is a good man trained in speaking."

It is significant that wherever distinctive growth of speech training has occurred it has been closely associated with democracy. Through speech, freemen have always indicated the purposes in their lives and have obtained the action they wanted. Tyranny and dictatorship always suppress speech education as a threat to their survival. Under such governments little progress is made in teaching men to think clearly, to find the truth, and to express it freely and effectively. In totalitarian countries, all training is dominated by a state-controlled propaganda machine that captures the minds of men to serve the ends of party leaders.

Other divisions of speech also have distinguished origins. Drama began in ancient tribal ceremonies. The earliest form is found in the Greek theater, centering around the Dionysian Festival about 500 years before Christ. Early ideas about play writing, acting, production, and the use of masks and costumes are found in *Antigone, Medea, Oedipus the King, The Trojan Women, The Birds,* and other Greek dramas.

Various countries have made contributions to the theater as we know it in the twentieth century. Your high-school program is part of an expanding educational theater that produces over 75,000 plays each year.

The oral interpetation of literature predates the theater. In Greece, poets chose skilled performers to read their works at competitions and drama festivals. Choric interpretation was first used in Greek plays as a means of expressing, through the voices and actions of the chorus, ideas and emotions important to the plot. Often the chorus expressed the ideas of the playwright and served as a commentary on the acting. The use of choric interpretation in modern times is really not the discovery of a new art, but a revival of a very interesting old one.

Radio, television, and films are of recent origin because of their dependence on technical invention. Actually they provide electronic and photographic means for transmitting the basic forms of speech and drama that were previously developed. They are, of course, responsible for the development of some new techiques adapted to their needs.

Speech skills do not apply only to public life. You will find them of great use in your private life. You know from experience that you are more likely to be permitted the use of the family car if you want it for a good purpose and ask for it politely, than if you demand it without explaining why you want it. You may want it for the same reason in both instances. But in the former your oral communication was good; in the latter instance you simply failed to communicate. There are many ways to ask a girl for a date or the boss for a raise, or to promote an interscholastic basketball game. The effective way is the way that results in the response you want, that leads to the right action. The important word here is "right." Do not be misled into the folly of the Sophists. Honesty and sin-

SPEECH ACTS
IN DEMOCRACY

In town meetings such as this one the individual citizen's voice is heard. Residents of the town participate directly in their government, and take part in debate and discussion with one another and with their elected officials.

At state and national party conventions such as these, party members meet to choose the candidates who will represent them in elections. They also choose the party's platform—the issues on which their candidates will campaign.

Candidates campaign for election: each candidate tries to reach as many of the people as he possibly can. On the street, on public transportation, on radio and TV, at organized meetings and rallies, the candidate uses speech to reach the voters.

It is the duty of every citizen to listen to the candidates, consider their statements and records, and indicate his choice at the polls. The votes, whether registered by machine or by paper ballots, are counted; the candidate who is the choice of the majority is elected.

14

Votes are tallied, results are announced, the candidate is elected. He then uses speech in administering his office—to persuade voters to support his programs, and legislators to adopt them, to define policy—to communicate in democracy.

cerity cannot be faked. If you do not believe what you are saying, listeners will not believe you and you will not gain the response you want. People, either individually or in groups, are rarely deceived for very long.

WHAT MODERN SPEECH TRAINING IS ABOUT

Speech is a learned activity. From the time you first learned to talk you have been building habits of oral communication. Some of these are assets—you should keep them. Others are liabilities—these you should change. A desire to improve and some hard work will help you establish effective speech habits.

All forms of speech activity employ audible symbols (sounds) and visible symbols (actions) that you (as a speaker, reader, or actor) produce to convey your ideas and feelings to one or more persons (listeners, observers, audience) in order to gain a desired response from them.

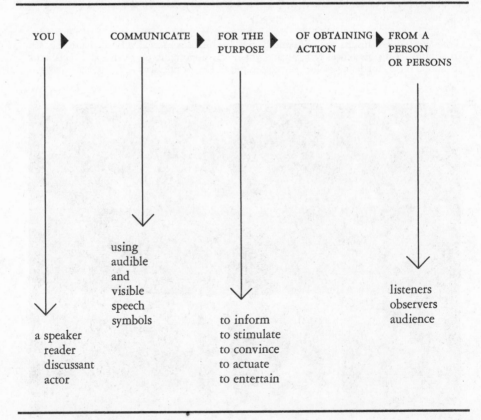

YOU ▶ COMMUNICATE ▶ FOR THE PURPOSE ▶ OF OBTAINING ACTION ▶ FROM A PERSON OR PERSONS

using
audible
and
visible
speech
symbols

a speaker
reader
discussant
actor

to inform
to stimulate
to convince
to actuate
to entertain

listeners
observers
audience

The areas of speech activity which you will study include fundamentals, or basic elements; informal speaking; public speaking; discussion; debate and parliamentary procedure; interpretation; drama and theater; radio and television. You will find it helpful to have a brief description of each area.

Fundamentals are the basic elements of all forms of speech. In this text they relate to both speaking and reading aloud (interpretation). They include attitude or emotional adjustment; personality; ability to organize ideas, information, and content; speech production, voice, articulation and pronunciation; language; materials for oral listening.

Informal speaking treats speech of an individual in conversation, interviewing, and telephoning.

Public speaking deals with an individual speaking before an audience. It covers the preparation and delivery of speeches.

Discussion is a group activity. It includes the philosophy of group thinking, problem solving, and techniques in preparation and leadership of discussions. It is related to debate and other forms of argumentation.

Debate and parliamentary procedure are two special situations requiring exact knowledge. The nature of argumentation, propositions, analysis, evidence, and reasoning, and methods of interscholastic debate are fully developed. The rules of parliamentary procedure, essential for good citizenship, are also included.

Interpretation covers the selection and analysis of prose, drama, and poetry, with attention given to the techniques which must be developed to recreate literature for an audience.

The drama and theater section consists of practical suggestions on the selection, directing, acting, scenery, lighting, properties, costuming, production, house and publicity management, etc., of plays.

Radio and television depend on your school and local facilities, your interests, and those of your teacher. Your study may range from evaluation of current programs to a thorough coverage of the history, pattern, and methods of broadcasting.

Basic Principles in Speaking

EFFECTIVE SPEAKING IS FOR COMMUNICATION, NOT EXHIBITION.

Some people have the idea that they must put on a show when they talk to an audience. They believe that a few funny stories or gimmicks will captivate the audience and guarantee success. Others believe that fancy language, smoothness, and a resonant voice will impress listeners. Both assumptions are incorrect. These tricks will never persuade your listeners to act in behalf of a cause or a principle. Remember, your basic function is to *communicate* your ideas, information, and feelings so that you can gain the response you desire from the audience. Artificiality, or putting on an act, has no place in the proper conception of the rôle of a speaker.

EFFECTIVE SPEAKING DEPENDS ON THE INTELLIGENCE, KNOWLEDGE, CHARACTER, AND GOOD WILL OF THE SPEAKER.

Since speaking effectively is *not* a show, you should know the qualities that make a speaker a good communicator. He must be reasonably intelligent if the audience is to respect him. He must have a thorough knowledge of his subject; too often speakers are evaluated by these devastating words, "He talked a lot, but he didn't say anything!" There is no substitute for *content* (knowledge) in a speech. Honesty and sincerity are also among a speaker's greatest assets. His rating by the audience depends on its belief that he is telling the truth. His evidence of friendliness, high motives, and solid values establishes good will with his audience.

EFFECTIVE SPEAKING IS PURPOSEFUL AND WELL ORGANIZED.

In addition to knowledge and sincerity, the speaker must have a purpose; his speech must have a *direction* or *target*. The purpose provides this. Clear and careful organization of your knowledge and content with respect to your purpose, or intention, is essential. Lyman Beecher said, "Eloquence is logic on fire." Your purpose controls the manner in which you use and organize your knowledge. It determines how you point up your ideas as you deliver your talk.

EFFECTIVE SPEAKING GETS THE DESIRED RESPONSE FROM THE AUDIENCE.

Achieving your purpose is the ultimate test of your effectiveness as a speaker. If the audience *understands* your explanation, *accepts* your ideas, and *does* what you propose, you have succeeded in winning the response you desire.

It is said of Cicero that once, being complimented by a flatterer, he replied, "When Cicero finishes his talk the people say, 'How well Cicero spoke!' but when Demosthenes addressed the Athenians, the people rose and with one voice shouted, 'Let us go and fight the Macedonians!'" Cicero, because he could not move his listeners to action, considered his speech a failure.

EFFECTIVE SPEAKING COMMANDS AND HOLDS ATTENTION.

Although you may have knowledge, sincerity, purpose, and clear organization, you have nothing unless your material and delivery command and hold the attention of the audience. Your choice of ideas, examples, and illustrations, along with their arrangement, contribute to keeping your audience interested. You will never achieve your purpose unless you keep your audience listening to you.

EFFECTIVE SPEAKING DEPENDS ON ANIMATED DELIVERY IN VOICE AND IN ACTION.

What you say will be of no importance unless you are able to convey it to your listeners so that they will understand it. In speaking, there is no substitute for constructive, appropriate bodily action and a direct, lively vocal delivery.

EFFECTIVE SPEAKING IS APPROPRIATE TO THE SPEAKER, THE OCCASION, AND THE AUDIENCE.

Although you may have prepared well and delivered your talk with suitable enthusiasm and vigor, you must still check your performance with respect to good taste and appropriateness. Remember how Fidel Castro and Nikita Khrushchev shocked and alienated their audiences when they spoke to the United Nations in New York in 1960. In one instance Khrushchev was cut off the public-address system because of his offensiveness and a violation of the rules of debate. Castro put his audience to sleep with a four-hour tirade. Much of your effectiveness comes from your ability to adapt the subject, materials, language, and delivery to your audience and the occasion. Careful planning and tactful presentation will help you win your audience.

CHAPTER 3

LISTENING:
THE
COUNTERPART
OF
SPEAKING

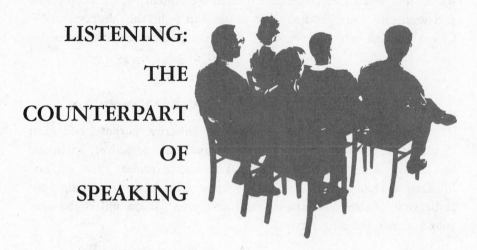

Give us grace to listen well
—PALM SUNDAY PRAYER of JOHN KEBLE

The art of good listening is a skill you develop, just as you train yourself to be a good speaker. It is a mistake to assume that just because a person hears, he is listening. Hearing is the physical ability to receive sounds, listening is interpreting them—understanding the message the words are intended to convey.

Communication is a two-way process involving a communicator and a receiver. No study of speech is complete without learning the second part of the process, listening. It is only because other people listen that what you say is communicated. Without a listener there would be no response to your spoken language. Your purpose would not be accomplished, your wants and desires would not be satisfied. Ambrose Bierce, in *The Devil's Dictionary,* defined a bore as a person who talks when we wish he'd listen.

We have all met people who never bother to listen to anyone else. They are never popular.

Of the four language arts—writing, reading, speaking, and listening—research shows we spend more time in listening than in any of the others.

20

We listen for entertainment and information. Notice how carefully you listen when a friend tells you a joke, so that you will not miss the "point," or when someone tells you about a good mechanic or hairdresser. In the first case you listen for amusement, in the second for information. A dramatist, Wilson Mizner, said that a good listener is not only popular everywhere, but after a while he knows something.

ARE WE EFFICIENT LISTENERS?

In spite of the amount of time we spend listening, most people are not particularly good at it. Research studies show that people in general are only about 25 per cent efficient (they miss 75 per cent of the content); high school students retain 28 per cent of what they hear in class, and college students 50 per cent. Yet, most of these people *think* they listen carefully.

WHAT IS EFFICIENT LISTENING?

Efficient listening is the fast, accurate interpretation and comprehension of what has been said. It sounds simple. But it isn't always easy. Because many people do not enunciate clearly, you may misunderstand them. Most people do not use simple, clear English. You have to pay strict attention to get the "point," or meaning of what they are saying.

Today our survival may depend on our skill as listeners. To be effective we must stay "tuned in." Comprehension of words spoken face-to-face, over the telephone, on radio, television, and in films, may determine our destiny as people. Walter Lippmann wrote that "while the right to talk may be the beginning of freedom, the necessity of listening is what makes the right important." Wrong meanings given to words by those who listen could be the catalyst to plunge us into open conflict and perhaps destroy us.

THE PURPOSES OF LISTENING

The Greek slave, Epictetus, who taught in Rome in 90 A.D. said, "Nature has given to men one tongue, but two ears, that we may hear from others twice as much as we speak." You listen for a variety of purposes.

You Listen to Recognize and Understand Speech Sounds

This means that you identify sounds correctly and relate them to words you understand.

You listen to, and give meaning to, all aspects of inflection: emphasis, changes in voice quality, volume, pitch, speed, etc. This is the basic purpose of listening, and the foundation for all of the meanings you obtain from the spoken language.

You Listen to Get Information

This is the heart of listening and learning depends upon it. Lectures, discussions, newscasts—all bring you new ideas, facts, and points of view. Your whole life is a continuing learning process.

Your increasing store of information, as a student, or on the job, or as a responsible citizen and member of your community, depends on your mastering this listening skill.

You Listen for Entertainment

A large proportion of your enjoyment is obtained by listening—your pleasure from music, drama, radio, television, and scores of other things depends on your ability to listen. Even social conversation is dependent on listening.

You Listen to Evaluate Ideas (to Make an Intellectual Judgment)

Your reaction to what you hear goes beyond enjoyment. Whenever you agree, disagree, or are undecided about an idea, you are engaging in *critical* listening, and your reaction is the result of your own *intellectual* judgment.

This critical function is most important to you as a person, a voter, a student, and a consumer.

You Listen to Appreciate (to Make an Artistic Judgment)

This goes beyond enjoyment in that you add *your opinion or judgment* on the beauty, artistic worth or appropriateness of what you hear. If you listen to a jazz record as you dance to it, you listen only to enjoy. But, if you say "That recording has the best sax solo I have ever heard," you have listened to appreciate.

22

WHY WE LISTEN INEFFECTIVELY

Because most people assume that anybody who does not have a physical hearing defect must be able to listen, there is little formal training in the field. Most of us do not realize that good listening is a skill. Nichols[1] classifies the causes of ineffective listening as (1) false assumptions about listening and (2) bad listening habits.

False Assumptions

Many assume that "bright" people listen well and "dull" ones listen poorly. The facts show that poor listeners are not always stupid.

Another assumption is that poor listeners have poor hearing. Statistics prove only 6 per cent of students have a hearing defect.

A third assumption is that training in listening is unnecessary because everyone gets so much practice at it. But practice is no guarantee of efficiency, especially if you are practicing the wrong things. Finally, it is assumed that learning to read will automatically teach us to listen.

[1]Ralph Nichols and Leonard Stevens. *Are You Listening?* New York: McGraw-Hill (1957), 10-14.

There are differences between reading and listening that negate this: reading is done alone, listening is a social activity. A listener must adjust to the pace of the speakers; a reader can set his own pace. The listener hears the words only once; the reader can go back and re-read.

Bad Listening Habits

Without instruction to improve listening skills many students develop bad habits they retain through life. Unless these habits are changed there will be no gain in listening ability. Nichols[1] report of research at the University of Minnesota lists six bad listening habits that are nearly universal. Do any of them apply to you?

FAKING ATTENTION. In this the student goes through all of the outward behavior of really listening. He assumes the posture of listening, he looks at the speaker, perhaps nods understandingly now and then. But his mind is far away. He is thinking his own thoughts. John Ruskin, the English critic, said, "When a man is wrapped up in himself he makes a pretty small package." He fools only himself. What he misses, he will never recover.

"I-GET-THE-FACTS" LISTENING. This bad habit is developed because the student believes he must get all of the facts. The method consists of trying to memorize in order *every* fact the speaker presents. The student generally bogs down when the facts pile up, and suddenly discovers he has missed the *point* of the speech. Memorizing facts is not the way to listen. Ideas are the important thing; facts merely support them.

AVOIDING DIFFICULT LISTENING. Often the first impression of a lecture or a speech is that understanding the material is going to require some effort and concentration. After a few words the student concludes that "It's too hard to listen to. I'll pass it up." The result is a decreasing efficiency in all listening, because the student did not try hard enough.

---

[1]Nichols and Stevens. 104-112.

Theodore Roethke, educator and author, addresses students. Though the address is informal, the audience gives its undivided attention to the speaker.

QUICK REJECTION OF A SUBJECT AS UNINTERESTING. After a short period of listening, this student comes to the conclusion that the subject is boring. This becomes his excuse for not listening. Both the idea and the information are lost. Never stop listening prematurely; stay with the speaker and you may get a pleasant surprise.

CRITICIZING DELIVERY AND PHYSICAL APPEARANCE. Faced with a speaker he does not want to listen to, the student finds fault with his dress, his vocal pitch, the size of his nose, the way he combs his hair. These dislikes become the reason for not listening to his ideas.

Dress, voice, appearance and mannerisms are important, and as a speaker you should be aware of their influence. But they are not alibis for failure to listen to the content of a speech. Never use such criticisms as an excuse for not listening.

YIELDING EASILY TO DISTRACTIONS. Scarcely any speaking situation is free from distractions. In school, a plane roars overhead, students are noisy in the hall outside—all these and more can occur when you are trying to listen. A good listener will learn to tolerate these things. The bad listener uses minor distractions as an excuse to stop listening and say to himself, "I can't hear the speaker and I'm not going to try."

Analyze yourself and see whether any of these bad habits decrease your skill as a listener.

Guides to Good Listening

Nichols,[1] from his research and experience, provides ten guides to help you improve your listening efficiency.

1. FIND SUBJECTS OF INTEREST. You increase your effectiveness if you are interested in what is being discussed. As you listen to a speech, be alert for facts that will be useful to you, information to add to your knowledge about things you are already interested in. Trying to discover such items will make you a better listener.

2. JUDGE CONTENT, NOT DELIVERY. Focus your attention on ideas and content. "Listen with your own experience" to what the speaker says, never to his manner of saying it. Raise your level of understanding and you will be a more effective listener.

3. HEAR THE MAN OUT. This is an antidote: for those who prematurely reject a subject; for getting too excited over a minor point to understand the main idea; or for being hurt if a pet idea is attacked. Learn to defer your judgment until you hear the end of the speech.

4. LISTEN FOR IDEAS. As we have said, good listeners focus on ideas; they don't try to memorize facts. It is better to study the language in which central ideas are expressed, recognize the way in which the speaker connects his ideas, and note his summary of the key themes. Concentration on ideas will improve your listening skill.

5. BE FLEXIBLE. In recording what you hear, remember that notetaking is not outlining. Some speeches cannot be outlined; others demand a shift in method in order to record important facts and principles. Adjust your method to the needs of the talk. Be flexible and adaptable.

6. WORK AT LISTENING. Good listening takes energy. Help yourself by investing your energy wisely and efficiently. Give conscious attention through your posture, eyes, and reactions. This will help both you and the speaker.

7. RESIST DISTRACTIONS. Adjust quickly to the "normal" distractions in the listening-speaking situation. Remember this is the noisy century—expect distractions, live with them, learn to listen in spite of them.

8. EXERCISE YOUR MIND. It is probable that you have rarely been challenged by speeches that spurred you to use all your faculties. Arnold Toynbee, one of our most important historians, says all civilization is based on challenge and response. Your response to a challenge of this sort may help decide the type of person you become. To increase your skill try listening to some difficult lectures. You may develop a real enthusiasm for them.

9. KEEP AN OPEN MIND. Your convictions, emotions, and prejudices are all potential blocks to effective listening. Too often we stop listening when a word, phrase, or idea offends us. Don't shut your mind—let communication reach you freely at all times.

10. CAPITALIZE ON "THOUGHT SPEED." Most people speak about 125 words per minute, but they can think at least four times that fast. Conse-

---

[1]Quoted by permission of Tangley Oaks Educational Center, publishers, Lake Bluff, Illinois, from the reprint of "Ten Guides to Good Listening" from the *American Educator Encyclopedia.*

A man who knows the value of listening looks and is attentive and thoughtful. A good listener is easy to talk to. This is Dr. Arthur Kornberg, biochemist and co-winner of the Nobel prize in medicine in 1959.

quently you can be "way ahead" of the speaker. What do you do with this extra thinking time? Do you use your thought speed to advantage in the following ways: (1) anticipate what the speaker is going to say; (2) summarize what has been said; (3) weigh the speaker's material by raising questions, or check it for accuracy in your mind; (4) listen between the lines—discover things not expressed in words, but implied by inflection, or gesture.

HOW TO LISTEN

During this course you will listen to many talks. Your listening will be easier and more effective if, in addition to following the suggestions above, you know that a speech should follow a basic pattern.

You will hear speeches that (1) give information, (2) try to convince you to accept a given argument, (3) are designed to entertain, and (4) attempt to rouse you to action. All are similar in their basic plan. This plan has been in existence for over two thousand years, and is still in use.

The trained speaker uses an *introduction* to gain your attention and arouse your interest. He tries to establish contact so you and he are on a common ground. Listen for the way a speaker uses this short section of his talk—often it will be a startling statement, a humorous story, a quotation, or some similar attention-getter.

Next he reveals his central idea in the main part of the talk, the *body*. Some writers call this central idea the thesis of the talk. It is short, often simply a topic sentence, or it may be in the form of a question.

The body, which is the longest section, develops the central idea and divides it into sub-topics. Listen for these and note what they are specifically. Be sure to note the supporting evidence, examples, or illustrations which the speaker uses to prove his main points.

Finally, there is the *conclusion*. Listen for the summary, short appeal, or suggestion for action. In the conclusion you have your last opportunity to check the central idea against the facts.

When you understand the elements comprising a speech, and use the guides to good listening to develop your skill as a listener, you will find your enjoyment increasing and your studies easier because you will have learned to grasp the important "point" the speaker or teacher was trying to make.

ACTIVITIES

1. Take an inventory of your listening and speaking habits. Do you speak more than you listen? If so, attempt to bring the situation into closer balance.

2. Get a standardized test of listening, or ask your teacher to procure one. Take the test and compare your listening score with that of others. One good one is the *Brown-Carlsen Listening Comprehension Test,* Harcourt, Brace & World, Inc., New York, N.Y.

3. Test yourself by checking these items from the *Communication Skills Syllabus,* Michigan State University:
   Do you have a majority of checks in the "Good Listener" column? Which can you improve?

CHARACTERISTICS OF GOOD AND POOR LISTENER

Good Listener	Poor Listener

A. Have you the following attitudes toward the listening situation:

1. Do you want to listen?	1. Are you indifferent or bored?
2. Do you find a personal reason for listening?	2. Are you not clear about why you are listening?
3. Are you willing to do your part in the listening situation?	3. Do you expect the speaker to do all the work?

B. Have you the following attitudes toward the speech:

4. Are you receptive and open-minded?	4. Are you suspicious or antagonistic?
5. Are you aware of the effect of your own prejudices?	5. Are you unaware of the effect of your own prejudices?
6. Are you willing to hear the speaker out?	6. Do you stop listening at the slightest provocation?
7. Do you make understanding your most important objective?	7. Do you make agreement or disagreement your most important objective?

C. Do you have the following attitudes toward the speaker:

8. Are you friendly and sympathetic?	8. Are you indifferent or hostile?
9. Do you respect the speaker as a person?	9. Are you critical or suspicious?

D. Do you prepare to listen in the following ways:

10. Try to learn about the subject.	10. Aren't interested in subject, speaker, or situation.
11. Sit where you can see and hear.	11. Sit where you can avoid listening or leave first.
12. Try to eliminate distractions in your environment.	12. Welcome distractions in your environment.
13. Are you ready to take notes when appropriate?	13. Can't decide when and how to take notes.

E. Do you do the following things while listening:

14. Relate what the speaker is saying to past knowledge and experience.	14. Think of other things during your extra thinking time.
15. Look in the direction of the speaker.	15. Doodle, look out the window, or watch other listeners.
16. Evaluate the speech as you hear and understand it.	16. Pre-judge the speech on the basis of speaker, subject, or situation.

17. Are you attentive, accepting your responsibility as a listener?

18. Eliminate or quickly adjust to distractions in yourself.

19. Takes notes suitable for your purpose.

20. Try to reconstruct the organizational pattern of the speech.

21. Try to locate the central idea.

22. Consider relationship between points made by the speaker.

23. Recognize the difference between facts and opinions.

24. Recognize the purpose of illustrations and examples used.

25. Do you understand the figurative language used—analogy, metaphor, etc.?

26. Select important details for retention.

27. Are you aware of implications and inferences in what is said?

28. Can you distinguish relevant from irrelevant material in the speech?

29. Determining new word meanings by reference to context.

30. Are you aware of loaded words, emotional slanting, and semantics errors?

31. Try to relate what is said to yourself and your interests.

32. Overlook any inadequacies in speech content and delivery.

33. Recognize use of devices such as: introduction, transition, repetition, summary, conclusion.

---

17. Fake attention or expect the speaker to command your attention.

18. Dwell on the distractions within yourself or create them.

19. Take the same kind of notes in all situations.

20. Are you unaware of the structure or organization of the speech?

21. Listen for facts.

22. Are you unaware of or unwilling to look for relationships between points?

23. Confuse facts and opinions.

24. Are you confused and diverted by examples and illustrations?

25. Do you fail to understand the figures of speech used?

26. Try to remember all details.

27. Are you unaware of implications in a speech?

28. Do you fail to discover which material is relevant and which is irrelevant?

29. Ignore new words in the speech or try to recall dictionary definitions.

30. Are you swayed unknowingly by emotional language and propaganda appeals?

31. Do you get nothing "out of the speech" which is helpful to yourself?

32. Do you dwell on inadequacies in content and delivery?

33. Do you fail to recognize compositional and structural devices?

34. Recognize the effect of emphasis, inflection, rate, volume, gesture, and quality on meaning.

34. Are you unaware of influence factors of delivery on meaning?

35. Interpret what you hear in terms of the speaker's stated or implied purpose.

35. Do you fail to recognize the speaker's purpose?

F. Follow up your listening in the following ways:

36. Be able to give an accurate restatement of the main points in the speech.

36. Recall disconnected points or unimportant details.

37. Ask questions of the speaker if there is an opportunity.

37. Ask no questions and are impatient with those who do.

38. Talk about what has been said with others.

38. Talk about the speaker rather than what he said.

39. Construct an outline of the speech from your notes.

39. Neither make an outline nor review your notes.

40. Look for opportunities to refer to what was said in speaking or writing.

40. Want to forget the whole affair as quickly as possible.

4. Read aloud a description of a physical scene. Have each listener (1) list the items mentioned and (2) read them aloud (3) sketch the scene as he "sees" it.

5. Read aloud a poem. After reading, ask each listener to (1) tell the *ideas* in the poem (2) discuss his feelings or emotional reaction.

6. Seat the students in a circle. Whisper a simple statement of fact to the first student, have him whisper it to the next, and so on. Have the last student repeat the statement aloud. Check this with the original for accuracy, and wording.

7. Read a short narrative. Have the students act out what they have heard.

8. Play a recording of a speech by a famous person. Have the class listen carefully, then state the central idea and purpose. Outline the main points and the supporting examples and material. Discuss the reports. Then re-play the record and allow each student to check his notes.

9. Use a similar method on the next round of speeches in class.

10. Hold a class discussion on "How can I improve my listening manners?"

11. Give directions on how to get to a building in town or on the campus. Have each student repeat these instructions.

12. Listen to a radio or television newscast. Summarize the content. Write or give orally a criticism of the delivery of the newscaster.

31

CHAPTER 4

INFORMAL
SPEAKING

Conversation is an art in which a man has all mankind
for his competitors, for it is that which all
are practicing every day while they live.
—RALPH WALDO EMERSON

The least formal speaking situation is conversation. It is so ordinary and obvious a part of our daily lives that it hardly seems worthy of comment. Yet if we were to keep track, we might find we use about 20,000 words of conversation for every *one* we use in formal speaking situations. Therefore it would seem a most important use of speech.

But there is more to conversation—which includes any oral exchange of ideas or information in an informal situation—than just a lot of talk. In its highest form it has serious purposes and values; it has quality. The greatest teachers, from Socrates down to those of today, have used conversation as a method of imparting knowledge to their students. Today major business transactions are often made verbally at a luncheon, or during informal talk on a golf course. In our complicated world, political leaders first talk over major problems in informal conversation. They often reach important decisions under the same conditions.

Conversation need have no ulterior motive. Emerson pointed out that "Wise, cultivated, genial conversation is the last flower of civilization." It is an art that is practiced on all social and economic levels, in all areas of man's activity. Sydney Smith, the English essayist and wit, said, "One of the greatest pleasures of life is conversation." In our era of spectator sports and TV, many people claim that conversation is becoming a lost art, but the good conversationalist is still the most popular person in the room. No professional comedian on TV can compete with the presence of a friend who has interesting things to say in an interesting way. David Hume, Scottish philosopher and historian and himself a renowned talker, said, "The free conversation of a friend is what I prefer to any entertainment." Conversation is the lifeblood of any social situation. A party where nobody talks is deadly dull.

Although conversation is one of the most common and ordinary uses of speech, it is also one of your most important tools for achieving success on any level of activity. How effective is your conversation? What does it accomplish?

Do you feel comfortable about meeting the many situations that confront you? What impression do you make at a party—are you alive and interesting, or silent and dull? Have you ever felt left out of a situation because someone else talked all the time? Have you ever "put your foot into it" because you said the wrong thing? Did you ever sit at the phone hesitating to call a new friend because you weren't quite sure what to say? Have you ever stumbled miserably through introductions? And how about your last interview for a summer job—was it a success?

In addition to the significance of conversation in your daily life, consider the advantages you gain from mastering it:

You Can Make Friends

If you have ever been a stranger in a group, remember how much it meant to you when someone came up and said, "Hello!" That offer of conversation is an opportunity to start a new friendship. Most of us are anxious to talk with someone who looks attractive or interesting. The right words of introduction, interesting questions and answers, and you have started something through a conversation that may develop into an enduring relationship. Mark Twain, the American writer, said, "I can live

A good speaker, even in conversation, thinks about what he is saying and chooses his words well. This is Dr. Eleazer Krumbein, educational psychologist.

two months on a good compliment." A sincere compliment is one of the easiest ways to win friends, but sometimes we have to learn to *say* the complimentary things we often think but don't say.

You Can Learn Interesting Facts

A high-school student sat beside a jet pilot on a bus; in an hour's conversation he learned hundreds of things about flying. Another student talked to a doctor just returned from the Congo and was fascinated by the knowledge she gained about Africa. Nearly everyone you meet—including your classmates—has some specialized knowledge that he is willing to share. There is no limit to what you may learn from chance conversation.

You Can Develop Important Ideas

Two girls, in casual conversation, found they were both disappointed to find so few recordings of living authors and their works. They began to talk about what could be done about it. The discussion led to founding a company, and their first attempt was a recording by Dylan Thomas, the Welsh poet. It sold 500 copies the first week, and in a few years sold over 125,000 copies. This was the beginning of Caedmon records.

34

In any serious conversation each person stimulates the other, and such stimulation produces many new and important ideas.

You Can Develop Your Personality

Every experience affects your personality. Through conversation you gain new information that broadens you, important ideas and attitudes that make you more mature. Hearing the viewpoints of others develops tolerance and tact. And you gain sincerity and stature as a person by learning to express your own beliefs and convictions. Ralph Waldo Emerson observed that conversation is our account of ourselves.

You Can Become a Better Speaker

Conversation offers you the greatest opportunity you have to practice and improve your speech. You can use all the fundamental skills in conversation, and your attitudes toward speaking, your knowledge and ideas affect it strongly. You have to organize thoughts clearly and quickly to make them count in conversation. Appropriate, spontaneous wording and fluency are great assets in informal talk. Your speech must be intelligible, or your ideas will be lost. "Conversation is the image of the mind. As a man is, so is his talk," was said in the first century by Publilius Syrus, a Latin writer, and it bears repetition today. In such a casual atmosphere, voice and action make the most subtle meanings very obvious to your listeners. In this atmosphere you can afford to experiment, something you cannot risk in formal speaking situations. Try saying the same thing in different ways to two different groups of classmates. Choose different words, different types of sentences, different approaches. See which is the most successful.

Appreciating the importance of conversation and the benefits to be gained from it, what can you do to improve yours?

HOW TO IMPROVE YOUR CONVERSATION

There are several ways to improve your conversation. Some may require important changes in your habits; others will call for improving things you are now doing.

Remember That Conversation Is a "Sharing" Experience

There are "hungry" talkers—they never quit. They are so eager to hold the spotlight that they interrupt the moment anyone tries to speak. They never pass the verbal ball. They break every rule of courtesy, and violate the basic purpose of conversation. Sydney Smith, whom we quoted before, said of a friend, "He has occasional flashes of silence that make his conversation perfectly delightful."

By definition, conversation is an "oral exchange." Both parties must be able to participate or little is gained. You will want to share your best, your *real* self in conversation. Be genuine and sincere. "Words, words, words, no matter from the heart," William Shakespeare wrote of those who speak without sincerity. If you are affected or try to show off, you are displaying yourself at a disadvantage.

Make Yourself Worth Listening To

Much conversation is dull because those speaking have shallow, empty minds. Conversation is limited by lack of knowledge, experience, and imagination. It is not difficult to become more interesting. Each book you read will give you ideas and information for discussion. Agree or disagree with the author. A concert gives you a topic. Was it good or bad, and why? If you watch the launching of an astronaut on television, you can share in conversation with others the feeling of tension and suspense. A football game between your school and a traditional rival should give you conversational material for a week or more.

Through every avenue of experience you can fill the reservoir of your mind. If you develop this storehouse, it will serve you well, not only in your conversation, but also as you respond to what others say.

Be Adaptable in Conversation

A skilled conversationalist can adapt to almost any situation. Adapting is changing your manner, ideas, language, voice, or actions to fit any situation. If you're with young children, you change your vocabulary and adjust to their interests and ideas. You try to enter their world.

You adjust when you visit your grandparents. Here, there is a great age difference, and their interests, problems, and activities are far different from yours. Yet you can adapt yourself to this situation because you love them and share with them many common interests.

The lunch-hour baseball talk of boys is an easy situation, and most boys feel right at home. But when a girl approaches, a change in subject often occurs. If you are versatile and adaptable, you can meet this situation easily.

36

Develop Skill in Conversation

Conversation offers many opportunities for you to become a better speaker, but good conversation *depends* on your ability to speak fluently. We have mentioned the importance of ideas. Equally important to good conversation is the organization of your ideas and information. Make your points stand out. Pindar, the Greek lyric poet, said, "For whatsoever one hath said well goeth forth with a voice that never dieth." Choose words that are interesting. Build a vocabulary that fits your ideas and the occasions you meet. Slang will not always do the job; learn new words that will. Use them often to gain ease and fluency with them.

Speak distinctly; deliver your message clearly the first time. Be aware of your vocal quality; you can make your voice a friendly, attractive, forceful part of your personality and gain interest through more variety or better pitch.

Develop personal vitality and enthusiasm. Conversation needs sparkle—you can provide it by improving your skill in speaking. But bear in mind the advice of Cervantes, the author of *Don Quixote,* that jests that give pain are no jests.

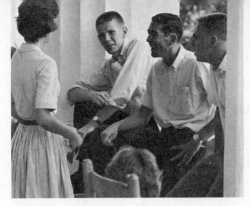

Evaluate Your Success in Conversation
and Work on Your Weak Points

No one perfects a skill like good conversation overnight. It takes time, and requires constant checking to find out how well you are doing. There *are* ways to do this. Your best yardstick is to watch the attitudes and reactions of others to your conversation.

If people look interested and respond readily to you, it is a good sign. Next, observe what others say in reply to you. If their remarks are "in tune," and follow your meaning, these too are good signs.

If you have been through a difficult social or conversational situation, ask a member of your family or a friend to tell you how you did. They are interested in you and will give you an honest opinion.

Finally, ask yourself: "How effective was I in achieving the various values of conversation?" "How could I improve my attitude, my subjects, my ideas, my speaking?"

Do everything you can to overcome your weaknesses, but be conscious of your successes, too. La Rochefoucauld, a Frenchman famous for his epigrams, wrote, "Confidence does more to make conversation than wit."

Lord Chesterfield, an English statesman and man of letters of the eighteenth century, was concerned about the education of his son. He wanted him to have a brilliant career and, as with most doting parents, he worked too hard at it. His efforts took the form of letters to his son, full of excellent and often lengthy advice. His son never profited much from the letters, but the world has treasured them. He considered the art of conversation one of the most important attributes of a gentleman. The following is taken from a long letter written from Bath, October 19, 1748. You may find the language a bit stilted, and the choice of words quaint; but Lord Chesterfield had the root of the matter in him and his advice is still sound.

Talk often, but never long: in that case, if you do not please, at least you are sure not to tire your hearers.

Tell stories very seldom, and absolutely never but where they are very apt and very short.

Never hold anybody by the button or the hand, in order to be heard out; for, if people are not willing to hear you, you had much better hold your tongue than them.

Most long talkers single out one unfortunate man in company (commonly him whom they observe to be the most silent, or their next neighbor) to whisper, or at least in a half voice, to convey a continuity of words to. This is excessively ill-bred, and in some degree a fraud; conversation-stock being a joint and common property.

Take, rather than give, the tone of the company you are in.

Avoid as much as you can, in mixed companies, argumentative, polemical conversations; which, though they should not, yet certainly do, indispose for a time the contending parties toward each other; and if the controversy grows warm and noisy, endeavor to put an end to it by some genteel levity or joke.

Above all things, and upon all occasions avoid speaking of yourself, if it be possible.

Take care never to seem dark and mysterious; which is not only a very unamiable character, but a very suspicious one too; if you seem mysterious with others, they will be really so with you, and you will know nothing.

Neither retail or receive scandal willingly; defamation of others may for the present gratify the malignity of the pride of our hearts; cool reflection will draw very disadvantageous conclusions from such a disposition; and in the case of scandal, as in that of robbery, the receiver is always thought as bad as the thief.

Mimicry, which is the common and favorite amusement of little low minds, is in the utmost contempt with great ones. It is the lowest and most illiberal of all buffoonery.

I need not (I believe) advise you to adapt your conversation to the people you are conversing with: for I suppose you would not, without this caution, have talked upon the same subject, and in the same manner, to a minister of state, a bishop, a philosopher, a captain, and a woman.

One word only as to swearing, and that, I hope and believe, is more than is necessary. You may sometimes hear some people in good company interlard their discourse with oaths, by way of embellishment, as they think, but you must observe, too, that those who do so are never those who contribute, in any degree, to give that company the denomination of good company.

Loud laughter is the mirth of the mob, who are only pleased with silly things; for true wit or good sense never excited a laugh since the creation of the world. Whatever you say, if you say it with a supercilious, cynical grin, will be ill received. If, into the bargain, you mutter it, or utter it indistinctly and ungracefully, it will be still worse received. If your air and address are vulgar, awkward, and *gauche*, you may be esteemed indeed, if you have great intrinsic merit; but you will never please; and without pleasing you will rise but heavily.

THE SPECIAL SITUATIONS

Among the various types of conversation, two or three, because they are especially important or require certain forms, deserve particular attention.

Introductions

In the social situation nothing is a greater conversation-blocker than not knowing the people around you.

Correct and prompt introductions do much to "break the ice" and help to get conversation going. Fortunately you do not have to be inventive or imaginative in this matter. Forms for introductions have been established for generations and cover all possible situations. They are not subject to change or variation. Once you have learned them you have nothing further to worry about.

Men are introduced to women. "Miss Davis, may I present Mr. McCarthy?" or "Peggy, this is Jim."

Young people are introduced to older people. "Mother, may I introduce Tommy Jones?" or "Father, this is Sue Brown."

At school, your parents are presented to your teachers. "Mr. Brown, this is my mother, Mrs. Drake."

Distinguished persons have others introduced to them. "Senator Wilson, may I present James Thompson?"

All guests are introduced to the hostess. "Mrs. Miller, may I present Miss Van Dyke?"

All persons are introduced to clergymen. "Reverend Ward, may I present Miss Davis?"

Acknowledgment consists of a polite nod or a handshake where indicated. Men and boys shake hands with each other. Your handshake should be firm enough to seem sincere. Avoid the "bonecrusher" and especially the "dead-fish" handshake—both leave an unpleasant impression. A woman offers her hand to a man or a boy if she wishes. A young woman does not offer to shake hands with an older woman but waits until the other offers. Men do not offer to shake hands with women but respond at once if a woman offers her hand.

As a rule, mere exchange of names will start conversation. However, it is considerate to mention something about the person introduced, such as his business, hobby, education, achievements, or place of residence to give people something besides the weather to talk about.

40

At a large gathering, you will not be expected to introduce each person to everyone. You will find you can start by introducing strangers to a few people or a small group, and they will continue introductions on their own.

Inability to remember names is one of the most embarrassing social situations. Most of us feel slighted when someone cannot remember our name—yet we often find ourselves incapable of repeating the name of a person to whom we have just been introduced.

Everyone likes to be called by name. If you want to become proficient in this, you must work at it.

Repeat the name of the person when you are introduced. Keep thinking of that name as you talk, identify *that* name with *that* person, by noting his features, color of hair, clothes. Use the name as many times as possible while you are talking; say "Mr. James," instead of "you." Let him talk a little about himself, so you can build an association of his name with his business, school, hobby, or family.

By mastering introductions and remembering names accurately, you can add to your own social conversational acceptability.

Use of the Telephone

Using the telephone is both an opportunity and a responsibility. It is an opportunity, because it permits you to converse anytime with people separated from you by distance. You may call your friends whenever you want companionship or help. You may call dozens of people you do not know as well for goods or services, such as your dentist, a shopping service, or a garage mechanic.

But remember in telephoning that the impression you create is formed entirely by what you say and how you say it. Teen-agers are sometimes criticized for the length of their conversations. However, a reminder to use the telephone with tact and consideration for others who depend upon it for personal and business reasons should curb those who are inconsiderate.

There are accepted rules of behavior for telephone use. The telephone companies have done a masterful public service in preparing materials for free distribution to schools, and in Teletrainer equipment for use in developing more effective telephone usage.[1] Here is a summary of some of their major suggestions:

---

[1]See Bell System pamphlet, *Telephone Pointers,* summaries reprinted by permission. "Teletraining for English and Speech" (1960) and teletraining equipment are available through the local Bell System representative.

1. IN RECEIVING CALLS: Answer promptly and identify yourself at once; it saves time and possible confusion. Take calls for other persons courteously, and write down all messages. In a business office, if you receive a call by mistake, take time to see that it is transferred to the proper person.

2. IN MAKING CALLS: Plan outgoing calls before you make them. Place calls correctly; this can be done by using the directory. For out-of-town calls be sure you have the area code number and the right exchange and number before you place the call. For person-to-person and other special calls, give the operator all the information she needs to place the call for you.

3. IN SPEAKING ON CALLS: Reflect a pleasant personality; be sincere and helpful. Use a normal conversational voice and speak distinctly at an appropriate speed. Simple, understandable language is best, and a low-pitched voice with good variation in tone. Always end calls pleasantly.

Interviews

Interviews are planned or directed conversations with a specific purpose. Regardless of the purpose, certain fundamental and obvious rules apply to all interviews. The most common reasons for interviews are: to obtain

43

information, to apply for a position, and to sell merchandise or services.

An interview to obtain information is the tool of many professions —and a tool that is often misused. Learn to use it well; you will need it to get facts for a report, to obtain opinions or news for your school paper, or to learn about schools or career opportunities.

Make an appointment, and be sure that you arrive at the appointed time.

Know the purpose for your interview, and what you wish to accomplish by it.

Prepare thoroughly what you are going to say.

During the interview cover your subject as clearly and as quickly as possible.

End the interview at the appointed time, without cutting off the interviewee's statement, and always with thanks for the time of the person with whom you have talked.

Be prepared for interviews—have both answers and questions ready for the interviewer.

Usually you are assigned a subject to cover in an interview. This is the purpose; try to determine ahead of time what you want to learn about the subject. Write out the questions you want answered. During the interview, present your questions clearly, and write down the answers clearly and accurately.

Nobody likes to be misquoted. But remember that an interview is a "shared" experience. The person you are talking to may not have the information you came to get, or he may not want to talk about it. He may have something different to offer, something even more important than what you came to get. As in all conversation situations, you have to remain flexible and adapt yourself to circumstances. Offer to leave as soon as you have the information you came to get, or a substitute for it, but do not leave too abruptly.

Since you came to learn something, give the person time to tell you as much of the story as he wants to. It is common courtesy to thank the person for the time he has given you.

Even though you may have written a letter, sent recommendations, and filled out forms, you will eventually be interviewed by your prospective employer. He wants to see you in person so he can judge your suitability for the job by your appearance, manner, and speech. There are many things you wish to learn about the position, things that were not described by the agency that sent you; you will have questions that were not answered by the ad you are responding to.

You will want to present yourself in the most favorable light, and will take as much care to present your personal qualifications as you do with your appearance. Plan your questions about the job, the organization, and your possible future in it. During the interview, give your reasons for wanting the job, and present your qualifications clearly and briefly. This interview differs, however, from the one in which you seek information, in that *you* are the person interviewed. The initiative is not yours; you respond. Be sure to listen carefully to what the personnel representative has to say and convey an attitude of interest and willingness to learn. The company is not interested in what they can do for you, but in what you can do for them. Don't worry about how to end this interview; that matter will be taken care of by the person interviewing you. He, or she, will signify when the interview is over, and then you should leave promptly.

The best salesmen are great conversationalists and, although their conversation may seem spontaneous, it has been carefully planned to achieve the desired effect.

Every successful sales person has interest and confidence in his product or service. Your purpose in this type of interview is to arouse the same interest and confidence in your customer. In order to do this you must organize clearly, and know thoroughly, the essential reasons why your product or service is needed, the ways in which it is beneficial to the customer, and why it is better than a competitor's product.

Try to gain the customer's attention and confidence in you as an

authority in your field. The best salesman establishes an atmosphere of friendliness and honesty. He makes it pleasant to do business with him. And he gains the loyalty of his customers because they are also his friends.

If you have done the above successfully, the interview will end with your closing the sale. In all cases, thank the customer for his time.

Regarded as opportunities rather than difficulties, the situations outlined in this chapter can be used to develop your skill in informal speaking to the point where your conversation will be one of your strongest assets.

ACTIVITIES

1. Prepare a list of test questions you could use in evaluating conversation. Test your own conversation, using these questions.

2. Listen to, and if possible tape, several conversations among your schoolmates or friends. List the chief weaknesses you observe and suggest ways of eliminating them; or, as a group, discuss ways in which the conversation could have been improved.

3. Describe the characteristics of a person you consider a superior conversationalist. Use these characteristics as guides for improving your own conversational skills.

4. Secure the *Teletrainer Exercises for Secondary School Students* and the accompanying equipment available from the American Telephone and Telegraph Company representative in your area. Use these aids in developing your individual telephone skill.

5. Tape the best and worst examples of telephone conversation done in this exercise. Play them back, evaluate them, and begin to make a file of such tapes for your speech class.

6. Stage (and tape if possible) the following interviews, with speech class members taking the various parts:

   a. A reporter from your school paper interviewing a celebrity who is visiting your community.

   b. An employment interview following your written application for a position advertised in the newspaper.

   c. A conference between a teacher and a pupil who needs help in his speech assignment.

   d. A conference between a parent and a teacher concerning a student's work.

   e. A conference between the student council president and the school principal regarding needed funds for a selected student activity.

7. Develop a rôle-playing situation for a discussion on any school or community problem you wish to consider. Assign the various parts and positions you wish represented. If possible, tape the discussion and play it back for listening and evaluation.

8. Stage a reception or party in which you are the host or hostess and are obliged to introduce any or all of the following persons: the school principal, the grandmother of your class president, a visiting high-school boy and a local girl, a science teacher, the mayor, a famous athlete, a movie star of the silent screen, a concert violinist, a priest from a seminary, a grade-school sister of yours, the president of General Motors, and a member of the House of Representatives.

CHAPTER 5

DEVELOPING
CONFIDENCE

Confidence is that feeling by which the mind embarks
in great and honorable courses with a sure
hope and trust in itself.

—CICERO

One of the advantages of taking a course in speech is that it helps you gain poise in speaking in public. You will find this poise a valuable asset throughout your life.

If you have some misgivings at the prospect of appearing before an audience, remember a certain amount of nervous tension is common to all of us. It is just as natural for you to be tense before you begin to speak as it is for a halfback to tighten up as he waits to catch the opening kickoff. Both of you feel the challenge and excitement of a new situation and are eager to excel in what you are doing. In either situation it is the over-confident who are most apt to come to grief. "The best way to preserve confidence," Henry C. Alexander said, "is to prevent it from turning into overconfidence."

Nervous tension should not be upsetting—it happens to the best people. Outstanding speakers, teachers, and political leaders, actors and actresses on the stage, in television, and in films recognize nervous tension as a natural experience and have learned to make it serve them.

Among those who have admitted to stage fright are Cicero, William Jennings Bryan, Henry Ward Beecher, Franklin Roosevelt, Bing Crosby, Jack Benny, Steve Allen, and Helen Hayes. Obviously their stage fright was not an insurmountable handicap. Actually this tension is nature's way of helping us out. When we are frightened, angry, or excited, the adrenaline glands become active, adding certain elements to our blood stream that enable us to act at the top of our power. Stage fright is your insurance that you will do your best.

There are several things you can do that will help you make public appearances with greater assurance. Emerson said, "Self trust is the secret of success." If you follow these suggestions, you can learn to trust yourself and will be able to dismiss all problems that are imaginary or unfounded. Then you can work directly on any real problems that exist.

Think of yourself first as a communicator. This is a fundamental principle of effective speaking. The real reason you are speaking is to communicate an idea to your audience and get a particular response from them. You are not showing off your voice, clothing, hairdo, or vocabulary. Your concern is to get your message across. Try to forget yourself and concentrate on the purpose, the information, and the organization of your speech. If you talk enthusiastically to your listeners, they will respond by being enthusiastic.

Develop the attitude "I have interesting and important information; I'd like to share it with you." When you know you have ideas and facts that are important, novel, or interesting, you become eager to share your knowledge. Your principal objective is to be the means through which your audience can obtain that knowledge. Such an attitude will soon establish you as an individual worth listening to.

When you are thoroughly convinced that you are right and that the things for which you stand are worth while, you won't have time to worry about your own emotional state. Your sincere belief will so dominate you that you will find yourself eager to jump to your feet and present your position or defend your ideals. When you are completely convinced of

Poise comes with practice. Which of these speakers would you rather hear?

the justice of your cause, you dedicate yourself to gaining acceptance for it. Such dedication is important to effective speaking in any situation; it not only increases the confidence of the speaker but convinces an audience as well. The great speakers of the world have been the ones most strongly dedicated to the causes in which they believed.

Confidence is born of a person's knowledge, acquired through experience of his ability to do the job at hand. Each time you speak before an audience, you gain confidence. Success is never achieved by the person who says, "I'll never make it; I know I can't do it." Believe in yourself and your abilities and take every opportunity to test them. Say, "I can do this; I will succeed." And supplement your belief by every bit of application and energy at your disposal.

The most valuable insurance for success in speaking in public is careful and thorough advance preparation. Confucius, the great Chinese sage, said, "In all things success depends on previous preparation, and without such preparation there is sure to be failure." Here is a list of steps in preparation that will be more fully treated in later chapters. They are listed now because they are the foundation on which you will build your own confidence in speaking and to help you develop useful work habits.

50

Allow plenty of time for preparation.

Select a subject suitable to the audience and the occasion—one in which you have a genuine interest and, if possible, some previous knowledge.

Have a worthy purpose.

Supplement your information and background with ample reading.

Organize your material in a detailed outline.

Write legibly or type your notes; learn to use notes smoothly and easily.

If necessary, write out the first few sentences and practice speaking them or memorize them. This will lessen your tension at the opening of your speech and get you off to a good start.

Run through your entire speech from outline at least twice before giving it. State the basic ideas in usable language, but do not try to memorize. Keep your language varied and alive. Try expressing the same idea in more than one way.

If you are using charts, objects, or mechanical equipment, check them to be sure everything is in order. Work out in advance more than one method for using them.

If you understand that you are a communicator and not an exhibitor, if you have interesting ideas and believe in them strongly, and if you have prepared your talk adequately, you will have every reason for confidence as you face your audience. With this security you can gradually develop a habit of conscious mental relaxation before you appear in front of your audience.

You can use physical activity and control to reduce your tensions. Before speaking, force yourself to relax physically. When you reach the platform, deliberately assume a relaxed posture. You can control your breathing in these dependable ways: Before you enter the auditorium,

Here again is a contrast in speakers. Assuming a relaxed pose helps you to relax.

breathe deeply in order to fill your lungs with fresh air. When you reach the platform, take a deep breath before you say a word. During your speech, pause at frequent intervals to draw a deep breath. Never speak so fast your breathing becomes shallow. But do not allow your deep breaths to be noticeable to the audience.

During the first minute or two on the platform you may want to handle some unobtrusive object, such as a book. The gesture will ease tension and help you feel more comfortable. Use free bodily action. Properly motivated, this freedom of action will do more than any other single physical factor to help you acquire self-control and release your speaking power.

One person you can depend on to understand your difficulties and be able to help you overcome them is your teacher. Don't hesitate to take your problems to your teacher or to ask for suggestions on preparing and delivering your speech. Take advantage of his knowledge and his desire to help you—you will soon realize that he is interested in your improvement and will help you achieve success. Apply any suggestions as soon as possible after they are given.

"Practice" alone does not make "perfect." It only makes "permanent," and practicing unsuccessful methods may exaggerate existing faults. Therefore, *immediate application* of constructive criticism is necessary for improvement. This the very essence of learning. *Repeated* performance is needed if you are to gain the benefits of confidence and security that experience gives. By seeking opportunities to speak in school and in the community, you will speed your development and "set" the new habits you want to acquire.

ACTIVITIES

1. Prepare a three-minute talk on a subject on which you have a strong personal conviction. Make your position clear and support it with your best arguments, evidence, and examples. Deliver it with enthusiasm, vigor, and sincerity. Be ready to answer questions following your talk.

2. Under the direction of your teacher, select a subject for a two-man, six-minute debate. Prepare a three-minute talk on your side of the question. Be ready to answer the arguments of your opponent in a short reply following his speech.

3. Organize a symposium of three or four speakers on a current question. Decide ahead of time if each speaker will discuss his views on the whole question, or on an assigned part of the problem. The speakers must be prepared to defend their positions.

4. Assume the rôle of a radio announcer describing a special event, such as a championship basketball game, a boxing match, a spectacular fire, a horse race, a flying exhibition by the Blue Angels, a space rocket launching, or some similar event. Lose yourself in the experience of making your listeners see the details and excitement of the thing you are reporting. If possible, you may want to do this over a public address system.

5. Describe, with as much physical activity as is needed and possible, a thrilling or impressive sight you have seen. Use action to convey the size, location, shape, or other details of the scene. Examples of such possibilities include the Grand Canyon, an airplane view of New York, Niagara Falls, Glacier Park, the Mississippi River from a boat or a barge, the San Francisco skyline, the fiords of Norway, Paris at night, or any others you may have seen.

6. Tell the class about your hobby, showing them any of the things you need, do, or collect in following the hobby. Try to interest everyone in having a hobby, either yours or another.

7. Play the game of charades with two teams from the class. Use book titles, plays, movies, or titles of songs or musical compositions. Concentrate on the ideas and your means of communicating them.

8. Give a chalk talk or board demonstration. To explain your materials or ideas, develop the details of your sketch as fully as you can.

CHAPTER 6

PRELIMINARY
PREPARATION

The beginning is the most important part of the work.
—PLATO

Some people think successful speakers just "have a way with words." They think the flow of ideas, the exact phrase, and the impressive delivery of the experienced speaker just happen. Nothing is further from the truth.

Most successful speakers, like outstanding athletes, have spent much time in preparation. Mark Twain, who was famous as a speaker, said, "It usually takes about three weeks to prepare a good impromptu speech." What the audience hears is the result of study, wide reading, careful organization, audience analysis, and practice in delivery. The confidence with which a good speaker faces an audience is the result of his preparation.

Preparing a speech is an entirely different process from that of preparing a daily lesson. A speech demands much greater development and practice. It takes time. It draws on your background and observations and represents your best efforts to get your ideas across and make yourself worth listening to.

YOUR PREPARATION DEPENDS ON THE TYPE OF DELIVERY

Every plan for preparing a speech is closely related to the method of speaking, or delivery, that is used. There are four types: impromptu, memorized, reading from a manuscript, and extemporaneous.

Impromptu speaking is best described as speaking without previous preparation. It is often confused with extemporaneous speaking, that is, giving a speech that is fully prepared but not memorized. Useful as impromptu speaking is in emergencies or in special situations, it is not the speaking technique recommended for general use. Some students may attempt to practice this method. However, sad experiences—when they fumble for ideas and stumble over words, and when "fuzzy" organization makes them ridiculous before an alert audience and teacher—usually convince them that such a method is not successful. Important as the ability to meet unexpected situations may be, greater skill is gained by the student who prepares his material and practices effective habits of delivery. Then he finds he can use his increased ability to greater advantage when he is called on in an impromptu situation.

Certain speakers feel they have greater security if they write every word of their speeches and memorize them word for word. This method has the advantage of being exactly worded. However, it has disadvantages that outweigh the precise language that results. First, such a talk usually sounds stilted and mechanical. Attention is directed to words rather than ideas; the speaker concentrates on accurate recall of language rather than on meaning. Second, the speech is inflexible and cannot be adapted to either the audience or conditions. Third, the speaker faces a burden of remembering the exact words he wrote. This may lead to his downfall if he cannot recall a key word.

Under certain conditions speakers may write a speech and read it to an audience. While these occasions are not numerous, you should recognize the circumstances under which reading may occur.

The pressure of accuracy of quotation in a newspaper or magazine forces certain speakers to prepare manuscript speeches and deliver them as written. This is often done by public officials, such as the President, the Secretary of State, the mayor of a city, the head of a company or a labor group, or the superintendent of schools. What they say may affect or determine policy. Their talks are often subject to study and reply by foreign diplomats, political opponents, or citizens in the community. Another factor is the need to edit or censor. Officers in the armed forces, certain industrial employees, and transportation officials must usually clear their material with superiors in their departments before delivering it.

Both of these factors contribute to the use of this method in radio and television performance. These media, however, add another factor that makes manuscript speaking necessary. This is time. Broadcasting stations insist on the clearance of materials, and demand that the speech be timed to the second to fit the air time allowed.

For most persons, reading from manuscript provides an accurate method, but one subject to the same inflexibility as memorized copy. It adds the dangers of losing audience contact—because the speaker's eyes are glued to the manuscript—and of putting the andience to sleep with a monotonous reading pattern.

If you must work under these conditions, you should make every effort to develop both reading and speaking skill. Certain professionals are so accomplished that their reading presentation is conversational and sounds exactly like spontaneous speaking.

The extemporaneous method is practical, and therefore the one ordinarily used. It is not, as some think, a method requiring no time for preparation. The speech is fully prepared and outlined; however, the wording is not set, and the speech is not committed to memory. The speaker chooses the wording as he proceeds. This method permits him to adapt his language to his audience and the occasion, while using the outline as the basic guide for his ideas and their organization. By concentrating on ideas and expressing them in language that is appropriate, the speaker has a method that is spontaneous, flexible, and expressive.

The extemporaneous method takes more time and experience to develop than any of the others. It is subject to some inaccuracies, to repetition of words, and possibly to hesitation and breaks in fluency as the speaker learns to use it. Once mastered, however, it is the most satisfactory of all.

PREPARING YOUR SPEECH

Preparation is closely related to delivery methods. Cicero warned almost two thousand years ago that as a field, however fertile, cannot be fruitful without cultivation, neither can a mind without learning. There are certain essential and usable steps in preparing a speech. Nearly every person has

his own way of doing things; it fits his abilities, temperament, and personal characteristics. The steps listed here are basic steps that you can adapt to meet your particular needs.

Select a suitable subject.
Decide on the general purpose.
Word the specific purpose (or central idea)
    in terms of the audience and occasion.
Gather materials for your speech.
Organize and outline your speech.
Word and practice your speech, using notes,
    an outline, and audio-visual aids.

Select a suitable subject

In most of your talks you will be permitted to choose your own subject. You will have an opportunity to share your ideas, knowledge, and beliefs with your classmates. However, you have the responsibility of interesting your audience.

Whenever you give a three-minute talk to twenty-five people, you are using seventy-five minutes of listening time. Therefore, each speaking experience should be of some profit to you and your listeners.

Your speech class should be a place where you discuss significant areas of interest and important issues and problems that you face. For the first speech you deliver, however, you need not select the most profound or difficult subject.

Many people think that for a speech to be interesting it must be about a big, important subject, such as the United Nations, world disarmament, or racial integration. This is not necessarily true. Such a subject is so big, and three minutes is so short a time that you can talk of nothing but generalities everyone else already knows. You have to narrow your subject, go from the general to the specific. What happened the day you visited the United Nations can offer you an opportunity to describe a world personality who might well prove interesting to your classmates.

The best starting point to find a good subject is your own knowledge and experience. You have had many experiences that are good speech material: your summer job, trips you have taken, amusing people you have met, visits to fairs or expositions. You also have knowledge about interesting subjects; for example, you may have a hobby you know more about than anyone else in the class does. Any of these and more provide subjects on which you can speak as an expert—and this will help give you confidence. Much of the fun and benefit in speech class come from sharing and exchanging your knowledge and experience with your classmates.

You will find something else must be considered if you are to choose a suitable subject. This is your desire to talk about it and your enthusiasm for it. Speakers who talk just because they must say something lack the sparkle and zest that come from a desire to communicate. The job they do is half-hearted, and the audience knows it.

You have another important source of subjects—your beliefs and convictions. If you feel strongly that testing of atomic weapons should be stopped and that you would like to do something about it, you probably would give a good speech on the subject. If you are convinced that action should be taken against the alliance of crime and government in your city, you have another compelling subject. If you believe that teen-age drivers are in need of systematic, careful training, you can probably present a strong case for your position.

In speech classes and in the discussions and debates of the inter-scholastic speech programs, many of the leaders of our democracy have discovered the great causes they believe in and fight for. Be courageous enough to state your convictions, explore and test them, and learn how

to present them effectively.

Although your first talks will be given in class, you may, as you progress, be called on to speak in other school situations or before an outside organization. Different occasions have different conditions, objectives, and kinds of audiences, and a subject appropriate for one may not be suitable for another. Learn all you can about the occasion before you select your subject. Don't speak on the mechanics of an internal-combustion engine at a women's club Fourth of July meeting.

In choosing a subject, find one that will interest your listeners and invite their response. Arthur Phillips, an early writer on speech, said, "Get into the experience of the audience if you wish to arouse its interest." You must start with your listeners—observe and study the things that reveal their interests and select subjects close to them.

One high-school boy announced "Pets" as his subject for his first three-minute class talk. After questions from his classmates and teacher he decided "Dogs" would be a more suitable choice. Another series of questions changed his subject to "The Cocker Spaniel." After further thought he made still another change; "How I Wash My Cocker Spaniel" was his final effort, and, when he made his speech, it proved to be both instructive and humorous.

Decide on the general purpose

Closely related to selecting your subject is your general purpose in speaking. The general purposes of speaking are as old as mankind. They have been listed in speech textbooks from the time of Aristotle (330 B.C.) to the present. They developed from situations in which one human being tried to influence others to respond in a certain way to what he said. The general purpose controls how you will use your material to obtain the response you seek and provides you with a broad objective.

59

Purpose	*Response desired*
1. To inform	understanding
2. To convince	belief; acceptance of one's argument
3. To actuate	action—definite and obvious
4. To stimulate	emotion; inspiration
5. To entertain	enjoyment; pleasure

Although there are five possible purposes, do not conclude that your speech must fall completely under one of them. Quite often you will have more than one purpose in a single talk. A speech primarily to inform may also entertain. Always plan your talk around the primary purpose.

If your general purpose is to inform, you hope to make the audience understand the facts or information you present. Their understanding may be the basis for their use of, or action on, what you have told them. Suppose that you want to explain to a group of freshmen students the rules for taking books from the school library. The test of your success rests on the clarity of your talk in informing them of school rules.

If your general purpose is to convince, you are trying to make the audience believe what you believe. You want acceptance of your position on a question, or agreement with you. The talk to convince attempts to prove something; your target is the belief of the audience. Your materials consist of arguments supported by evidence (opinions, figures, etc.) and reasoning that will get your listeners to accept your ideas.

When your purpose is to actuate, you wish to secure a definite, observable action from your audience. You want them to do something you can see or hear in their basic response to your talk. The chief difference between the speech to convince and the speech to actuate is one of degree. The second goes further—it seeks observable action as the response.

When you wish to stir up the audience emotionally, your general purpose is to stimulate. For this purpose the speaker usually tries to reinforce, or strengthen, feelings that already exist—as at homecoming you would try to reinforce established loyalties and traditions. Thus, you would try to inspire members of the football team to use greater effort, members of the student body to compete for higher scholastic records, members of a Sunday-school class to practice Christian virtues.

When you want your audience to enjoy themselves, your general purpose is to entertain. Although this purpose is usually associated with after-dinner speeches and straight humor, there are other kinds of speeches whose purpose is to entertain.

60

Word the specific purpose in terms of the audience and the occasion

Part of your training as a speaker is to learn to see things from the point of view of the audience. This ability affects your choice of a subject, both broad and specific purposes, the content of your talk, its length, its organization, and the way in which you deliver your speech. You must learn to put yourself in the place of your listeners and hope to judge accurately the effect your talk will have on them.

Here are some guides that should help you analyze the occasion. Where and under what conditions will you have to speak? Will the talk be given indoors or outdoors? If indoors, in what kind of room or auditorium will you speak? Can the speaker be heard and seen easily in this room? How will the audience be located? Directly in front of the speaker or widely spread and on either side? Will they be seated or standing? Crowded or comfortably placed? Will a public address system be used? Is there a speaker's stand? Will there be distractions and noise conditions either from within the audience or from outside?

Ask yourself about the purpose of the occasion. Is this a special occasion, such as an anniversary, homecoming, honors banquet? Is this a regular meeting of an organization or club? Are you the principal speaker or are there several? Is the meeting formal with a definite procedure or ritual, or is it informal and casual? Are the subject and purpose of your talk dictated by a special event, or have you freedom to select the subject and purpose?

What rules and procedure exist for the occasion? Is there a regular order of business or a planned program that includes your speech? Are officials, celebrities, or guests present whom you should mention and possibly compliment? Who will introduce you? Will you be expected to answer questions following your talk?

What are the details of the program on which you will speak? What is the hour (time of day) of your speech? Is your talk to be given following dinner? Luncheon? What events precede your talk—music, announcements, business, introductions? Do other important events directly follow your speech?

The second part of this step in your preparation concerns your analysis of the audience. What general facts can you secure about the age of the members of the audience? A wide difference in age causes you to adapt to this range in both your subject and your materials. What is the size of the audience? Is the audience mixed or of a single sex? Women have definite interests not shared by many men. Some subjects suitable for one sex would be out of the question for the other. Is the audience composed of a certain occupational group? Interests are closely allied with occupations. A group of day laborers would have different knowledge and interests from college professors. The tastes and interests of housewives are different from those of school children. Does the audience belong to a single religion? Knowledge of their religious beliefs would aid you in stressing or avoiding certain issues. As a speaker, you should respect the things that certain sects respect and hold sacred. What is the education of members of the audience? Are they members of professional, business, or social groups? Organizations tend to influence the interests, views, and activities of their members. Do they represent special political beliefs?

What facts can you learn about the members of the audience that relate *specifically* to *your* speech? What is their knowledge of the subject? If you are sure that they know very little about your subject, you can depend on interest because of the novelty of your content. If you discover that they are extremely well informed on your subject, you will need to prepare more carefully. Get greater amounts of material, select it, be

extremely accurate, and plan to present it vividly. What is their attitude toward your purpose or position on the subject? As soon as you reveal your purpose in speaking, the attitude of your audience will fall into three classes. It will be favorable, neutral, or opposed. Advance knowledge of their attitude toward your purpose determines the approach and delivery of your speech.

Wording the specific purpose (and response) requires that you limit your subject to fit the speech situation. Here are two examples in which the first steps in preparation are outlined. (Note the italicized statement of the specific purpose and subject in relation to other items.)

SPEECH A

1. Subject:	Rules for using the school library.
2. General Purpose:	To inform.
3. Specific Purpose:	*To explain to high-school freshmen how to procure overnight books from the school library.*
4. Specific Audience:	Freshmen students of Senior High School, Ann Arbor, Michigan.
5. Specific Occasion:	Orientation talks conducted by Student Council 9:00 A.M., Sept. 9, 1959, freshman study hall, Senior High School, Ann Arbor, Michigan. Time 20 minutes. Introduction by president of Student Council; other talks on various subjects to follow.

SPEECH B

1. Subject:	Safety belts.
2. General Purpose:	To actuate.
3. Specific Purpose:	*To cause high-school students to have safety belts installed in personal and family cars.*
4. Specific Audience:	High-school senior students enrolled in driver education, fall quarter, at West High School, Aurora, Illinois.
5. Specific Occasion:	Discussion session on modern safety equipment needed in automobiles at present time. Program planned by students under instructor supervision. All talks to be 10 minutes in length, September 14, 1959, 10:45 A.M., in high-school building, driver education classroom.

Gather material for your speech

You now know the limits of your subject for your audience and the occasion. A sensible method is to start with what you know about the subject, and add to it what you need. List the principal ideas and information you have on the subject as topics on your work sheet.

Let's use Speech B on safety belts as an example. Bear in mind that the general purpose is to actuate, and the specific purpose is to cause high-school students to have safety belts installed in cars. Your work sheet might look like this:

List of Ideas and Information
1. Most high-school students drive or ride in cars.
2. Traffic accidents are steadily increasing.
3. Teen-age drivers have been charged with a high percentage of accidents.
4. Injuries and fatalities are numerous among high-school drivers.
5. In collisions the principal injuries occur because the driver and passengers are thrown against the windshield or out of the car.
6. Safety belts are not standard equipment in all cars.
7. Our car does/does not have safety belts.
8. Such belts are used in airplanes and by stunt drivers.

Review your subject and be sure to check any additional information you need before you put your talk in outline form. You have not answered these questions about safety belts:

1. How effective are safety belts in preventing or reducing injuries in accidents?
2. If they are so important, why are they not installed in all cars now?
3. Are they difficult to install?
4. Are they expensive to install?
5. Do they spoil the appearance of a car?
6. Do they interfere with the driver's operation of the car?
7. Are they uncomfortable for passengers who wear them?

Such a work sheet gives you a blueprint to work from. Now you proceed to get the additional material you need, by reading or in other ways.

For your first speeches you may select subjects that require little or no search for materials. If you speak on "My Coin Collection," you may draw on your own knowledge and experience for all the information you need. However, if you plan to speak on a more difficult subject, you will probably have to add to what you know.

You look for materials that will arouse interest in your speech, hold attention, make points clear, support them strongly, and provide variety for your audience. What kinds of materials achieve these ends? They must be vivid, familiar, novel, concrete, alive, and stimulating. They must be within the experience of the audience. In what form should they be? In general they should be short, well organized, and in language instantly

grasped. They should be from sources which your audience will accept as authorities. A second kind of material is nonverbal. You should never overlook this. It includes visual and audio-visual aids that often are more effective than words and not too difficult to obtain. All types of materials can furnish you with support for the points in your speeches.

There are many sources for material. They are listed here as a guide in your search. We will explain them more fully later and show how they can support ideas in a speech.

Facts and Statistics: items of known truth.

Testimony and Quotations: statements of opinion.

Narratives, Illustrations, Examples: stories or instances used to clarify points.

Comparisons, Analogies, and Contrasts: similarities or differences to emphasize points.

Definitions, Explanations, Descriptions: give similarities or relationships of points.

Epigrams: sum up points in a witty fashion.

There are many places to find materials you need. Remember to start with your own knowledge, and add to what you know.

You may do this by direct experience and observation. Do the things you want to talk about yourself. In some cases such experiences satisfy an immediate need in preparing materials; in others they are long-range. If your talk deals with bus service in your city, you could answer most of the questions about it with facts you get in making a planned cross-town bus trip. Or you may watch others do what you cannot do. Observation is an opportunity for you to gain knowledge. Most class trips or individual visits allow you to see what is going on. You can't make steel yourself, but a trip to an open-hearth mill will furnish you with a great deal of material for a speech.

Use interviews and conversation to gain much valuable material from talking with informed people. This can be done informally in conversation or through a planned interview, for which you make an appointment with an expert source.

Use letters and questionnaires. A great deal of knowledge is available to you in sources you can reach by letter. Businesses, industries, schools, chambers of commerce, churches—all receive hundreds of inquiries by letter each year from persons who merely wish to know about or who want to give talks about these organizations. Quite often they have brochures or pamphlets they will send on request.

Listening to the radio and watching television and movies will give you special knowledge on current events. Documentaries, selected dramas, interviews, special news coverage, and educational films may furnish material not otherwise available.

Reading, however, remains the greatest source of speech materials. Get the reading habit if you wish to be successful as a student and a speaker. Read because you desire to know and to possess knowledge of the thousands of wonderful things that man has recorded in stone, script, or print since the beginning of time. Don't wait until your teacher pushes you into the library. Learn to go under your own power. Go because you realize that libraries have collected for your use the best books, periodicals, and pamphlets they can purchase. These materials can answer the questions and fill the gaps in your knowledge on your speech subject. They can widen your horizon by giving you new ideas and facts—things you did not know before. Learn what to read and how to use the library to get results.

Use newspapers to keep up with world and local events; and magazines and periodicals for a wide variety of information and current material not in books. *The Readers' Guide to Periodical Literature* will help you find the specific information for which you are looking.

Books are the best source of information and background. Become familiar with *general reference books,* which will provide basic material, facts, statistics, biography, quotations, epigrams, debates, discussions—and much more that may never even occur to you to want to know about! Learn how to use the card catalogue to find the particular books that will give you the specific information you need.

Bulletins and pamphlets contain extensive and valuable information published by state and national governments, business organizations, religious and educational societies, and many other agencies.

Speakers often need appropriate quotations, terse "capsule" statements (epigrams), and humorous stories that are suitable. Books of these are available; for example, Bartlett, John, *Familiar Quotations; Brewer's Dictionary of Phrase and Fable;* Cerf, Bennett, *Try and Stop Me;* Edwards, Tryan, *Dictionary of Thoughts;* Fuller, Edward, *Thesaurus of Epigrams; Granger's Index to Poetry and Recitations;* Prochnow, Herbert, *Public Speaker's Treasure Chest; Speaker's Handbook of Epigrams and Witticisms;* and *The New Speaker's Treasury of Wit and Wisdom;* Roberts, Kate, *Hoyt's New Cyclopedia of Practical Quotations;* Stevenson, Burton, *The Home Book of Quotations;* Untermeyer, Louis, *Treasury of Laughter.*

Perhaps you think you do not need to take notes on your material. However, a person forgets 40 per cent of what he reads within an hour

after he has read it. You need something more reliable than your memory. You need a filing system to help you find your material when you want it. You cannot afford just to have it "somewhere."

Taking notes is an individual matter, and you need to develop a method that works for you. You may want to keep a notebook in speech class for all outlines, materials, speech observations, criticism sheets, tests, and clippings. A notebook has many advantages; however, you cannot easily shuffle and rearrange individual items of material if there are several written on one page. This is why you may prefer to use a card system in recording material or to combine the use of cards and the use of a notebook.

Cards have the advantage of quick, easy filing. Materials can be easily rearranged, and new items added in proper sequence. Individual cards can be removed and used for quotations or facts in a speech, and returned to your file. Because of their size and greater firmness, they are popular among public speakers. In using cards, many people prefer the 3" x 5" size. However, you may find the 4" x 6" a bit more practical because it allows you more space.

Be careful and systematic in making out cards. Place a *main* heading in the top left-hand corner. Next to it list the *part* or *subhead* of the main subject.

Here is an example of a card.

> Speech Correction: Speech Defect (Definition)
> Speech is defective when it deviates so far from speech of other people that it calls attention to itself, interferes with communication, or causes its possessor to be maladjusted.
> Van Riper, Charles, *Speech Correction -- Principles* and *Methods* (Prentice-Hall, Inc., 1954), p. 19.

Put one quotation or set of facts on each card. Always write the source in the following order: (1) author, (2) title of article and publication or title of book, (3) volume, (4) date, (5) pages.

Be accurate! You may be challenged by an opponent or a member of the audience. Exact wording of your quotation and correct statement of your source are essential, especially in debate or discussion.

Whatever your note-filing method, the important thing is for you to develop a way of making your information *permanent* and *easily available.*

Now let's study each kind of material and see how it can best be used to make your meanings more clear and vivid, your speech more convincing. We will explain each type of material and suggest its use.

FACTS. These are known truths or events. They have been verified by actual experience or observation. They constitute the largest body of supporting materials. They may be used to support any of the five purposes; however, they are most often used in speeches to inform. Example: Leaves on the trees turn color in the fall because of the lack of chlorophyll in the leaf cells.

STATISTICS. Numerical facts are called statistics. But they are more than mere numbers. They are compiled to show the proportion of cases of a certain kind. Although any speech may contain statistics, they are most frequent in speeches to inform or to convince.
Example: Labor Day traffic deaths in 1958 were 420 for the three-day period. Experts predicted a 1959 total of 450. By the end of the first 24-hour period, 125 traffic deaths were reported in 1959. The three-day total was 438 deaths.

TESTIMONY AND QUOTATIONS. These are statements of opinion from ordinary persons or authorities. Facts, statistics, and testimony together are called *evidence* when used to *prove* a point. Expert testimony (or quotation) is most often used in speeches to inform, to convince, or to actuate. If his testimony is to be effective, the expert should meet the following tests: (1) He should be recognized as an expert. (2) He should be qualified. (3) He should be unprejudiced or unbiased. (4) He should be quoted in the field in which he *is* an expert. You should distinguish between statements that make interesting support for your point (literary quotations) and those used to prove points (expert testimony.)
Example: *Literary quotations:* " 'Tis with our judgments as our watches, —none/Go just alike, yet each believes his own."—Alexander Pope.

EXPERT TESTIMONY. "Radioactive fall-out from *all* atomic tests to date will increase your radiation exposure by only 3 to 6 percent over the natural background radiation that everyone receives."—(Sept. 1959) U.S. Congressional Committee on Atomic Energy.

NARRATIVES. These are materials in story form used to support points in your speech. They make the points clear, arouse interest, and provide the human touch. An effective form of narrative is the *anecdote*—brief and usually humorous. Your selection should be based on novelty, appropriateness to the point, and suitability for the audience and occasion.

Example: Parents and teachers, especially, note the changing times as they observe the behavior of children. One older teacher in a metropolitan neighborhood was used to scrawls on the sidewalk and masonry. "Jimmy is a meanie" was a common sight. Imagine her amusement when she noted this change: "Jimmy is a nasty boron isotope."

ILLUSTRATIONS. A detailed example, narrative in form and vivid in detail, is an illustration. Its strongest use is in drawing comparisons that help make meaning clear. There are two principal types: the *real* illustration—which actually occurred—and the *planned,* or general, illustration—which is not an actual happening. It may be imagined and constructed by the user to fit his point and support it.

EXAMPLES. An example is a *specific instance* of a rule or point, but usually it is not a fully developed illustration. Examples are useful in all types of speeches to answer the audience's eternal questions, "For instance?" or "Name one!" Examples pin down and make specific your general points.

Example: In America success is not reserved for the rich man or one of distinguished ancestry. Great desire, ability, hard work, and the opportunity to use all of these are more important. Consider Andrew Carnegie, Abraham Lincoln, and Henry Ford; all of them came from lowly backgrounds and achieved great things.

COMPARISONS, ANALOGIES, AND CONTRASTS. Expressing vividly the *similarities* between two objects makes them clearer. This is *comparison* or *analogy.* Figures of speech such as *metaphors* and *similes* are comparisons and are very useful in achieving vividness. Contrasts rely on showing *differences* between two objects in order to make their relationship sharp and clear.

You should recognize the difference between the *figurative analogy,* useful in making an instance more clear, and the *literal analogy,* important in proving a point. The former is based on a similarity of relationships; the latter is based on *actual* similarities.

Examples: *Figurative analogy.* The circulation of blood is similar to the circulation of money. The heart, like the mint, could be said to be a starting point, from which the purified blood proceeds to circulate through the body. When it is filled with impurities, it returns through the lungs to the heart, and the process starts all over again. *Literal analogy.* A short time ago Highland Park (Illinois) High School initiated a classroom and interscholastic debate program. Parents had for years observed the benefits of the strong debate program at New Trier, a neighboring high school of the same size, type of student body, and financial status. Highland Park parents wished to provide the same training and benefits for their own children. *Simile.* He had a mind like a steel trap. It snapped up everything that came its way. *Metaphor.* His voice boomed from a cannon of a mouth. She stroked her hair with red lacquered talons. When I tried to persuade them I ran into a brick wall.

EPIGRAMS. A terse, witty saying that sums up the point is an epigram. Epigrams help provide variety and hold audience interest in any kind of speech.

Example: Oliver Wendell Holmes' sign on his medical office: "Small fevers gratefully received."

Select your materials carefully and learn to use them wisely in supporting your points. Thus, you will gain the attention of your audience, hold its interest, and achieve the responses you seek.

NONVERBAL MATERIALS

The materials discussed above have all been verbal or printed. There are other materials that will be very important to you—those of the visual, audible, and audio-visual types. Although they are often described as aids, they are actually materials in a different form; you can use them to support the ideas in your speech.

VISUAL MATERIALS. These include paintings, sketches, prints, posters, charts, diagrams, models, objects themselves, flannel board displays, chalkboard sketches, slides or filmstrips, and silent motion pictures. With these visual aids you can often cover more subject matter than you can with verbal materials alone. You can find such aids or prepare them yourself; they will have a strong and vivid effect upon your audience.

AUDIBLE MATERIALS. These obviously are those that can be *heard* by the audience. We live in an age of electronics, that has made it possible to record, preserve, and play back the sounds in our world. These aids should not be a *substitute* for your speech. The chief kinds are magnetic tapes and disk recordings. Again you may make such materials in your preparation period.

AUDIO-VISUAL MATERIALS. These combine visual and auditory presentation, and an increasing store of such items is available. They include sound motion pictures, filmstrips with a sound track or disk recording to fit the frames of the film, your own slides with your live comment or recorded tape to accompany them, commercial or educational kinescopes, video tape, and television. They provide you with vivid materials with which to support the idea in your speech. A list of professional sources of these materials is given at the end of this chapter.

Nonverbal materials can be well related to the points of the speech they support, and they are useful in all the types of speeches we have discussed.

There are, however, some special suggestions for their use: Be sure they are exactly what you need and are relevant to the points you wish them to support. They should be correct and accurate in all details. Be sure that they are clearly visible (and legible) and/or clearly audible to the audience. Be sure to link the material to your speech, as follows: (1) State your point. (2) Introduce your verbal support, e.g., example or illustration. (3) Offer the nonverbal material and clearly show its relationship to the point it supports. (4) Allow enough time for the audience to absorb the material and its relationship.

ACTIVITIES

1. Recall speeches you have heard, either live or over radio or television. Select one that you believe exemplifies each of the four methods of delivery mentioned in this chapter. Relate the delivery to the preparation involved in each method. Evaluate the effectiveness of the speech as you listened to it, and in terms of audience reaction.

2. Prepare a four-minute speech to inform, following the steps suggested in the text. Keep a record of the amount of time you spend on each of the steps. Indicate how you might change this time distribution for your next talk. Justify the allotment of time you use.

3. Evaluate your methods in the preparation and use of notes in the speech you prepared and gave for exercise 2. Determine what changes you can make to improve your effectiveness in the organization and delivery of your talk?

4. Organize the class into groups of four members each. Have each group select a single subject that is of interest to all. Then have each speaker use this subject for his talk, one giving a speech to inform, the next a speech to stimulate, another a speech to convince, and one a speech to entertain.

5. Choose a speech from a collection of speeches, from *Vital Speeches* magazine, or from a similar source. Read it carefully, then analyze it, indicating in an outline the following: the subject, the title, the general purpose, the specific purpose or central idea, the major points of the body with their supporting materials, the introduction, the conclusion, the reported response to the talk, if this information is available.

6. Prepare a list of ten possible speech subjects, drawing on your own interests or experiences. Draw up a similar list of subjects on contemporary affairs. Continue this process, as time permits, to form a speaker's reference file for use in class or outside it.

7. Go to your school library. By title and author, list the books of quotations that would provide useful materials for you as a speaker. Also list the almanacs, books of facts, encyclopedias, and other general reference works available to you.

8. Start a file of anecdotes, both humorous and serious, that might serve you in speech introductions or as supporting materials.

9. After a few days of observation, prepare an analysis of the interests, hobbies, beliefs, experiences, and values of members of your speech class. Keep these on file for use in the preparation of your future speeches.

10. Develop a speech in which you use the life of a famous person as the subject. Select someone who interests you greatly. Read his biography and writings, newspaper interviews, discussions of his work, and the like. Examples of such persons are: Albert Schweitzer, George Bernard Shaw, Abraham Lincoln, Frank Lloyd Wright, Mark Twain, Babe Ruth, Eleanor Roosevelt, Madame Curie, and any others you might know.

CHAPTER 7

ORGANIZING
AND
OUTLINING
YOUR
SPEECH

...to follow that way straight forward, to carry out the plan without being obliged to deviate from it a thousand times by a thousand varying influences, requires, besides great strength of character, great clearness and steadiness of mind.

—KARL VON CLAUSEWITZ

Many students wonder why, when speech is primarily a matter of oral communication, they should have to make a written outline. The reason is that it is difficult for any of us under ordinary circumstances to keep to the point. In conversation (or argument) you and your friends may begin by discussing a particular actor, then go on to mention this actor's performance in a popular movie, pass from that to the movie, to the role of movies in our social and cultural life, to the function of the director, the importance of the playwright, and on to special lighting and photographic effects. It may be a stimulating conversation, and most entertaining, but it is not a speech.

A speech has a subject, a specific purpose, and an audience. If you are to keep to the subject and achieve your purpose, you will need an outline to guide you; otherwise you will scatter your points, wander from the subject, and fail to achieve your object.

ORGANIZING YOUR SPEECH

Good organization does not occur because you scribble a few notes on a scrap of paper. It results from good thinking, careful planning, originality, and practical use of an outline. You must think clearly in order to plan the way your points or ideas relate to the specific purpose of your speech and to each other. You need to exercise care in fitting in the details of your materials. Originality gives your talk novelty and sparkle. And, of course, there is no substitute for well-prepared notes or a logical outline.

There are certain things that will aid you in your work. The first is knowledge of the basic structure of a speech—the three parts, their purposes, and what each contains. The next is to understand that there are many ways to arrange your ideas and materials: topical, time, space, and many others.

Most modern authorities agree that the three parts of a speech are the introduction, the body, and the conclusion.

The body is the longest part of a speech and requires the greatest study and care in the arrangement of the material. You plan the body first because it contains the principal content, and this carries out your purpose and develops the central idea. The introduction and the conclusion are planned in relationship to the body—the one to lead into it, the other to summarize or reinforce it.

The Body: Ways of Arranging Ideas and Materials

The general ways of arranging ideas are useful in organizing the body of your speech. Your subject, specific purpose, and audience strongly influence your organization. You must develop an organized sequence that proceeds clearly and effectively from start to finish. If you achieve this, your audience will be able to follow your thoughts. We will study seven ways of arranging the materials in the body: topical, time, space, cause-effect, problem-solution, logical, and climactic. Let us examine the first kind of arrangement.

TOPICAL ARRANGEMENT. Certain subjects and types of information fall easily into subdivisions that seem natural. They may represent parts of an organization, company, or subject that offer units convenient to handle in speaking. At times questions or issues in the minds of the audience will provide a topical arrangement. Example:

PURCHASING A HI-FI SYSTEM

I. Cost
II. Space
III. Manufacturers of equipment
IV. The amplifier
V. The turntable or changer
VI. The speakers
VII. The cabinet or housing

TIME ARRANGEMENT. Some subjects and materials are best organized in the order in which they happened. This is called chronological arrangement. Here you start with the point that came first in time, and follow in order with the second, third, fourth, fifth items, until you reach the last. A time arrangement can also be used backward. Example:

THE DEVELOPMENT OF THE AUTOMOBILE

I. The first automobile
II. Automobiles 1910-1915
III. Automobiles 1915-1925, etc.

SPACE ARRANGEMENT. Certain subjects and materials are best organized according to their geographical or physical location. This means that instead of arranging your points on the basis of *when* they happened, you arrange them on the basis of *where* they are. If you talk on the Empire State Building, you can discuss the way it is constructed floor by floor. Example:

TROUBLE SPOTS IN THE CARIBBEAN

I. Cuba—Communist thorn in our side
II. Guatemala
III. El Salvador
IV. Honduras
V. Nicaragua

Good organization is the result of careful planning and thorough research.

CAUSE-EFFECT ARRANGEMENT. At times your talk can be best organized in a way that allows you to discuss a number of actual conditions and then point to the results of these conditions. This is called a cause-effect arrangement because the conditions produce the effects, or results, that you point out.

Social, political, or historical materials often are nicely organized in such an arrangement. The subject of Salk polio vaccine can be handled in this way:

I. Development of the Salk polio vaccine was a great medical achievement (*cause*).
    A. The virus was discovered and isolated.
    B. The vaccine was made in the laboratory.
    C. The vaccine was tested on animals in the laboratory.
II. The real test was its use on human beings (*effect*).
    A. In 1958 with limited use the number of polio cases was greatly reduced.
    B. In 1959 with wider use there were no epidemics of polio.
    C. In 1960 polio cases were still further reduced.

PROBLEM-SOLUTION ARRANGEMENT. Often it is more effective to organize your points and the supporting materials into two principal sections; the first would be the explanation of a problem and the second the solution or solutions to the problem. Many issues in our social, political, economic, or educational life are best handled by such an arrangement. This method can be used for those issues that already exist or for those that may arise in the future.

In some cases you may suggest several solutions in a speech of this type, but each individual solution must be developed clearly and related to the problem as described.

Here is an example of the problem-solution arrangement from an actual student outline for a speech on traffic safety and driver education.

MAKE TODAY'S DIEWAYS TOMORROW'S HIWAYS

Problem

I. Deaths on the highways are a major problem in the United States.
A. In 1963 there were 43,600 deaths and 1,600,000 disabling injuries in traffic accidents.
B. In the Korean war an average of 8500 people were killed in each year of fighting.
C. The causes of these accidents are known:
1. Speed and higher horsepower of cars are the greatest.
a. Speed caused 19,500 of the deaths, or one of every two; it caused one of every four injuries.
b. Careless or untrained, irresponsible drivers caused close to a majority of accidents.
c. Faulty equipment was responsible for only 5 per cent of the accidents.
2. The toll is increasing despite steel car bodies, safety glass, seat belts, padded dashboards, and power brakes.

Solution

II. Driver education is the solution for the major causes.
A. In grade school, children can be taught:
1. Rules of the road.
2. Road signs.
3. Proper driving courtesy.
B. In high school, training can be continued:

78

1. Proper driving techniques and habits.
2. Careful driving.
3. Further knowledge of laws, etc., to qualify them for safe driving (less speed) and their licenses.
C. This training will remedy the problem by getting at the major causes, the careless driver and excessive speed.

LOGICAL ARRANGEMENT. In arguing that your audience accept your points, you are immediately challenged to prove what you say. This means you must arrange your material in such a way that each sub point proves the truth or reasoned acceptance of the point it supports. Each sub point is thus a reason for the acceptance of the main argument preceding it. In the outline of "Today's Dieways," you see such an arrangement of points, in which the supporting subheads are reasons for your acceptance of the main point.

In setting forth the problem of deaths on the highway, the speaker cites the official statistics of 43,600 deaths. He also lists the major causes, showing that the driver and his handling of the car—not defective equipment—cause the majority of deaths.

This is a good example of logical arrangement, a pattern that you can use effectively whenever your speech demands that you prove something. Here is another example:

OUR CITY SHOULD CONDUCT A CAMPAIGN AGAINST FLIES

I. Thousands of flies infest the city every year.
   A. They breed everywhere.
   B. They buzz at every kitchen door.
II. Flies spread disease.
   A. They carry germs.
   B. They contaminate food.
III. Flies can be eliminated easily.
   A. Widespread use of DDT kills them.
   B. Cleaning up refuse prevents their breeding.

CLIMACTIC ARRANGEMENT. In speeches to inform, convince, and actuate, you can often get understanding and acceptance of your materials by arranging them in the order of climax. This means that you put your least important point first and support it well. Next, place your second most important point with its material, and continue this through to your last and most significant point, which becomes your climax. In other words, your speech builds as you progress from the least to the most important point, from the weakest argument to the strongest, from the least exciting to the most exciting. If you plan well, the climax should convince and impress the audience.

There is a certain audience psychology necessary for correct use of climactic organization. If you gain audience interest, understanding, or belief in your weakest point, and the audience senses that you are building, they will listen, accept, or act on the stronger parts of your talk. The climax should literally bowl the audience over if you have planned well. The body of the speech below is outlined in climactic arrangement:

MOUNTAINS THRILL ME

I. The Bad Lands are mountainlike formations caused by erosion of wind and water.
>A. Location is in western South Dakota.
>B. There are interesting colors and shapes, but there is little height.

II. The Black Hills are mountains but not of extreme altitude.
>A. They present beautiful color scenes and interesting vegetation in South Dakota.
>B. The Needles are very striking.
>C. Mount Rushmore, with the carved figures of the four Presidents, is most impressive.

III. Rocky Mountain National Park (Colorado) contains the highest peaks I have seen.
>A. Long's Peak and over twenty others are over 14,000 feet, but they are not so overpowering as others I have seen.
>B. Bear Lake and others high up in the range are picturesque.
>C. Trail Ridge Road is the highest traveled road in North America and permits a view of the whole range.

IV. The Grand Tetons (Wyoming) are much like the European Alps.
>A. They rise abruptly from the floor of Jackson Hole.
>B. Jenny Lake and Jackson Lake are directly at the foot of the huge peaks.
>C. The Tetons have a rugged beauty, but are not so high as Long's Peak.

V. Glacier National Park (Montana) gives me my greatest thrill.

A. There are four gorgeous mountain areas, with peaks surrounding the lakes in each case.

B. The scenery in each area is distinctive and almost overpowering, with rugged peaks everywhere.

1. The East Glacier area has peaks around Two Medicine and St. Mary's Lakes.

2. Around Swift Current and Josephine Lakes there are many glacial areas.

3. Waterton Lake and the peaks are like the fiords in Norway.

4. Lake McDonald is different, with its peaks set in green slopes and forests, and is very lovely.

C. The fifty glaciers on the mountains make them unique.

D. The Going-to-the-Sun Highway and Logan Pass are more thrilling to me than Trail Ridge Road in Colorado.

The Introduction: Ways of Arranging Ideas and Materials

The introduction has three important purposes: (1) to gain contact with the audience, (2) to secure attention and arouse interest in your

subject, and (3) to reveal the specific purpose and central idea of your talk. The content of your introduction is important; use significant material to gain contact with the audience and arouse their interest.

AN APPROPRIATE QUOTATION. It is not difficult to find a quotation appropriate to your subject, audience, and the occasion. Be sure it is brief, to the point, unusual, and from someone the audience knows and respects. To start his speech on the importance of reading wisely, a high-school senior used this quotation from Francis Bacon: "Some books are to be tasted, others to be swallowed, and some few to be chewed and digested."

A STARTLING STATEMENT. At times you may want to jolt your audience to arouse their interest and capture their attention. In the first class of a course in flight training, the officer said to his class, "Look at the man on your right long and carefully, and remember what I say to you now—in one month one of you will not be here!" He then went on to discuss the rigors and opportunities of the program.

A CHALLENGING QUESTION OR SERIES OF QUESTIONS. The speaker can sometimes arouse attention and set the key points of his talk by a question or a series of questions to start the audience thinking in a way that will lead to the response he seeks. In beginning his talk "Losing Weight Easily," a doctor asked an audience of women, "What would you do if your husband *forced* you to carry a twenty-pound sack of groceries ten miles every day?" He then explained that they were doing exactly that because of their own foolish eating habits.

A HUMOROUS STORY. Some people think a humorous story or anecdote is the only good way to begin a speech. In learning the speaker's art, don't overlook the value of humor, but don't be misled into believing that telling a funny story will make you a success.

Be sure that your anecdote is carefully chosen. It must be to the point—useful in leading your audience into your subject. It must not offend anyone in the audience, and it must be in good taste. If you are not sure whether your story is appropriate, don't use it—get one that is. Finally, be certain that it is genuinely funny to the majority of people. Tastes in humor differ vastly. If you can satisfy these requirements, your story should serve as a good introduction.

A SHORT DEMONSTRATION. You can use nonverbal materials to introduce a speech. Show or demonstrate an object, hold up a picture, play a few measures of a record, flash a picture on a screen, or briefly display a chart. In introducing her talk, a girl walked to the front of the room. After a momentary pause she opened her purse and took out her lipstick; she quickly painted a pair of lips on her face, produced some rouge, and in an instant smeared a blob on each cheek. "Now," she said, "most of you do not need cosmetics. But if you must, you should learn to use them properly. Today I will explain how to apply make-up properly."

AN ATTENTION-CAPTURING INCIDENT OR ILLUSTRATION. Similar to the humorous story is the incident that instantly grasps the attention of the audience. Try to select one that leads directly into the subject of your talk. Relate it clearly, smoothly, and vividly. A high-school junior opened his talk in this way:

"Last evening as I sat in my room studying, I was interrupted by the furious barking of our dog, which we keep tied near the garage. I dashed downstairs and out the back door in time to hear the sound of footsteps fading away. The dog continued to bark, and as I approached him I passed our car, parked in the drive. I noticed that two of the hub caps were missing and one tire was flat. It had been punctured or cut by some sharp object, perhaps a knife. This made me very angry, and that is my reason for talking to you today on 'Why Teen-age Vandalism?'"

AN IMMEDIATE ISSUE OR CHALLENGE. At times the best way to start your talk is to state a critical issue or a challenging situation. Here is an example of such a beginning on the subject of good sportsmanship:

"You all know we lost the basketball game with Parkersburg last night by one point. You know that our fans started booing and yelling whenever Parkersburg tried to make a free throw. Then Parkersburg fans started doing the same thing to our players. What happened? Our boys couldn't take it. We lost by a margin of one free shot. I believe we need to talk turkey among ourselves about good sportsmanship."

A PERSONAL REFERENCE OR GREETING. One of the quickest ways to establish a common bond with your audience is to say something of a personal nature. This is how an alumnus began his talk to a high-school group:

"Two years ago I sat in row three, seat number four, of this assembly hall. In some ways I wish I were sitting in that very seat right now. As I look down there, I see a very pretty girl in seat number five!"

83

A REFERENCE TO SOMETHING RELATED TO THE OCCASION. You can plan one of the simplest and best introductions by referring to the occasion. Select something appropriate, pleasing to the audience, and timely, to lead into your subject. There are many possibilities: a casual comment on something you noticed; a genuine compliment or sincere expression of pleasure regarding the town or its people; reference to a special or local interest; a remark linking your talk to that of a previous speaker; a gracious, sincere acknowledgment of the chairman's introduction. All of these are useful and help raise interest and establish contact with your audience.

A BRIEF REFERENCE TO YOUR SUBJECT OR PROBLEM. When you know that your audience is interested in your subject, you can move much more directly in your opening remarks. Recently a college guidance counselor, in his talk before high-school students on college admissions, started with the following statement:

"All of you are interested in attending college. The chief questions facing you are these: (1) How do I go about applying for admission? (2) When do I make my application? In the next hour I intend to help you answer these questions."

The Conclusion: Ways of Arranging Ideas and Materials

The chief purpose of any kind of conclusion is to clinch the central idea. You want to reinforce the central idea and summarize your main points. You want also to direct attention to your specific purpose and to the response you hope to gain. But this response is not limited to your content. You want to leave your listeners in the proper emotional state or attitude.

In addition, you wish the audience to realize that this is the end of your talk. By all means avoid the situation of Melopemus Jones in one of Stephen Leacock's essays. A guest at a tea, Jones did not know how to say good-by. The result was they discovered the poor fellow thirty days later amidst a heap of dirty teacups, mumbling to himself, "Well, I guess I better go—but—" When you quit, quit all over and for keeps.

In planning your conclusion consider what mood would be most favorable to the response you wish to achieve. Should it be enthusiastic, angry, thoughtful, logical? When you have decided, organize your conclusion to obtain this effect. There are numerous ways in which to do this. Learn to select and use the most practical.

The simplest kind of conclusion is a summary. There are several types.

The formal summary repeats briefly the main points of your speech. If you had a single point, this single idea is your summary; if the talk was more complex, you have a series of points. As a rule, it helps if you state your ideas in ways slightly different from the ones used in the body; it sharpens your focus.

The "in other words" summary. A change of the statement, a summary which says, "In other words, I mean this," or "I want you to remember this," is often effective. It is sometimes called a common-sense summary because you strip the idea down and reword it in common-sense language.

The epigram, which should be an old friend by now, is a summary worded with wit and is a most effective conclusion. It ties things together in a short, pithy phrase containing the heart of your talk. As one speech teacher said about rambling, unprepared speakers: "Many can rise to the occasion, but few know when to sit down." He then followed with another epigram. "A good speech has a good beginning and a good ending, which are kept close together."

An appropriate quotation is just as valuable for use in a conclusion as in an introduction. It can express briefly, vividly, and dramatically, the key idea in your talk.

An illustration or striking incident also has the attention-getting power to clinch the main idea of your conclusion. But be sure it is really striking and completely applicable to your point.

An appeal or challenge is a means of emphasizing the main point of your speech by associating it with the drives or emotions that stir the audience to action or acceptance. Add emotion to your logic and ideas to reinforce the points developed in the body of your talk.

A specific procedure applied to audience interests asks the audience to take a specific action that will further their interests. These are examples: "Vote for Tom Smith for class president and reduce senior dues"; or "Boycott the Strand theater and get rid of dirty movies"; or "Let's whip polio; get your shot today."

A picture of better things to come may sound like the standard conclusion of a political speech, but it can be a very useful and strong conclusion. Add some originality to the picture and it becomes even more effective. The body of the talk usually exposes weaknesses, describes bad conditions, or expresses disapproval of established things. The conclusion describes sincerely, enthusiastically, vividly, and optimistically a picture of better times to come.

OUTLINING YOUR SPEECH

The basic purposes of an outline are to ensure proper preparation and guide you in delivery. Your outline is the blueprint of your talk—and it is also tangible evidence that you have made careful preparation. A good outline relieves you of the burden of remembering every detail; you may rarely refer to it, but it is there when you need it. It represents your best in terms of specific purpose, central idea, main points, and supporting materials, all organized in the best way possible.

Your outline is related to the four methods of speaking. When you use the extemporaneous method, you must develop notes and outlines that ensure the greatest effectiveness in your speech.

List of Words Outline

This outline is the shortest and simplest type. It is practical for the experienced or talented speaker who has poise, fluency, and an excellent memory. The example below develops the body of the talk only:

AMERICAN RECREATION IS A BALL

I. Baseball
II. Basketball
III. Football
IV. Volleyball
V. Handball
VI. Tennis
VII. Golf

Short-Phrase Outline

This type of outline helps you because of its brevity. Each short phrase suggests an idea. If properly written, the catch phrases help you to remember your particular points as well as their arrangement. However, this type may bother you when you are speaking if you cannot remember what follows the catch phrase.

BABY-SITTING: EDUCATION FOR PARENTHOOD

A Liberal Education

Introduction

   I. My financial depression
      A. Big expenses
      B. Small allowance
  II. The neighbors' babies—my gold mine
      A. Close to me
      B. One year old
      C. Parents on the go

Body

   I. My publicity campaign
      A. Phone calls
      B. Card in mail
  II. The campaign pays off
      A. Two jobs
      B. Preparing to mine gold
 III. My liberal education
      A. Meeting the parents
      B. Learning the house
      C. "Getting to Know You"
         1. Awake or sleeping!
         2. Feeding
         3. Burping
         4. Spitting up
         5. Changing
         6. Entertaining
         7. Sleeping—or awake!

Conclusion

   I. It's worth it—$$$$
  II. Try it sometime

Complete Sentence Outline

The most practical outline for you as a beginning speaker is that in which complete sentences are used throughout. It has numerous advantages. First, it requires that you develop your points in formal language when you prepare your speech. Next, if you glance at the outline during delivery you will find completely worded ideas. No guesswork or interpretation is needed. Finally, it is especially helpful in the introduction and conclusion because it supplies you with the exact wording you wish to use. This example brings out these advantages clearly:

AMERICA'S ANSWER TO SMALL FOREIGN CARS

Introduction

I. Since 1955, a million small, economical foreign cars have been sold in the United States.
  A. France has sold many Renaults.
  B. West Germany has led with the Volkswagen.
  C. Great Britain has been selling Austins, Vauxhalls, and others.
II. There were four major reasons for their sale here.
  A. They are small, easy to handle, and solve parking problems.
  B. They are economical on gas, oil, and operation cost.
  C. They are stripped of useless, showy accessories.
  D. They sell at a price far below that of most American cars.

Body

I. America's answer began in 1957 with the AMC Rambler, a smaller car.
II. It was followed by the Studebaker Lark in 1958.
III. In 1959, the three manufacturers, General Motors, Ford, and Chrysler, gave their answer with completely new models for 1960.
  A. Ford introduced the Falcon, with an 85-horsepower engine mounted in front, single headlights, and claimed 32 miles to a gallon of gasoline; it was 109 inches long and 67 inches high.
  B. General Motors produced the Corvair, with an 80-horsepower, air-cooled engine mounted in the rear; the car was 108 inches long and is only 51 inches high.
  C. Chrysler developed the Valiant, with an engine of similar power; it was 184 inches long and about the height of the Falcon.
  D. All cars were stripped of costly accessories and were about 1000 pounds lighter than standard models.
  E. The price is just over $2000.

Conclusion

I.   The success of America's answer will depend on the acceptance of these American-made cars by the public.

II. The dealers believe that they have correctly sensed the demand for small, economical cars and that they can meet foreign competition by their new products.

Principles and Suggestions for Outlining

As you read through the sample outlines you will notice a consistent pattern in all of them. This list will help you understand the pattern and principles of good outlining.

1.   Center your speech title at the top of the outline.

2.   Mark the main parts: introduction, body, and conclusion.

3.   Leave a double space between parts of your outline. Proper spacing makes it easier to read at a glance.

4.   Within each main part, use a system of symbols in a consistent scheme to show the relationship between main points and sub points. Your main points will be I, II, III, etc. The first supporting points will be A, B, C, etc. To support these, you will probably have sub points marked 1, 2, 3, and other sub points as needed.

    I.

       A.

          1.

            a.

               (1)

                   (a)

                   (b)

               (2)

                   (a)

                   (b)

            b.

               (1)

                   (a)

                   (b)

          2.

            a.

               (1)   etc., etc.

5. Place only one point in each numbered or lettered division.

6. Indent points of equal importance the same distance from the left margin and use corresponding symbols for them.

7. In the introduction be sure to state the central idea and make your specific purpose clear.

8. The order of points in the body should be consistent with the kind of arrangement you select for your talk (See types of arrangement).

9. Use suitable connectives where they are necessary to link points in your speech or the major parts of your talk.

10. Write out in your outline the opening and closing sentences of your speech.

WORD AND PRACTICE YOUR SPEECH, USING NOTES, AN OUTLINE, AND AUDIO-VISUAL AIDS

Having organized and outlined your material, you are ready to word and practice your speech. Remember we are stressing the extemporaneous as the soundest speaking method; the object of your practice is not to memorize, but to become effective in on-the-spot wording and convincing delivery.

Working from your outline, practice *aloud* putting each idea, each important point, into effective oral language. Refer to Chapter 8 for help in choosing language that is clear and easily understood, persuasive, and suitable to the audience and the occasion. Only key points that require absolute accuracy, such as quotations or statistics, should be written in your outline so that you will have the exact wording when needed.

How to Link the Materials and Points of Your Speech

Pay careful attention to how you fit your speech materials together. As you build your outline you begin to see that you are not aimlessly piling up one point upon another. It becomes clear that every example, fact, or illustration is related to another. You need a means of expressing that relationship—a means of fastening your materials together to make a strong, solid speech.

Transitions are the means you use. These are words or phrases that carry the meaning from one point to the next, or from a point to the example, statistic, or illustration you use to support the point. Transitions are the important links that hold the parts of your speech together.

You can tie the parts of your talk together by numbering your points for the audience or by using linking words, such as *therefore, consequently, my next point, for example, let's quote from, let's look at the record, here are the figures, I recall a case, you have seen the problem— now we can try to solve it.* These phrases link materials closely to the points they support so the audience understands them easily. Transitions "tighten up" your talk and give it clarity and strength.

Suggestions for the Use of Audio-Visual Materials

If you plan to use any of these materials in your speech they will require some special preparation. Nothing is more embarrassing than a mechanical failure of this type.

1. Rehearse with your audio-visual materials exactly as you plan to present them in your speech, linking them smoothly to the points they are intended to support. This will help you time your speech correctly.

2. If you use objects such as flip charts, make sure you can move them easily. If you use anything mechanical, practice with it often enough to know how to operate it smoothly—and check to see that it is running properly.

3. If you play only a portion of a tape or recording, mark the starting and ending points so you use only this section in your talk.

4. In advance of performance, check the recording tape or film by actually running it to hear that everything is operating as you planned it. Check your projection equipment at the same time.

5. If necessary, get a classmate to help operate equipment so you can devote maximum time to the actual communication of your speech.

In the speeches outlined below, you will note the types of materials used to support the ideas of the students who planned the talks.

SUPPORT STUDENT ACTIVITIES

Specific purpose: To actuate students to buy their activity tickets now.
  I. What is a student activity ticket?
      A. It is a single ticket sold in advance that admits you to all
      school events.   (*definition*)
          1. It admits you to athletic events: football, basketball, swim-
          ming.   (*examples*)
          2. It admits you to plays and debates.

3. It admits you to two all-school parties.

4. It admits you to the Fall Carnival.

5. It gives you weekly copies of the school paper.

II. Why buy a student activity ticket?

    A. It is more convenient.

      1. ONE ticket takes the place of individual tickets to various events.   *(fact)*

                                       (reference to definition)

      2. It saves you money.

        a. Total price of the ticket is $8.00.

        b. Individual tickets to all events would cost $17.50.

        c. Even if you attend only part of the activities, you save money; individual admissions to football and basketball would be $10.50.

      3. It finances *in advance* the student activities in all of these departments.

        a. Funds are distributed on a percentage basis to departments involved.

        b. Such a guarantee allows sponsors to budget safely.

      4. The student body supports this plan.

        a. Last year 75 per cent of the freshmen and 80 per cent of sophomore, junior, and senior classes subscribed.

                            (statistics)

      5. The faculty supports the plan.

        a. Principal James Russell states: "This is the best method we have found for financing student activities."

                            (authority or expert opinion)

        b. Business Manager Tom Ewing says: "Student activity tickets are most satisfactory for both the school program and the students."

      6. Parents are in favor also.

        a. Mrs. Sam Roberts, President of the Parent-Teacher association, says: "My children not only save money but develop interests in all kinds of school events."

                            (quotation and evidence)

b. Mrs. John Ainslee, parent of a freshman girl, says: "My daughter not only attended fine educational activities but was able to meet many students because she bought a ticket in her first year."

III. Where, how, and when can tickets be purchased?

A. Each homeroom has salesmen.

B. Tickets may be paid for over a four-week period.

C. Students sign up and may pay the whole amount or the first $2.00 in the first week of school.

(*additional facts*)

TRAFFIC LAWS

<table>
<tr><td>General statement</td><td>I.</td><td>There is a need for better traffic regulation.</td></tr>
<tr><td>Planned illustration</td><td></td><td>A. Suppose you had an experience like this:</td></tr>
</table>

General statement
Planned illustration

I. There is a need for better traffic regulation.

A. Suppose you had an experience like this:

1. You parked just at the end of a parking zone.

2. Someone else pushed your car out of the zone.

3. You were arrested and fined.

Factual illustration

B. Son of the mayor of Fort Bend, Illinois, was stopped eighteen times but not arrested.

1. Officer stopped the car.

2. Began argument.

3. Discovered boy's identity.

4. Apologized and released him.

Specific examples

C. There are many similar cases:

1. Elmer Jay interrupted an unmarked funeral procession in Sheboygan, Wisconsin.

2. Henry Black violated six traffic rules in Lansing, Michigan, without penalty.

3. Frequent double-parking occurs in downtown sections of Lafayette, Indiana.

Statistics

D. Figures show the extent of traffic law violation.

1. In New York last year 300,000 motorists were arrested.

2. New York motorists paid one million dollars in fines.

    a. This is more than the total paid in all England, Scotland and Wales.

Expert evidence

E. Prevalence of this condition is recognized by experts.

    1. Testimony of R. L. Burgess, special investigator for *American Magazine* who traveled 8000 miles through cities in 21 states:

        a. "There is ample justification for a growing bitterness among our millions of car owners who have come to resent and ridicule an outrageous system of traffic law enforcement which violates almost every American principle of justice and equity."

Analogy

F. It would be almost as easy for an American to eat with chopsticks as to keep track of the traffic regulations of neighboring cities.

Restatement

II. Traffic reform is an urgent American problem.

ACTIVITIES

1. For future use in class, select speech subjects that could be developed using each of the seven ways of arranging materials: topical, time, space, cause-effect, problem-solution, logical, and climactic. Outline each potential speech, giving the main points of the body in appropriate arrangement.

2. Select a speech from a collection, from the newspaper, or from *Vital Speeches*. Outline it, listing main points, sub points, and supporting materials. Identify the kind of arrangement used and evaluate its appropriateness for the talk selected.

3. Listen to the speech of a classmate. Identify the kind of arrangement used, outline the main points, and offer suggestions on its organization.

4. Select, as in the second activity, a speech. List the main points and identify the kinds of supporting material used under each point. Comment upon the effectiveness of the speech.

5. Plan a complete outline for a speech you will deliver in class. Select an appropriate subject, indicate general and specific purposes, plan the arrangement of the body. Check the outline form and the use of coördination and subordination. Select the type of introduction and conclusion from the types contained in the text. Identify the kind of outline you are using, justifying its use for this speech and occasion.

6. Plan a speech outline in which you concentrate upon the use of audio-visual aids in your presentation. Indicate the kind of aid to be used in each part of the speech and develop the use of the aids carefully and completely. Deliver the talk, comparing this method with a talk in which you have not employed such aids.

7. Explain and justify your method of practicing a speech. Discuss time, spacing of practice periods, and ways to ensure freshness in delivery.

8. Prepare a short talk in which you advise a beginning speaker on the best ways to use notes in presenting a talk.

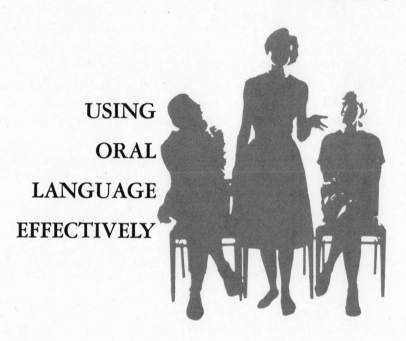

CHAPTER 8

USING
ORAL
LANGUAGE
EFFECTIVELY

*Words are the dress of thoughts; which should no
more be presented in rags, tatters, and dirt, than
your person should.*

—LORD CHESTERFIELD

Although you may speak distinctly, choose your ideas carefully, and organize them clearly, you still have to consider the effect your choice of
words will have on your audience. Remember that language consists of
words, but words are not things. They are merely symbols that stand for,
or *represent,* things. Words are handy tools which you, as a speaker, use
to call up meanings (about objects, facts, or relationships) in the minds
of your listeners. They mean different things at different times, and they
often mean different things to different people. The same word may have
a number of dictionary meanings.

Take the simple word *cat.* It may mean the domestic animal; or be a term of contempt for a human being, as a spiteful woman; it may refer to any member of the genus feline, as a lion, tiger, leopard or panther; or to one of their cousins, the civet. To a furrier it may mean a skin; to a military man a movable penthouse to protect besiegers approaching a fortification; to a sailor part of a contrivance for raising an anchor; it may be a whip; or in certain games, a stick; a double tripod; a mess of meal placed in a dovecot; or a bundle of hay worked with clay in making mud walls; or a kind of vessel used in coastal trade. Or among your friends it may mean someone who is either cool or smooth, but who does not have four legs and certainly doesn't say "Meow!" You learn the *meaning* of the word from the context in which it is used.

Lewis Carroll in *Through the Looking Glass* has Alice ask, "The question is whether you *can* make words mean so many things."

"The question is," said Humpty Dumpty, "which is to be master—that's all."

If you are going to master the use of words you will first have to understand the difference between written and spoken English, and some general requirements of spoken English. The chief requirements are: (1) clarity, (2) correct grammatical use, (3) persuasiveness, and (4) accuracy. Rose Macauley, the novelist, has pointed out, "Language should do anything it is told, undertake any job required, not be a stubborn one-idea thing." That is exactly what you can make language do, once you have mastered it.

THE DIFFERENCE BETWEEN WRITTEN
AND SPOKEN LANGUAGE

The writer selects his own subject. He writes a manuscript and turns it over to a publisher, who prints and distributes it. It is read in various situations—at home, in an office, on a train. It may be reread, studied. If there is a reaction, either favorable or unfavorable, the writer is not immediately aware of it. He is interested in the language of literature, and its appearance on a printed page. If he repeats, he will be criticized. He is concerned with style, with the effect he will have on a single reader. The writer cannot change anything, once the book is printed.

In contrast, the speaker often has his subject chosen for him. He prepares it with a specific purpose for a specific audience. He appears before his audience, delivers his talk *once,* and hopes he will succeed in obtaining the response he wants. It is certain that he will get some sort of on-the-spot reaction. Unlike the writer, he can judge from applause or interest whether he is succeeding. If the audience is restless, bored, or hostile, he can modify his speech.

The speaker is concerned with the sound of language. By careful use of voice he can influence understanding as he speaks or overcome distractions in the audience situation. He uses the language of practical discourse. He employs repetition to make his meaning clear or emphatic. His fluency is affected by conditions at the time he speaks.

Because of these differences, there are special conditions the speaker must meet, and the general requirements below are especially important.

General Requirements for Spoken Language

1. YOUR SPEECH SHOULD BE INSTANTLY UNDERSTOOD. As a speaker you must gain the response you want in a single performance. The people in your audience cannot go back to reread your talk—you must hit the mark with a single shot. Your language must be instantly understandable. Unless your listeners understand you immediately, they probably never will. For clarity and accuracy, use short sentences and simple language.

2. YOUR SPEECH SHOULD BE SUITABLE TO YOU AND TYPICAL OF YOUR OWN STYLE. Your language should fit you, as a person. You have a typical conversational style; you use words suited to your ideas, feelings, and interests. Only you are you. Only you can say it in your way. So be forthright and be yourself. Ralph Waldo Emerson, the American essayist, said, "Insist on yourself; never imitate." He also said that a man's style is his mind's voice. Your vocabulary is a product of your learning, experience, reading, and observation.

However, the language you use for a public speech will differ from language you use in everyday conversations. Use your *best* style in speaking before an audience.

3. YOUR LANGUAGE SHOULD FIT THE AUDIENCE AND THE OCCASION. Audiences vary in age, interests, sex, intelligence, and many other qualities—and occasions vary, too. Some are relaxed and informal; others demand special, sometimes formal, treatment. There is a great difference between speaking before a small committee in a classroom and before the school assembly on honors day. Select the language and style appropriate to the occasion and to your listeners.

Pleasant-sounding words are easier to listen to and easier to say than unpleasant-sounding ones. Check your entire speech, if possible by taping it, to see how it "listens." Deliberately select words and combinations of words that sound well together.

4. YOUR LANGUAGE SHOULD BE PERSONAL AND DIRECT. As a speaker, you seek a close relationship with your audience, one which says to them, "He's speaking to me." You achieve this by using personal pronouns, including direct address. You develop the *"you* attitude" and the *"we* feeling" in your speech by using personal pronouns to create a common bond with the audience.

5. YOUR SPEECH SHOULD HAVE VARIETY IN SENTENCE STRUCTURE AND VOCABULARY. Language, like voice or action, becomes monotonous if it has no change of pace. How do you achieve the variety you need? First, by using sentences of varying length. A mixture of short, medium, and long sentences, appropriately suited to the ideas is the most effective way. But don't make any sentences too long for your audience to follow easily.

Second, use variety in the structure of your sentences. Declarative sentences make statements; imperative sentences call on the audience to

Your choice of words will depend a great deal on your audience.

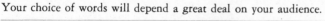

accept, to believe, or to do; exclamatory sentences (by definition) contain heightened feeling; interrogatory sentences ask questions. Intelligent variation in the kind of sentence helps you keep the audience interested because of the contrast it provides.

Variety in choice of words helps, too. Enlarge your vocabulary so you can use the most vivid, graphic, exact word available. Study examples of good written and spoken language. This will help you avoid old, trite expressions, and provide freshness in your speech. It will help you emphasize ideas to restate them in different language, language that sounds original to your audience.

Special Suggestions for Achieving Clarity

We have noted the *general* requirements for spoken language—now let's observe some *specific ways of making meanings clearer* through oral language.

1. KEEP YOUR SENTENCE LENGTH RELATIVELY SHORT. Most authorities on listening agree that many long sentences, complex in character, can be booby traps for both speaker and listener. A length of under twenty words is usually best for your purposes.

Note how much easier the second of these two sentences is to understand:

"Applications for admission and financial assistance in six schools of the university were examined by the admissions committee, and additional sums were voted to help incoming students."

"The university admissions office voted increased funds to meet requests for aid of incoming students."

Doing all you can to keep sentence length short will make the speech easier to deliver and easier to understand. Look for long sentences and try to break them into shorter ones. One editor said, "Use periods. They take no more room than commas and less room than 'whichs'."

2. AVOID MANY-SYLLABLE WORDS WHEN SHORTER WORDS WILL DO. Your choice of words should favor those that are easy to say and to understand. Mark Twain said: "I never write 'metropolis' for seven cents when I can get the same price for 'city'."

Use words that can be delivered easily. Although certain words may be appropriate, you need to be sure they can be *said* easily and smoothly— and therefore clearly. Avoid tongue twisters. Marcellinus Ammianus, the Roman historian, said 1500 years ago that the language of truth is unadorned and always simple. It's still true.

3. GET RID OF UNNECESSARY WORDS. Many words that are spoken are not needed to make the meaning clear. People afflicted with excess verbiage, which obscures clarity and weakens the argument, are called "windjammers." Don't be one. Say what you have to say in as few words as possible. Keep the meaning clear, but economize in the *amount* of language you use. Note the difference in the salutation of these two speakers. "Mr. Chairman, members of the senior class, distinguished teachers, representatives of the Board of Education, honored guests, and ladies and gentlemen." "Mr. Chairman, ladies and gentlemen."

4. USE WORDS FAMILIAR TO YOUR LISTENERS, BUT AVOID TRITE WORDS. A speaker reaches his listeners best with words they know and understand. Some educators caution against the COIK fault—giving explanations that are Clear Only If Known. If your listeners do not understand the words you use, your meaning will be lost. The simple word is often the clearest, most vivid one.

But you can overwork familiar words and use words and phrases so common and shopworn that they have lost their luster. Clichés or trite expressions are tired language. Use as few of these as possible.

John Galsworthy, the English novelist, has this advice to speakers and writers: "The soul of good expression is an unexpectedness, which still keeps to the mark of meaning, and does not betray truth."

Suggestions for Achieving Persuasiveness

To persuade is one of the most common and one of the most important uses of language. We are surrounded by people trying to persuade us, and we in our turn try to persuade others. The clergyman urges us to love good and shun evil, the patriot wants us to fight for our country, the social-minded ask us to give money to our Community Drive. Appeals are made to us to fight cancer and tuberculosis, aid Boys' Town, buy a certain soap powder or shaving cream.

You try to persuade your father to let you use the car, go to the Junior Prom, or be allowed to take a job. We persuade an employer to hire us; even courtship is a form of persuasion. Much of our happiness depends on how successful we are as persuaders.

Bruce Barton, American writer and clergyman, has said, "No man can persuade people to do what he wants them to do, unless he genuinely likes people, and believes that what he wants them to do is for their own advantage." Mr. Barton is writing about sincerity, and it is the first and most important ingredient of persuasion.

Adjectives are among the language tools of the persuader, but the listener becomes "tone-deaf" to them if they are over-used. Never fill your speech with adjectives; strive instead for fresh, concrete, honest, persuasive wording.

Those who wish to persuade must arouse the interest and secure the attention of the audience. Then they must hold that attention, while they try to influence the listener to the desired action.

1. USE WORDS THAT STIR UP SENSORY IMAGES OR "PICTURES." Learning takes place through the senses of sight, hearing, smell, taste, touch, or muscle response. This is important to you as a speaker because in speech you can appeal to *all senses,* either by recalling memories of past sensations or by describing imagined sensations. The selection below is from Charles Dickens' *A Christmas Carol.* Notice how the writer appeals to all five senses. Make a list of the sensory images. Listen for them in ordinary conversations, try to use them in your own speech, and note how effective they are. You can "push the right buttons" with the words you use if you choose them wisely.

Choose your words for connotations as well as literal meanings.

102

The Grocers'! oh the Grocers'! nearly closed with perhaps two shutters down, or one; but through those gaps such glimpses! It was not alone that the scales descending on the counter made a merry sound, or that the twine and roller parted company so briskly, or that the canisters were rattled up and down like juggling tricks, or even that the blended scents of tea and coffee were so grateful to the nose, or even that the raisins were so plentiful and rare, the almonds so extremely white, the sticks of cinnamon so long and straight, the other spices so delicious, the candied fruits so caked and spotted with molten sugar as to make the coldest lookers-on feel faint and subsequently bilious. Nor was it that the figs were moist and pulpy, or that the French plums blushed in modest tartness from their highly-decorated boxes, or that everything was good to eat and in its Christmas dress; but the customers were all so hurried and so eager in the hopeful promise of the day, that they tumbled up against each other at the door, clashing their wicker baskets wildly, and left their purchases upon the counter, and came running back to fetch them, and committed hundreds of the like mistakes in the best humor possible; while the Grocer and his people were so frank and fresh that the polished hearts with which they fastened their aprons behind might have been their own, worn outside for general inspection, and for Christmas daws to peck at if they chose.

2. USE WORDS THAT ARE WITHIN THE EXPERIENCE OF THE AUDIENCE. The strength of your words lies in enabling people to connect an experience they did not have, with feelings they *have experienced*. Always check your language and select the parts that strike within the range of your listeners' experience. Examine Dickens' use of familiar, simple words that are easy enough to grasp—almost common, but used in a special way.

3. USE SPECIFIC WORDS. The more general or abstract the word, the less definite is its appeal to the senses and the less effective is any association your listener may have. Note the series below. The first word is a general or class name, followed by more specific nouns, and at last by the name of a particular person. Concreteness increases as you move through the words to the proper name, where the end result suggests a clear picture if the person's face is known to you.

man — writer — poet — modern poet — Carl Sandburg
woman — musician — vocalist — contralto — Marian Anderson

4. USE LOADED WORDS WITH CARE TO GAIN PARTICULAR EMOTIONAL REACTIONS. Loaded words are those that have certain associated meanings (connotations) in addition to the basic meaning of the word (denotation). "Freedom" and "communist" are two of the most loaded words in our language today. You touch off a whole cluster of emotions

103

when you employ a loaded word. This passage, taken from a commencement address on "Learning to Speak" by Ernest Fremont Tittle,[1] is an example of the usefulness of loaded words:

> There are colorful words that are as beautiful as red roses; and there are drab words that are as unlovely as an anemic-looking woman. There are concrete words that keep people awake; and there are abstract words that put them to sleep. There are strong words that can punch like a prizefighter; and weak words that are as insipid as a 'mama's boy.' There are warm, sympathetic words that grip men's hearts; and cold, detached words that leave an audience unmoved: . . .

Do not use loaded words unfairly, however, because they can act as an intellectual blackjack. Socrates warned against using false words. He said that they were not only evil in themselves, but that they also infected the soul with evil.

Suggestions for Speaking Better English

Anyone speaking in public makes every effort to speak with grammatical correctness. Grammatical mistakes in written material will be corrected before they are published. But one grammatical error in a speech can be fatal. It can destroy not only the effectiveness of the speech but make the audience lose respect for the speaker.

Obviously, your use of correct grammar is imperative in public speaking. In order to be sure of yourself in public you must make a practice of correctness in private. It is equally important in your everyday language, both oral and written.

1. DEVELOP A MATURE ATTITUDE TOWARD GRAMMAR. The first step is to *want* to speak correctly. Nothing labels a person more quickly than his manner of speaking. Speaking incorrect English puts a person at a disadvantage in business and in social situations. As Shakespeare said long ago, "Mend your speech a little, lest you mar your fortunes." It is not stuffy to speak correct English, and it is a sign of maturity to be able to express yourself well.

2. TAKE INVENTORY OF YOUR ERRORS. Make a list of those blue-penciled mistakes on your themes. List any errors pointed out in your everyday speech. Ask your speech teacher for an analysis after he has lis-

---

[1]From a commencement address before the Northwestern University School of Speech, by Ernest F. Tittle, June 1924.

tened to several of your talks. Listen to yourself while you speak; make tapes to help you find mistakes. Now go to work on *all* the errors that you have found!

3. SECURE A GOOD REVIEW GRAMMAR OR HANDBOOK ON USAGE. To help you learn the correct forms, refer to a reliable source. You should have in your possession such books as Corbin's *Guide to Modern English, Book 10 or 11* (Chicago: Scott, Foresman and Company, 1960 and 1963). These books are organized so that you will find it easy to locate common errors and the correct forms to replace them.

4. KEEP WORKING ON YOUR SPECIFIC PROBLEMS. Once you have found your mistakes, watch for them. Application is the real test—keep listening carefully for errors whenever you speak and weed them out. Tape and listen to your talks so you can catch every possible mistake. Old habits are hard to change, but you can do it if you *want* to.

Achieving Greater Accuracy

Accuracy is one of your most important considerations. This means that you will try to fit your spoken language as closely as possible to the *life facts* that the language seeks to represent.

Language is a *map*. Words *represent* or *stand for* the territory. The *real* territory consists of the things, facts, or relationships that you would find if you went to the territory. If you are careless and inaccurate in the words you use to *represent* the territory, your audience will not understand the *real* territory. Their response to you may not be the one you wanted. Similarly, much of their thinking is based on a reaction to words they hear and see, rather than to the *actual* things the words represent.

Semantics, or the study of language, seeks to clear up inaccuracy through: (1) understanding the nature of language; (2) analyzing existing language habits; and (3) developing *suitable* methods to remedy undesirable habits so that language can more accurately represent reality.

Understanding language rests not only on *your* use of a word, but on *what that word means to your listener.* Remember that any word (depending upon the experience, age, education, sex, intelligence, religion, race, political beliefs, or nationality, of the listeners) can have an almost infinite number of meanings. To put it differently: *A definite number of words can represent an infinite number of things.* Your first consideration in improving accuracy in language rests in your knowing and analyzing your audience.

105

To do this try to imagine what each word will mean to *them* and see if it is different from what the words mean to *you.*

We all have language habits that cause us trouble in conveying accurate meaning and in understanding other people. Sometimes the fault lies in us, sometimes in others. We can at least correct our half of the trouble.

Some Faulty Language Habits and Their Remedies

1. ALLNESS. This is the tendency to confuse *all* members of a classification with only part of it. Or, when someone else is talking, assuming that he means *all,* when he means only *some.* This can make a person jump to a hasty generalization about the *thing.*

A simple example of allness in the thinking of some adults is contained in their reaction to the word "teen-ager." Too often they judge *all* teen-agers by the few who make the front pages of the newspapers.

Word each description or statement so that your listeners will know when you do not mean *all* has been said on the subject. Limit your statement by using language that clearly defines the territory you mean to cover.

2. EITHER/OR THINKING. This is the habit of thinking in terms of either black or white, forgetting or ignoring the gradations between. You may classify, by your use of words, all behavior as "good" or "bad." Your language may insist that a listener accept a case as "right" or "wrong."

There are many situations in which you cannot place things in the either/or categories; circumstances demand that language describe the conditions more exactly. Father Flanagan blasts the either/or thinking when he says, "There is no such thing as a *bad* boy."

Examine the middle ground between two "opposites." This way you will discover the errors in either/or thinking and use language to say exactly what you mean.

3. QUICK EMOTIONAL REACTIONS. Sometimes we react immediately to a word, not thinking, but allowing our emotions to take over. The word "liar" often gets this response; the word "spy," used in international relations, is another such word.

Emotional reactions to derogatory names of national or racial groups create one of our most serious problems at present. They violate the "allness" principle, too, because they assume a whole group is like one obnoxious person somebody may have known.

106

Admit to yourself that you sometimes react without thinking, and reflect *before* you speak so that you can check your reactions and your listeners' reactions to *loaded* words.

Trends today indicate that the *best* persuasive methods move toward honest, semantically accurate use of language, rather than toward the use of emotionally weighted words in both speaking and writing.

If you understand how language and words work, you will remember to choose your words with your audience in mind and to choose the clearest, most accurate word to convey your meaning. You will not find yourself in the position of Alice in Wonderland as Lewis Carroll described her.

"Then you should say what you mean," the March Hare went on.

"I do," Alice hastily replied; "at least—at least I mean what I say—that's the same thing, you know."

"Not the same thing a bit!" said the Hatter.

The best way to increase and reinforce your vocabulary is by reading. Read widely; notice new words, or new meanings for old words; use your dictionary.

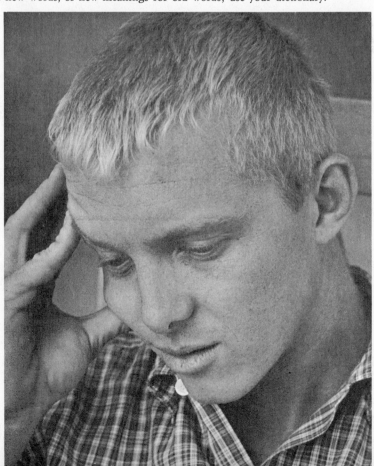

CHAPTER 9

CONTROLLING
YOUR
VOICE

*Surely whoever speaks to
me in the right voice,
him or her I shall follow.*
—WALT WHITMAN

Very few of us know how we sound to others. We use our voices care-
lessly, content to mumble along, mouthing our words until an exasperated
listener interrupts too often with, "What? What did you say?" Then we
usually increase our volume and assume the listener has a hearing defect.

The first time you record your voice and listen to the playback, you
will probably say, "That doesn't sound like me!" You may even be shocked
at the way you sound. You're right. It doesn't sound like you because you
are not familiar with the sound of your own voice. Your own impression of
how you sound comes largely through the bones of your head, which add
resonance, and not through your ears.

The voice you hear on a recording comes to you principally from outside your head, the way others hear you. The voice that you accept as satisfactory may affect others differently.

Studies of the speech of high-school students indicate that only half of them have pleasant voices; a third speak distinctly and can be easily understood. Electronic devices such as recorders, telephones, radio, and television transmit all the bad as well as the good qualities of a voice. Thus it should not surprise you if your voice does not sound satisfactory.

It is not only high-school students who fail to use their voices effectively. Many adults have bad speaking habits. Even professional speakers are too often guilty of poor voice control and careless pronunciation. John Davenport describes this situation in an article, "Slurvian Self-Taught."[1]

> Listening to a well-known Hollywood radio commentator some time back, I heard her say that she had just returned from a Yerpeen trip, and had had a lovely time nittly. I at once recognized her as an accomplished Slurvian linguist and, being a student of Slurvian, readily understood that she had just returned from a European trip, and while there (in Yerp) had had a lovely time in Italy.
>
> Slurvian is coming into common use in the United States, but I am, so far as I know, the only scholar to have made a start toward recording it. There is no official written Slurvian language, but it is possible, by means of phonetic spelling, for me to offer a brief course of instruction in it. In a short time, the student can learn enough to add immeasurably to his understanding and enjoyment of conversation wherever he travels in the country.
>
> I first heard pure Slurvian fluently spoken by a co-worker of mine who told me that his closest friend was a man named Hard, "Howard." Hard was once in an automobile accident, his car unfortunately cliding with another, causing Hard's wife Dorthy, who was with him, to claps. Dorthy didn't have much stamina but was a sweet woman—sweet as surp.
>
> I soon discovered I had an ear for Slurvian, and since I began to recognize the language, I have encountered many Slurvians. At ballparks, they keep track of hits, runs, and airs. On farms, they plow furs. In florist shops, they buy flars. When hard up they bar money from banks, and spend it for everything from fewl for the furnace to grum crackers for the children.
>
> When Slurvians travel abroad, they go to visit farn (or forn) countries to see what the farners do that's different from the way we Murcans do things. While in farn countries, they refer to themselves as Murcan tersts, and usually say they will be might glad to get back to Murca. A Slurvian I once met on a train told me he had just returned from a visit to Mexico. He deplored the lack of automobiles down there, and said that the natives ride around on little burrs.

[1]Reprinted by permission of the author; first published in The New Yorker. Copyright © 1949 by the New Yorker Magazine, Inc.

...Surnames cannot be considered subject to the ordinary rules of pronunciation. In fact the only one I have positively identified in Slurvian is Faggott, the name of the American admiral who won the Battle of Mobile Bay.

The name Faggott brings me to a discussion of what I designate as "pure" Slurvian. This includes those Slurvian words that, when spelled exactly as pronounced, also make good English words (such as "Faggot," "burr," and "claps"). The day I can add to the lexicon such a word, hitherto unrecorded, is a happy day for me. Here are some examples of pure Slurvian, alphabetically listed:

bean, n.	A living creature, as in human bean.
cactus, n. pl.	The people in a play or story.
course, n.	A group of singers.
fiscal, adj.	Pertaining to the body, as opposed to the spurt.
form, n.	Gathering place of the ancient Romans.
gnome, n.	Contraction for "no, Ma'am." Colloq.
line, n.	The king of beasts.
lore, n.	The more desirable of the two berths in a Pullman section.
myrrh, n.	A looking glass.
par, n.	An attribute of strength, as in the par and the glory.
plight, adj.	Courteous.
sears, adj.	Grave, intent.
sport, v.t.	To hold up, to bear the weight of.
wreckers, n. pl.	Discs on which music is recorded for phonographs.

I am presently engaged in compiling a dictionary of Slurvian words, which I hope will prove to be the definitive work on the subject. The help of any interested students is welcomed, but I must caution such students to be certain the words are genuine Slurvian, and not merely regional speech, such as that of Alabama, Texas, or New England....

At first reading you may think that Mr. Davenport's comments refer principally to articulation and pronunciation, but a little study will convince you that many of these laughable errors are due to poor quality of voice control. "Yerpeen," for example, can be traced to a nasal quality, as well as the mispronunciation. You cannot develop a good speaking voice by concentrating on pronunciation alone. It must be coupled with control of the quality and quantity of your voice and the development of good breathing habits.

To change your voice, you will have to do three things: (1) learn to listen to your voice objectively so that you know how you sound; (2) change your habits in order to secure the best possible voice; (3) through practice, set and control those habits. However, before you start a program, you might like to know something about how you produce voice and speech sounds.

110

You may be surprised the first time you hear a recording of your voice.

HOW THE BODY PRODUCES SPEECH SOUNDS

Your body has no separate mechanism for the production of speech. The human body, with amazing economy, uses the same organ for a number of functions. All parts of the body used in the production of speech have other primary functions. Human beings survive without the ability to speak, but they cannot survive without breathing, eating, or drinking.

It is obvious that the mouth, lips, tongue, teeth, and throat are concerned first with biting, chewing, and swallowing. The windpipe and lungs are basically designed to get air into the body so that oxygen can purify the blood. Breathing, accomplished by the lungs with the help of many muscles, is not primarily a speech function. Breathing is necessary for survival, and in diseases such as the common cold, the secondary function, speech, may be lost while the primary function continues.

Let us consider how these organs, all with primary functions not concerned with speech, produce your voice. Wind instruments, from the clarinet to the pipe organ, have certain parts in common essential to the production of a musical tone. These parts are the same used to produce sound in the human body: (1) *a source of energy* (the lungs, diaphragm, and accompanying muscles); (2) *a vibrator* (the vocal folds in the larynx); (3) *the resonators* (the upper part of the larynx, the throat, mouth, and nasal cavities); (4) *the articulators* (the teeth, jaws, lips, tongue, hard and soft palates). Each of these parts performs a basic function in speech production.

The energy to produce a musical tone with a wind instrument or a vocal tone in the human body is provided by a current of air. In breathing, the muscles of the lower chest, abdomen, and diaphragm work together to obtain that current of air as you inhale and exhale. *Inhalation* gives you the supply of air you need for speech; *exhalation* enables you to produce a vocal tone. To be adequate for good speech, breathing must provide plenty of power or support for the tone. Most important, however, is control of breath, which enables you to produce a sustained or intermittent tone necessary for effective, audible speech.

The second element needed for speech is a vibrator. In the clarinet this element is the reed, which vibrates when a current of air strikes it. In the human body short, fibrous structures called the *vocal folds* provide the vibrating element. Muscular action pulls them close together horizontally across the opening of the larynx or voice box. When air passes between them as you exhale, it causes them to vibrate and produce a vocal tone. Variations in the force of the expelled air and the tension of the folds determine the degrees of pitch and loudness. This process is called *phonation*.

Once the basic tone is phonated, it passes through other parts of the body that help enrich and amplify it. The throat, the pharynx, the nasal cavity, and the mouth are active in the process of *resonation*. By controlling their use, you help the tone become pleasant, smooth, well-rounded, and suitable for speaking.

To produce the many sounds of speech, the tone must be further shaped or modified. The vocal passage is narrowed or widened by the hard and soft palates, tongue, jaws, lips, and teeth to produce vowel sounds. They also interrupt the tone, or stop it either partially or completely, to form consonant sounds. The process of shaping the speech sounds by using these various structures is called *articulation*.

HOW TO DEVELOP A GOOD SPEAKING VOICE

You need a good supply of breath for vocal power even in ordinary conversation. Tests show that only a fifth of us use the proper energy, or breathing, to produce good resonance; the other four fifths haven't enough energy for even normal conversation. When you address a large audience in a large room, the demands on your vocal power increase greatly. You use sixty-six times as much energy in such a situation as you do in ordinary conversation. By exercise and practice you can develop the breath supply that produces both good tone and vocal power.

In addition to such power, you need better control of your breath. Speech requires some sustained tone, although not nearly so much as singing, because in speaking the sounds are relatively short and precise. Your greatest need, therefore, is to develop control of exhalation, so you can obtain the desired variety in pitch and loudness as air strikes the vocal folds.

Some persons develop so much tension in the throat and neck while speaking that their voices are harsh and monotonous. Relaxation of the throat and neck provides the flexibility and vocal contrast needed for an expressive, interesting voice. There are numerous exercises at the end of the chapter to help you achieve relaxation.

The beauty and distinctness of human speech come from active, careful use of the articulators—lips, jaws, tongue, teeth, and palates. More than eighty per cent of indistinct speech comes from careless habits in using these articulators. Develop more active, accurate use of them by daily work on good exercises.

Use the Elements of Voice to Develop More Expressive Speech

There are four elements, or attributes, of voice—quality, pitch, time, and force. In order to convey meaning clearly, correctly, and expressively, you need to understand these elements and use them intelligently.

When we say someone's voice is nasal, harsh, or throaty, we are talking about its quality. Each person's voice quality differs from that of all others. You recognize one person by his nasal quality, another by her thin quality, and another by his full, resonant quality.

Harshness and huskiness are two undesirable voice qualities. They are the results of tension in the throat or forcing too much air between the vocal folds. People have been known to injure or tear these folds by shouting or yelling sharply, and then huskiness remains unless surgery corrects it. Certain diseases or inflammation can have a similar effect; however, if examination reveals no such condition, suitable exercises will help. Relaxation of the throat and proper breath control are the basic ways to overcome this problem.

Weak or thin quality is another fault. Illness affecting the condition or use of the muscles, or inactivity of the resonators, may contribute to this weakness. Lack of power because of ineffective breathing sometimes produces a weak voice. Good muscle support in breathing and stronger use of vocal energy may help, plus a fuller use of the throat and mouth for more resonance.

A nasal quality is not uncommon, and in most instances results from too limited a use of the nasal cavity. Exercises to activate the soft palate and gain control over it will help in some cases. However, it takes time and expert assistance, usually at a speech clinic, to overcome nasality of long standing.

Older books on speech and elocution classified eight types of vocal quality: normal, oral, falsetto, orotund, guttural, aspirate, nasal, and pectoral. These terms described what were then believed to be usable qualities for speaking, impersonation, and acting. These qualities were associated with certain emotional states or moods.

Thus normal, with an equal balance between mouth and nasal resonance was used for ordinary conversation; oral, a light, higher-pitched quality, was employed for amorous sentiment or weakness; falsetto, extremely high-pitched, was used in impersonation or to express fatigue; orotund, a full, round tone, was indicated for public oratory; guttural, a

114

throaty quality, was linked with anger; aspirate, extreme breathiness, was the stage whisper; nasal, a poor quality, was employed to characterize country yokels; and pectoral, a deep chesty quality, suggested awe or mystery.

Such mechanical attempts to reveal feeling by vocal quality may well be questioned, and there is no need to study these types for that purpose. However, there is some value in the description of the qualities and in using them as exercises to increase vocal flexibility. This flexibility of voice is most important in conveying genuine emotion.

In genuinely motivated vocal change, the emotion develops within the person first, and the resulting vocal quality reveals it. When you feel happy, your vocal quality is gay and lively. When you feel weak and tired, your vocal quality is thin and high-pitched. Effective use of vocal quality results from developing the ability to respond to the conditions and meaning of the immediate situation.

Reversing this process by learning the qualities and using them artificially to superimpose a veneer of emotion would result in affectation and insincerity, readily detected by listeners. Once you recognize that vocal quality reflects emotion, you can practice suitable qualities to develop greater flexibility and expressiveness.

Some voices normally sound high, others sound low, and you can vary your own voice to produce high or low tones. These variations are changes in *pitch,* the position or location of your voice on the musical scale. As you vary the tone to express different meanings, your voice moves up and down the scale from its normal pitch. For best use, your normal pitch should be somewhere in the lower half of your range.

Changes in pitch that follow a pattern result in a melody. In a song the composer writes the melody, or the changes in pitch, in a tune. But in speech there is no tune; your interpretation of meaning by vocal changes establishes the melody. Beware of the monotonous pattern, in which each sentence has the same changes repeated mechanically. Keep your control of pitch responsive to the differences which ideas and emotions impose on your speech.

There are certain commonly recognized ways of varying pitch. They are called *slides* and *steps.*

Many schools have language laboratories which students may use to improve their vocal quality and enunciation.

A continuous and gradual change of pitch within a syllable or word is a slide. In the phrase below, you can observe that the meaning is carried by the gradual, yet continuing pitch change, especially in the "Oh."

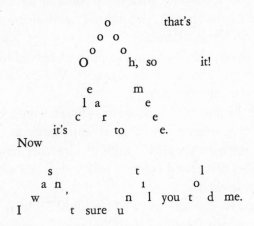

```
                    o           that's
                  o  o
                o    o
        O         h, so        it!

              e         m
            l   a         e
          c     r         e
        it's        to    e.
    Now


            s           t         l
          a n   ,           l       o
        w                 n  l you t  d  me.
      I       t sure u
```

An abrupt change in pitch when there is a definite break from one syllable to the next is a step. In the following sentence, note the abrupt changes, or steps, that occur.

```
                right,              in?
        If you are      then why give
```

Here the meaning hinges upon the two words *right* and *in*. In order to convey it correctly, two definite vocal steps are used.

The above sentence does not contain extreme emotion or a vigorous mood. However, note the question below, in which surprise and fright are indicated.

```
                                    shot
            earth         doing with      gun?
    What on        are you          that
```

Wider steps and a greater range of pitch are utilized to express vigorous emotion.

Learn to use all pitch variations to give life, color, and meaning to your voice.

Time, or tempo, has the common meaning of *rate,* or the number of words you speak per minute. The normal rate for speakers is 120 to 150 words per minute. However, rate varies with the meaning expressed, and may exceed a normal one if meaning demands it.

A sportscaster is obliged to maintain a fast rate to convey excitement and to keep pace with the action. A minister usually has a slower, more dignified rate. Rate of speaking then is the result of the meaning, the emotional condition of the speaker, the normal habit of the speaker, and the need for intelligibility in utterance.

Variation in rate, like variation in pitch, is needed for expressiveness and for holding the interest of the listeners. Variety in rate depends on two things: *pauses* and *quantity.*

A pause is the length of time spent *between* words; the more pauses, the slower the rate. Pauses are of great importance as emphasis: when they are placed immediately after a word or idea, they let the idea sink in; when these pauses are placed before a word, they add suspense or a dramatic effect to your words.

Some speakers fear the pause. They dislike silence and think talk must go on incessantly. Nothing could be more untrue. Action and good eye contact will hold audience interest when you pause. Remember that pauses for emphasis or effect are an indication of control and poise, not of timidity or confusion.

There are certain kinds of pauses that are detrimental to smooth delivery. These are the typical "uh," or "er-uh," sometimes called vocalized pauses. You can eliminate these if you understand some of their causes.

Some people pause with an "er-uh" because they need time to formulate the next idea or think of the next word or sentence. The way to avoid this is to prepare more completely, paying particular attention to your choice of language. Sometimes speakers use a vocalized pause because they lack suitable linking or transitional words to connect ideas or carry the meaning from one part of the speech to the next. It is quite easy to avoid this error if you make a short list of transitional words—and put these words in action.

Quantity is the length of time used to say one syllable or sound *within* a word. The longer or greater the quantity, the slower the rate.

By lengthening or shortening the duration of syllables, quantity becomes an important means of setting the mood or indicating a sentiment. It is most effective when utilized properly. The impressiveness of "In my father's house are many mansions; I go to prepare a place for you..." is achieved by suitable use of quantity on the key words. If you read this in the sharp, staccato sportscaster's use of quantity, you ruin it. Similarly, the sportscaster would defeat his purpose if he said slowly, and with great quantity, "Theeey—aare—on-the-baaack stretch—Beeetlebaum is leading-he-is-ahead—by three-ee lengths—aand—gaining faast."

As in good use of voice quality, the meaning or emotion dictates the use of this aspect of rate.

One of the fundamental principles of good delivery is that the speaker must speak loudly enough to be heard easily in all parts of the room. A voice of adequate force, used with the proper emphasis, will carry conviction.

If you have ever heard an average seventh-grade "orator" proclaim in a small voice, "I am sure that democracy and freedom will endure forever," at that moment you may have entertained some doubts about the fate of democracy. He was ineffective for two reasons: he could not be heard easily, and he did not have enough *force,* or vocal energy, to suggest that his statement is true.

As important as achieving force is your ability to control it so that you can use it to convey a variety of meanings. The amount of force and the way it is used are two essential factors in achieving necessary variety. Monotony in force kills interest; varying the amount will hold attention. The need for change is the reason for increasing or decreasing force. A powerful voice that never changes soon irritates listeners, while a soft, quiet voice that is always the same will put an audience to sleep. You need a change of pace to keep listeners alert.

The way that you use force should be closely related to your emotional meaning or attitude. A gradual, firm application of force indicates awe, dignity, or reverence. Firm use of force, with more rapidity and more vigor, expresses determination, extreme sincerity, or conviction. A sudden or explosive use of force suggests an emotion that may be uncontrolled, such as anger, disgust, or fear.

Remember that your application of force should be in response to the real, inner meaning of the words you are speaking. Mechanical vocal changes sound insincere and affected. Develop the kind of control that allows you to employ force intelligently and purposefully.

By this time you have seen that all the elements of voice are useful in producing meaningful changes. These meaningful changes are known as *emphasis.* Quality plays a role in emphasis; so do time, pitch, and force. You become more skillful in delivery as you learn to use these elements to convey the precise, subtle meaning that your speech demands.

119

ACTIVITIES

Exercises for Breathing

1. Take a full breath. Avoiding any tension, count from one to twenty. Keep your rate constant, about two counts per second. Be especially careful in forming the sounds as you say the numbers. Use a normal conversational tone. Do this easily without "squeezing" or "pinching" at the end.

2. Now try the same exercise, counting to thirty, thirty-five, forty, and as far as your air supply will allow. What was the highest count you reached? Be sure not to strain, and stop before you have used all your breath. Try this daily, extending your count while maintaining control.

3. Try the same exercise, using the letters of the alphabet. When you reach z, start over with a without a break. How many times can you go through the alphabet without stopping and still retain control without strain? Use this exercise to lengthen your breath span and control.

4. Read the following selection. Prolong the vowel sounds and read each group or phrase with no break between words in the phrase. Breathe to fit the phrases and the punctuation. Allow pitch to follow the meaning.

> The day is done, and darkness
> Falls from the wings of Night,
> As a feather is wafted downward
> From an eagle in his flight.
>
> *   *   *
>
> And the night shall be filled with music
> And the cares, that infest the day,
> Shall fold their tents, like the Arabs,
> And as silently steal away.

> —*Henry Wadsworth Longfellow*

Exercises for Pitch and Rate

1. Choose an exciting description in a story, or write a short sportscast or newscast of a thrilling incident. Read your selection aloud, using a wide variety of pitch. Now record your reading, play it back, and note your range in pitch and its relationship to meaning. Note how the rate helps convey the excitement of the description. Repeat the exercise, making appropriate changes in pitch and rate to suit the content. Compare the two recordings.

2. Listen to a professional recording of a similar event. Analyze it as you did your own. Compare its general effectiveness with that of your own performance.

3. Choose a poem or passage of prose requiring a medium or lower pitch than you normally use. Try modifying your pitch.

Exercises for Rate and Time: Intelligibility

1. Select an expository prose passage, a page in length, from a novel. Read it aloud at your normal tempo with your usual expressiveness for a period of two minutes. Then count the number of words you read. Divide this by two, and you will have your rate of words per minute. Repeat this process for another two minutes, and recheck your rate per minute. Now classify yourself by this scale: *excellent*—160-170; *satisfactory*—150-160 or 170-180; doubtful—all rates either above or below the limits set (150 to 180 words per minute).

2. Using the same rate and volume, read the same passage aloud to a person seated with his back to you about fifteen feet away. Have him note any sounds he cannot hear easily.

3. Repeat the exercise, increasing your rate about one third. Be particularly careful in shaping the sounds as you read. Have your listener report any unintelligible portions under these conditions.

Exercises for Volume and Force

1. Read the following passage silently. Then underscore the words you believe important for a clear understanding of its meaning. Read the selection aloud stressing the words you marked. Have a listener with a similarly marked copy report on your success.

> Years from now, streaking through the deadness of space toward the moon or perhaps a planet, some astronaut will watch his crewmates sleep. Reflecting on how he got there, he may think back to the years he spent at the United States Air Force Academy, in the early days of space conquest.
>
> For him, and for earthbound hundreds of other Academy graduates, one image is almost certain to return more sharply than all the rest; seventeen silvery spires in perfect alignment, etched against the dark flank of the Rockies, pointing to the heavens.
>
> So, too, will those spires of the Cadet Chapel be the USAFA symbol best remembered by millions of visitors who stroll across the beautiful Academy campus in coming years.

2. After your listener reports, try the exercise again, making any changes in stress you believe needed.

3. Listen to a similar performance of classmates and note the differences in stress they indicate to convey the meaning.

4. Read the following sentences, giving the correct stress to convey the meaning indicated by the words in italics.

a. It is a *man* who is standing in the *shadows*.
b. It is a man *standing* in the *shadows*.
c. It was a *roan* horse that won the race for the *first* prize.
d. It *was* a roan horse that won the race for the first *prize*.
e. It was a roan *horse* that won the *race* for the first prize.

CHAPTER 10

IMPROVING
YOUR
ARTICULATION

Speak the speech, I pray you, as I pronounc'd
it to you, trippingly on the tongue.

—WILLIAM SHAKESPEARE

Your speech may be well prepared, well organized, and well worded, but if it lacks clarity and distinctness—if it does not have perfect *diction*—your meaning will be lost. Listeners suffer when someone mumbles or slurs speech sounds. John Davenport, in *The New Yorker,* has described Americans as a nation of "Slurvians" because of our careless speaking habits. (See the excerpt from this article in Chapter 9.)

In judging your own diction you might ask yourself these questions: "Do people ask me to repeat because they can't hear what I say?" "Do they miss certain parts of my sentences (beginning, middle, end)?" "Do they fail to understand certain words, or word endings?"

The answers may give you some clues to your own articulation, or the making of speech sounds. Articulation is the key to good diction.

FAULTY DICTION AND ITS CAUSES

You can improve your diction by understanding the causes of your mistakes and working to remove them. Basic causes are: (1) *not knowing the proper sounds,* (2) *not understanding how to produce them correctly,* and (3) *bad habits,* resulting from carelessness, or lack of pride in good speech. The speech of people with whom you are associated influences the form and standards you develop.

Defective hearing may be the cause of omitting or distorting sounds, because the affected person has never heard the correct sounds.

Disease or illness that impairs the function of the muscles, jaws, lips, and palate may, of course, have serious effects. *Poorly formed structures* of the speaking mechanism can affect articulation.

However, the greatest number of articulatory defects come from the first three causes, and it is within everyone's ability to overcome them.

Kinds of Errors

There are three principal kinds of errors. An individual may (1) *omit* sounds, (2) *substitute* one sound for another, or (3) *distort* sounds.

You will notice that young children frequently omit sounds. *Omissions* occur when they cannot easily utter the correct sound, or because of carelessness, or sometimes they are the result of foreign dialects. Examples such as *reconize* for *recognize, libery* for *library* are types of omissions.

In *substitution* the correct sound is replaced by an incorrect one. *Rabbit* becomes *wabbit, these* becomes *dese,* and the lisper says *thoup* instead of *soup.* The person of Spanish origin substitutes for our short *i* and *a* sounds when he says *thees ahpul* for *this apple.* He does not have these sounds in his language.

When you *distort* a sound you approximate but fail to produce the correct sound. The sound of *s* is often distorted. The boy who did not have *toime* to work and the girl who is *goingk* home are both distorting sounds.

WAYS TO IMPROVE ARTICULATION

Know the Proper Sounds and How to Produce Them

Knowing and understanding the correct production of the sounds is the first step toward improvement. There are two kinds of sounds—*vowels* and *consonants.*

VOWELS. Depending upon which classification is used, there are from fourteen to nineteen vowel sounds, or tones. They are produced in the larynx by vibrating the vocal cords. There is little narrowing of the vocal passage in the production of vowel tones; the throat is left "open." Differences in tone are produced principally by the tongue, lips, and jaws.

Below is a list of vowels with their markings as used in the Thorndike-Barnhart Dictionaries. There are corresponding symbols in the International Phonetic Alphabet (IPA). We are concerned primarily with dictionary markings as the basis for our study and practice of these sounds. English is not always pronounced the way it is spelled. The Thorndike-Barnhart Dictionary and the phonetic alphabet use symbols designed to represent the ways sounds are *spoken*.

VOWEL SOUNDS

Thorndike-Barnhart Dictionary	Key words
a	hat, cap
ā	age, face
ã	care, air
ä	father, far
e	let, best
ē	equal, see
ėr	term, learn
i	it, pin
ī	ice, five
o	hot, rock
ō	open, go
ô	order, all
oi	oil, voice
ou	house, out
u	cup, butter
ů	full, put
ü	rule, move
ū	use, music
ə represents	a in about
	e in taken
	i in pencil
	o in lemon
	u in circus

124

CONSONANTS. Consonants are described as noises, rather than tones. By narrowing or constricting the vocal passage above the larynx you produce a great number of such sounds—most classifications list about twenty-five. Different speech organs interrupt, stop, or in some way alter the breath as it is exhaled, so that the vowels in speech are combined with the consonants to form syllables and words. The teeth, tongue, jaws, lips, and hard and soft palates are used in shaping consonant sounds.

CONSONANT SOUNDS

Thorndike-Barnhart Dictionary	Key words
p	paper, cup
b	bad, rob
t	tell, it
d	did, red
m	me, am
n	no, in
ng	long, bring
f	fat, if
v	very, save
k	kind, seek, cat
g	go, bag
r	run, try
l	land, coal
th	thin, both
TH	then, smooth
s	say, yes
z	zero, breeze, ease
sh	she, rush
zh	measure, seizure
w	will, woman
hw	wheat, when
y	young, yet
ch	child, much
j	jam, enjoy
h	he, how

Consonants are classified in terms of (1) the *kind of action* that produces them; (2) the *part of,* or *place in,* the speaking mechanism that is involved; (3) whether or not production of the consonant involves *vibration* of the vocal cords. Consonants having such vibration are *voiced;* those without it are *voiceless.* In pairs, such as *b* and *p, z* and *s, d* and *t, v* and *f,* the first sound in each pair is voiced, the second voiceless.

PLOSIVES OR STOPS. By a momentary and complete *stopping* of the air stream in the vocal tract, pressure is built up and *suddenly released*. This action causes the consonant sounds of this group. There are six, classified in terms of the part of the speaking mechanism which does the stopping. For example, *b* and *p* are stopped by lips; *d* and *t* by the tongue against the teeth ridge, just behind the upper teeth; *g* and *k*, by the action of the soft palate. In pairs, the first sound in each is voiced.

FRICATIVES are produced by narrowing the vocal passage so that the air is set into vibration by forcing it through a restricted opening. The sound is the result of *friction* between the air stream and the structure, hence the name. Sounds in this group include *z* and *s*, *v* and *f*, *th* (voiced), as in *then*; and *th* (voiceless), as in *thin*; *zh* (voiced), as in *azure* and *sh* (voiceless), as in *short*.

NASALS. Sounds in which there is a complete shutting off of the nasal or oral cavity are called nasals. The vibrating breath stream is diverted through the nasal *passages*. The sounds of *m, n,* and *ng* are in this group, *Man, never,* and *sing* are examples.

GLIDES are characterized by a particular placement of the lips and tongue, with some movement involved in their production. Sounds in this group include *w, wh, r* and *l*.

126

In exercises at the end of the chapter you will find lists of words and sentences that will help you produce correctly these different types of consonants.

Know the Errors You Make

By careful listening to your own speech as you talk, or as recorded on tape, and by analyzing it with your teacher, you can discover which sounds you need to correct. Such an analysis requires that you be able to discriminate between the correct and incorrect sounds.

There are several ways of testing that will help you:

1. TEST SENTENCES.[1] Each of the following is planned to test a particular sound as it is used in each of three positions—at the beginning of a word, in the middle of a word, and at the end of a word. These sentences cover the most *common errors*. Read them aloud with a partner or your teacher, listening carefully as you read. Check any that you believe you say incorrectly, and ask your partner to check you also. Keep a record of your mistakes and start consciously to correct yourself.

(*r*)   Our barn is covered with brilliant red roses. The broad crimson roof draws admiring crowds from far and near.

(*l*)   Lawyer Clark held his little felt hat and his black gloves in his lap. He silently placed the will on the table.

(*w*)   Wait until the weather is warm. Then everyone will want to walk in the woods.

(*wh*)   "What is that?" he whispered. Somewhere from the left came the whistle of a bobwhite.

(*th*)   We thought that the theory was pathetic. But we had faith that something would lead to the truth.

(*TH*) My father finds it hard to breathe in this weather. Even the heather withers.

(*s*)   The successful student does not assume that class exercise is sufficient. He also practices by himself outside.

(*z*)   My cousin's play, "The Zero Zone," is amusing. But it won't be chosen for a prize because it doesn't deserve it.

(*sh*)   The fishing ship was in shallows near the shore. In one motion a wave crushed it on the shoal.

(*zh*)   I make no allusion to sabotage. But an explosion near the garage is unusual.

(*ch*)   Mitchell was a righteous old bachelor. He watched for a chance to chase children out of the neighborhood.

(*j*)   All but Judge Johnson pledged allegiance to the legislation. He objected that it was unjust to the soldiers.

---

[1] From Grant Fairbanks, *Voice and Articulation Drillbook* (Second edition), New York: Harper and Brothers, 1960, xiv. Test sentences for all sounds are in the Foreword, v-xix.

127

2. A LOADED PASSAGE. The paragraph below contains all of the sounds that might be uttered incorrectly. Read the passage aloud with a partner or your teacher. Mark any errors you make.

MY GRANDFATHER[1]

You wished to know all about my grandfather. Well, he is nearly ninety-three years old; he dresses himself in an ancient black frock coat, usually minus several buttons; yet he still thinks as swiftly as ever. A long, flowing beard clings to his chin, giving those who observe him a pronounced feeling of the utmost respect. When he speaks, his voice is just a bit cracked and quivers a trifle. Twice each day he plays skillfully and with zest upon our small organ. Except in the winter when the ooze or snow or ice prevents, he slowly takes a short walk in the open air each day. We have often urged him to walk more and smoke less, but he always answers, "Banana oil!" Grandfather likes to be modern in his language!

3. WATCH YOUR CONVERSATION. In all conversations with your classmates listen carefully for errors that occur in your speech. If possible, tape a conversation. Note your errors, then replay the tape and check your analysis. If the replay confirms your original observations, keep the list of sounds you need to work on; add to it if necessary. Compare this list with any errors you detected by the other methods of analysis.

---

[1]From Charles Van Riper, *Speech Correction: Principles and Methods.* © 1954, Prentice-Hall, Inc., p. 178.

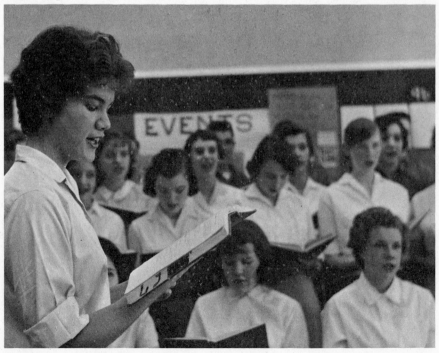

128

4. LEARN TO PRODUCE THE CORRECT SOUND. Having selected one particular sound for improvement, learn to produce it correctly. Pay particular attention to efficient use of the various parts of the speech mechanism involved. Continue your practice until you never fail to produce the sound correctly.

5. PRACTICE THE CORRECT SOUND IN SYLLABLES AND WORDS. When you are absolutely sure of success in producing the correct sound by itself, use it in words and syllables, so that you can employ it correctly in any position in a word, and in combination with other sounds.

6. USE FULL SOUND IN ALL SPEAKING SITUATIONS. Employ the sound in all forms of speech and in all situations—conversation, discussion, public speaking, oral reading, etc. As you fit it into your everyday speech practices, it comes to "belong to you."

PRONUNCIATION

I was settin' on the front steps when a feller drove up in a genuine sports car. He jumped out over the side—like a athalete—and come toward the house. "Kin you tell me how to git to the Park theayter?" he sez. "Nope," I sez, "I can't becuz I just spend my time settin' here. I find that prefERable to goin' to shows."

There are at least eleven errors in pronunciation in the above paragraph. Many of the errors occur in the pronunciation of high-school students, and they are not trying to be comedians.

To master correct diction you will have to add to your skill in articulation a knowledge of the commonly accepted ways of pronouncing all the words you use. Errors distract listeners and give a bad impression that no one can afford. Eliminate any unusual or peculiar pronunciations; get rid of incorrectly accented syllables in the words you use. (There were two in the quoted paragraph; did you notice them?) Avoid adding sounds. (There was one of these.) Be careful not to substitute incorrect sounds. (There were four of these.)

Because the spelling is not a good guide on how to pronounce a word, you can be confused in pronunciation. If you listen to *good* radio or television announcers (not all are good guides) you will note the care and accuracy with which they articulate their words. Compare your pronunciation with that of trained, educated people in your locality. It will help you to improve your pronunciation.

Regional Pronunciations Vary

If you were asked to characterize a girl from the deep South, a farmer from Kansas, and a high-school boy from Boston you could show certain interesting differences in changes of pronunciation.

Dictionary editors agree that acceptable pronunciation is based on the actual speech of various communities. This is mentioned in all good dictionaries, including the *Thorndike-Barnhart Dictionary,* and Kenyon and Knott's Phonetic Dictionary, *Pronouncing Dictionary of American English,* and *Webster's New International Dictionary.*

Professor Albert C. Baugh, University of Pennsylvania, believes that "in the present state of our knowledge it seems best to recognize seven regional dialects in the United States." You will notice that all Professor Baugh's dialects occur in regions that were settled prior to 1812. It takes about a hundred and fifty years for a dialect to develop. However, people living in distinct geographical areas frequently take great pride in certain localized pronunciations and special uses of words. Such use is not necessarily incorrect, even though it may not fall within one of the recognized dialects.

1. *Eastern New England.* This includes the area east of the Green Mountains and the Connecticut River. There is usually the retention of the rounded vowel in *hot* and *top,* the use of the broad *a* in *fast, path, grass,* etc., and the loss of the *r* in *car, hard,* etc. Boston is its focal area.

2. *New York City.* While often considered part of New England, New York City and adjacent counties have a speech that is wholly different. The *o* in *hot* and *top* is unrounded, the *r* is usually lost, *curl* becomes *coil,* and *third* becomes *toid,* although this last is infrequent in cultivated New Yorkers.

3. *Middle Atlantic.* The Eastern third of Pennsylvania, southern New Jersey, Delaware, and parts of Maryland all preserve the *r* in all positions, have unrounded vowels in *forest* and *hot,* always pronounce *æ* in *fast, ask,* and *grass.* The focal area is Philadelphia.

4. *Western Pennsylvania,* or more correctly, Western Midland, as it spreads into adjacent parts of Maryland and West Virginia. It resembles General American with the *r* always pronounced, and with *æ* in *ask, path,* etc. *Cot* and *caught* are generally homonyms.

5. *Southern Mountain,* with rather vague boundaries settled from both Pennsylvania and the South, shows the influence of both.

130

6. *Southern,* covers a large area—all the old plantation lands—and is not of uniform character. It agrees with New England in the loss of the *r* finally and before consonants, and tends to go even farther and omit the *r* before a word beginning with a vowel, as in *far away.* But it does not have the rounded vowel in *hot* and *top,* or a broad *a* in *grass* and *dance.* The diphthong in *out* begins with *æ, eu,* or *au.* Slower enunciation produces the "Southern drawl." Final consonant groups are likely to suffer from a weakened articulation: *las', kep', fin'.*

7. *General American* is characterized by the flat *a* in *fast, path,* etc., the unrounded vowel in *hot* and *top,* the retention of a strong *r* in all positions. There is also less tendency than in British English to glide after the vowels.

STAGE DICTION AND YOUR PRONUNCIATION. For years professional actors have used Standard English, which is essentially what is used in the Southern part of England. Do not assume that you will become successful by using this diction—unless your part, your director, and your community accept it for such purposes. You should not affect it in everyday speech as a means of calling attention to your interest in the theater. Modern usage is moving away from such pronunciation, and use of it might only cause people to think your speech is affected—not a desirable impression to make.

WAYS TO IMPROVE PRONUNCIATION

Your best standard of pronunciation is that of your region. Check your pronunciation against it, and maintain this standard. The steps for improvement are the same as those for articulation—practice the correct pronunciation, and make a point of using it in everyday speech.

Plosives

Repeat these words, exaggerating the stop sound at first. Then produce them in the normal manner; note the sensation and action that produces them. Be sure your production is clear and definite.

bear	pear	dean	teen	goal	coal
bop	pop	dear	tier	gap	cap
beak	peak	doll	tall	goat	coat
beer	peer	dress	tress	grab	crab
bees	peas	candy	later	again	cocoa
baby	upon	today	atlas	began	local
fable	apron	under	utter	forget	second
table	oppose	fad	fat	bag	seek
rabbit	report	and	ant	keg	like
bob	bop	had	hat	log	luck
cab	cap	kid	kite	pig	pick
scrub	ship	need	neat	bug	buck
web	stop	feed	feet	leg	work

Note that in the first few words in each column the stop sound is at the beginning of the word (initial); in the next group it is in the middle (medial); in the last it is at the end (final). Check yourself on your ability to produce in each position.

Speak the following sentences, listening carefully to your production of the plosives. Be sure you do each correctly.

1. Some people prefer plum pie or plum pudding, but I like pumpkin pie better.
2. The pig pulled so hard on the rope that he broke both posts, the rope, and a blackboard.
3. Do you suppose that Peter planned purposely to propose a big basketball game?
4. The ripples in the water in the brook began because the boys threw pebbles.

132

Fricatives

Pronounce each word, stressing the key sound. Then pronounce in the normal manner, hearing the sound and feeling the action that forms it.

s and *z*		*th*			*th* and *s*		*sh* and *s*	
sing	zing	thin	then		thin	sin	sheen	seen
sag	zag	thick	this		theme	seem	sheet	seat
grace	graze	oath	wreathe		kith	kiss	clash	class
price	prize	ether	either		myth	miss	mash	mass

f and *v*		*sh* and *zh*	
feel	veal	glacier	glazier
fat	vat	dilution	delusion
safe	save	assure	azure
strife	strive	Aleutian	allusion

Speak the following sentences. Note all fricative sounds.

1. Last Thursday Theodore went to the theological seminary.
2. Following a fast thaw, the thick fog floated slowly through the thicket.
3. Few very vicious or violent fish were found in the fast flowing foamy waves of the coast waters.
4. It is not healthful for small children to put their thumbs in their mouths.
5. Beige camouflage shrouded the shore near the battered ships and edges of the bomb shelters.

Nasals

Pronounce each of the words, stressing the key sound in your first attempt. Listen to the sound and feel the vocal action needed to produce it. Then pronounce the words in a normal fashion. Be sure to discriminate carefully between similar sounds.

n and *m*		*ng*, *n*, and *m*		
name	make	sing	sun	sum
need	me	rung	run	rum
born	sum	tang	tin	tam
can	time	rang	ran	ram

panel	lemon
senses	rumor
round	stamp
tent	jumps

Speak these sentences, noting your production of all nasal sounds. Be sure that you do not carry the nasal tone into the vowels after *m* or *n*.

1. Pam, find your napkin and come to dinner.
2. The moon shines at night but the sun shines during the day.
3. Running, jumping, and singing are sometimes done at the same time.
4. Nineteen funny little chickens ran from the incubator to find their meal.
5. Tiny gnats milled around the lamp and settled in the vines.

Glides

Pronounce each word, stressing the key sound. Then try the list again, listening carefully, feeling the action you use for each sound.

w and *wh*		*r* and *l*	
wig	Whig	rabbit	leave
wear	where	ran	lake
wet	whet	are	call
wail	whale	bear	girl
will	while	every	pallid
		organ	film

Speak these sentences. Be sure that you give each consonant its proper production.

134

1. What whim led Whitney White to whistle *Whippoorwill?*

2. The swimmer swam the swollen waters of the whirling river on a sweltering day.

3. The little lake was full of large lily pads.

4. The merry waitress had pretty, rosy red cheeks.

5. The rules of the road restrict driving sports cars over the stretch running near the river.

ACTIVITIES

1. Make your lips and tongue more active in speech by rapidly repeating the "a, b, c's" with your teeth tightly clenched. Exaggerate the action of the lips and tongue.

2. Practice saying "lay, lee, lie, low, lou," slowly, then gradually increase the tempo until you go as fast as you can. Be sure that your tongue is active and precisely employed.

3. Count to fifty as distinctly and clearly as you can with your teeth clenched. Exaggerate the lip action. Count to fifty again, opening the mouth wider and activating the lips and tongue. Continue the exercise, increasing speed and precision.

4. Open your mouth easily, dropping your lower jaw. Place the forefinger of your right hand on the lower jaw, just below the lip, in order to make sure the jaw does not assist the tongue. Then say lightly, rapidly and with the precise rhythm of a drumbeat, the following syllables:

    NAH   nah — nah — nah   NAH   NAH — NAH — NAH
    DAH   dah — dah — dah   DAH   DAH — DAH — DAH
    TAH   tah — tah — tah   TAH   TAH — TAH — TAH

5. Using active lip and tongue action, say each of these phrases slowly, then rapidly:
    a. Rubber baby buggy bumpers.
    b. Peter Piper picked a peck of pickled peppers.
    c. Good blood, bad blood; good blood, bad blood.
    d. Five wives wearily weave bright red rugs.
    e. He who laughs last laughs best.
    f. Theophilus Thistle, the thistle thruster, thrust three thousand thistles through the thick of his thumb.
    g. Around the rough and rugged rock the ragged rascal ran.

Develop similar exercises of your own and write them in your notebook. Learn to say them correctly and rapidly. Then bring them to class and introduce them to your friends.

CHAPTER 11

USING
ACTION
EFFECTIVELY

Suit the action to the word, the word to the
action; with this observance, that you o'erstep not the
modesty of nature.

—WILLIAM SHAKESPEARE

You sit watching a rather ordinary interview on television one evening when the sound goes off. You continue to watch, but it quickly becomes meaningless—because the participants do nothing to convey their ideas to you, and you turn off the set. A week later the same thing happens, but this time the program holds you. The performer conveys meaning by his facial expression and excellent use of action. Instead of turning off the set you watch until the sound returns.

Such an experience makes you aware of the importance of visible signals. As a speaker you rely heavily on visible signals as well as audible sounds to communicate ideas.

EFFECTIVE ACTION—A BASIC MEANS OF COMMUNICATION

Action is easily perceived and instantly intelligible. When someone beckons, thumbs a request for a ride, shakes his head to mean "no," or nods in approval, we know what he means.

You convey many ideas and emotions through gestures. You may shrug your shoulders, raise your eyebrows, tilt your chin, smile, or slouch down in your chair. All these gestures are ways of indicating meaning by use of your body. You can tell someone you like him, you can disagree with him, approve of him, or express anger—all without uttering a sound. You may have seen Marcel Marceau, the celebrated French pantomimist, convey a whole series of emotional reactions with subtle movements of his mouth or eyebrows. You may do the same thing when you speak.

Action by its very nature conveys meanings words alone cannot express. An audience responds to the actions of a speaker more quickly than to the words he says. When you appear before an audience you communicate a great deal before you speak one word. The chances are they have not missed a thing about your clothes, posture, walk, or gestures.

They have read your face—did it say "I'm glad to be here." or "I'm scared stiff! I wish I'd prepared better."? They have noticed your walk as you moved to the speaker's stand. Was it hesitant and halting—or rapid and nervous? Such impressions are created before you speak.

Your audience learns about you from your posture. Do you lean on the speaker's stand, or drape yourself over it? Do you fumble in your pockets for your notes? Do you hold your head down and look at the floor? Or do you stand erect, with your head up, looking at the faces before you? All these physical attitudes are revealing; you have already "talked" to your audience. Remember you always give two speeches— one that the audience *sees* and one that the audience *hears*. Your job is to be successful in *both!*

How Action Helps the Speaker

Your ability to control your body and use action is important to you as a speaker. There are several specific reasons why it helps you.

ACTION HELPS YOU ESTABLISH AND MAINTAIN PERSONAL CONTACT WITH THE AUDIENCE. As a speaker you do not just talk *before* an audience. Your purpose is to speak *to* them so that they feel personal contact with you. Your actions establish such contact, and in this case the eye is the means by which it is made. As you speak, hold the eye of first one person for a short time, then switch to another. You want to reach each individual. This personal contact can be established throughout your talk. If the members of the audience are aware of your concern for each of them, they will respond quicker. This is the essence of good communication, and your eyes are the heart of it.

ACTION HELPS YOU CONTROL TENSION. Tension comes from the surge of energy as you anticipate your performance. Action is the normal outlet for this energy and it helps you relax. Physical relaxation cuts down emotional tension.

ACTION HELPS YOU CONTROL YOUR VOICE. As a speaker, you soon realize that breathing and the production of the speech are related to bodily control. As you relax and control your muscles by action you find that your voice is more controlled. Its quality is more pleasant, and your rate of speech and expressiveness improve.

ACTION AIDS THINKING AND FLUENCY. Since we use the muscles and nervous system in thinking, better physical control aids us in thinking. Some people find that standing up, moving around, and using hands and arms help to break mental blocks and stimulate thinking. With your mind working at top speed it is easier to select the words you want, and consequently your fluency is increased.

How Action Helps the Audience

The effect of action on the audience is significant because of the high visibility of gestures and the speed with which the meaning is transmitted. There are several specific ways in which action helps your listeners.

THE SPEAKER'S ACTION PRODUCES A SIMILAR ACTION IN THE AUDIENCE. As you watch a track meet, have you ever caught yourself straining, leaning forward, even rising from your seat, as the runners approach the finish line? Or have you seen people at a football game leap to their feet, some of them even reaching forward to "help" as an end leaps to catch a pass?

If you have, you were exhibiting the fundamental physical reaction of imitating the action you saw. This is *empathy.* In the same way you respond to the actions of a speaker or actor. Silly, giggly behavior by a speaker produces a like reaction in the audience. Lazy, sloppy posture and weak gestures induce weak, spineless responses. Enthusiastic, vigorous, controlled action by a speaker "perks up" the audience; they make a similar response.

138

ACTION CONVEYS SPECIFIC MEANINGS TO THE AUDIENCE. By using gestures you convey ideas and emotions more *specifically*. You can describe, indicate size, point out location—all by your actions. Actions indicate your attitude: enthusiasm, seriousness, amusement, anger, etc.

ACTION REINFORCES SPEECH FOR THE AUDIENCE. Often you need something to give greater impact to what you say. Gestures and facial expression provide such emphasis for your voice. The Churchill frown was a means of underscoring an important point. Teddy Roosevelt used vigorous gestures to drive home an argument. You will find that when you are aroused or concentrating on ideas, you will use action naturally.

ACTION AROUSES INTEREST AND HOLDS ATTENTION. An audience does not voluntarily give its attention to a speaker for a long time. Listeners are constantly "dialing the speaker in and out" of their attention. If there is little variety in your delivery, you may lose your audience. Action furnishes a way to capture and hold attention. Movement from one location to another on the platform, a change of stance, descriptive gestures, an emphatic nod of the head—always related to and motivated by the content of your speech—are means of holding attention.

KINDS OF ACTION AND HOW TO USE THEM

You cannot learn to use physical action by following a list of rules or by imitating pictures in a book. Do not consciously imitate any other speaker—develop action that is right for *you*. Your gestures should develop *within you*, to communicate ideas *you know* and emotions *you feel*. Then your actions are spontaneous.

POINTS TO REMEMBER. There are several kinds of action: posture, movement, gestures and facial expression.

1. Understand the basic nature of action for communication.

2. Learn to relax and ease tensions. Then use abundant, natural actions.

3. Develop control in your gestures—become more specific in each action you employ.

4. Polish and develop techniques that are most effective for you.

Posture

Posture is the way you "carry" your body while sitting, standing or walking. Remember your speech begins before you say a word; you are conveying the first part of your message by the way you sit on the platform before you have been called upon.

Your posture is something you developed long before you entered a speech class or stood before an audience. It is the result of lifelong habits of carrying your body.

In a single day you use many postures. You may sit hunched over at the breakfast table, as you eat. This posture is probably one you always use when you eat breakfast. You stand on the bus, balancing to remain upright as the vehicle lurches. Your particular stance is the one you usually employ, and it will be the same tomorrow unless unusual conditions change it. You sit upright, trying to look poised, when you talk to the principal in his office—perhaps you have adopted your "official" posture for this occasion. You have certain ways of holding your body, which have become habits. Posture depends on your mental attitude, on how you feel physically, and on the situation in which you find yourself.

When you speak to an audience you have a new posture situation to meet. You are the center of attraction for a group of people. There are no strict rules governing what you do; however, you want to look and act like a speaker. You want to meet the situation and do those things that will help you. You may have some doubt about how a speaker should look, you may even cite an exception who succeeds with poor posture.

Years ago Will Rogers, the gum-chewing cowboy humorist and philosopher, violated all of the *usual* rules of behavior and succeeded. He sat on the edge of the stage, reclined on the floor, or draped himself over a chair while he talked. Basically he was an entertainer, and those postures fitted his "official" personality, habits, attitude, and material. But there is no second Will Rogers. Each of us has to develop a speaking posture that is an expression of our own personality. Through experience and suggestions you can change your posture habits so they will be assets to you always. Such improvement comes from inside you; you have to *want* it. Then you have to do what is necessary to achieve it.

IMPROVE YOUR POSTURE: STAND "TALL." Good standing posture depends to a large extent on how you hold your head and what you do with it. Since your whole skeleton can be said to be "suspended" from your head, you can change the line of the neck, the spinal column, and the whole skeleton by raising the head or "reaching up" with it. Experts describe this action as "standing tall." When you "reach up," you pull the spine into a better line. The shoulders, hips, and others parts of the lower skeleton fall into place. If you make a habit of "standing tall" you will naturally acquire good posture.

How you support your body influences your posture. By bad placement of weight you can quickly destroy the good body line you developed by standing tall. The position of your feet can ruin the appearance of your whole body. Place your feet at a comfortable angle, with one foot slightly ahead of the other. Distribute your weight so that you feel at ease and can readily shift it when needed. This will help make your platform movements easy.

When you wish to urge a point you may shift your weight forward on one or both feet, and coordinate with your gestures. When you are explaining a point you may relax by shifting your weight to the rear foot. With a little practice you can control the distribution of your weight easily and naturally.

YOUR POSTURE REVEALS A FAVORABLE MENTAL ATTITUDE. Since posture tells the audience so much, it is important that it reveal a good mental attitude. Some people think it desirable to appear casual, bored, or uninterested. Nothing could be further from the truth when you are dealing with an audience. Audiences tend to react in the same fashion. If you have a "dead fish" posture you will get a "dead fish" reaction. If your posture reveals enthusiasm, energy, and sincerity, your listeners will tend to believe in you. No one can afford to "telegraph" anything but positive, favorable things.

DEVELOP A POSTURE THAT INCREASES YOUR CHANCES OF SUCCESS. "Standing tall" and distributing and controlling your weight properly contribute to your success as a speaker. Posture affects the action of your breathing mechanism and influences the control of your voice. It has much to do with your control of *all* the actions you make in your delivery.

DEVELOP AND SET GOOD HABITS OF POSTURE. They will ensure your ability to handle your body so it will perform in its most efficient way whenever you address an audience.

Movement

Movement is a change of location. It simply means walking. Movement, like posture, starts communication with your audience before you utter a word.

One of the first movements you make is going from your desk to the front of the room. If you move with assurance, vitality, and poise, your audience will be interested in you. If you hesitate, they may think, "He's scared!" Make your first impression a favorable one.

142

Beginners often start to speak too quickly, usually when they are still walking across the platform. The audience is watching but is not ready to listen. If you do this they may miss the *spoken* opening of the talk. If you walk with assurance to your place on the platform, get set, look momentarily at the audience, and *then* begin to talk, you will create a better impression.

Changing your location on the platform helps you relax, helps arouse interest and hold attention. It will punctuate your speech for the audience. Movement *toward* the audience is usually interpreted as an appeal or presentation. Movement *backward* or *away from* the audience denotes withdrawal or concession. *Movement to the right* or *to the left* can punctuate for you as you proceed from one section of your speech to another. Always integrate such movements with the content; link the visible and audible message.

Make your movements purposeful—do not become a "pacer." Such speakers lack real purpose in movement; they end by annoying the audience. In moving to the right or left, turn and walk easily to your new position—do not sidestep.

Some beginning speakers are overanxious to leave the platform—they start before they've finished speaking. Do not give in to that impulse. Bring both your audible and visible speeches to an end at the same time; then pause briefly and walk back to your seat. Be sure not to slouch off, or in any way imply "I'm glad that's over!" Keep your poise, and avoid spoiling the effect your words have created.

Gestures and Facial Expression

Gestures include movements of all parts of your body to convey meaning. Effective gestures come from within; they result from natural impulses to say things with action. Use action freely at first, because it helps you express things vividly and clearly. But do not try to *learn* a gesture mechanically and then "lay it on," using it just for the sake of gesturing. Such artificial actions call attention to themselves because they are "tacked on" for effect only, and do not come from within you. Mark Twain in *Tom Sawyer* describes a small boy speaking his piece, "accompanying himself with the painfully exact and spasmodic gestures which a machine might have used—supposing the machine to be a trifle out of order."

Good gestures are beneficial in four ways: (1) they help you relax muscle tensions; (2) they help you gain confidence; (3) they communicate ideas; and (4) they capture and hold attention.

Gestures may be roughly divided into two types: those of the head, including facial expression, and those of the hands, arms, and shoulders.

THE HEAD AND FACIAL EXPRESSION. Although it is not generally considered a gesture, facial expression is probably the most basic, universal, and understandable means of communicating. An audience usually looks at the speaker's face, and what it reads there is decisive. The smile, frown, or set of your jaw conveys much more to the audience than many hand gestures. Coupled with the use of natural movements (or gestures) of the head, facial expression reveals a wide range of meanings.

GESTURES OF THE HANDS, ARMS, SHOULDERS. Certain basic gestures of the hands and arms are very important.

Pointing. The index finger, and sometimes the thumb, with the accompanying movement of the arm, provide the means for indicating direction or location.

Accepting or giving. Extending the hand with the palm up is a natural gesture for presenting or giving, and for appeal or acceptance.

Refusing or rejecting. Quite as naturally you use a gesture with the palm down or outward to refuse an object or reject an idea.

Describing. You often use your hands to tell the size, shape, height, or action of a thing. Such gestures give specific meaning as well as suggestiveness to your language when you build word pictures for your audience.

Emphasizing. You may clench your fist, shake your index finger, or employ similar gestures to reinforce your words. Strong feelings inevitably evoke such gestures.

Dividing or relating. The parts of your talk, or key ideas, can be demonstrated more vividly by using your hands to indicate separation, location, or spatial relationship. Time intervals, order, or sequence are made clear with such gestures.

Principles of Effective Gesture

ALL GESTURES ORIGINATE WITHIN YOU. Gestures are not something that can be added as an afterthought to decorate your speech. They must come from a genuine desire to convey certain *meanings.* No gesture is effective if it is "tacked on." Your inner purpose must touch off the action.

GESTURES SHOULD BE APPROPRIATE TO BOTH AUDIENCE AND OCCASION. If your gestures are too numerous they will lose their effect because they call attention to the gesturing. You are better off to use too few gestures than too many. If gestures are not suitable to the audience and the occasion, they seem ridiculous or in bad taste.

Broad, expansive gestures are more appropriate to large audiences in auditoriums or convention halls; in a schoolroom before a small audience they are out of place.

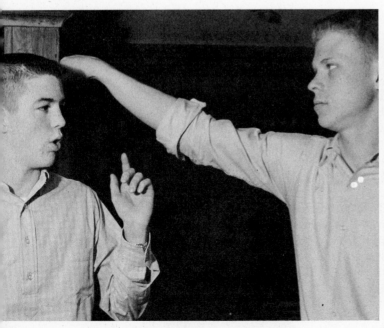

GOOD GESTURES HAVE EASE AND COORDINATION. If gestures are smoothly made, they will not call attention to themselves but will be a part of the delivery. Such ease and coordination are developed only by experience and practice.

GESTURES ARE MADE WITH THE WHOLE BODY. The whole body is involved in achieving smoothness and unity of any action. There must be "follow through." Your face, hands, trunk, and legs must all say the same thing to present a *total* and convincing effect as you gesture.

GESTURES HAVE VIGOR, STRENGTH AND RELAXATION. If your gestures are flabby or weak they will not be convincing; or adequately convey your meaning; or impress your audience. The relaxation of muscles allows flexible use of the wrists and full control of the hands, arms, and fingers. Such control gives you the proper muscle tension needed for vigor and grace in making effective gestures.

GESTURES ARE SUITABLY TIMED. As a rule an effective gesture slightly precedes the words to which it refers. However, the finishing movement of the gesture should be exactly timed to fit the word or phrase which it stresses. Practice will help you most in learning good timing.

GESTURES ARE DEFINITE AND PRECISE. If you point to an object, do it exactly and definitely. Make each gesture clear and distinct, so there is no confusion about the location, description, or importance of the thing your gesture is meant to indicate or describe.

ACTIVITIES

1. You have just returned from a trip which included travel by bus, railroad, and plane. At the bus depot, the railroad terminal, and the airport you saw many interesting people. You wish to share these experiences with your friends. Impersonate the actions of any of the following, or add others you wish to create. Be funny without being unkind.

A fat woman with numerous packages filling both of her arms. Her hat, which has a long feather, starts to slip down over her eyes so the feather tickles her nose. She has problems!

A man, carrying a large bag in one hand, tries with the other to keep his hat from blowing away.

A beautiful young lady doing her makeup while using a small mirror held in one hand.

A girl, unaccustomed to high heels, has broken the heel on her left shoe. She tries to run to catch the bus, which is about to leave. Her shoe comes off, etc.

146

A small newsboy with a large bundle of papers; in his circuit around the waiting room he tries to sell papers to everyone.

A man making a phone call cannot get his bag into the booth with him, and is afraid to leave it outside.

An elderly lady in tight shoes walking with a cane to the ticket window, where she fidgets while awaiting her turn. In the process she drops her purse.

A fashionable matron approaching the station with her head in the air, escorts a French poodle pulling at the leash. As she draws close to some interested people on the platform, the dog spies a stray cat and quickly changes direction. He gets the leash tangled around the woman's legs.

The cashier in the lunchroom, taking checks: she re-adds them, puts them on a spindle, punches cash register key, and makes change.

A Texas cowboy in high-heeled boots trying to walk swiftly and smoothly on a slippery floor.

A mother with a baby in her arms and two small children tries to get safely through a revolving door.

2. Do any of the following individual pantomimes or any of your choice.
   Cooking bacon
   Making fudge and testing it
   Ironing a dress with pleats
   Pressing a pair of trousers
   Doing your setting-up exercises
   Washing a dog
   Casting a plug or fly
   Jacking up a car and removing the wheel
   Conducting a band
   Playing a violin
   Dusting a table top filled with small objects and a lamp
   Putting up pin curls

3. Develop a pantomime of two minutes in which you reveal a series of happenings in a given situation. Include an entrance and an appropriate exit for your scene.

4. Using a group of three people, devise a pantomime for any of the following situations: (create your own if you wish)
   Fisherman on a pier—on a good day
   Members of a golf threesome
   Woman hanging pictures and curtains
   Policeman and pedestrians on a busy corner
   Women at a glove counter
   Basketball players warming up at free-throw line

Family planting a garden

Group of high-school students cleaning up leaves

Women in a beauty parlor

Cooks and waiters at a short-order counter in a restaurant

People in a self-service grocery store

5. Bring to class and demonstrate in a five minute talk an object you can operate, take apart, or assemble as you explain its use. Be prepared to answer questions about it.

6. Using the blackboard, draw a sketch revealing a "layout" or operation. Explain all parts clearly as you draw or label the sketch.

7. Without any props or sketch, describe vividly a scene, or explain how to do some complex process. Use your hands, arms, etc., to emphasize and clarify your material.

Posture

1. Use the proper posture for each of the following:

Putting a golf ball

Shooting a free throw

Facing off in hockey

Pitching horseshoes

Standing at bat

Serving a tennis ball

Standing at attention

Reaching up to pick an apple

Reacting to a stomach cramp

Relaxing and being casual

Acknowledging an introduction

Shooting a bow and arrow

Starting to mount a horse

Looking through a "scenic" telescope

Lifting one end of a plank

Stepping from one stone to another in crossing a stream

2. Try these additional ones:

"Stay away from me!"

"Please come this way."

"Turn to the right at the next corner."

"Climb higher!"

"Move over one seat, will you please?"

"Put the things on the table right here."

"What on earth did you do?"

Movement: Walking

1. Each member of the class should walk from his seat to the front of the room or the platform. He should stop, assume a suitable speaker's posture, and look at the audience briefly. Then he should return to his seat. Teacher and/or pupil evaluations of walk and posture may follow.

2. Place four chairs on the platform or at the front of the room. In groups of four, the class members will walk to the platform and seat themselves in the chairs. Each student should assume a suitable sitting posture for a speaker seated before an audience. Each student will then rise and walk to his seat. The teacher and pupils should give constructive suggestions.

3. Each student will rise, acknowledge an imaginary introduction with a nod, and step forward as if to speak. Then he should return to his seat.

4. Using a suitable walk, proceed to the platform or to the front of the room. Walk across to the speaker's stand and place your notes upon it, arranging them as you wish to have them. Look up, facing the audience, and give the opening sentence of your talk. Be sure that you are "set" before you begin. Be aware of the importance of holding your head up and looking at the audience before you start to speak.

5. Practice moving from one side of the stand to the other. Do it naturally and easily.

6. Try a transitional movement forward toward the audience and from either side of the stand, as you say, "Now, I want you to understand this next point, etc." Step back and return to your place behind the stand as you refer to your notes.

Gesture

(In all of these exercises be sure your gestures are of the whole body and are well coordinated.)

1. *Pointing or locating.* Use your index finger, hand, and arm to point out at least three objects in the room as you name them.
   Indicate each of the four directions—north, south, east, or west—as you name them. Rotate or turn the body suitably to match this action.

2. *Accepting or giving.* Use the palm-up gesture, extending your hand toward the audience as you say, "This is for you." "Please accept my position." "I appeal to your understanding and better judgment."

3. *Refusing or rejecting.* Use the palm-down gesture as you say, "I cannot accept your proposal." "I will never do what you ask." "That is ridiculous."

4. *Describing.* Use both hands, gesture and say, "The stick was two feet long."
   Use one hand and say, "He ran in and out of the crowd." "The mountain towered over the lake." Create other descriptive phrases which you can invent gestures to describe.

CHAPTER 12

MEETING
SPECIAL
SPEAKING
SITUATIONS

To everything there is a season,

and a time to every purpose under heaven.

—ECCLESIASTES 3:1

There are many speaking situations in which the techniques of preparing and delivering a speech will not serve. You can hardly nominate a friend for a class office in the same way you make a formal speech on current American politics. There are many such special situations, and they can be arranged in three main categories—the meeting, the presentation of awards or gifts, and the special social occasion.

THE MEETING

Americans are famous for their meetings—Scout meetings, political meetings, P.T.A. meetings, professional meetings, and even meetings to prepare for future meetings. So you'll need to be able to deliver certain basic speeches necessary to carrying on a successful meeting. Announcements must be short and informative. Speakers must be introduced with enthusiasm, and the speaker must know how to respond effectively. Nominations must be made and accepted in a manner that keeps the meeting moving along. And new members or visitors must be greeted warmly, and should respond in the same way.

ANNOUNCEMENTS

Success in making announcements starts with understanding their purpose. Though they are short, they contain important information. Usually the information given leads to action on the part of the listeners. Consider this announcement: "Fifth-period classes will not meet today." And consider the results if the announcer made a mistake and said, "Fourth-period classes will not meet today." Accuracy is of primary importance.

Remember that announcements are often put in a part of the program where they are least conspicuous, or are given quickly under distracting conditions. In a short space of time you must meet all the following demands: (1) Know the facts: the event or action, its reason, how it is to be carried out; the date, hour, and place; the persons involved; the charges, if any. To call extra attention to the event, add any other interesting information you may have. (2) Organize your facts with great care. Accuracy is essential—you cannot afford misunderstanding.

The announcement is one type of speech that it is wise to write out in complete detail and read. List each item clearly and briefly, so there will be no misunderstanding. Make certain that you read loudly enough so that everyone in the room can hear you.

Check your audience to be sure everyone has understood. If necessary, restate the essentials facts in a summary.

INTRODUCING A SPEAKER

Your purpose in introducing a speaker is to acquaint the audience with him and his qualifications to handle the subject. You want to accomplish this as courteously as possible. Therefore, you tell them the essential things: his subject, his name, and any brief but important information

151

about him. On some occasions you may tell him something about the audience and the occasion. Thus, you will interest the audience in the speaker, and the speaker in his listeners.

Write or talk to the speaker in advance. Learn the essential facts about him that will interest the audience he is addressing. If it is a group of teachers, the speaker's own educational background and his accomplishments in the field will be important. If other facts about him—his hobbies, travels, experiences—are of interest, add them to your list. But the essential information is what makes him especially fitted to discuss his subject. Be sure you know how to pronounce his name correctly!

Organize your facts in clear sequence and make your remarks to the point. Don't overpraise the speaker. The more distinguished he is, the less introduction he needs. Deliver the introduction warmly and with enthusiasm. Leave his name until the last, and say it distinctly.

Keep your introduction brief; the audience came to hear the speaker, not you. Do not discuss the subject the speaker has chosen. This is his privilege. State it, *clearly* and audibly, and sit down.

RESPONDING TO AN INTRODUCTION

As a speech student you may be asked to speak before a school or neighborhood audience. Just what will you say after the chairman has introduced you?

First, remember your response should be brief and appropriate. When the chairman completes his introduction, take your place before the audience. Recognize the chairman by calling him by his name and title, and thank him for what he has said. Then turn to your audience.

It is not necessary for you to call the roll of persons present. The best salutation is "Ladies and Gentlemen." If important persons are present and you believe it appropriate to mention them, state their names and titles after you have addressed the audience. Never list the guests first and then, as an afterthought, add "Ladies and Gentlemen."

NOMINATING A CANDIDATE

If you want to name a person for nomination to an office, you must acquaint the members of the group with his abilities that make him a good choice for that office. Clarity, sincerity, and relevant details are all part of a good nomination speech. Organize your talk around these essential points: (1) State the office for which you are making the nomination. (2) List and develop the abilities needed in that office. (3) Name your candidate and tell how he qualifies for the office. (4) Predict that your candidate will do an excellent job for the organization.

ACCEPTING A NOMINATION

Your purpose in accepting a nomination is to assure those supporting you that you are a competent candidate and that you appreciate being selected to run for that office. These hints may assist you: (1) Briefly thank the group for nominating you. (2) Discuss the plans and achievements of the organization you will represent if elected. (3) Mention any new or interesting ideas you think will strengthen that program. (4) Modestly, seriously, and briefly state your intentions.

WELCOMING NEW MEMBERS OR VISITORS

A speech of welcome should make your visitors glad to be present. As speaker, you are the host, and by your remarks you must try to make your guests feel at ease and genuinely welcome. The situation and what you say are not unlike those in your own home when you have guests.

Keep in mind these suggestions: (1) Be warm and sincere; those you are welcoming will appreciate such an attitude. (2) Refer to the occasion and your rôle in greeting the new members or visitors. (3) Include the name and point of view of your school or organization in your remarks. (4) Mention the special qualities of your visitors and identify individuals by name. (5) Offer to be of help. (6) Keep your remarks short.

ACKNOWLEDGING A WELCOME

The response to a speech of welcome is a courteous acknowledgment of the words of greeting just described. Again, be brief, sincere, and specific to the occasion. These are a few points to remember: (1) Express thanks for the opportunity to visit and pleasure at being there. (2) Compliment the host and his organization on their kindness and hospitality. (3) Offer to return their hospitality when they visit you. (4) Mention any reasons you may have for enjoying your visit.

THE PRESENTATION OF AWARDS OR GIFTS

For the presentation of an award or gift to have true meaning, the speaker must be able to express sincerely why the award is being made; and the person who receives an award must express his gratitude with dignity and warmth.

The purpose of this type of speech is to call attention to the character or achievements of the person to whom the award is given, or any special reason for the gift.

Your talk may, if you wish, have touches of optimism and humor, and, since this situation is frequently one of farewell, it may also include your sincere regret. The content of the speech may draw specifically on one of these subjects: The award is presented because of distinctive achievement—individual merit or result of competition, and you explain the details.

The gift is made because of long and faithful service. Develop a short biography. The gift is given because the recipient is leaving. Refer to a possible use of the gift in new circumstances and express regret at the person's going away.

The talk usually concludes with an expression of best wishes for happiness and success.

RESPONDING TO AN AWARD OR GIFT

In accepting a gift or an award, you express your thanks for the recognition you have received. Make a brief reply, marked by seriousness, sincerity, and modesty. A touch of humor may be appropriate in certain situations.

These suggestions may help you in responding to an award: (1) Be sure to thank the donors of the gift. (2) State that you are honored by the occasion and the award and express your hope that you can continue to maintain the standards that merited it. (3) Explain what you intend to do with the award. (4) Reminiscences or anecdotes appropriate to the occasion or to your service may be useful in your response.

THE SPECIAL SOCIAL SITUATION

Now, let's consider those speeches that are delivered on special occasions —the after-dinner speech, the toastmaster's speech, and the commemorative speech. Each of these speeches has particular qualities.

156

THE AFTER-DINNER SPEECH

Membership in clubs, service organizations, and business groups seems to be an American characteristic. With the growth of these groups, the occasions for after-dinner speeches have multiplied in direct proportion to the increase in the number of meetings. You may soon find yourself invited to speak after dinner without having asked for the opportunity.

The traditional after-dinner speech is primarily to entertain. People gathered for a pleasant, satisfying experience after a meal should be in a pleasant mood. They enjoy congenial companionship, and want to relax and have a good time; humor and laughter are part of the scene. Serious thoughts can enter, but they should not be deep or heavy. Good feeling, liveliness, and geniality dominate the occasion.

At some banquets a theme is set. This is true of alumni meetings for the purpose of reunion and good fellowship, birthdays, certain anniversaries, and special occasions of celebration. As a rule, the theme permits seriousness and levity, with the latter predominating. The light touch characterizes most of the speeches. Whether a particular theme is used or not, it is to your advantage to know how to make a speech appropriate to the occasion.

There is no definite formula for the after-dinner talk. You will be quite safe if you catch the spirit of the occasion and then follow the typical pattern—an interesting talk, spiced with suitable humor. The choices of material and the humor vary as widely as the people who gather at these dinners.

Originality and imagination are important in speeches of this type. Some people write out all or parts of their speeches because they rely on puns, twists of language, and humorous phrases. Learn to develop your own special abilities along this line—most successful speakers of this type are made, *not* born. Very few people are just naturally funny.

If you do this kind of speaking often, you may want to build a file of appropriate stories by clipping quips from newspapers and magazines. Add to your file any stories that "click" when you hear experienced speakers tell them.

Here are some suggestions that may guide you in planning such a talk: (1) Open with a story or incident, related to the theme or occasion, that illustrates the particular point you wish to make. (2) Develop your point briefly, supporting it with further humorous incidents, anecdotes, or quotations adapted to the situation. Keep your development brief. (3) Be sure the humor is in good taste. If you are in doubt, discuss it with a friend or with your teacher. (4) Close with a brief restatement of your point. (5) "Toss the ball" back to the toastmaster or to the next speaker.

THE TOASTMASTER AND THE AFTER-DINNER SPEECH

The presiding officer of the after-dinner program is the toastmaster, and he has complete charge of it. His job requires that he be congenial, avoid controversy and criticism, create a suitable atmosphere, and be efficient. His specific duties are important.

He starts the meeting appropriately and on time. He tactfully calls the meeting to order, welcomes the audience, briefly introduces any special guests, and clearly states the purpose of the meeting. Such an opening is never left to chance; it must be well planned.

He sets the atmosphere of the meeting. Everything the toastmaster does affects the atmosphere of the occasion. His informality, light touch,

Historian Arnold Toynbee gives an after-dinner speech.

158

or casual manner will move the meeting in that direction. If he is serious, he will develop that kind of tone for the group. He keeps things moving. The time schedule of the program is the toastmaster's job. By careful planning, conferences with his speakers, and an inconspicuous system of warning them as speaking time passes, he can effectively keep things running on schedule.

He is the one person completely informed about names, titles of speeches, personal information, theme, objectives of the meeting, and time limits. He should use this knowledge to produce a superior program.

Success of his program rests upon its being molded into an effective whole. Speeches are linked together by his comments, both planned and ad-libbed. It is he who provides the appropriate story, the amusing quip to carry over an effect, and the spark that will ignite the next bit of rhetorical powder.

His final duty is to provide a conclusion for the session, one that leaves the audience and the participants with a glow of good feeling. Planning is necessary for this, and skill in making use of any materials or events that develop during the session is very helpful.

THE COMMEMORATIVE SPEECH

Many kinds of events are commemorated: the anniversary of a significant event, the birthday of a famous person, the dedication of a new theater, the opening of a superhighway. In a commemorative talk, you mark the importance of the particular event. Your rôle is to praise or pay tribute to someone or something in a way that will leave a vivid and lasting impression with your listeners.

Whether it is for Father's Day ceremonies, an assembly honoring school athletes, or a Fourth of July celebration, the pattern of all commemorative speeches is the same: (1) Learn all you can about the person, the group, or the event to be commemorated. (2) Start by referring to the event or the person. (3) Explain the reason why this recognition is deserved; give details of achievements; cite the events that have led to the present event. (4) Introduce human interest material if you are praising a person; use examples, anecdotes, and stories. (5) Read famous commemorative speeches to help you learn the attitude and the type of content desired. (6) Deliver your talk in a sincere, straightforward manner. Be yourself.

THE EULOGY

A eulogy is a speech praising someone who has made an outstanding contribution to religion, science, academic life, government, society, education, or literature. A eulogy is usually delivered after the death of the individual.

The method used in constructing a eulogy is to cause the celebrated person to live again in the minds and emotions of the audience. You should have a rich supply of human interest material about the person—anecdotes, illustrations, examples, and incidents. Recall personal actions, interviews, and conversations, if possible.

Two basic ways of organizing the material are available. Develop the speech in a time sequence, re-creating the events of his life as the basis. The second is to arrange the materials around certain subjects or topics that were most prominent in the achievements of the individual. Unless you have much time and skill, it is desirable to maintain one or the other of these patterns rather than attempt to combine them.

Your delivery should be sincere, straightforward, and communicative. As a high-school student, you should not seek to achieve an exalted or affected manner in such a presentation.

ACTIVITIES

Introductions

1. Pairs of students should prepare introductions and suitable responses for situations suggested by the teacher or developed by you. Allow one minute for introducing a speaker. Each speaker introduced should give a twenty-second response. Your teacher or the student in charge can arrange the speaking schedule in advance. Confer with your partner about personal information, his subject, and other matters. The last speaker on the list introduces the first speaker, to start the activity. If this is not practicable, prepare both an introduction of an imaginary person and his response to that introduction.

2. Give a short introduction for one of these speakers:
   a. An outstanding alumnus at a class reunion
   b. Your student body president at an assembly
   c. A faculty advisor at a class election of officers
   d. Other situations suggested by your teacher or developed by you

Nominations

1. With students working as partners, each pair prepares and presents a suitable nomination speech and acceptance for any office.

160

2. Prepare a nomination speech for one of these positions:
   a. President of the Student Council
   b. Chairman of the school talent show
   c. President of the debate club; representative to Boys' or Girls' State Chapter of National Forensic League
   d. Secretary of Girls' Athletic Association
   e. Treasurer of your class

Welcome and Response

Using partners, prepare welcome and response speeches for these situations, or others approved by your teacher.
1. A group of students, from a school nearby, attending an exchange assembly
2. Students attending a debate tournament in your school
3. Alumni returning at homecoming time
4. A visiting young people's group at your church
5. A state convention of 4-H or Future Farmers of America
6. A visiting actor who is to address your drama club

Presentation and Acceptance

Prepare a presentation speech and the acceptance speech in response to it. Plan a particular situation and accept a particular award or gift. Use originality.

After-Dinner Activities

1. Divide the class into groups, each with a toastmaster and speakers, each group to plan an after-dinner program and give the speeches for occasions they select.
2. Plan an after-dinner speaking program suitable to a speech-awards dinner that your school might give annually.
3. As the toastmaster in charge, plan and carry out a program for any one of these: a science club dinner, a football banquet, a Hi-Y meeting, a G.A.A. meeting, a National Thespian banquet.
4. Write and present an after-dinner speech on any of the following subjects: patience, moonbeams, rockets, faith, words, dreams, or others suitable for a banquet theme you select.

Commemorative Speech

1. Prepare a commemorative talk for any of the following occasions: Lincoln's Birthday, Armed Forces Day, Mother's Day, Father's Day, recognition of a championship baseball team, recognition of scholarship winners.
2. Prepare a speech eulogizing any of the following: a great writer, an outstanding musician, a great athlete, a pioneer in science, a famous speaker, a leader in government, a leader in aviation.

CHAPTER 13

DISCUSSIONS

AND

CONFERENCES

Before you begin, take counsel, and when you have
taken counsel, is full time for action.

—SALLUST

The faculty and students in a small consolidated high school faced a problem: the noon hour was hectic in bad weather. Two thirds of the pupils came from outlying parts of the school district, brought their lunches, and ate in the lunchroom. The other third lived in town and went home for lunch. Two hundred students ate lunch in about half an hour, which left thirty minutes before the next class. In bad weather most of the town students did not go home, but joined the others and ate lunch at school.

Two hundred fifty students had nothing to do during the half-hour before class, and neither they nor the faculty were very happy. The halls were jammed; the gymnasium was overcrowded, as it was the only room open. It was suggested that teachers be posted as guards, but the principal, rather than give such an order, decided to ask the Student Council for help. This group wanted to coöperate. Their president appointed a committee to study the situation, talk with both students and faculty, and to make recommendations.

The committee started by analyzing the existing conditions. They recognized that the pupils didn't intend to cause trouble; they simply had no adequate place to go during the after-lunch period nor any activity program. The gymnasium was small; its basketball courts and ping-pong table accommodated twenty-eight students. The rest concentrated in the lower halls, played pranks, and made noise. The teachers assigned to hall duty did not enjoy giving up half their lunch hour to act as policemen. Both students and faculty wanted to find some activity and facility so the congestion and chaos could be eliminated.

Several suggestions were made: (1) organize group games in the gymnasium that would accommodate more students; (2) supervise the games; (3) open the library the last half of the lunch hour so pupils could read or study; (4) ask the audio-visual department to show motion pictures in the lecture room; (5) open the band room and permit dancing to the hi-fi set there; (6) obtain a television set for students to watch.

The Student Council submitted these suggestions to the principal and the faculty. After discussion it was decided to carry out suggestions 1, 2, 3, and 5. On the first rainy day this plan was put in effect, and it immediately cut down the congestion and reduced the noise. Later the P.T.A. purchased a television set, and in three weeks the problem was solved. A chaotic noon hour turned into a pleasant, worth-while period for all. This is only one of many problems that exist in schools; most of them can be lessened or solved if you know how to use an important speech method—group discussion.

THE NATURE OF GROUP DISCUSSIONS

In this method of communication you exchange ideas, information, and opinions in order to learn and think together to solve problems. Discussion is directed by a leader, either previously appointed or selected during the meeting. It may occur in a closed session or before an audience. In order to understand the process, let us use the case of the hectic lunch period to discover the characteristics of this way of solving problems.

Discussion is an oral method. Instead of speaking alone before an audience, you are a member of a group in which everyone may participate and express his opinions. All the qualities of good speaking are just as important in groups as when you speak alone. Speech is the sole means of communication in a discussion. The Student Council committee members "talked over" the lunch-hour problem and suggested solutions.

Discussion is coöperative, not competitive. In group discussion you coöperate in *exchanging of ideas, information, and opinions* in order to learn, or you *think together* to solve a problem. You are not trying to win arguments or compete with anyone.

Discussion is a group way of solving problems. Probably the most important function of discussion is that it uses the abilities of a number of people to solve a problem. The lunch period problem and solution contain all the steps of group problem solving.

1. Statement of the problem: "How can we improve the conditions in the halls during the lunch hour?"

2. Exploration of the problem. During discussion certain points are noted. *Obvious effects:* noise, confusion, misbehavior, breakdown of discipline. *Causes:* increased number of students, inadequacy of the gymnasium, lack of space and activities, inability of the teachers to supervise the situation. *Determination of the values and standards that should govern the solution:* proposed activities should be constructive, provide for a variety of interests, be supervised by responsible persons; and additional space, properly distributed, should be provided.

3. Suggestion of solutions and their evaluation. In consideration of the effects, causes, and standards, the students proposed various solutions: conducting group games to give more students the use of the gymnasium, supervising games, opening the library for reading and study, showing motion pictures in the lecture room, allowing social dancing in the band room, and procuring a television set for viewing in the study hall. All of these solutions were discussed and evaluated.

4. Selection of the best solution (or solutions). After step three, the committee decided to use four of the proposed solutions, because they seemed most practicable and could quickly be put into effect: the revised gym program with supervision, social dancing, and opening the library.

5. Suggestions for trying out the solutions. With the coöperation of the faculty, the new program was announced by the Student Council leaders. The pupils welcomed the proposals and agreed to try them on the next rainy day. The first result was that the halls were cleared; constructive recreation attracted students to different areas of the building, and supervision became much simpler. Some time later, after the purchase of a television set, the last of the solutions was in operation.

Discussion is directed. In a small group the leader may be appointed, as the chairman in the Student Council committee was appointed by the principal. But leadership does not mean domination. The leader *guides* discussion according to a pattern, as in the five-step pattern outlined above, that ensures a systematic attack on the problem. Some discussions do not follow this pattern or have a preappointed leader. In such cases the group chooses a leader, because most persons inexperienced in discussion are more successful with a designated leader. Leadership places responsibility and ensures against aimless procedure.

Discussion is dynamic. By *dynamic* we mean that the thinking of each member of the group is not set, but is subject to change. Ideas develop or are altered as the discussion proceeds. The phrase *thought in process* describes this situation. When new, challenging information is introduced, it is possible to change your opinion if you wish.

Discussion is democratic. Every person in the group has an equal right to express himself as he wishes and should have an equal opportunity to do so. With skillful leadership and a coöperative attitude among the members, discussion becomes one of the most democratic forms of speech activity. Because all viewpoints may be heard, a conference often takes longer to reach a decision than other methods of problem solving. However, this loss of time is more than compensated by the benefits gained by pooling information and knowledge.

Discussion is based on sound information and good preparation. Some people have the mistaken idea that you don't have to prepare for a discussion. Or as one student put it, "All you do is hold a bull session." If this was true, a discussion would be nothing but a pooling of ignorance. Good discussion rests on accurate knowledge, good analysis, a thorough search for solutions, and careful consideration of the quality of the solutions. Opportunities develop for expression of new ideas as discussion progresses; but basic knowledge is the foundation on which creative thinking is based.

Discussion may be done in public or in a closed session. At times, discussion can serve its purpose best when it takes place before an audience. Everyone interested can hear the analyses and suggestions, and sometimes the public is allowed to ask questions or make comments. At other times, discussion is limited to the members of a committee. Those working on the noon-hour problem operated in closed sessions and reported to the principal and the Student Council.

THE RELATION OF DISCUSSION TO DEBATE

Discussion is a coöperative method in which people talk together in order to exchange and develop ideas and find a solution to a problem. Sometimes, even though they have done careful work and used all the steps in group thinking, they cannot reach agreement. The next logical step is to debate the question.

In debate, the speakers each seek to win approval for the position they uphold. They are in favor (affirmative) or opposed (negative). There is no middle ground in debate. Each opponent uses all his skill to convince the judges (members of a group, an audience, voters, or a jury) to decide in favor of his position. In discussion one may take any position one desires on the question. Discussion seeks *coöperatively* to reach a decision; debate is used to reach a decision by *competitive* means.

The two columns show the relationships and the differences between discussion and debate.

Discussion	*Debate*
coöperative	competitive
no decision; perhaps an agreement or consensus	decision by vote, action
dynamic: changing or "developing" reasoning	static: position and lines of reasoning are set
shift of opinion is characteristic	shift of opinion impossible—original position must be kept throughout
informal: usually no set rules for number of speakers, or time limit	formal: school debates permit one affirmative and one rebuttal speech per person with strict time limits
objective: start with a problem and find the best solution	objective: start with a proposal and win the decision for your side
delivery: conversational, expository	delivery: argumentative, persuasive

SUBJECTS FOR DISCUSSION

There are three kinds of subjects suitable for discussion and debate. If the subject is concerned with truth or falsity, it is a question of *fact*. "Is the moon capable of sustaining human life?" is such a subject. By thorough research and study, scientists (or discussion participants) could answer this question. If the subject raises the issue of goodness or badness, it is a question of *value*. "Is a natural pearl superior to a cultured pearl?" is such a question. If the problem is whether something should or should not be done, it is a question of *policy*. "Should the United States abandon its foreign aid program?" is a question of policy.

166

Types of Discussion

There are several types of discussion, each with its own particular features. Your success in using discussion lies in your selection of the best one for the occasion.

INFORMAL DISCUSSION. Many discussions grow out of social conversations. When the persons talking move to serious purposes, they pass from conversation to discussion. Discussion can be carried on informally and yet follow a pattern. Such exchanges of ideas and opinions are common among young people who are intellectually alert and well informed.

SMALL CONFERENCE OR ROUND TABLE. The degree of formality may vary in these as much as in a committee meeting. An actual table may be used to help keep the face-to-face quality in your discussion; however, the same thing may be achieved if you are seated in a small circle. A round-table discussion is a closed session. You and the other members of the group privately share ideas, analyze, and solve the problems before you. There is no audience participation. Discussions of this type appear on TV and in radio programs.

PANEL DISCUSSION. In a panel discussion a small group is presented to an audience. Four to eight persons make a good panel. Seat them in a semicircle or hollow square, so they can see and hear each other and so the audience can hear and see them. A true panel is a spontaneous discussion directed by a leader. It is not a series of prepared speeches. This method ordinarily follows the steps in group discussions, so there is a plan that covers the problem for both panelists and audience. Panel discussion may be followed by a question period or *forum*. The panel is frequently used in radio and TV.

THE DIALOGUE OR INTERVIEW. Two persons participate; one asks questions and the other answers them, while the questioner acts as a discussion leader. His partner is usually an expert on the problem. A skilled questioner asks prepared questions in such a way that the audience feels he represents them. The answers of the expert become the principal content of the program. This form, too, is often used in radio and TV.

THE SYMPOSIUM. In the symposium each speaker presents a prepared speech on a single subject before an audience. The chairman opens the discussion by stating the subject and introduces each speaker. He may provide relevant comments to connect the several talks and summarizes if necessary. As a rule a question period follows a symposium.

There are two methods of presenting a symposium. In the first, the problem is divided, and each speaker is assigned a particular section. For example, in a symposium on the question "Should two years of oral communication work be required of all high-school students?" one speaker could define the question and explain its importance, another could analyze the problem, another could present solutions and plans, still another could evaluate them.

In the second method, each speaker presents his own views on the entire subject, outlines the existing conditions, and suggests a remedy. Under this plan speakers may be chosen to represent different points of view, giving the audience an interesting contrast in material. The speaker under each plan prepares his talk carefully, but is adaptable enough to discuss any important points that may arise.

In the symposium there must be definite knowledge of the material, and speakers prepare in advance. Its chief disadvantage is that it is not so flexible as a panel discussion.

THE LECTURE-FORUM. The lecture-forum consists of a speech by one speaker followed by a question period. The chairman introduces the speaker and the topic. The speaker should be an authority on the subject,

and there are two kinds of speeches he may make. The first is an expository talk that includes background material and extensive facts. In the second, the speaker may present his views, his reasons for them, and leave the question open for the audience to explore. Either is an effective opener for a forum discussion.

THE FORUM

The forum is an audience question and discussion period following a panel, dialogue, symposium, or speech. It varies in the way it is conducted, depending upon the size and kind of audience. In a small, interested group, questions and comments can be handled with a minimum of direction. Free and spontaneous audience participation can then be achieved without obvious planning.

CONDUCTING A FORUM

A large audience cannot be handled so informally. In large groups individuals may not respond readily, or too many may wish to talk at once. Special techniques are required on these occasions, or the forum may get out of hand.

The chairman tells the audience at the beginning of the meeting if there is to be a question period. If they know this, they will listen more carefully, take notes, and prepare their questions during the first part of the program.

Opening the forum provides a link between the two parts of the program. As chairman, you restate the issues and summarize important items to make this transition.

Invite the audience to follow vital points with questions. Usually, such an opening will produce questions. If there is no response, ask the first question yourself. If a panel has preceded the forum, direct a question on a controversial issue to a member of the panel. The chairman's rôle is to "stir up" the audience.

If questions are to be directed first to individual members of the panel, as chairman you explain this. If all panel members are to participate and statements of opinion as well as questions from the audience are to be allowed, this should be stated. Indicate the time speakers from the floor will be allowed.

If written questions are to be used, explain the procedure. Attendants usually distribute cards for this purpose and collect them, preferably at the beginning of the forum. As chairman, you sort them, select those you wish to use, and direct them to the individual speaker as you read them aloud. However, questions are usually asked orally from the floor. As chairman, repeat each question so all will hear. If necessary, restate the question but be sure to keep the same meaning.

Some leaders attempt to divide the problem into areas for discussion and move from one issue to another. This does not always succeed, because some listeners may wish to follow their own interests rather than the planned order. It is better to permit the audience to determine the order rather than curb their enthusiasm by insisting upon a prearranged plan.

Be interested and enthusiastic and help create an atmosphere of lively participation in the discussion that you are leading. By combining these qualities with sincerity and skill, you can secure the same reaction from the audience.

The average length of a forum period is a half-hour. In a class period, with a panel or symposium preceding the forum, this may be too long. It is better to allow more time for the prepared introductory phase of the discussion program. A fifty-minute period divided to allow thirty minutes for the panel and a twenty-minute forum is a sensible plan. In an outside meeting, it might be better to allow forty minutes for the panel, thirty for the forum, and five minutes for announcements or introductions.

In concluding the forum, anticipate the conclusion. Two or three minutes before the adjournment, announce that there will be time for only one more question. Then when the last question has been answered, you can conclude by either summarizing or making a statement of appreciation to the speakers.

The Film Forum

Today, when there are excellent films available, the problem for discussion can be presented by showing a film. The background presented by the film gives the group the material for the discussion that follows. Certain useful suggestions will help such a situation: (1) Be sure that facilities are available to permit satisfactory viewing of the film; (2) be sure to preview the film for content, length, and critical points; (3) plan the questions you use in starting the forum, moving from the general to specific points; (4) before showing the film, list on a chalkboard the points to look for in viewing; (5) allow everyone an opportunity to ask questions or make comments; (6) conclude the forum while it is still alive, and summarize the contributions of the group.

The Buzz Session or Phillips 66

Originally devised by J. Donald Phillips, this form of discussion is used primarily to aid a large group in preparing questions for a forum. It is used following a lecture that presents a problem. The procedure is: (1) the chairman divides the audience into groups of six pairs, who confer together; (2) each group discusses the problem for a short time (six minutes is a common time); (3) each group selects a representative to present one question to the audience for consideration; (4) the chairman calls for these questions, which are briefly presented by each group representative; (5) the chairman summarizes the questions, pointing out their relationship to the problem; (6) the chairman then leads the discussion by the whole group, being sure that each question is considered and that the decisions are the result of group deliberation.

The buzz session is a method of involving the entire audience in the solving of a problem. It allows for quick coverage of a group reaction and concentrates attention on the most important questions. It is not ordinarily needed in a small group.

THE PARTICIPANT IN DISCUSSION

Your preparation for discussion will be of two kinds: general education, as it relates to the discussion for which you prepare, and specific preparation, from investigation for this particular discussion. Both kinds of preparation are of value. Your methods of specific research are similar to those employed in getting materials for a speech. Draw on all the sources you use to keep yourself well informed. Weekly news magazines such as *Newsweek, Time,* and *U.S. News and World Report;* newspapers such as The *New York Times* and *Christian Science Monitor;* periodicals such as *Harper's Magazine, The Atlantic Monthly, Saturday Review, Current History, The New Republic,* and many others—all should be part of your general and sometimes immediate preparation. Publications on the subject, either in pamphlet or book form, supply valuable information. Know how to use them and where to find them.

As a participant, make an inventory of your ideas and information in a systematic outline following the pattern of discussion. Recall the basic purpose of the discussion: it is coöperative—a group working together to solve a problem. Do not seek to win an argument or show off your knowledge. You must expect differences and changes of opinion. New evidence and sound reasoning should be the basis for modifying your views.

Try to keep your emotions under control and develop an attitude of objectivity apart from your own political or religious beliefs or your social or economic background. Such an attitude helps you fulfill your responsibility to contribute a clear analysis and arrive at the best solution to the problem under discussion.

Be enthusiastic and eager to contribute. Add to your factual knowledge enthusiasm for contributing your knowledge, thinking, and reactions. The success of the process depends on your desire to do the job well and a positive approach toward it. The leader will appreciate your enthusiasm, because obviously the discussion cannot move ahead if everyone sits back and does not speak! Be relevant in your comments. You must stay "on the subject" of the particular issue at hand and not talk just for the sake of talking. You contribute only if what you say is relevant and applies to the point being considered.

Listen carefully and courteously. Careful and courteous listening ensures a good discussion atmosphere. It guarantees that your remarks will be relevant and in tune with the discussion pattern as it develops. Be tactful and aware of human relations. Since group thinking rests upon the joint effort of people, you must remember that tact and consideration are important. Avoid dogmatic, overpositive comments. If you disagree, do so politely. Use phrases such as "I see your point clearly; however, it seems to me..." or "Your facts are accurate, yet I draw a different conclusion from yours."

Procedures and Techniques

Procedure varies widely in formality. The panel is less formal than the symposium. The committee session is often conducted much like conversation. In most small groups you can talk without asking leave to speak, and you "come in" at the appropriate moment. Get your ideas "into circulation" in a way suitable for the occasion. Don't interrupt others or try to dominate the scene; think and observe before you speak. If several are eager to talk at once, raise your hand or let the leader know that you want his permission to speak.

Your technique in participating follows a practical formula. State your opinion; then give the reasons or facts you have to support it; tell why it is important to the discussion; then explain how you arrived at this conclusion. Using this method, you will be clear, relevant, strong, and objective.

THE LEADER IN DISCUSSION

If you are asked to lead a discussion, you will prepare thoroughly and carefully, as any participant would. However, you have a responsibility to put your preparation on paper in outline form. Your leadership responsibilities influence this preparation, and your discussion outline is specifically planned to help you carry them out.

You may wish to write and then read your introductory remarks and introductions of speakers. But for the main part of the discussion use basic steps as divisions of your outline.

Since the leader's purpose is to stimulate discussion, prepare questions rather than statements to get members of the group talking. Base your questions on the content the group should explore under each division. But the major challenge is to prepare the best questions you can, to get the right responses from the discussion members. One question in each division may not be enough. Prepare a series of related questions that allow you to follow up the replies and keep the discussion going. In form, your outline will be sequences of questions. Be ready to modify your scheme on the spot or take immediate advantage of points or good ideas that develop. Make notes in your outline so that you can question especially qualified persons to utilize their knowledge. Be ready with a tentative plan for closing the discussion.

While you know that discussions are not rehearsed or closely planned, it is good insurance for the leader to have a briefing or preplanning session with members of a panel. As leader at such a session, usually held several days ahead, explain your plans for introducing the subject, set the mechanical details, get information about your members, and if possible, agree on definitions and limitations of the question. Learn the ideas of the members and the information they have acquired and suggest directions for further exploration. Consider the basic sequence of key issues to be introduced so that points of conflict may be formed.

For beginners, preplanning usually helps develop a smoother, more effective discussion. You should remember, however, that the purpose of such preparation is *not* to rehearse lines or "set" the participations; it is a *planning* operation to clear up details so that the actual discussion time can be used to develop the vital issues of the problem.

Local conditions influence the amount of control you will have over the physical arrangements, but always arrange the chairs so members of the group can see each other. For small groups, seating the members around a table is best. Then you have a face-to-face situation that builds a group feeling, and encourages shy or inexperienced persons. In a panel of six or more members, a semicircle or hollow square is desirable. The use of visual aids, displays, or chalkboards will affect the arrangement. Chairs should be placed so that these items are visible to the audience and can be used easily by the members.

Other physical arrangements you need to consider in advance are name cards for the participants, ventilation, lighting, noise conditions, paper or writing materials, an easel for charts, and ash trays if needed.

The leader has important responsibilities in starting the discussion. But certain routine duties come first: He must introduce the members of the group to the audience, announce the subject, explain the purpose and importance of discussing the problem, inform the audience of the time limits and whether they will be allowed to ask questions or speak from the floor, supply any other information, and direct the opening question to the group.

This is the simplest and most direct way of opening a discussion. Another method you can use after introductions includes using a quotation, stating the major points of disagreement, defining the problem, sketching the history of a typical case, or setting up two opposing positions on the problem.

Following the opening you can use questions in these specific ways: (1) Use one or more prepared questions. Start with a general question that sets a logical beginning according to your outline. Follow with a specific question to an individual (by name) who you know has a definite position on the problem. Avoid questions that can be answered by "yes" or "no." (2) Plant starter questions. These touch off quick response and begin the opening analysis you believe basic to further comments from the group. (3) Use a *what* question to get individual reactions. For example, "*What* is your position?" or "*What* are the present conditions as you see them?" or "*What* is your analysis?" (4) Follow this with *why* questions. They keep things going and search for reasons and facts behind the positions.

You understand that the leader must keep the discussion going and give it order and direction. There are several methods you can use to achieve this. (1) Follow the steps in the pattern. Use the basic steps in group thinking and fit your outline to it, assuming it is sufficiently flexible. Guide the thinking of the group through these phases, and the discussion will be orderly and systematic, and have a definite opening and conclusion. As a beginning leader, this is probably the best method. It suits most situations in high-school speech classes. (2) Develop key issues and then "point up." In this method, used by experienced leaders, you start the discussion at the point of greatest interest and build the other points around this. Use key issues as the heart of your plan; do not follow the five steps in the pattern, but "point up" or tie in the contributions to the basic problem as they are developed. An able leader thus capitalizes on *interest* as the heart of the discussion and relies upon his skill in linking points of interest to provide order and direction. (3) Link parts of the discussion clearly. Use good transitions as you move from one part of the discussion to another. It is important for you to relate the new to the old, the unfamiliar to the known by *your* comments. (4) Use summaries intelligently. Appropriately placed summaries of content are important in keeping audience and panel together in their thinking. Learn to state the heart of an issue in simple, clear language, so you can develop this ability.

Concluding the Discussion

While you hope that the panel may reach an agreement (or consensus) or that specific action will be recommended or taken, neither may be the case. It may be necessary to refer to your notes and observations made during the discussion, so you can readjust your original plan. Your responsibility is to present a brief, concise summary in conclusion that states fairly what the group has accomplished. As a discussion leader, you must know the techniques for covering this significant material.

News reporters use a formula for getting facts about a story. It is based on these questions: *Who? When? Why? What? Where? How?* As a leader you learn to use these in ways that serve the particular discussion. You know that through a *what* question you can learn a person's position, and a *why* question helps you discover the reasons and facts for holding that position. *How* questions are useful to learn solutions and methods of solving the problem. *Who* questions lead to expert opinions and sources. *When* and *where* locate information in time and place.

Every leader wants the speakers to make statements that are clear and understandable as well as interesting. Do not hesitate to ask a participant for an example or illustration for concreteness and clarity.

Many high-school students fail to support or prove their general statements. As a leader you can ask for such proof by evidence—facts, statistics, or quotations. You may also cite such material and ask the speakers for their reactions to it. Both methods help give logical strength and support to a discussion.

Although you may find some conflicts of opinion difficult to use, you can generally help keep the discussion moving by tactfully pointing out differences and the bases for them. The mere expression of such conflicts opens the problem to honest and clear thinking, which is a basic purpose of discussion.

176

Typical Discussion Situations

As a leader you will find that a few people waste time with dull, useless talk. You must be able to stop such unproductive periods by learning to handle people in typical discussion situations. Below are some of the most common methods[1]:

1. To call attention to a point that has not been considered: "Has anyone thought about this phase of the problem?"

2. To question the strength of an argument: "What reasons do we have for accepting this argument?"

3. To question the source of information or argument: "Who gathered these statistics that you mentioned?" "Who is Mr. Gish whose opinion has been quoted?" "Do you know that as a fact, or is it an opinion?"

4. To suggest that the discussion is wandering from the point: "Can someone tell me what bearing this has on our problem?" "Your point is an interesting one, but can't we get back to our subject?"

5. To register steps of agreement (or disagreement): "Am I correct in assuming that we all agree (or disagree) on this point?"

6. To bring the generalizing speaker down to earth: "Can you give us a specific example on that point?" "Your general idea is good, but I wonder if we can't make it more concrete. Does anyone know of a case...?"

7. To suggest that some are talking too much: "Are there those who haven't spoken who have ideas they would like to present?"

8. To draw the timid but informed member into the discussion: "Spelvin, here, lived for quite a while in China. Suppose we ask him whether he ever saw...?"

9. To cut off a speaker who is too long-winded: "While we're on this point, let's hear from some of the others. Can we save your point until later?"

10. To break up a heated argument: "I think we all know how Jones and Smith feel about this. Now who else would like to get in on it?"

EVALUATING DISCUSSION

For purposes of evaluating discussion, various check sheets may be devised. The one reproduced here allows your teacher or observer to judge the work of the leader and participants in a panel discussion. Use such a list to evaluate your own discussion.

[1]Abridgment of pp. 59-61 HANDBOOK FOR DISCUSSION LEADERS by J. Jeffery Auer and Henry Lee Ewbank. Copyright 1947 by Harper & Brothers, and reprinted with the permission of the publisher.

CHECK LIST FOR DISCUSSION*

Participants								
Names of Participants								
Knowledge of the problem (Information)								
Logic in reasoning								
Skill in following the "pattern"								
Willingness to promote discussion								
Cooperation in thinking and contributing								
Skill in speaking: voice, etc.								
Totals								

The Leader

Skill in stating the problem		Skill in clarifying and summarizing and "pointing up"	
Skill in stimulating participation without intruding		Skill in handling the various kinds of conflict	
Skill in guiding in pattern of reflective thinking		Skill in stimulating cooperative spirit	
Skill in encouraging statement of all points of view		Skill in controlling pace suitable to members and time	

RATING: (1) Poor; (2) Fair; (3) Adequate; (4) Good; (5) Excellent

*Courtesy of Kenneth G. Hance, Department of Speech, Michigan State University.

ACTIVITIES

1. Prepare a panel discussion for your class. Select the leader and members carefully. Make all necessary mechanical arrangements. Prepare outlines to guide both the participants and the leader. Evaluate the results of the panel after its conclusion, using the items on the check sheet as a guide.

2. Plan a lecture-forum for a class meeting. Invite an outside speaker to deliver this lecture. Appoint a student chairman to conduct the meeting. Evaluate the results: leadership, audience participation, effectiveness of the lecture, etc. Compare your results with those of the panel.

3. Plan a similar program with one of your class members as a lecturer. Use a student chairman and develop all details of the program.

4. Prepare a symposium on a subject of your choice, assigning suitable speeches to selected class members. With a student chairman, run the program during a regular class session. Evaluate it and compare your results with those of the panel and lecture-forum.

5. Watch a television discussion program and write a report on what you observed. Compare the organization and techniques with those you have used in class.

DISCUSSION SUBJECTS

Personal or educational problems

1. How much homework should high-school students be expected to do each night?
2. How can better scholarship be developed in our school?
3. How should a student select a college or university?
4. Should the legal age for required school attendance be changed?
5. How much control should parents exercise over teen-agers' dating?
6. Should driver training be required in all high schools?
7. Should ability grouping in high-school courses be discontinued?
8. How can high-school students improve their study habits?
9. How can grading be improved in high-school courses?
10. Should high-school students go steady?
11. Should participation in extra-class activities be limited by school regulation?

Current affairs

1. What should be the policy of the United States toward Cuba?
2. How can the United States improve its relations with the free world?
3. How can the farm problem be solved?
4. Should the testing of nuclear weapons be discontinued?
5. How can the quality of radio and television programs be improved?
6. Should the United States substantially reduce its foreign aid payments?
7. What should be the policy of the United States toward Red China?
8. Should national censorship of motion-picture films be required?
9. What policy of medical care for the aged is best for the United States?
10. What are practical methods for handling problems of racial integration in the public schools?
11. Should federal aid to education be authorized for all schools?
12. What plan of military training is most satisfactory for young men in our country?
13. How can the image of America be improved in foreign countries?
14. How can automobile accidents on our highways be reduced?
15. How can the narcotics problem in America be solved?

CHAPTER 14

PARLIAMENTARY PROCEDURE

Order is heaven's first law.
—ALEXANDER POPE

Whenever a large group of people want to transact the business of a club, society, or government they have to follow a set of rules; otherwise everyone will try to talk at once, and jump from subject to subject without ever coming to a firm resolution on any one matter. The system they usually follow is Parliamentary law. It derives from the rules and customs developed over generations by the British Parliament, and modified and reaffirmed in *Robert's Rules of Order*. It is based on principles essential to the democratic way of life: the right of the majority to decide, the right of the minority to be heard, and the right of absentees to be protected.

Following parliamentary procedure will ensure that these rights are respected *only when the rules are properly understood and applied*. This method can be twisted by unscrupulous and unprincipled men. Such men, by a misuse of these rules, can use them to suppress the liberty they are designed to protect. Ignorance on the part of the governed will leave them open to such attacks. Since these rules are followed in our national and local governments, as well as in our clubs and societies, it is essential that each citizen understand just how this system works.

Suppose you attend a meeting of your high-school club, the purpose of which is to elect a new secretary. You go because you want to nominate a friend for the office.

The president declares the meeting open for nominations. A girl jumps up and says, "I nominate Judy Mills." A boy rises immediately and says, "Mr. Chairman, I move the nominations be closed." Another student calls out, "I second the motion." The president says, "All in favor of closing the nominations say 'Aye.' " You hear a modest chorus of ayes. "All opposed say 'No.' " Then the president abruptly turns and announces, "Well, Judy, I guess you are the new secretary."

Now you don't have to be an expert at parliamentary law to know that the right of the majority to decide, the right of the minority to be heard, and the right of absentees to be protected have been violated. But just what do you do? It isn't very pleasant to sit helpless and unable to protect yourself against the knowledge and skill of another group.

What you need to do is rise to your feet when the boy moves to close the nominations and say, "Mr. Chairman, I rise to a point of order. According to *Robert's Rules of Order* a reasonable time must be given before a motion to close nominations is in order. Also, a motion to close nominations requires a two-thirds vote, not a majority vote." This is an incidental motion, it needs no second, it is not debatable or amendable, and you may interrupt any speaker to make it. The decision, however, lies with the chairman. Should he still try to force the issue, by deciding against you, you may appeal from the decision of the chair. This motion requires a second, may be debated, is not amendable, and requires a majority vote to pass.

Now suppose you and your friends are trying to make a change in the form of student government. You feel that it is a good change and will benefit the entire student body, but the idea is a little slow to catch on, and the opposition is well organized. They bring the matter up at a meeting before you are ready, and you realize that the debate is going against you. What can you do to protect your idea?

If you want to stop all discussion of the subject, you can move to table it. This motion is undebatable and requires only a majority to pass. With this motion you and your friends could probably succeed in stopping the immediate discussion.

But suppose you and your friends want to see just how many students you have on your side and would like the matter discussed further without its actually being brought to a vote. In that case someone moves to postpone indefinitely, which means that the matter cannot be brought up again at that session. If this motion is narrowly defeated, it would lead you to believe the main motion would be defeated, so in effect you would have achieved a test vote.

But if your purpose is to delay, while the debate on postponement is in progress, you can have someone move to amend the motion and someone else move a second amendment. All these motions are debatable and must be disposed of before the meeting can return to the main motion. Such motions also suggest needed changes in the main motion, and so the main issue is kept alive and has the opportunity to gain support from other members present.

If more time is needed, someone can move to refer the matter to committee, another debatable motion. Then someone can rise and move to postpone to a given time, and this motion supersedes the motion to refer. By this time things may be getting a little restive, and it is a good strategy to have one of your friends move to limit the time of debate on any, or all, of the motions to ten minutes. This motion is not debatable and takes a two-thirds majority to pass. At this point someone else can move to amend the last motion to twenty minutes. If you and your friends muster the two-thirds vote to pass the motion regarding time, you may feel that your position is strong enough for you to rise and move the previous question, on the main motion, and bring the matter to a vote. If the voting on the time motion shows you will probably lose, you can then move to table the motion, and come back to the issue at a future meeting.

You can easily see that you can learn to handle meetings only if you study the "rules of the game." You need to learn the basic principles of parliamentary procedure.

PRINCIPLES OF PARLIAMENTARY PROCEDURE

Parliamentary procedure is a democratic method. It is a means by which people can work together, discuss problems, vote on them, and take action.

The purposes of parliamentary procedure are to provide an orderly and efficient guide for all kinds of meetings and to ensure that every member of the assembly has an equal chance to introduce business, discuss or debate it, and vote on it.

182

Certain basic principles underlie parliamentary procedure. The first of these is the rule by the majority. This means that in exchange for the privilege of participating, each member agrees to accept the decision of the majority. An important part of this principle is that the minority has the right to be heard and represented. Certain rules, such as the two-thirds vote on any motion to restrict or close debate, protect this minority.

The second principle is that each member is expected to support his privileges by accepting his share of the responsibility for the operation of the organization. If you belong to a club, you do not just enjoy your privilege of debate and voting—you also pay dues, serve on committees, hold office, and work. You give of your ideas and energy to make the club a success. This is the principle of citizenship in our democracy. Citizenship gives you certain rights; it also gives you responsibilities.

The third operating principle is that only one question or proposal at a time shall be immediately pending before the assembly. This means that only one question at a time shall be discussed and subject to vote by the assembly.

The fourth guarantees respect for the rights of individuals and the assembly. This means that every person receives the same courteous treatment. It means that the members respect the organization and its purposes as binding upon the members, once they belong to it.

The fifth principle is that the right of free debate (discussion) shall always be safeguarded. It is restricted only when the welfare of the whole group is bettered by such action.

The parliamentary terms used in formal meetings may seem strange to you. Even experienced club members often need to refresh their knowledge of certain details. Here are the basic terms you must know and use.

Chair: the chairman or presiding officer.

Floor: the right to speak; *i.e.,* by obtaining the floor.

Recognize: the act of the chairman which permits a member to speak. Ordinarily the chair nods to the member when he rises, or calls him by name as a sign that he is given the floor.

Obtain the floor: this action consists of the member standing, addressing the chairman ("Mr. Chairman," "Madame Chairman"), and being recognized by the chair. In some groups you obtain the floor by raising your hand and being recognized by the chair.

Minutes: the record, kept by the secretary, of what happens in the meeting.

Motion: a proposal for action by the assembly. Typical accepted form is "I move that..."; avoid "I make a move to" or "I make a motion that."

Second: the support given a motion by a second person in the group. Typical accepted form is "I second the motion."

Order of business: the sequence of procedure in the meeting.

In order: correct according to rules of procedure.

Not in order or out of order: incorrect according to rules of procedure.

Majority: one more than half of all of the votes cast.

Plurality: the highest number of votes cast. If three candidates were running for office and *A* received 14 votes, *B* 13, and *C* 10, *A* would have a plurality, not a majority. In some groups a plurality is accepted in elections.

Debate: discussion or remarks upon a motion.

State: state or repeat the motion.

Put: restate the motion so that it can be voted upon.

Adjourn: conclude or close the meeting.

Convene: assemble and start the meeting.

Call to order: The chairman states "The meeting will please come to order." In so doing he stops noise and confusion.

Quorum: the number of members present officially designated as those necessary to conduct business.

The rules of parliamentary procedure help create an atmosphere of order and fairness in dealing with problems during a meeting. Without rules, confusion would reign and the rights of an individual or a minority group would be lost. Parliamentary procedure speeds the handling of business and helps operate meetings more efficiently. Use it where it is needed, but do not insist on it in small, informal sessions where problems can be solved effectively by ordinary discussion methods.

TYPES OF MEETINGS

Organized meetings are of two types, relatively short *temporary* ones, such as rallies or mass meetings, and *permanent* organization meetings, such as those of clubs, legislatures, and student councils. The temporary meeting usually has no elected officers; a chairman or community leader presides. A permanent organization has a regular time and place to meet, a set of elected officers, and a constitution and bylaws.

The steps in forming a permanent organization are not difficult. First ask interested persons to come to an initial meeting where a temporary chairman and secretary are elected. At this meeting the nature and purposes of the organization are discussed. Check your school rules for creating new organizations and conform to them. Appoint a committee to write a constitution for the organization.

The committee writes the constitution, making sure it contains the name of the organization, its purposes, qualifications for membership, time and place of meetings, officers, and ways of amending the constitution. Bylaws covering dues, size of the quorum, the order of business, and a list of standing committees are formulated next.

Last steps involve studying the constitution paragraph by paragraph, making needed changes, and adopting it by vote of the members. Finally, permanent officers are elected and all necessary business transacted, depending on the occasion and the group.

Having organized your permanent group, you will use parliamentary procedure to conduct its meetings.

PROCEDURE IN A MEETING

All meetings follow a certain order in conducting business. The order may vary with the class, organization, or club, but the essential steps are:

1. The chairman calls the meeting to order.
2. The secretary calls the roll. (This step may be omitted if an oral check on attendance is not needed.)
3. The reading of the minutes (by the secretary) and their approval.
4. Reports of officers.
5. Reports of boards and standing committees.
6. Reports of special committees.
7. Unfinished business.
8. New business.
9. Adjournment.

In calling the meeting to order, the chairman states, "The meeting is called to order," or, "The meeting will please come to order." He then asks the secretary to call the roll, and to read the minutes of the last meeting. Then he asks, "Are there any additions or corrections to the minutes?" If there are none, he says, "If not, the minutes stand approved as read." If

corrections are made, he directs the secretary to make the necessary corrections, and says, "The minutes stand approved as corrected."

Reports from all officers may not be made at each meeting, but as a rule the treasurer's report is essential. The treasurer includes money received and money spent and states the balance on hand in the treasury.

The chairman then calls for reports from boards and standing committees. Standing committees are appointed for the duration of the term of the officers or annually. Such committees are membership, finance, house, entertainment, and program. In certain organizations each committee reports at each meeting to the whole group. In others a committee may report only when it has something of importance to bring before the meeting. Usually reports of standing committees are also presented in writing to the secretary.

Unfinished business is the next item. The chairman asks "Is there any unfinished business?" It is best to turn to the secretary at this point, since that officer has a record in the minutes and a list of items not completed at the last meeting. The items are considered as they were introduced by the members. Following unfinished business, items of new business are considered. These are brought up by members after the chairman asks, "Is there any new business?" Upon the conclusion of this section of the meeting, adjournment is in order.

186

VOTING

There are several methods of voting on motions and in elections. Most small business meetings vote by voice. This method is most suitable for motions requiring a majority vote. It is not employed on motions requiring a two-thirds vote where exact count of votes is needed.

The correct form is for the chairman to say, "All those in favor of the motion say 'Aye.'" After this vote is recorded, he says, "All opposed say 'No.'" It is incorrect to say, "All in favor say 'Aye.' All not in favor same sign." The opposite of *Aye* is *No,* and any other response is confusing.

If you are presiding and it seems obvious that a motion has strong support, you can speed the meeting by asking, "Are there any objections to this motion?" If there are none, you conclude that the motion is passed and so state. However, if there is any objection from the floor, put the motion to a vote.

Another standard method used when votes are to be counted is to ask members to raise their hands. The chairman then asks the secretary to help him check the tally. He should also ask members to keep their hands raised until he finishes his tabulation.

When a close vote is expected and the count may be difficult, he asks the members to stand so he can be sure of accuracy. Although this method is time-consuming, it is easier to count than a show of hands.

If a secret vote is needed, any member may move to vote by ballot. This becomes a regular motion from the floor to be seconded and approved by a majority. It is not debatable. Voting in elections is customarily done by ballot unless the bylaws contain other provisions.

In larger assemblies, when a record of each vote is required, the roll is called and each member's vote is recorded after his name by the secretary or clerk. This is not usual in small meetings.

ELECTIONS

Every permanent organization elects officers at specified times. The most efficient method is to appoint a nominating committee that submits a list of candidates. After this committee reports, members have the privilege of nominating additional candidates from the floor.

If you wish to nominate from the floor, you say (after being recognized), "Mr. Chairman, I nominate Sarah Johnson." The chairman repeats the name, and instructs the secretary to record it. He does not call for a second. Nominations do not regularly take a second, though in some groups a second may be required. The nominating continues until all desired nominations are made.

If there is no nominating committee, the chairman uses nominations from the floor to procure candidates for offices, handling them in order: president, vice-president, and so on.

Nominations may be closed at any time by a motion from the floor. Such a motion is not debatable and requires a two-thirds vote.

A vote is then taken on the candidates, usually by secret ballot. Tellers appointed by the chairman distribute ballots and collect and count them. They give the results to the chairman, preferably in writing, using this form:

TELLER'S REPORT—ELECTIONS—May 24, 1964	
Number of votes cast	30
Number necessary for election	16
Candidate A received	17
Candidate B received	7
Candidate C received	3
Illegal votes (2 names listed)	3
Total	30

Candidate A is elected.

Respectfully submitted,

John Dykstra

Helen Johnson

Tellers.

DUTIES OF OFFICERS

Each organization elects specific officers to do certain specific tasks. These responsibilities do not overlap, although one officer may assume another's duties when that officer is absent. But one does not expect the president to prepare the treasurer's report, or the secretary to conduct the meeting.

The Chairman

The chairman or president conducts an organization's business by presiding at all meetings, conducting debates, helping to determine policies, and making committee appointments. As the highest executive officer, he provides leadership and represents the group in all of its relationships with the school and community.

The Secretary

Every organization has a person who keeps its records, the minutes of meetings, roll call of members, and programs. Some groups also have a recording secretary to write letters and other communications, but these functions are usually handled by one person in school organizations.

The Treasurer

This officer is responsible for all financial business. His duties include collecting dues, receiving and paying bills, and reporting on finances.

COMMITTEES

Organizations have two kinds of committees: *standing* committees and *special* committees. Standing committees are appointed annually or for the duration of time from one election of officers to the next. They carry out the work of membership, programs, finance, social affairs, house maintenance, and similar necessary and continuing responsibilities.

Special committees perform a particular function or a particular project, usually one of short duration, such as planning a party. The committee ceases to exist as soon as the job is completed.

Committees are groups of three, five, seven, or any other odd number of persons. As a rule, the person sponsoring the project is appointed chairman if he is able to serve. If he cannot serve, he should be given the opportunity to decline.

Hasty appointment of committees is not advisable. The chairman makes a better selection of persons if he is allowed to announce committee members later. When the committee is formed, it has its own chairman responsible for calling meetings and getting the work done. All members should coöperate by doing their share of the work and help to formulate the report to be presented.

PARTICIPATING IN A MEETING

Every member of an assembly has the right to speak his mind upon debatable motions before the house. Usually all main or original motions, as well as numerous subsidiary motions and others so designated, are debatable.

In order to participate in debate on a motion, you first obtain the floor by addressing the chairman as "Mr. Chairman" or if a woman is presiding, "Madame Chairman." The chairman recognizes you by nodding or calling you by name.

Certain general rules prevail in debate. When a man and a woman rise at the same time, the floor should be granted to the woman unless some other factor makes such action improper. If a person who has not spoken previously rises at the same time as one who has already spoken, the floor is ordinarily given to the one who has not had an opportunity to speak. It is usually desirable to recognize anyone whose point of view has not yet been heard.

In debate, names of persons are usually not mentioned. This is in line with the policy of keeping a debate impersonal, so the facts, evidence, and reasoning, rather than personalities, play the important role in making decisions. It is proper to say, "the previous speaker" or "the person who seconded the motion."

In any meeting the time for the session is limited. If your club meets in an activity period of fifty minutes, you should try to finish the meeting in that time. Even if your group meets after school, you should set some time limits to the meeting. Because of this, some organizations limit debate in order to get their business done in the proper time.

The two most common ways of restricting discussion are to limit the total time for debate on a particular motion to ten minutes per motion or to limit the length of time each member may speak to three minutes.

Such restrictions interfere with the right of free debate. However, they are for the "welfare of the whole group." Any *standing rule* of this sort would have to be approved by the organization and placed in its bylaws. But a motion to limit debate can be made at any meeting and requires a two-thirds vote for approval.

If it is not desirable to limit debate, an important or difficult motion can be referred to a committee for study and then reported on at a later meeting for final action.

KINDS OF MOTIONS AND GENERAL PROCEDURE

The basic purpose of parliamentary procedure is to expedite the business of a meeting. All business is introduced by *a proposal for action by the assembly*—or *a motion.* There are essential facts about motions you need to know in order to take part in such a meeting.

Precedence means that certain motions, because of their importance, have a higher rank than other motions. A higher ranking motion must be considered before one over which it takes precedence.

Motions have certain qualifications that influence their use. You can remember the qualifications if you ask these questions: What is the purpose of the motion? Does it take a second? Is it debatable? Can it be amended? What vote does it require? May it interrupt the speaker?

A Table of
COMMONLY USED PARLIAMENTARY MOTIONS

Motion	Purpose	Needs Second	Debatable	Amendable	Vote	May Interrupt Speaker	Subsidiary Motion Applied
I. ORIGINAL OR PRINCIPAL MOTION							
1. Main Motion (general) Main Motions (specific)	To introduce business	Yes	Yes	Yes	Majority	No	Yes
a. To reconsider	To reconsider previous motion	Yes	When original motion is	No	Majority	Yes	No
b. To rescind	To nullify or wipe out previous action	Yes	Yes	Yes	Majority or two-thirds	No	No
c. To take from the table	To consider tabled motion	Yes	No	No	Majority	No	No
II. SUBSIDIARY MOTIONS							
2. To lay on the table	To defer action	Yes	No	No	Majority	No	No
3. To call for previous question	To close debate and force vote	Yes	No	No	Two-thirds	No	Yes
4. To limit or extend limits of debate	To control time of debate	Yes	No	Yes	Two-thirds	No	Yes
5. To postpone to a certain time	To defer action	Yes	Yes	Yes	Majority	No	Yes
6. To refer to a committee	To provide for special study	Yes	Yes	Yes	Majority	No	Yes
7. To amend	To modify a motion	Yes	When original motion is	Yes (once only)	Majority	No	Yes
8. To postpone indefinitely	To suppress action	Yes	Yes	No	Majority	No	Yes
III. INCIDENTAL MOTIONS							
9. To rise to point of order	To correct error in procedure	No	No	No	Decision of chair	Yes	No

10. To appeal from decision of chair	To change decision on procedure	Yes	No, if made when another question is before the assembly	No	Majority or tie	Yes	No
11. To suspend rules	To alter existing rules and order of business	Yes	No	No	Two-thirds	No	No
12. To object to consideration	To suppress action	No	No	No	Two-thirds	Yes	Yes
13. To call for division of house	To secure a countable vote	No	No	No	Majority if chair desires	Yes	Yes
14. To close nominations	To stop nomination of officers	Yes	No	Yes	Two-thirds	No	Yes
15. To reopen nominations	To permit additional nominations	Yes	No	Yes	Majority	No	Yes
16. To withdraw a motion	To remove a motion	No	No	No	Majority	No	No
17. To divide motion	To modify motion	No*	No	Yes	Majority	No*	Yes

IV. PRIVILEGED MOTIONS

18. To fix time of next meeting	To set time of next meeting	Yes	No, if made when another question is before the assembly	Yes	Majority	No	Yes
19. To adjourn	To dismiss meeting	Yes	No	Yes	Majority	No	No
20. To take a recess	To dismiss meeting for specific time	Yes	No, if made when another question is before the assembly	Yes	Majority	No	Yes
21. To raise question of privilege	To make a request concerning rights of the assembly	No	No	No	Decision of chair	Yes	No
22. To call for orders of the day	To keep assembly to order of business	No	No	No	None unless objection	Yes	No
23. To make a special order	To ensure consideration at specified time	Yes	Yes	Yes	Two-thirds	No	Yes

*See text

STEPS IN PASSING A MOTION

Before studying a specific motion, you need to know the basic method of handling all motions. These steps are listed below.

1.   A member obtains the floor: he rises and addresses the chair: "Mr. Chairman" or "Madame Chairman." He is recognized by the chairman: "Mr. Smith" or a nod if the name is not known.

2.   The member presents the motion: "I move that our organization hold a student conference on November 21."

3.   Another member seconds this motion: "I second the motion."

4.   The chairman then states the motion: "It has been moved and seconded that our organization hold a student conference on November 21."

5.   The chairman calls for debate (discussion): "The motion is now open for debate (discussion)."

6.   Debate takes place on the motion: each member wishing to speak must first obtain the floor before speaking to the group. If no one wishes to speak, the chairman proceeds to step seven.

7.   When debate seems to have been concluded, the chairman checks to see whether the members wish to continue the debate or wish to vote. Chairman: "Are you ready for the question?" The audience response to this inquiry is, "Question!" if the members wish to vote on the motion.

8.   The chairman "puts" the motion: "The motion before the house is that our club hold a student conference on November 21."

9.   The chairman asks for a vote on the motion: "All those in favor of the motion please say 'Aye.' Those opposed say 'No.' "

10.   The chairman states the result of the vote: "The motion is carried" or "The motion is lost."

PRINCIPAL MOTIONS

A main motion is used to introduce original business before the assembly. Such proposals are also called general motions because of their broad use. They must be seconded, debated, and voted on—unless they are disposed of in some way by a subsidiary motion. A majority vote is required to pass a main motion.

Some books on parliamentary procedure list certain *specific* main motions because they require consideration of and action by the assembly. Specific main motions include:

Reconsider

If a motion has been passed, and at the same or the next meeting, a member who voted on the prevailing side wants to have it brought up again, he moves to reconsider. The motion to reconsider is in order when another has the floor; it requires a second and a majority vote, and is debatable if the motion to which it applies was debatable. It takes precedence over all incidental motions.

The correct form is "I move to reconsider the vote on. . . ."

This motion when passed reopens debate on the previous motion (if it was debatable) and/or to take another vote on it. If the new vote differs from the first one, the new vote stands.

Rescind

If members wish to wipe out a previous action of the assembly, they move to rescind it. Notice of a motion to rescind must be given at an earlier meeting and a majority vote is sufficient to carry it. However, if immediate action to rescind is desired, a two-thirds vote is required. This motion requires a second, is debatable, and can be amended.

The proper form is "I move to rescind the vote on. . . ." In case of strong disapproval of the previous action, "to expunge it from the record" is added.

When carried, this motion nullifies the previous action, whereas a motion to reconsider merely reopens the issue for debate and/or another vote.

To Take from the Table

This motion is used to gain further consideration of a matter that has been postponed by laying it on the table, usually at the same meeting. The motion requires a second, is undebatable, cannot be amended, and requires a majority vote.

The form is "I move to take from the table the motion to . . . ."

If this motion passes, the original motion is reopened for debate and a possible vote.

SUBSIDIARY MOTIONS

Subsidiary motions are used to dispose of motions by speeding up voting, delaying action upon them, changing the wording, or referring them to a committee. Subsidiary motions are made during the regular time of debate on the motion affected, and voted on before the motion affected is voted on.

Lay on the Table

(Sometimes called "tabling a motion.") This motion is used to defer action when the assembly cannot settle the question or has other urgent business. This motion facilitates quick action because, although it takes a second, it does not require debate and must be voted on immediately after it is stated by the chairman. Its effect is to defer consideration until later in the same meeting or to a subsequent meeting. It can be used to suppress a question.

The form of the motion is "I move that we lay the question on the table." Any motion that is laid on the table may be reopened by the motion to take from the table.

Previous Question

This motion is used to stop debate. The name of the motion comes from the action desired, that debate cease and the question be voted on. During debate on a motion, any member may call for the previous question. The motion requires a second and a two-thirds vote because it suppresses debate and is undebatable. If it carries, the motion is voted on immediately.

The correct form of the motion is "I move" or, "I call for the previous question."

Limit, or Extend the Limits of, Debate

The purpose of this motion is to establish the amount of time for debate on a motion being considered. The motion may be made at any time during debate. It requires a second and a two-thirds vote.

The form for the motion is "I move that debate on the question be limited to three minutes per person" or "I move that the total debate be limited to fifteen minutes."

Postpone to a Definite Time

The motion to postpone to a definite time is used to defer action until a specific date and/or hour. It requires a second and is debatable.

The form is "I move that the question under consideration be postponed until the next regular meeting and be the first item considered under unfinished business."

196

Refer to a Committee

When an assembly is considering a motion that can more suitably be handled by a smaller group or that calls for further study before a vote, it is frequently referred to a committee. Such a motion always specifies certain things: (1) who is to appoint the committee, (2) how many are to be on it, and (3) when it is to report. The motion takes a second and is debatable.

The form for the motion is "I move that the chairman appoint a committee of three to study this problem and that the committee report at the next meeting."

Amend

Motions often need to be changed or amended. These fall into three groups: those that add words; those that strike out words; and those that substitute words. Such an amendment must be made *before* the main motion has been voted on.

To Postpone Indefinitely

Another motion used to defer action is the motion to postpone indefinitely. Unlike the motion to postpone to a certain time, it does not specify when the matter will be considered. Therefore its effect may be to suppress the question by causing it to die a lingering death.

The correct form of the motion is, "I move to postpone the matter indefinitely."

A main motion may have a motion to amend it; this amendment may in turn have an amendment. But only one amendment to an amendment may be pending at a time. After one amendment is disposed of, another may be presented.

In voting on an amendment, the last one introduced is voted on first. If the amendment passes, the main motion is voted on as amended. If the amendment does not pass, the main motion may be debated further and then voted on.

The proper form is "I move to amend the motion by striking out the words...and inserting the words...so that the motion will read... (amended form of motion)."

INCIDENTAL MOTIONS

Incidental motions arise out of the business at hand. They are matters that must be settled before the motions out of which they come can be voted on. They take precedence over all main and subsidiary motions, but yield to a privileged motion, which will be discussed later. Incidental motions are undebatable, except an appeal from the decision of the chair. Two of them, suspension of the rules and objection to consideration, require a two-thirds vote.

Point of Order

Whenever a member notices an error in procedure, he may, without being recognized, rise and say, "Mr. Chairman, I rise to a point of order." The chairman asks him to state his point of order. After the member quotes the rule, the chairman either affirms or denies it. If he affirms it, he then makes the necessary correction in procedure.

Appeal from the Decision of the Chair

If a member believes the chairman has made a mistake in *ruling* on a parliamentary matter, he may appeal from the decision of the chair. If the appeal is seconded, the chairman must submit it to the vote of the assembly. A majority affirmative vote sustains the appeal.

Suspension of the Rules

There are occasions when it is wise to suspend parliamentary rules in order to accomplish a particular purpose. A motion to suspend the rules, supported by a two-thirds vote, accomplishes this.

Objection to Consideration

An objection may be made to the consideration of any main motion. The purpose may be to suppress it or to save time if the motion is irrelevant. However, the objection must be made before debate begins or before any subsidiary motion is applied.

The form is "Mr. Chairman, I object to consideration of the motion." Since this motion needs no second and is undebatable, the chairman must immediately put it to a vote. It requires a two-thirds vote to sustain it; otherwise debate on the main motion begins.

Division of the Assembly

When in a voice vote the Ayes and Noes seem about equal, a member may call for a division of the assembly. This means the chairman must order a vote, by show of hands or standing, that can be accurately counted.

Make, Close or Reopen Nominations

These were discussed under elections.

Leave to Withdraw a Motion

To withdraw a motion that, after consideration, seems unnecessary, the maker of the original motion says, "Mr. Chairman, I wish to withdraw my motion." Because this motion is made after the original motion has been seconded, it must secure the approval of the person who seconded the original motion. If he consents, the chairman rules that the motion may be withdrawn.

To Divide the Motion

When a motion relating to a subject contains several parts, each of which is capable of standing as a complete proposition if the others are removed, it is advisable to divide the motion for more efficient consideration. Such action should be proposed when the matter is first introduced. It can be taken only on main motions and amendments.

In wording the motion a member states: "I move to divide the motion," and indicates specifically how he wishes it to be divided. If the motion is passed, each section designated is then considered and voted upon.

Request for Information, Parliamentary Inquiry

A request for information, or parliamentary inquiry, may be made at any time. The member rises, addresses the chair, and says, "I rise to a question of information." The chairman says, "What is your question?" Upon hearing it, the chairman answers the question or refers it to the speaker or member who can answer it. All inquiries and questions must be asked *through* the chairman.

PRIVILEGED MOTIONS

Privileged motions deal with the needs and privileges of the members of the assembly. They take precedence over all motions and may be presented when main and subsidiary motions are before the house.

Fix Time to Which to Adjourn

The purpose of this motion is to set the time for the next meeting; it is *not* a motion to adjourn. The motion may be amended, takes a majority vote, and is debatable only when there is no other business before the house. It takes precedence over all other motions.

The form of the motion is "I move that when we adjourn, we adjourn until tomorrow morning at 9:30, when we shall meet in this room."

Adjourn

This motion is to close the meeting. It takes precedence over all motions except the motion to fix the time to adjourn. It takes a second, is undebatable, cannot be amended, may not have a subsidiary motion applied to it, and takes a majority vote. It is in order at any time except when a speaker has the floor, during voting, while votes are being counted, or when the chairman is stating or putting a motion.

The usual form is "I move that we adjourn."

Take a Recess

This motion is used when the members of the assembly are tired or a recess is indicated. It is undebatable, can be amended, and requires a second.

The proper form is "I move that we take a recess of one hour."

Raise a Question of Privilege

A question of privilege covers the safety, comfort, dignity, reputation, or freedom from disturbance of the assembly. Because it helps preserve the rights or privileges of free debate, this motion has high rank. It can interrupt a speaker who has the floor. It is undebatable, can be amended, laid on the table, or postponed indefinitely.

The correct form is "I rise to a question of privilege."

Call for the Order of the Day

Most assemblies have an order of procedure. If this is not adhered to, a member may insist on the prescribed order being followed. He may interrupt a speaker to introduce the motion, which does not take a second and is undebatable.

The proper form is "I call for the order of the day."

To Make a Special Order

There are times when a matter is of such importance that a member desires it to be considered at the next meeting, before any unfinished or new business.

To accomplish this he states: "I move to make a special order of this matter for (specifying the time)."

Because the effect of this motion is to postpone the pending question and to change the place of the matter in the regular order of business, it requires a two-thirds vote. The secretary records special orders and calls them to the attention of the chairman at the next meeting.

ACTIVITIES

1. Organize your class into a *temporary* body with a rotating chairmanship and secretaryship. Each secretary serves for half a period during a business meeting; the person serving at the end of the period writes the minutes and has them ready for the next day's session. Each chairman serves until he makes an error in procedure detected either by students or teacher. Then your teacher appoints a new chairman, who picks up the business at the point of the error, corrects it, and proceeds with the meeting.

You may organize standing committees and special committees, to learn the procedure and duties of members of an assembly.

2. Organize your class as a club (*permanent* organization). Hold a first meeting with temporary officers. Appoint the necessary committees for writing a constitution and bylaws. At your second and subsequent meetings, elect permanent officers, present and approve a constitution, and appoint necessary committees. Conduct your class meetings on the basic form of permanent organization following *Robert's Rules of Order.* Or use the work of your class to form a permanent school organization to encourage drama, radio-TV, or a combination of speech arts.

3. Prepare visual materials, such as charts or a flannel board, useful in learning types of motions, their qualifications, and precedence. Committees for this purpose can function in your organized class pattern.

4. Using your class organization, plan any of the following activities: a tournament or festival in which you entertain visiting schools, a play to be given before the school, a speech assembly, a radio or television program to be done over a local station. Use the parliamentary methods of a business meeting to develop all details for the project you select.

5. Organize the class as a legislature in which two parties are represented. Elect floor leaders, a chairman, and a clerk. Plan sessions in which each party introduces opposing bills, debates them, and tries to gain passage of its own measure.

Some Problems in Parliamentary Procedures

Can you meet the problems in parliamentary procedure listed below? If not, work on this unit and discover the solutions. You may have additional questions you want to ask in class; do not hesitate to do so.

You are the chairman of a business meeting. What would you *do* and *say* in these situations?

1. To call the meeting to order?

2. To secure approval of the minutes?

3. A member moves that certain action be taken; when you begin to state the motion you find you cannot remember the correct wording?

4. Two members rise and address the chair at the same time. To which will you give the floor? Why?

5. You have just called for a voice vote on a motion. Before you can announce the result of the vote, a member rises and says, "I call for a division of the house."

6. After debate on a motion a member obtains the floor and says, "I move the previous question."

7. In an election you are receiving nominations from the floor. At the conclusion of the first nomination, a member rises and says, "I rise to a point of order. Nominations require a second."

8. A main motion has already had two amendments made to it. A member rises and proposes further amendment.

9. While a member is speaking on a question before the house, another member jumps to his feet and calls out, "Mr. Chairman, I rise to a question of privilege."

10. A main motion has been made and seconded. You have not yet stated it. A member rises and after obtaining the floor says, "I move to lay the question on the table." What would you do if he made this motion after you had stated the motion and called for debate?

As a member of the assembly you wish to do certain things. What motions will you use? State the qualifications of each.

1. You cannot hear the member who is speaking.

2. You detect an error in procedure by the chairman.

3. You wish to change the wording of the main motion. What motion will you use? What are the various ways of changing the wording of a motion?

4. You wish to have a committee consider the business pending before the house. What things must you always specify in your motion?

5. You have at least two thirds of the group supporting you. You wish to kill a motion before it is debated. What do you do?

6. You have only a minority you can count on. What is the quickest and best means of suppressing a motion under debate?

7. You wish to close debate at once and get a vote on a motion before the house.

8. The assembly has passed a motion. What action can you propose at the same meeting to nullify this action?

9. You wish to have a rest and time for a short conference, but the meeting is in session. What do you do?

10. You wish to defer action on a question until the opening of the next session. What motion will you use?

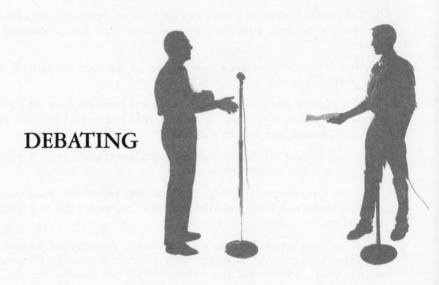

CHAPTER 15

DEBATING

It is better to debate a question without settling
it, than to settle it without debate.

—JOSEPH JOUBERT

You have studied the use of conferences as a way to solve problems. But sometimes you and your classmates could not agree on the solution. Analyses or conclusions differed. What can be done if you wish to take action or reach a decision? You may vote on it and follow the decision of the majority. This is the democratic method. But it is more logical to debate the question first.

Debate allows those with opposing views to present both affirmative and negative arguments before an individual, or an audience, who then judges the merits of the respective positions. Based on the strength of your case, the judge will accept your views or reject them. Debate grows out of a real need to try to settle unresolved questions. Debate may be said to complement discussion in solving problems.

Debate is one of the oldest, most valuable forms of speech. Historically it was used to deal with crucial issues in Rome and Athens.

There were famous debates in the British Parliament, the Continental Congress, the House of Representatives and Senate of the United States. It has been used in Presidential campaigns as recently as 1960. Many leaders in our government have gained prominence because of their skill in debate: Patrick Henry, Webster, Clay, Calhoun, Lincoln, Lodge and Borah are some of these.

Debate is characterized by these qualities: (1) it is competitive, leading to a decision by vote; (2) it requires that the participants take a definite position, either affirmative or negative, which cannot be changed; (3) it is more formal than discussion and follows rules of procedure; (4) its objective is to start with a proposal, make the best case for it, and win approval for that side; (5) the style is argumentative and persuasive.

You follow the basic pattern of debate whenever you argue: a person tries to convince you to take a certain action and you disagree; to explain your position you present reasons and facts as you do in debate. George Berkeley, the Irish prelate, put the matter briefly, "The end of debating is to persuade."

You find forms of debate in many situations in everyday life. In student council business meetings you use *legislative* debate. This type is used in city council meetings, in state legislatures, and in the United States Congress. Debate is found in courtrooms. Here it is *judicial* debate, one lawyer taking the side of the prosecution, the other that of the defense. Judges and juries make the decisions in judicial debate. The use of *political* debate, as in the 1960 Presidential campaign, is an effort to win the decision of the voters.

Interscholastic debate is a more formal situation. These debates are a specialized form of oral argument, carried on under definite rules. Two teams, usually of two speakers each, agree on a subject, the time and place for the debate, the time limits and the kind of decision to be reached. Each team, one affirmative and one negative, presents its arguments on the question (proposition), and a critic judge, board of judges, or the audience makes the decision.

In all types of debate opposing speakers try to influence others to *believe* or to *act* as they wish them to believe or to act.

The best strategy for persuading the audience to agree with you and your colleague is to promote a full, honest, and accurate discussion of the proposition. The team that tackles every major issue, replies to every major argument, and stays close to sound reasoning and reliable evidence is the team most likely to win the support of the audience.

As soon as a team tries to avoid discussing the major issues, seeks to cloud and avoid the major arguments of the opposition, or resorts to careless reasoning and doubtful evidence, the audience suspects that it is not able to present fairly or defend adequately its case. When an audience has such a suspicion it is apt to join your opponents in looking for your weak arguments and evasions. No member of an audience, least of all a debate judge, likes to feel that he is being duped or tricked.

In debate the effectiveness of everything you have prepared depends on your delivery. You are *judged* on your speaking ability and your case and argument. A machine-gun style contributes little to good communication; if you try to crowd ten minutes of material into an eight-minute constructive speech you may lose more points in delivery than you gain in argument.

You will not gain many points in either delivery or argument if you attempt to shout down your opposition or blister him with sarcasm. Samuel Johnson, the English lexicographer and critic, gave the sharp edge of his wit to one such bombastic debater when he said, "You raise your voice when you should reinforce your argument."

The speaking style that lends itself most readily to debating is that of lively, or animated, conversation. Your posture should be erect, your gestures natural and meaningful, your voice adequately projected and interestingly varied, and your eye contact direct and personal. Strive for a delivery that will suggest lively *thinking aloud* about the issues before you. *Communicate* persuasively each argument you develop.

CHOOSING A DEBATE QUESTION

A wide variety of subjects is possible in debating. You may start with local questions or ones that you have considerable basic information about. Perhaps you will decide to debate a question that you could not agree on when you discussed it. Discussion normally precedes debate and is part of the preparation of debaters. In discussion they explore the *whole* problem, gather evidence, and begin to observe the disagreements which arise. Several debate questions may grow out of one discussion.

For example, a speech class discussed the question: "How can final examinations in this high school be improved?" The current plan was analyzed, and from the discussion three debate questions were formulated, all worded as formal resolutions:

(1) Resolved: That multiple-choice questions replace essay questions in all final examinations.

(2) Resolved: That College Board examinations be given as final examinations in all subjects.

(3) Resolved: That all students having *A* grades in full-credit subjects be excused from final examinations in those courses.

Each question, or resolution, recommends a change in the current plan. The first suggests a change in the *form* of examination, the second recommends standardization on a national basis, and the third proposes excusing certain superior students. Resolutions are called *propositions* in debate terminology.

Qualities of Good Debate Propositions

Each of the above resolutions has the qualities of a good proposition:

1. IT SHOULD BE STATED AS A FORMAL RESOLUTION. A formal resolution is a statement, not a question, and is introduced by the words, "Resolved: That," etc.

2. IT SHOULD BE DEBATABLE. This means the question is not settled, that there is good material and weight of argument on each side. If we had stated as a proposition, "Resolved: That Hawaii should be admitted as a state," there would be no use in debating it.

3. IT SHOULD BE INTERESTING, IMPORTANT, AND UP-TO-DATE. Resolutions should be chosen because they arouse the interest of the debaters and the audience, are of some significance, and are timely. William Hazlitt, the English essayist, points out that, "When a thing ceases to be a subject of controversy, it ceases to be a subject of interest."

4. IT SHOULD BE WORDED SO THAT THE AFFIRMATIVE SUPPORTS THE PROPOSED CHANGE. In each of the propositions about examinations, the affirmative advocates that something in the present situation be changed. This causes the negative to *disagree* and oppose the change. Such wording for a proposition is "natural"—the affirmative says "Yes," and the negative says "No." Ordinarily, such wording retains the nominal *sides* in the debate.

5. IT SHOULD CONTAIN ONE AND ONLY ONE PROBLEM. If you changed the first proposition on examinations by adding "and that College

Board examinations be given in all subjects," you would have a *double* proposition, one that contains two problems. It is impossible to debate such a question satisfactorily; both sides are confused, and the debaters might never argue the same issues in either problem.

6. IT SHOULD CONTAIN NO CONFUSING OR AMBIGUOUS WORDS. Some words in a proposition may be clear to you, but not understood by others. This causes definitions to vary and results in differences in arguments based on different definitions. The three propositions *seem* to have no words with more than one meaning, or with confusing meanings. However, "College Board examinations" might be mistaken for the Scholastic Aptitude tests. The words "multiple-choice" and "essay" questions could be confused by some, even though they seem perfectly clear to you.

7. IT SHOULD BE APPROPRIATE TO THE DEBATERS. Sometimes a proposition meets the first six requirements, but when selected by a national committee, it is inappropriate to the age, intelligence, ability, or interests of those supposed to debate it. If you are responsible for selecting a question, be sure to check it in terms of the debaters.

Types of Debate Propositions

All the propositions noted above are of the same type. They are questions of *policy,* because they state that something should or should not be done. Questions of policy are the most practicable for school debates, and over 90 per cent are of this type.

However, there are two other types—propositions of *fact* and propositions of *value.*

A question of *fact* states that something *is* or *is not true.* Most questions of fact are not debatable because they can be settled by a brief investigation. "Resolved: That the Renault Dauphine car gets thirty miles to a gallon of gasoline," could probably be settled by a few tests. It is not a good debate proposition.

A question of *value* states that something is *better than* or *worse than something else.* "Resolved: That Washington was a greater man than Jefferson" is a question of value. Some debaters use this type, but it is not ordinarily used in interscholastic debate.

INVESTIGATING THE PROPOSITION

Successful debating depends on thorough, careful preparation. Nothing is so disastrous as lack of knowledge when you try to defend yourself publicly against an informed opponent. The Greeks, who first established the form of debates, had a proverb: "We should not investigate facts by the light of argument, but arguments by the light of facts."

Finding Materials

The same general sources and methods used to find and record information for speeches apply in gathering material for debates. The debater's arguments, supporting evidence, and skill in organizing his case depend on the strength of his preparation. Daily trips to the library are the only way to become completely informed on a debate subject.

Original research through reading is the best way to proceed. Below is a list of sources for use in debating:

> *The Annual Debater's Handbook.* National University Extension Association. Eugene, Oregon: The University of Oregon.

> *The Reference Shelf.* New York: H. W. Wilson Co. Annual volumes on current debate questions. Each volume contains articles, briefs, and bibliography.

> *The University Debater's Annual.* New York: H. W. Wilson Co. Transcribed debates with briefs of the opposing teams.

> *The Debater's Handbook Series.* New York: H. W. Wilson Co. Similar to the annual above.

> *The Congressional Digest.* Washington, D.C.: U.S. Govt. Printing Ofc. A monthly publication on the issues before Congress. The fall issue (October) usually contains a pro and con discussion of the current debate proposition.

> *The Congressional Record.* Washington, D.C.: U.S. Govt. Printing Ofc. The published remarks of all speakers in the U.S. Senate and House of Representatives upon bills considered before these two bodies. Back copies and current issues are to be found in your school or public library.

> Package kits of debate materials are available from your state library, university extension division, or the headquarters of your state debating league.

> Government publications listed in the U.S. Government Printing Office, Washington, D.C. Write for their list of publications.

> News magazines, These include *U.S. News and World Report, Time, Newsweek, The American Platform, Vital Speeches, The New York Times Index,* and others.

After these sources, develop a working list of references (bibliography) from the card catalogue in your library, the *Readers' Guide to Periodical Literature,* and the *National University Extension Bibliography.*

Outlining Guides Your Investigation

The following outline gives the major guide posts around which your analysis and investigation should be organized:

I. Survey the background
  A. Origin and history
  B. Immediate cause for debate

II. Learn definitions of important words and terms
  A. Terms in the proposition
  B. Terms related to the proposition

III. Set up the goals and their underlying values of the action that will be proposed
  A. General goals
  B. Specific goals

IV. Survey and study the present situation (need for action)
  A. Its nature: how it operates; conditions that affect it
  B. Its strong and weak points at present
  C. Decide whether these points are inherent or the result of human error or weakness
  D. Determine whether the weaknesses outweigh the strong points
  E. If so, do they justify the changes to be made:

V. Study the affirmative proposal (the solution or plan)
  A. Its nature
  B. Its features, good and bad
  C. Decide whether it can meet the conditions that need to be changed (IV-A, B, C, D)
  D. Try to discover whether the affirmative plan has been tried anywhere and has been successful
  E. Discover the benefits of the proposal *in addition to* its ability to take care of the weaknesses of the present situation
  F. Find the weaknesses of the affirmative proposal

VI. Carefully search to discover other, or alternative, proposals that would take care of the situation
    A. Determine whether revising or repairing the present plan would solve the need for change
    B. Find plans *other* than that of the affirmative (counterproposals) that would do the job
    C. List their strong and weak points

Recording Your Materials Systematically

Use a card filing system to record your materials. Major headings should follow the above outline: background, definitions, goals and values, criteria for the proposal, and the present situation, solution or affirmative plan, counterproposals. Establish your own subheads as your material expands. Some students use a notebook or sheets for clippings, graphs, and charts. However, the cards allow you to rearrange items, take them from the file, use them in debate, and reurn them to your file. You soon evolve a plan to suit your individual needs.

Use care and accuracy in recording. Copy arguments, facts, and opinions exactly, and do not fail to list the citation giving publication, title, author, date, and page number for each item. Do this from the start and you'll save much time.

Analyzing the Proposition

Analyzing the debate question is how you discover the issues. The basis of your analysis is your own research and thinking. As you read and analyze, you find the basic contentions around which the debate swings.

GENERAL ISSUES. The issues are the bedrock contentions that *support* the proposition. They are the main points on which there is a direct clash between the affirmative and the negative. Ordinarily the issues are stated as questions. To these questions the affirmative always answers "Yes," and the negative "No."

1. Do conditions exist at present which make a change necessary? (The *need* issue)

2. Will the proposed change remedy or improve these conditions?

3. Will the proposed change bring new and greater benefits than those that exist at present?

4. Is the proposed plan the best?

5. Are there other proposals or plans better than the one suggested?

While not all of these questions are considered in every debate, the first three are very important.

SPECIFIC ISSUES. On the general issues are built the specific issues for a particular debate. To determine the specific issues, the general issues are adapted to the material found in investigating the propostion. In the question, "Resolved: That the Federal Government should own and operate all commercial television stations," here are examples of how certain *specific* (sometimes called "fighting") issues are based on general issues.

1. Are present TV programs of poor quality? Are they harmful to children? Adults?

2. Is the present TV system so commercially dominated that its basic educational purposes are lost?

3. Is commercial TV abusing its use of the broadcasting channels? (Quiz show and Payola scandals)

All three of these issues are adaptations of general issue number one: Do conditions exist at present which make a change necessary?

4. Would a system of government ownership and operation remedy the existing conditions in TV?

5. Would the benefits of government ownership and control be greater than the present weaknesses under private ownership and operation?

6. Is government ownership better than a strict system of government control under private ownership?

Specific issue number four is an adaptation to the TV question of general issue number two. Specific issues number five and number six are developed from general issues number three and number four.

Proving the Proposition

After you have found the specific issues in your debate question, proceed to organize and use the materials you have gathered to support these issues and prove the proposition. Proof includes all the means you can use to influence the listeners to believe your arguments.

There are three kinds of proof, their names coming down to us from classical times: *ethos,* ethical proof, resulting from the personal qualities and manner of the debater; *pathos,* emotional proof, obtained by arousing the interests and desires of the audience; and *logos,* logical proof, that comes from the facts and reasoning presented in the debate.

Our concern is with logical proof. To understand it you need to learn about evidence and study the types of reasoning.

USING EVIDENCE IN DEBATE

Evidence consists of *facts* and *opinions* (sometimes actual objects or things) that are used as proof. In your investigation you sought arguments, which we define as contentions or statements, to support the main issues of the proposition. You looked for evidence to support these arguments.

For example, your reading and observation of TV furnishes evidence that allows you to *contend* or *state* that TV programs are of poor quality. But most of your evidence is in written form. You obtained it from printed sources: questionnaires containing opinions and statistics, reports from bulletins and pamphlets, and books.

Sometimes you may bring *objects* to help prove a point. When the question of chain stores was debated students brought samples of merchandise in varying sizes and qualities to the debate table. However, this is not a common practice in debates.

Through your card file you have classified and organized your evidence, according to headings suitable to the proposition. You should know certain questions and tests that help you decide whether your evidence is honest and strong enough for use in debate.

How to Test Your Evidence: The Quality

The evidence should be consistent with human experience. Neither you nor your opponent will accept evidence that is contrary to ordinary human experience. Check to see that your evidence is acceptable in those terms.

The evidence should be consistent with facts already known. Test your evidence in relation to known facts. Items that seem contradictory or extreme may not be believable.

The evidence should be consistent with itself. Test your evidence carefully to see that it contains no contradictions. If you or your opponents can discover inconsistencies within your own material, these will be most damaging. Eliminate such items.

214

The evidence should be able to pass the hearsay test. Evidence passed from mouth to mouth is called hearsay. It is best to avoid such evidence if possible. However, if you ever do employ it, be sure that the mouths through which it has passed are completely reliable and trustworthy.

How to Test Your Evidence: The Source

Facts and statistics are no better than their sources. Apply these tests to be sure that your evidence is satisfactory: Who collected the evidence? What are his qualifications? Is he competent? Is he unprejudiced and free from influence or financial pressure? Is he honest? If a group made the study, what are its qualifications? Where were the findings published? Is the publication regarded as reliable and objective? When were the facts obtained and when published? Are they outmoded? Are they current and up-to-date? What methods were used in obtaining the facts? Under what conditions were the data gathered?

Apply the following tests to an ordinary witness: Is he mentally, physically, morally qualified, and in a position to know the facts?

Apply the following tests to an expert witness: Is he qualified as an authority? Is he recognized as an authority? Is he unbiased? Is he quoted in the field in which he is an expert? Is expert opinion needed in this case?

How to Test Your Evidence: The Amount

It is not enough to present one item of evidence to prove a point, unless the evidence is unusually strong. To establish a generalization, you need several typical, well-selected items. To support a strong argument, you have to set forth three or four items of evidence. If time restricts you, you will find it both tactful and convincing to state as many items as you can, then indicate that you have others, equally strong, that can be added if requested.

USING REASONING IN DEBATE

For many years the study of reasoning in debate was based on the use of the *syllogism,* and *deductive* and *inductive reasoning.* The syllogism is a three-part statement, with a major premise, a minor premise, and a conclusion. Deductive reasoning goes from the general to the specific, and inductive reasoning from the specific to the general.

Thus we use deductive reasoning in a syllogism as follows:

All trees that lose their leaves in fall are deciduous. (Major)
Oak trees lose their leaves in fall. (Minor)
Therefore, oak trees are deciduous. (Conclusion)

In inductive reasoning, you collect as many examples as possible. You observe many trees, not only oaks, that lose their leaves in fall. Your conclusion would be that all trees that lose their leaves are deciduous.

These examples are oversimplified. There are many kinds of syllogisms, and there are many examples of inductive reasoning; a full treatment of this subject would become extremely complicated.

Four methods of reasoning are described below. In debate it is essential to avoid mistakes in reasoning (fallacies). A set of questions is given with each method to help you test your ability to use these types.

Example or Generalization

The method of *example* or *generalization* consists in citing several examples and drawing a conclusion from them. Here is an illustration of this type of reasoning: Tom is a sophomore and is a good athlete. Fred is a sophomore and is a good athlete. Therefore, you conclude that sophomore boys are good athletes.

To test this example ask the following questions:

1. Have enough examples been stated?

2. Are the examples typical?

3. Are there negative examples? (How you account for them? In other words are there sophomore boys who are not good athletes? Why is this true? Can you give a reason?)

4. Does the relationship exist clearly in each example cited? (Is each sophomore boy mentioned definitely established as a good athlete?)

Cause to Effect

In this method you reason that the circumstance you assume is the cause is the *actual reason for the existence* of the effect. You may proceed from the cause to the effect or from the effect to the cause. For example, if your mother reasoned that you and your two brothers have big appetites because you walk two miles to school each day, she would be reasoning from the effect (the appetite) to the cause (walking).

There are tests for evaluating this type of reasoning:

1. Is the cause sufficient to produce the effect?

2. Is the causal relationship complete? (Is there an actual connection between long walks and big appetites?)

3. Is the effect identified and known? (Is there evidence that you actually have a big appetite?)

4. Are there other causes or effects? (Could some other cause produce the big appetite? Hard work? Could long walks produce other effects, such as fatigue?)

Analogy

A third method of reasoning is by analogy. It is based on the comparison of two situations: whenever two situations are alike in certain essential respects, it follows that what is true of one is probably true of the other.

To be effective the two situations must be in the same class or category: for example, you compare two cities, two governments, two football teams, etc. If you argue that a system of socialized medicine in Great Britain produced great financial waste, therefore such a system of socialized medicine in the United States would also cause great waste of tax money, you are reasoning by analogy. Such a comparison, based on two situations in the same class, is called a *literal* analogy; there are actual resemblances.

Some persons misuse analogy by comparing two things *not* in the same class. They may say the circulation of money is like the circulation of blood. Here the analogy is a *figurative one*—and is based on a similarity of relationships, not on an actual resemblance. This has no value as proof, but only as illustration.

There are tests for analogy:

1. Are the two situations compared in the same class or category?

2. Do the points of resemblance outweigh the points of difference?

3. Even though there are numerous points of similarity, do the *essential* points outweigh them?

4. If so, will the action claimed for the first situation actually work in the second?

Sign

Reasoning from sign is sometimes confused with cause to effect reasoning. The difference is this: in cause to effect, the cause is the *reason for the existence* of the effect; in reasoning from sign, the sign is the reason for *knowing* or *recognizing* a relationship. For example, if you see a flag at half-mast and conclude that someone is dead, you are reasoning from sign. The flag did not cause the person to die, nor did the death cause the flag to be at half-mast. You *associate* the two and draw your conclusion on the basis of *recognizing* or *knowing* that a flag at half-mast often means the death of a public figure. As a matter of fact, the flag could be at half-mast because the rope stuck in the pulley.

A bell rings and you conclude lunch is ready. The bell did not cause dinner to be prepared; it is the *sign* which is your reason for knowing (or hoping) that lunch is ready.

There are certain tests for reasoning from sign:

1. Does the sign alleged to indicate a particular condition have a close and essential relation to it?

2. Does the sign occur so frequently in association with that condition that the probability is very high that the relationship exists?

3. Does this relationship exist regardless of time or changing conditions?

These methods of reasoning are useful in debating if you use them well.

ORGANIZING AND OUTLINING THE DEBATE CASE

Having investigated and analyzed the proposition, you face the problem of organizing and outlining your materials so they will be usable in debate. This is the preparing of the debate *case*.

A case is the stand or position an affirmative or negative team maintains in a debate. The situation is similar to one you have faced before. You say to a friend, "I believe it would be better to have five minutes between classes instead of three." Your friend answers, "I'd like to see you prove that!" The responsibility for proving the case is yours.

In debate the affirmative faces the same situation: it advocates a change and has to prove the need for it. Until proof is offered the presumption is that things should remain as they are; custom favors the negative. Therefore the affirmative must develop and prove a *prima facie* case—one that is strong enough to win if it is not refuted, and that builds a presumption in favor of the action set forth in the proposition.

Since you have studied the general issues and adapted them to your particular proposition, you understand the two positions, based on the issues, that exist on a question of policy:

218

Affirmative	*Negative*
1. The present policy needs to be changed.	1. There is no need to change the present policy.
2. The action proposed in the proposition is a practical way to change the policy.	2. The action proposed in the proposition is not a practical way to change the policy.
3. The change would be beneficial.	3. The change would be harmful.

In order to establish a prima facie case, the affirmative has to prove these three issues. But the negative can adopt any of four cases to defeat the affirmative: (1) it can *defend the present condition* (the status quo); (2) it can contend that although there is some weakness, it can be met by *repairing* or making a slight change; (3) it can admit there is a need to change the situation, and advocate an *alternative* or *counterproposal;* (4) it can use *direct attack* on the affirmative proposal, arguing that no matter how bad the present situation is, the plan proposed would be worse.

Ways of Outlining Argument

There are two ways of outlining material for a debate. One is to make a complete sentence outline of all available arguments and evidence on one side of the question. This is called a *brief.*

The second method is to prepare a *case outline;* that is, a sentence outline of the arguments and evidence to be used by the debaters in that particular debate. This way is most often used by coaches and experienced debaters.

THE PRINCIPAL SECTIONS OF AN AFFIRMATIVE CASE WOULD BE:

I. Introduction: brief history and statement of the proposition and position of the affirmative.
II. Definition of the terms of the proposition.
III. Basic issues to be proved with supporting evidence.
   A. There is a need to change the present conditions.
   B. The affirmative plan is a practical way of changing the present situation.
   C. The proposed change will bring definite benefits.
IV. Conclusion and summary of issues proved.

THE PRINCIPAL SECTIONS OF A TYPICAL NEGATIVE CASE WOULD BE:
(DIRECT ATTACK ON ALL ISSUES)

I. Introduction and statement of the negative position in the debate.

II. Definition of terms of the proposition.

III. Basic issues to be attacked:

    A. There is no need for a change.

    B. The affirmative plan is not practical.

    C. The proposed change would introduce many detrimental effects.

IV. Conclusion and summary of points proved.

Sample Case for Affirmative

This must always be done — **Definition of Terms:**
Resolved: That all United States aid should be administered through the United Nations.

May not be necessary — **Brief History**

1st Contention — I. The present method of giving foreign aid is unsatisfactory.

(Supporting argument or point) — A. Aid is given for political reasons instead of according to need.

(Explanation) — 1. To further U.S. interests, gain allies, we overlook needs.

(Evidence to support) — 2. Evidence: facts, opinions ...

B. Neutral nations are afraid to accept aid in present form.

220

<table>
</table>

          1. They think it will mean
"taking sides."

          2. Evidence: facts, opinions...

2nd Contention   II. Our plan is to give all aid through
the U.N.

    A. Congress appropriates.

    B. Economic and Social Council of
the UN administrates funds.

    C. Other nations could participate.

3rd Contention   III. Giving foreign aid through the
UN will help the U.S. and the free
world.

(Solution of problem)   A. Aid will be given according to
actual need.

    1. The agency will be impartial.

    2. Evidence: ...

    B. Small and neutral nations will
be more willing to accept aid.

    1. Aid will not come directly
from big power.

    2. Evidence: ...

    C. Other nations might join in.

    1. Evidence: ...

    D. The U.S. would gain prestige.

(Additional benefits)   1. We would not seem intent
on furthering our own
interests.

    2. Evidence: ...

Summary and conclusion.

221

REFUTATION AND REBUTTAL

Debating includes not only the affirmative or constructive case, but the attack on the case of your opponents. Refutation is the tearing down of the opposition's case. Successful refutation of the opponents' arguments depends on listening to what they say, on accurate recording of their case, and on convincing presentation of your reply.

First you must know where opportunities for refutation exist. Here are some questions that will help you discover weaknesses in your opponents' case:

(1) Have they met their obligation by dealing with the basic issues?
(2) Have they proved them satisfactorily? Is their reasoning clear and sound? Does it meet the tests for the various types of reasoning? (Identify the type and apply the tests for that type.)
(3) Is their evidence satisfactory? Have they failed to support any arguments? Is the evidence they offered sufficient in amount to prove their points? Does their evidence meet the tests of the quality of evidence? Is it consistent? Are the sources of evidence acceptable and reliable?
(4) Are their arguments and evidence relevant to the contentions they support?
(5) Have they met adequately the objections you raised against their case?
(6) Has the organization of their case and their rebuttal been clear and easy to follow?

From these questions it is clear that your preparation involves knowing as much, or more, about the case, arguments, and evidence of your opponent as you do about your own. You must be able to anticipate their points and prepare your statement in reply, along with any evidence you may use.

In refutation, make sure you see the opposing case as a whole. Then pick as your. target significant arguments closely related to the main issue, or *important* items of evidence. Don't waste time on small scattered points; such refutation takes valuable time and doesn't weaken your opponent's case. In handling refutation you can: point out that an argument is irrelevant, and toss it aside; admit the argument but contend that it does not harm your case to do so; match the argument by presenting one of equal strength of evidence of greater weight, thus neutralizing your opponent's argument; expose errors in reasoning, evidence, or organization that weaken or destroy the case of your opponent.

To help organize your refutation, here is a "capsule" guide: state what you are trying to refute, using the exact language of your opponent if possible; tell briefly how you plan to attack, *e.g.,* "I shall show this evidence is incorrect, and therefore their argument fails"; introduce the reasoning or evidence you will employ; show how it destroys the opponent's argument; link up what you did to show how this weakens the opponent's case and strengthens yours.

Rebuttal is the time indicated for presenting refutation. However, in the present style of debate, which is flexible, you may present refutation at any time you desire, using some portion of your time during the constructive speeches following the first affirmative. It is important that you answer all arguments as soon as possible after they have been presented by your opponents. Follow through on these arguments in refutation, handling a major point again and again if your opponents continue to stress it.

Your preparation for refutation can help you handle arguments quickly. Use topical headings on file cards; label each with the argument it covers and write the statement and evidence you plan to use. Then you can pull out each card as you need it.

Special Fallacies in Debate

As you know, fallacies are errors in the reasoning process. Such errors can be detected by test questions. There are a number of *special* fallacies that you should be aware of. In these the debater does not base his attack on the proposition, but upon something beside the point.

ARGUMENT TO THE MAN OR TO PERSONALITY. Here the debater does not prove the weakness or strength of the argument, but bases his attack on the character, motives, or personality of someone associated with it—the opposing debater, members of a political party, or an individual. For example: Foreign aid is undesirable because Franklin D. Roosevelt, a Democrat, supported it. The debater, in using this kind of proof, is not arguing the merits or defects of foreign aid. He is attacking a personality.

ARGUMENT TO THE PEOPLE. Here the truth, falsity, or strength of the proposition is not evaluated but attack is made on the basis that a great number of people are against it. For example: We should abolish Federal income tax because the majority is against it.

ARGUMENT TO IGNORANCE. A debater cannot establish proof of a point because his opponents are ignorant of the subject. Such an argument: This is a straight line because no one in the audience can prove it is crooked. Or: We should abandon use of ordinary submarines because our opponents cannot prove they are more efficient than atomic-powered submarines.

APPEAL TO WHAT INSPIRES REVERENCE. Here the stress is on a custom, a traditional or revered practice, rather than on the truth or falsity of the point in question. For example: All freshmen should wear green hats because they have always done so. Or: We should maintain the system of paying class dues among sophomores because every class since 1930 has paid class dues.

ARGUMENT TO PREJUDICE. A known dislike or bias cannot be used as proof of truth or falsity. Example: We should reject the proposal to hold the picnic at Harms Woods because the girls are too squeamish about bugs. Or: We should not admit Tom Lee to our club because his father runs a liquor store.

In most instances, debaters use these fallacies because they do not know better, because they do not have good supporting evidence, or because they deliberately try to win a point by using this invalid kind of proof.

CONDUCTING CONTEST DEBATE

Although contest debating is a specialized speech activity, used primarily in speech or social studies classes, its popularity among high-school students is increasing. Students enjoy the intellectual challenge of contest debate. It is often the principal event in school assemblies or community meetings and is broadcast by radio or television. But most contest debating is interscholastic, either in individual contests or tournaments.

Over forty state high-school leagues conduct debate competitions and many local and regional leagues add to the total. More than a thousand high schools are members of the National Forensic League and engage in state, regional, and national contests every year.

If you take part in such a debate, you will be amazed at the knowledge you gain about current problems. You will participate in exchanges of argument with other debaters and will hear leaders of business, industry, and government discuss critical issues. In addition to local or regional contests, many debaters attend state or national student congresses.

In contest debating each team has two speakers; there is a chairman, and there are timekeepers, ushers, judges, and an audience, even though this may sometimes consist only of the judges.

The debate is held in a room that has seats for an audience; tables, one for each team, are placed at the front where the debaters and the chairman sit. Each speaker is timed (by a watch with a second hand) and held to limits agreed on by both teams. Each judge has a sheet to mark during the speeches and a ballot to mark for the team he thinks has won.

The chairman's duties are to start the debate on time, make the opening remarks, state the proposition, introduce judges, indicate the timekeepers, and introduce each of the speakers in turn. He receives the judges' ballots and announces the result of the debate. He may conduct a forum after the debate. In tournament debating the chairman performs the same duties, but results are reported to the tournament manager, who tabulates decisions and points for all teams participating.

Timekeepers keep time for each speaker. By means of cards or other signals they notify him of the time he has used or how much time he has left. Ushers seat the audience, hand out programs, and collect ballots from the judges.

Members of the student body may serve as judges for class or assembly debates. In interscholastic debates judges are usually experts from high-school or college speech departments and are paid for their services.

FORMS OF CONTEST DEBATE

Organization may vary somewhat, but the following forms of debate are most often used.

Standard

The standard form of contest debate uses two-man teams, with the speeches arranged in this way:

First affirmative constructive speech	10 minutes
First negative constructive speech	10 minutes
Second affirmative constructive speech	10 minutes
Second negative constructive speech	10 minutes
First negative rebuttal speech	5 minutes
First affirmative rebuttal speech	5 minutes
Second negative rebuttal speech	5 minutes
Second affirmative rebuttal speech	5 minutes

Note that the affirmative always opens and closes the debate. The time limits are standard. For classroom debates they may be shortened to fit the class period; however, time limits that are too short destroy the effectiveness of a debate.

To fit a debate into a classroom situation one-man teams are often used.

Affirmative constructive speech (presents the whole case)	10 minutes
Negative constructive speech and reply to affirmative case	12 minutes
Affirmative rejoinder and rebuttal (answers negative and rebuilds his case)	4 minutes
Negative rebuttal and summary	6 minutes
Affirmative final rebuttal and summary	3 minutes

Cross-Examination

Cross-examination debate is used in National Forensic League contests, and has several forms designed to give variety and flexibility to the pattern and develop greater audience interest.

First affirmative constructive speech	8 minutes
Second negative questions the first affirmative	3 minutes
First negative constructive speech	8 minutes
First affirmative questions the first negative	3 minutes
Second affirmative constructive speech	8 minutes
First negative questions second affirmative	3 minutes
Second negative constructive speech	8 minutes
Second affirmative questions second negative	3 minutes
First negative rebuttal speech	4 minutes
First affirmative rebuttal speech	4 minutes
Second negative rebuttal speech	4 minutes
Second affirmative rebuttal speech	4 minutes

This debate can be run in an hour, the same length of time required for the standard two-man team debate.

Direct Clash

This form, which has several varieties, stresses quick adaptation and, after the opening speeches, develops around a series of rebuttal speeches:

First affirmative constructive speech	15 minutes
First negative constructive speech	10 minutes
Second affirmative constructive speech	5 minutes

The negative then starts an alternating sequence of four-minute rebuttal speeches in which one issue at a time is considered. Each issue is debated until the issue is awarded to one team by the judge. Then the negative starts the rebuttal on the next issue.

The direct clash debate has no hard and fast time limits and is excellent training. A number of speakers can be used on each side if desired. Both standard and cross-examination debates are used in tournaments; direct clash is not.

DUTIES OF SPEAKERS
(with a scheme for attack and defense)

CONSTRUCTIVE SPEECHES

First Affirmative

1. State the proposition and define the terms.

2. Give a brief background of the question.

3. Clearly state the affirmative position.

4. Prove the affirmative case: (a) Show the need for a change. (b) Establish that there is a need for a change of the policy which *this* affirmative proposes. (c) Summarize and press the negative to reply.

First Negative

1. Adjust to, or recognize the affirmative position, definition of terms etc., and clearly state the negative position.

2. Attack the affirmative case, hitting the major arguments.

3. Introduce and prove the negative case (status quo, repairs, counterproposal, etc.).

4. Summarize your presentation and press .the second affirmative to reply.

Second Affirmative

1. Reply to the attack of the first negative.

2. Attack the negative case.

3. Continue the proof of the affirmative case: (a) Restate the affirmative position and need. (b) Present the affirmative plan and benefits. (c) Summarize the entire affirmative case and press the second negative to reply.

Second Negative

1. Reply to the attack of the second affirmative.

2. Briefly restate the negative position and rebuild the negative case.

3. Relate this to the second part of the negative case and prove it.

4. Summarize the negative case and press the affirmative to reply.

REBUTTAL SPEECHES

First Affirmative

1. Reply to the major attacks against the affirmative case: (a) answer the first negative rebuttal; (b) reply to the second negative constructive speech.

2. Continue the attack on the negative case.

3. Press the second negative to reply.

First Negative (begins)

1. Attack the affirmative plan on practicability.

2. Attack the affirmative plan, pointing out the bad effects it will produce.

3. Press the first affirmative to reply to the arguments of the first and second negative speakers.

227

Second Affirmative (concludes the debate)	*Second Negative*

<table>
<tr>
<td>

Second Affirmative
(concludes the debate)

1. Rebuild the entire affirmative case by replying to the major arguments against it; be sure to include a reply to the key point of the second negative rebuttal in this review.

2. Advance the major affirmative arguments against the negative case. Show that they prevail.

3. *Strongly* urge the acceptance of the proposition.

</td>
<td>

Second Negative

1. Reply to the major attacks against the negative case; make sure to include your answer to the first affirmative rebuttal.

2. Advance each major negative argument against the affirmative case.

3. Press the second affirmative to reply.

4. Urge the audience to reject the proposition.

</td>
</tr>
</table>

JUDGING A DEBATE

Debaters ask this question many times: "How did he judge that debate?" The decision on any contest debate should be based on this question, "Which side did the best debating?" Ballots vary in their form and organization, but these are the points generally included:

(1)   Is the case, as outlined, logically adequate? Is it clearly organized and easy to follow?

(2)   Is the evidence pertinent, dependable, and sufficient, as submitted in the debate?

(3)   Are the arguments sound and comprehensive?

(4)   Is the defense well selected, thorough, and well organized? Have important points been chosen for refutation? Are they answered satisfactorily? Has the rebuttal work been well planned and organized?

(5)   A debater speaks extemporaneously. That is, he should be thoroughly prepared, but should compose his speech on his feet and adjust to changing situations. The *excessive* use of notes counts against a speaker. He should be direct, and speak to the audience. Is his delivery marked by courtesy, audibility, fluency, poise, and the use of good English?

Two kinds of evaluations are possible. Based on the above points, the judge may decide, "The affirmative did the better debating," and vote for that team. He may also give a quality or point rating to each speaker and each team, for example: superior—5; good—4; average—3; below average—2; inferior—1. These ratings make it possible for you to compare your effectiveness as an individual with others who took part, regardless of who won the decision.

The sample ballot below provides for both methods.

228

AFA DEBATE BALLOT

ROUND＿＿＿ ROOM＿＿＿ DATE＿＿＿＿＿＿＿＿ JUDGE＿＿＿＿＿＿＿＿

AFFIRMATIVE＿＿＿＿＿＿＿＿＿＿ NEGATIVE＿＿＿＿＿＿＿＿＿

Individual Ratings

Check the column on each item which, according to the following scale, best describes your evaluation of the Speaker's effectiveness:

1—poor   2—below average   3—average   4—good   5—superior

1st Affirmative＿＿＿＿＿＿＿＿＿ 1st Negative＿＿＿＿＿＿＿＿＿

	1	2	3	4	5
Analysis					
Evidence					
Argument					
Refutation					
Delivery					

Total＿＿＿

	1	2	3	4	5
Analysis					
Evidence					
Argument					
Refutation					
Delivery					

Total＿＿＿

2nd Affirmative＿＿＿＿＿＿＿＿＿ 2nd Negative＿＿＿＿＿＿＿＿＿

	1	2	3	4	5
Analysis					
Evidence					
Argument					
Refutation					
Delivery					

Total＿＿＿

	1	2	3	4	5
Analysis					
Evidence					
Argument					
Refutation					
Delivery					

Total＿＿＿

Team Ratings

Assign to each team the rating which best describes your judgment of its performance:

1—poor   2—below average   3—average   4—good   5—superior

AFFIRMATIVE＿＿＿＿＿＿＿＿＿＿ NEGATIVE＿＿＿＿＿＿＿＿＿

Decision

In my judgment, the better debating was done by the

＿＿＿＿＿＿＿＿＿＿＿＿
(AFFIRMATIVE OR NEGATIVE)

Reason for decision.

＿＿＿＿＿＿＿＿＿＿＿＿＿＿
(JUDGE'S SIGNATURE AND SCHOOL)

229

ACTIVITIES

After Propositions

1. List the five problem areas you consider important in contemporary affairs, education, or business. Under each, state at least two propositions suitably worded for debate.

2. From the list of problem areas below, choose one. Word three debate propositions for it, phrasing each properly;

College admissions
Honors courses
Space exploration
Military conscription
Federal aid to schools
Berlin
Communism in the Western Hemisphere
Driver training in high school
Labor unions and the 35-hour week
Scholarships for athletes
Family vacations
Teaching by television

After Investigation

1. Select a proposition and prepare a list of ten references for it (bibliography) by consulting the Readers' Guide, the card catalogue, and any specialized debate references you have.

2. Select a proposition, prepare a short bibliography, and read enough background to have the history of your question, plus the immediate causes for discussing it.

After Analysis

1. Select a proposition from your list and make an analysis of it in outline form, listing the following: (a) the stock or general issues; (b) the specific or fighting issues.

After Evidence

1. Using your proposition, read several articles and prepare five evidence cards with complete details of subject, subheads, source with author, publication, date, and pages. Be sure to have at least two authorities and at least two items of statistical evidence in your cards.

2. Select a short argumentative speech or article from your speech book, the newspaper, or a news publication. Find at least three examples of evidence used, and the arguments they support. Identify and test each item of evidence with the questions in this chapter on quality, amount, and source of evidence.

After Reasoning

1. Prepare an example of each of the four methods of reasoning. Identify each and test its soundness, using the questions in the text.

2. Listen to the informal debates of your classmates. Find an example of a fallacy, either a general type in which the methods of reasoning are involved, or a special type. Write it out, explain it, and tell how it could be corrected.

After the Debate Case

1. Working on a proposition in pairs, one affirmative and one negative, prepare a case outline for your side. Include all sub-arguments, and supporting evidence.

2. Present your case in an eight-minute speech prepared from the outline. Be prepared to present a three-minute rebuttal of your opponent's case.

After Refutation

1. For a class workout with your same opponent, prepare three major arguments on one set of cards. On another set prepare the refutation for each, using the "capsule" organization suggested in the text. Place the first set of cards face down on the table. Have your opponent select one and read the argument aloud. Then give the refutation you have prepared. Alternate by letting him refute arguments you choose from his cards. Continue around the class.

2. Select from a newspaper a provocative editorial. Choose one of its major arguments with the supporting material. Outline or write your refutation for it, and present it to the class.

For Contest Debate

1. With the help of your instructor and other members of your class, select a debatable proposition and plan all the details for a contest debate with teams selected from the class.

2. Assuming that your school enters interscholastic debate, plan a similar debate for an assembly to be given before the school.

3. Plan all the details for a debate tournament you will entertain at your school.

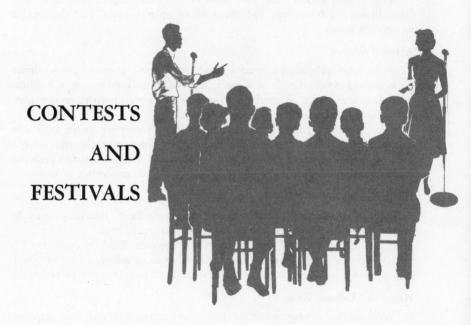

CHAPTER 16

CONTESTS
AND
FESTIVALS

Contests allow no excuses.

—IBYCUS

In different Midwestern high schools during the 1930's, three boys met regularly after school with their speech teachers. From these special sessions came achievements in debate and individual events that were outstanding. Later the boys attended the same state university, and became distinguished in debate, extemporaneous speaking, and oratory. They became leaders on campus. Since then, their serious interest in important issues and their skill in oral controversy have carried them far. One is a renowned international lecturer and the chairman of the English department at a major university; the second was elected to the United States Senate; the third, a former governor of his state, became a member of the President's cabinet.

Today students are able to participate in both speech *classes* and *contests*. However, over half of all high-school students get their training

232

in extra-class speech activities only. Like the three students, they start to develop their skills early. They enjoy the intellectual stimulation and the fun of after-school speech experiences, and continue such interests all their lives.

Speech activities include all organized, group, or individual speech performances conducted in or outside the classroom. Almost any speech activity can become a *contest* if the element of competition is introduced. Conversation, interviewing, and occasional speaking are more typically classroom experiences. Others are extra-class activities; some are speech contests, either in an intramural or an interscholastic program. These include extemporaneous speaking, oratory, debating, declamation, interpretative reading, and radio speaking. Choric interpretation, reader's theater, chamber theater, and plays are ordinarily given as public performances without contest emphasis.

Speech contests were a method of training as early as Greek civilization. Orations were common. Disputations, early forms of debate, were everyday experiences in the law courts. At the Dionysian festival, playwrights and poets presented their works in public performances before huge audiences at Athens. Prizes were awarded annually.

In the United States, speech activities were a regular part of college education as early as 1716. Harvard, Yale, Brown, and Princeton required students to give orations in Greek, Latin, and English at commencement. Forensic and syllogistic disputations were frequent events on college campuses in colonial times. Intercollegiate debates developed in the latter part of the nineteenth century and continue to the present. High-school debating first gained national attention in 1928, when the National University Extension Association became interested. In that year the first national championship debate was held before the House of Representatives in Washington, between Suffolk High School, Virginia, and Hartshorne High School, Oklahoma.

Today there are approximately forty-four state speech leagues. The NUEA furnishes the debate materials, and aids their programs in other ways. Each league has a publication describing its program, rules, and schedules. In the state leagues alone almost 15,000 schools and an estimated 300,000 students participate annually. Other privately sponsored high-school speech organizations are the National Forensic League, the National Thespian Society, and Masque and Gavel. They have active and alumni memberships totaling almost 600,000.

Another great part of contemporary programs in speech activities is the production of plays for school and community audiences. In April 1951, Rufus Jarman wrote in *The Saturday Evening Post*[1]:

> Not more than 2,000,000 Americans see professional plays of Broadway caliber regularly, and only about 5,000,000 see them occasionally. When Broadway numbers its actors by the hundreds, the huge amateur theater counts its performers by the hundreds of thousands and its audiences by the tens of millions. Its playwrights, unknown to the Great White Way, sometimes turn out a play that has 10,000 or more performances, which is more than Rodgers and Hammerstein ever did. Last year an estimated 100,000,000 Americans, counting repeaters, attended between 350,000 and 500,000 plays by amateur groups. The largest single group in this field of play givers was the nation's high schools, which, during 1950, produced about 75,000 full-length plays. These were viewed by between 18,000,000 and 25,000,000 persons.

In 1960-1961 the National Thespian Society reported that its member schools (1560 of 2221 schools) presented 2871 full-length plays, 251 children's theater shows, 1443 musicals, operettas, and pageants, and 3773 one-act plays. Projected to all high schools, the estimated total is well over 100,000 productions.

By taking part in a program in speech activities and contests you can gain substantial experience. Your interest in speech will be strengthened. You receive special training in the kind of speech performance you select. You find new friends and associates. If you enter contests, you have an opportunity to develop your skill because you want to excel in competition.

FORENSIC ACTIVITIES

These are all types of speeches designed to be given before the public. Forensic activity includes discussions and debates, as well as after-dinner speeches.

Extemporaneous Speaking

Developed in protest against "old-line" type of oratory, the first contests in extemporaneous speaking were held in 1926. Educators wanted to stress a more practical method of speaking than the memorization then

---

[1]Rufus Jarman, "To Heck with Broadway!" *Saturday Evening Post* (April 28, 1951), pp. 22-23.

used in contest oratory. The participant prepares a talk lasting from six to ten minutes, depending on the rules. Before the contest, he reads extensively on issues in the daily press or in designated news publications over a selected period of time. He then draws three subjects by lot from a large number prepared by a committee. He selects one of the three and is allowed not more than one hour to prepare. During the preparation he may use his own materials or the library. Then he gives his talk, which is judged on criteria for an effective extemporaneous speech. Time limits are carefully watched. In some states participants question one another after the speech. A reply to all questions is required. Both the prepared speech and the rejoinder affect the final rating.

If you are entering a contest in extemporaneous speaking, here are some suggestions for preparation:

READ EXTENSIVELY. First, acquire knowledge of current affairs. Make extensive use of town and school libraries and your own materials. Use television, film, and radio news programs, as well as special programs, to enrich your background.

TAKE ACCURATE NOTES ON YOUR READING. Use broad categories for listing your findings, such as civil rights, foreign aid, nuclear weapons, and similar subjects. Record details, including statistics and usable quotations. Develop a card file of materials.

MASTER BASIC PRINCIPLES OF SPEECH COMPOSITION. If you have not studied these principles, consult your teacher. If you have had a course in speech, review the essentials.

EVOLVE A PLAN FOR AN EFFECTIVE CONTEST SPEECH. As you prepare, develop a "capsule" plan that will appeal to your audience and the judges. Good texts in public speaking will direct you on general patterns of organization. Your originality and the experience of your speech director will add concrete details to ensure success.

PRACTICE DOING THE BASIC JOB, PREFERABLY UNDER CONTEST CONDITIONS. In practice sessions, have a "dress rehearsal." Draw your topics and select the best one for the contest. Consider audience interest, timeliness, and available information. Limit your preparation to one hour. Allow about two thirds of your time for composition and one third for delivery.

Give your talk before a "live" audience. This may be a high-school class, club, or community group. Observe exact time limits. Have your teacher evaluate you on the criteria and standards of the judges' ballot. Speak in an auditorium at least once a week, if you know that the contest is to be held in one. Adjust your talk to the various conditions you will meet.

ALLOW TIME FOR AN EXTENSIVE TRAINING PERIOD. The length of your training period will be influenced by your ability, your schedule, and the date of the contest. At least a month is needed for such preparation. Have daily sessions if possible, or practice several times each week.

Non-Original Oratory (Oratorical Declamation)

This activity requires the selection, memorization, and delivery of a part or the whole of the public speech of another person. Such speeches may be chosen from collections of student orations, such as *Winning Orations,* published by the Inter-State Oratorical Association, anthologies of famous speeches, and contemporary speeches found in *Vital Speeches* or *The New*

York Times. One of the great values of this event is the reading of superior speeches and the evaluation of them as significant pieces for presentation.

After studying available speeches, it is necessary to edit and cut the selection to have it meet the time limits of the contest. Student and teacher coöperate on this task.

Memorization of the text comes next, following the procedure best adapted to the student, with analysis and the development of the essentials of delivery, since the judging is primarily upon these essentials, using criteria and standards found in the rules.

This activity is employed extensively as a method of providing platform experience for young or less experienced participants.

Oratory

In oratory the student writes, memorizes, and delivers a persuasive speech arising from his personal feelings, convictions, or a source of irritation about something. In the best practice it is not a display of exhibitory speaking, although this unfortunate concept has often been held by some people. Oratory that is well done gives the student an opportunity to investigate a problem about which he feels strongly. It means the careful organization of his information. It requires skillful writing to achieve a desirable oral style. It demands straightforward, sincere, communicative delivery that is not artificial or burdened with ornamentation. To the extent that the student attempts to follow this formula, oratory is a profitable experience. To the extent that oration becomes a coach-written project, the only motivation being accurate memorization and mechanical delivery, it loses its value. Oratory can be handled as an activity; as persuasive speaking it is often taught in the classroom in advanced work in public speaking.

Should you enter a contest in oratory, these recommendations should help you[1]:

    I. READ EXTENSIVELY ON CURRENT PROBLEMS. (This is the preliminary exploration, and at least three weeks should be allowed for it.)
        A. Read daily newspapers and news magazines.
        B. Read special school publications on current problems, for example, *The American Observer.*

---

[1] Adapted by permission from Karl F. Robinson and E. J. Kerikas, *Teaching Speech—Methods and Materials.* New York: David McKay, 1963, pp. 397-402.

C. Make brief notations on the problems that seem to you to cry out for consideration or for remedial action.

D. List two or three current problems you would like to investigate further.

II. MAKE A BIBLIOGRAPHY ON EACH OF THE PROBLEMS CHOSEN FOR FURTHER INVESTIGATION.

A. Use the *Readers' Guide,* card catalogue, and special indexes.

B. List the names and addresses of persons who have special knowledge of the subject and arrange to interview these persons.

III. SELECT THE PROBLEM TO BE DEALT WITH IN THE ORATION.

A. Using your bibliography as a guide, review the most important material previously read and investigate new sources.

B. Consider the possible purpose for persuasive speeches involved in each problem. The result of the analysis may be conveniently represented, thus:

General Problem	Title of Oration	Specific Purpose of Oration
Crime	Children Cheated	To persuade the audience that slum clearance is essential to the success of a crime-prevention program.
Crime	"Pardon Me!"	To persuade the audience that the power to pardon and parole convicts should be taken from the governors of the respective states and given to non-partisan boards of expert criminologists.
Mental Health	Are We Our Brothers' Keepers?	To persuade the audience that better care is need for the mentally ill.

C. In the light of the analysis of the subjects, the specific purposes, the probable audience, and the self-examination of the speaker, choose the problem title, and specific purpose of the oration.

IV. COLLECT MATERIAL ON THE SPECIFIC SUBJECT AND PURPOSE CHOSEN.

A. Revise your bibliography; add new references on the specific subject chosen.

B. Take systematic notes on cards of uniform size.

V. ORGANIZE THE MATERIAL.

A. Place the cards in three stacks, one for the Introduction, the second for the Body, and the third for the Conclusion.

B. Outline the speech, selecting the best material; make full use of the possible elements of interest and persuasion.

C. Fix the outline in your mind.

VI. GIVE THE SPEECH EXTEMPORANEOUSLY WITHOUT NOTES. (Speak to a class or some other group, if this can possibly be arranged.)

VII. PROFITING BY YOUR EXPERIENCE IN EXTEMPORANEOUS PRESENTA-
TION, WRITE THE SPEECH IN FULL.
  A. Carry over the best attributes of your extemporaneous speaking
     into your style plus those refinements of language that increase the
     vividness, euphony, personal force, and moving power of the whole
     speech.
  B. Visualize the audience as you write.
  C. The style should be simple and clearcut, rather than ornate and
     highly involved.
  D. Concrete examples and illustrations pump lifeblood into the ora-
     tor's thesis.
VIII. READ THE SPEECH ALOUD.
  IX. REVISE THE SPEECH.
   X. PRACTICE THE DELIVERY OF THE SPEECH REGULARLY (over a period
     of several weeks, if possible).
  A. The presentation must be characterized by sincerity, animation, and
     directness of communication.
  B. Artificiality in voice and mere posing are to be avoided.
  C. Speak to real audiences (classes, home rooms, clubs, or other
     groups) whenever possible.

Analysis of Public Address

In order to train students in the analysis and criticism of various kinds of
speeches, the Oklahoma High School Speech League has recently initiated
this contest, and describes it in its *Official Handbook,* published at Nor-

man, Oklahoma. The first part of the activity necessitates extensive library research to find and select desirable examples of public address. The second stage demands careful analysis of content and organization. The last step requires the student to give a ten-minute speech presenting his findings to the audience and the judges. He is evaluated on his choice of speech, background information, the composition of his analysis, and his delivery. The event is growing in popularity and is an interesting contribution to speech training.

After-Dinner Speeches

Although this type of speech is often included in speech courses, it is also a part of many contest programs. The usual speaking situation is an *actual* dinner, such as the banquet at a festival, or a *simulated* one. The 1963 contest series in Illinois is typical of this event. An imaginary setting was specified—a banquet sponsored by a PTA, a booster organization, or a local service club. Participants prepared an eight-minute speech to entertain on any subject considered suitable by the contestant and his teacher.

This event is specifically identified as "a form of public address, and not an interpretative event. The speaker must be himself (a high school student) in a real situation. At the same time, the speech should have an evident theme. There must, in other words, be a reason for its existence. It is not merely a series of jokes or stories."

A typed copy of the speech is submitted in advance of the contest. Although Illinois requires that this speech be memorized, this is not the case in many other states. Contestants are seated around a table during the event. They stand and speak from a position behind the table. Judging is on subject, purpose, organization, supporting materials, and general presentation.

Students enjoy this event because of its opportunity for humor and originality.

Discussion

Directors of speech activity programs are placing greater emphasis on discussion as a tool for investigation of the problem area from which debate propositions are selected. The National University Extension Association announces annually the particular area for study. It lists three possible discussion subjects and three debate propositions to be used prior

240

to the announcement at Christmastime of the official proposition. Speech teachers stress discussion as a means of group thinking for problem solving. Many types of discussion are in use. Chapter 13 contains a detailed treatment of discussion.

Debate

The most widely developed group forensic activity is debating. It has no exact counterpart in life, but as a form of interscholastic competition is a means of training students in argumentation. A complete treatment of contest debating appears in Chapter 15.

INTERPRETATIVE ACTIVITIES

Oratorical declamation (non-original oratory) has been discussed under forensic activities. Two other types of declamation included in high-school speech contests are *humorous* declamation, utilizing a selection of prose or poetry considered funny by the participant, and *dramatic* declamation, employing a portion of prose or a cutting from a play involving dramatic qualities and characterization.

Declamation

In all of these contests the material is memorized and emphasis is placed on the delivery of the content. All selections are restricted as to time of performance. Criteria and standards are listed in the rules and judges' ballots. Effectively taught and presented, declamation is a valuable means of teaching delivery.

Poor material and exhibitory or unconvincing delivery are the greatest weaknesses in such contests. They smell of the lamp of elocution, the forerunner of declamation, where mechanistic techniques overwhelmed a meaningful presentation of a selection of humorous or dramatic material. Often commercial pieces dominate declamation contests, and are to be deplored. Modern speech education insists that the material stimulate and enrich the background of the participant. If it does not, the training in delivery can be better learned in other forms of speech activity.

Recently some organizations have dropped declamation as the name of the event, substituting reading instead. Changing the name *only* does not improve matters unless the nature of the contest is changed and the areas sensitive to criticism removed. The trend away from memorization and a declamatory attitude are noted in the discussion of interpretation.

Individual Interpretation

The trend in contemporary interpretation follows three significant directions: (1) selections must have high literary quality; (2) they necessitate thorough, careful analysis by the student; (3) they require *reading from the book* or evidence of relationship to it.

Interpretation may be conducted in festival form with no winners declared. Under these conditions, readers are classed as superior, excellent, good, or placed in some similar category. Several students may share one rating. The stress is on the interpreter's skill in sharing good literature. The University of Iowa has emphasized this kind of organization for many years.

A standard type of contest with winners determined by judges' ranks may also be used.

Choric Interpretation

The title indicates that this is a form of group interpretation using more than one person to interpret the same piece of literature. (See Part II, Chapter 5.)

Reader's Theater

A second group form, this activity presents challenging opportunities for interpreting a selection with each participant doing only one rôle. Drama and poetry are the types most frequently done, although prose may be used. This type of activity has been growing in popularity in recent years, not only because it is economical to present, but because it allows the group to present experimental and creative theater in a highly adaptable medium. (See Part II, Chapter 12.)

Chamber Theater

An experimental form pioneered by Dr. Robert Breen of Northwestern University, this activity uses several performers to present a selection of non-dramatic prose from a novel or short story in dramatic form.

Summer Speech Institutes

For the past thirty-four years students have been able to continue their speech activities by attending summer institutes sponsored by colleges and universities. In 1930, Northwestern University conducted its first national five-week program for high-school juniors. There are now over sixty such

242

programs for high-school students from grades nine through twelve. In most institutes the members live on campus, obtaining a bird's-eye view of college; some programs, however, accept day students.

They study intensively in the areas of their particular interest. Northwestern University gives training in basic skills to all, and allows specialization in one area—debate and discussion, drama, or radio-television-film. Classes and final performances in each area are used for observation by university students.

Members of the various institutes gain enrichment in their general education through trips, guest lecturers, conferences with professional performers, teaching by mature faculty specialists in communicative arts, and visits to cultural centers.

THEATER ACTIVITIES

Short Plays for Class or Contest

The short play, either a one-act, or a cutting from a longer play, is produced more often than any other type in high school. It not only requires less rehearsal time, but can be done more conveniently during a class period or an assembly, or as a noon-hour entertainment. It is an approved vehicle for the play festival or contest. In recent years, the festival has almost completely replaced the contest in state or regional speech conferences because it permits critics to evaluate and classify the productions entered as superior, excellent, good, rather than to select a single winner.

Participation in a play festival follows a typical pattern. In Illinois entries must be filed with the local manager one week before the date of the festival and consist of a complete plan of the play containing these items: name of play and author; director; cast of characters; setting, including a floor plan showing placement of all doors, windows, furniture, and properties; a list of properties to be furnished by the host school; a plot for lighting desired; acting time of the play. Any special charges for rental or transportation of properties or equipment must be paid in advance of performance by the school involved. The recommended length is thirty minutes. Plays running over forty minutes are disqualified.

The rules require all actors to be bona fide students of the school they represent. They specify no limit as to the sex or number of players in a cast. Directors may assist in preparation for the play. Prompting is permitted from the wings. Each cast must provide its own make-up, costumes, and special properties. Quality ratings are given by judges upon choice of the play, direction, staging, acting, and audience appeal.

Preparation of a contest play involves all of the steps needed in a three-act play—choosing the play; casting; rehearsing; preparing properties, lighting, and scenery, developing the best production possible.

Three-Act Plays and Long Productions

The significant place of theater in contemporary education is recognized in recent statements and actions by national groups. In 1960 the White House Conference on Children and Youth discussed ways by which youth could best be helped "to realize their *full potential for a creative life in freedom and dignity.*" Six hundred national organizations and six million people worked on preparation for the conference in which the delegates participated. Twenty-one of the final recommendations apply directly to education through theater. The most direct recommendation was that: public and voluntary agencies, schools, colleges, and communities should provide all children and youth with opportunities for participation in creative dramatics, creative writing, and dramatic production under qualified leadership, to develop their talents and give them basic understanding and critical appreciation of the theater arts.

Leaders in the Secondary School Theatre Conference, including Wallace Smith of Evanston (Illinois) Township High School, observe that the issue does not reside in the number of short or three-act plays being given each year, but in their quality. The nationwide problem is one of establishing goals and standards for drama programs, of integrating them with forward-looking educational ideals, and of encouraging the development of good programs in theater.

The 1963 *Course of Study in Theatre Arts at the Secondary School Level,* published by the Secondary School Theatre Conference of the American Educational Theatre Association, points definite directions for such activities with specific materials for students and teachers.

The school program may include course work, a drama club, and a season of plays to be given as an all-school program.

RADIO AND TELEVISION ACTIVITIES

The newest and most exciting of speech activities are in the media of radio and television. Each year more high schools offer training in these areas, but there are still definite limitations in courses in radio or tele-

244

vision because of the expense of equipment, heavily loaded school schedules, and lack of trained teachers.

Therefore, students secure their training through clubs, workshops, special activities, and contests. Numerous speech departments use the school public-address system with tape recorders or live programs to provide an in-school broadcasting set-up. In a few instances high schools have built FM radio stations, or installed closed-circuit television and vidiotape equipment. Actual aired broadcasting is done through the cooperation of local educational or commercial stations.

There are some developments in the contest field in these areas.

Individual Broadcasting Performance

The National Forensic League has radio speaking in its national tournament. The Iowa league asks participants to prepare an original expository script to be broadcast over closed-circuit television and evaluated by judges in the studio. Illinois has a radio speaking contest where contestants give a five-minute newscast from a prepared script.

Details of the contest are interesting. The state office furnishes a script for a prepared newscast containing fifteen minutes of material. From this the contestant is required to organize a five-minute newscast, including one or more commercials, in a preparation time of thirty minutes. Commercials may be prepared in advance of the contest. The *final* newscast must be presented verbatim from the contestant's *edited* copy of the original newscast. He is allowed to delete any portion of the long script, but can add only transitions, introductions, conclusions, and commercials. The newscast is presented over a public-address system with judges hearing (not seeing) the broadcasters. Timing must be "on the nose" at five minutes. Any speaker running under four minutes and forty-five seconds or over five minutes is disqualified.

Group Programs or Prepared Shows

A few secondary schools enter contests requiring dramatic shows, produced from original scripts, taped, broadcast, and evaluated by a panel of experts. Shows are judged on script, continuity, music, sound, acting, and direction. Winners receive awards of certificates or similar prizes.

By far the greater number of prepared shows are given under in-school workshop activity programs or on time spots donated by outside stations.

BIBLIOGRAPHY

Speaking and Listening

ILLINOIS CURRICULUM PROGRAM. Communication in the High School Program: Speaking and Listening. Bulletin D-1. Springfield, Ill. (October 1961), Chap. I.

ROBINSON, KARL F., and E. J. KERIKAS. *Teaching Speech.* New York: David McKay, Inc., 1963, Chap. I.

NICHOLS, RALPH, and STEVENS, LEONARD. *Are You Listening?* New York: McGraw-Hill Book Co., Inc., 1957.

Gaining Poise and Confidence

BAIRD, A. CRAIG, and FRANKLIN KNOWER. *Essentials of General Speech.* New York: McGraw-Hill Book Co., Inc., 1960.

Controlling Action

IRWIN, JOHN V., and MARJORIE ROSENBERGER. *Modern Speech.* New York: Holt, Rinehart and Winston, Inc., 1961. Chap. XIV.

MCBURNEY, JAMES H., and ERNEST J. WRAGE. *Guide to Good Speech.* Englewood Cliffs, N.J.: Prentice-Hall, Inc., 1960.

MONROE, ALAN H., and DOUGLAS EHNINGER. *Principles and Types of Speech.* Chicago: Scott, Foresman and Co., 1962. Chap. III.

Controlling Voice: Developing Articulation

AKIN, JOHNNYE. *And So We Speak: Voice and Articulation.* Englewood Cliffs, N.J.: Prentice-Hall, Inc., 1958.

EISENSON, JOH. *The Improvement of Voice and Diction.* New York: The Macmillan Co., 1958.

MULGRAVE, DOROTHY. *Speech: A Handbook of Voice Training, Diction and Public Speaking.* New York: Barnes and Noble, 1954. Chaps. XI-XVIII.

Preparing Your Speech

BAIRD, A. CRAIG, and FRANKLIN KNOWER. *Essentials of General Speech.* New York: McGraw-Hill Book Co., Inc., 1960.

BRIGANCE, W. NORWOOD. *Speech Communication.* New York: Appleton-Century-Crofts, Inc., 1955.

HANCE, KENNETH. "Public Address in the Secondary School," *Bulletin of the National Association of Secondary School Principals,* XXXVI, No. 187 (May 1952).

Using Language Effectively

CHASE, STUART. *The Tyranny of Words.* New York: Harcourt, Brace and Co., 1938.

HAYAKAWA, S. I. *Language in Thought and Action.* New York: Harcourt, Brace and Co., 1949.

HAYAKAWA, S. I. *Language: Meaning and Maturity.* New York: Harper and Bros., 1959.

Discussion

AUER, J. JEFFREY, and HENRY L. EUBANK. *Handbook for Discussion Leaders.* New York: Harper and Bros., 1954.

Debate

MCBURNEY, JAMES H., and GLEN E. MILLS. *Argumentation and Debate: Techniques of a Free Society* (Second Edition). New York: The Macmillan Co., 1964.

MCBATH, JAMES, Ed. *Argumentation and Debate.* New York: Holt, Rinehart and Winston, 1963.

Parliamentary Procedure

ROBERT, HENRY. *Robert's Rules of Order.* Chicago: Scott, Foresman and Co., 1951.

STURGIS, ALICE F. *Learning Parliamentary Procedure.* New York: McGraw-Hill Book Co., 1953.

FILMS AND KINESCOPES

Speech In Your World

Why Study Speech?	11 min.	YAF
Controversy, Freedom of Speech		
Majority Rule	30 min.	NET
Public Opinion	11 min.	EBF

Listening

Effective Listening	12 min.	McGraw

Informal Speaking

Ways to Better Conversation	11 min.	Coronet
Social Courtesy	11 min.	Coronet
How Do You Do?	14 min.	YAF

Developing Confidence

Overcoming Fear	14 min.	Coronet
Stage Fright and What to Do About It	10 min.	YAF

Speech Preparation

Speech Preparation	16 min.	C-B Films
Speech: Planning Your Talk	13 min.	YAF
Building an Outline	11 min.	Coronet

Using Language Effectively

Just What is Semantics?	30 min.	NET
Talking Ourselves into Trouble	30 min.	NET
Do Words Ever Fool You?	11 min.	Coronet
Words That Don't Inform	30 min.	NET

Controlling Your Voice: Articulation

Sound Waves and Their Sources	11 min.	EBF
Using Your Voice	10 min.	YAF
Your Voice	11 min.	EBF

Using Action Effectively

Public Speaking: Movement and Gesture	11 min.	Coronet
Using Visuals in Your Speech	14 min.	YAF
Platform Posture and Appearance	9 min.	YAF

Discussion

Organizing Discussion Groups	21 min.	EBF
Mr. Chairman	13 min.	EBF
Group Discussion	12 min.	YAF
How to Conduct a Discussion	24 min.	EBF

Parliamentary Procedure

Parliamentary Procedure	11 min.	Coronet
Conducting a Meeting	12 min.	YAF

FILM PRODUCERS AND DISTRIBUTORS

Coronet	Coronet Films, Coronet Bldg., Chicago 1, Ill.
EBF	Encyclopaedia Britannica Films, Inc., 1150 Wilmette, Wilmette, Ill.
McGraw	McGraw-Hill Co., Text Film Dept., 330 W. 42nd St., New York 36, N.Y.
NET	NET Film Service, Indiana University, Bloomington, Ind.
YAF	Young America Films, Inc., 18 East 41st St., New York 17, N.Y.

247

PART II

You now begin the art of communicating the ideas and feelings of others. You will use many of the techniques you learned in the first section, but there are some important differences between expressing your own ideas and feelings in your own words, and doing justice to the ideas and feelings of someone else.

When you communicate the ideas and feelings of an author, you are dealing with literature. *The art of analyzing a selection from literature and effectively communicating all of its elements to an audience is interpretation.*

Interpretation, instead of being concerned with conveying to your listeners exactly what *you* mean and how *you* mean it, makes clear exactly what *the author* meant and how *he* meant it. To do this, you must try to understand what he meant and how he meant it before you can convey it to others.

Although interpretation is a distinct

PRINCIPLES OF INTERPRETATION

speech skill, it is closely allied with all other forms of speech. It helps the public speaker who wishes to quote from an authority. The debater uses it to strengthen his case. Radio and television announcers rely heavily on interpretation for the response they want from their audiences. The actor finds that interpretation teaches him subtlety and broadens his appreciation of character differences. Singers use interpretation to make the lyrics of their songs meaningful.

A knowledge of interpretation increases your understanding and appreciation of all kinds of literature. It gives you added insight into what others think and feel. Finally, there is great personal satisfaction in sharing something you like with others, whether it be on a platform or in the company of a few friends.

THE TWO PARTS OF INTERPRETATION

Interpretation has two aspects. The first is analysis: to find out everything that is in a selection. This involves reading for the overall impression, then studying each detail and discovering its purpose, and then reassembling all the details so the audience receives a unified effect.

The second part of interpretation is the use of both voice and body to convey in the best way what you have found in the selection. Before you start using vocal and physical techniques, you must understand what the poem, play, or story is about. As an interpreter you must allow yourself to be directed by your author. He created the work, you re-create it.

In its broadest definition, literature includes all writing. The limits of good literature are not so narrow as you may think. Humorous stories, adventure stories, skillfully written sports stories, ghost stories, character sketches, nonsense verse, poetry, and drama can all be literature. You will find some writers you like very much, and wide reading will help you establish standards by which you can judge any author's writing.

It is not necessary that you like everything generally regarded as literature. No one does. But give enough consideration to anything you dislike so you know why you don't like it. You may start out liking what you know, and from that move to knowing what you like—and why you like it.

One of the tests of good literature is that it deals with universal experiences: things we all think about, such as remembered incidents from childhood, love, death, immortality. Faraway places, war, nature, patriotism are other things that interest most people.

There are many ways to write about the same thing, and the best literature is expressed in a fresh and individual way. Think of all the things you have read about a subject, such as early American history, adventure tales, or ghost stories. The ones that stand out are those that say what they have to say in a way that seems better to you than any other way you have ever heard it. They have individuality and style.

In addition to its universal appeal and individuality, literature stirs your imagination. This does not mean it must be imaginary. It means it makes you keep on thinking about the subject after you have closed the book.

Literature is not just facts. An encyclopedia or a scientific formula contains facts. Literature must go beyond facts. It is the author's evaluation and expansion of the facts that makes the difference. He has carefully thought out and organized the material, so that it conveys in the best possible way what the author feels and believes. Each word is exactly the right word. And they are put together in such a way that each sentence gives the precise meaning the author intended it to convey to his audience.

CHOOSING A SELECTION

In interpretation you do not have to think of something to make a speech about. You find a poem or story that says something you like

252

Take time to find a selection for interpretation. It should be suitable to your audience, and have individuality, appeal, and interest for *you*.

in a way you like. You may choose from among the best ideas of all the writers of all time. You need only find the ones that appeal to you. Your teacher can guide your selection by suggesting where to look for material. Some subjects suitable for the stage or TV are not suitable for classroom use.

Your first approach to any writing is bound to be subjective. Some authors you will like at once, perhaps for what they say rather than for the way they say it. Your own experience will have much to do with this. You may not know why you like one poem more than another until you have worked on it. For your first assignment it is enough that you are interested in the author's idea. If the poem or story deals with a universal experience, has individuality, and stirs your imagination even after you have finished reading it, you probably have found a good selection.

Libraries and your own books are full of good material. But do not expect to open a book or magazine and find the perfect selection immediately. You will do a great deal of reading before you find something that is just right. Start with the material in this book, or in your literature books, or with something you have read and liked. If you cannot find anything, look through the anthologies listed at the back of this book. Most of them are in your library.

Ask yourself what interests you. Do you like people, places, animals, or are you most interested in ideas? If you like places, do you prefer the city or the country? Do you prefer the part of the world where you spend your vacations, or where you live, or some place you have never been but would like to go? Find something to read that is about a subject you enjoy and get excited over. You will be much more successful in sharing your material with your audience if you like it yourself.

For your first reading choose a short selection to fit the time you need to prepare the assignment. Part of an interpreter's job is to consider the time it takes to perform a selection. If your first assignment is for five minutes, be sure your choice can be delivered within that time limit. Poetry is often brief and will fit these time limits easily. If you want to do a story that is much too long, select only a few paragraphs, or a description of the setting, or a character sketch as your unit for presentation. Be sure it has a beginning and an ending to make it satisfactory by itself.

HOW TO BEGIN THE ANALYSIS

As soon as you have made your selection you will be aware that, as an interpreter, you are relieved of another decision. You do not have to choose or organize the words for expressing the idea. The author has already done that. Your responsibility is to discover and make use of all the details he has given you to work with.

First decide exactly what the poem or story is about. You may find something you like, but do not completely understand. If it appeals to you, it will probably be worth while to work on it until you understand it.

Read it over many times to get the entire effect. Let the material work on you before you begin to work on it. Make your selection several days before your performance so you have plenty of time to think about it.

Sometimes it helps you to know something about the author. Be careful to keep your concentration on the selection itself. Do not attempt to read the author's entire biography and his deathbed message into something he wrote when he was twenty-five. Details of the author's life, his times, and his other writings are useful in helping you discover why he was interested in his subject, his attitude toward it, the mood he wanted to set, and the style in which he expressed it. Use whatever you find relevant to the selection you have chosen. But remember that the poem or story itself is the best place to look for clues about how to read it and what it means.

One of the best ways to begin is to look for clues in the title. Most authors spend a great deal of thought on the title in order to make it suggest without telling the whole story. Frequently the title provides a strong indication of the author's intention. The title of Shakespeare's *Romeo and Juliet* indicates that the play is about two people and not about a family feud, although the feud is necessary to the plot.

The Meaning of Words: Denotation and Connotation

It will be necessary to look up all unfamiliar words in the selection you intend to interpret. Don't be satisfied with an "almost" meaning. The author chose the words he used because they were the exact ones he wanted. He chose them for their *denotation,* which is their exact literal meaning, and for their *connotation,* which is their implied meaning.

Look at the three words *forest, woods,* and *orchard.* You know what each one means. According to the dictionary, they all mean "a piece of ground covered with trees." But there is a difference in connotation. A forest is bigger than a woods, and an orchard consists of fruit trees. Three writers have used these words to create different effects.

> This is the forest primeval.
> The murmuring pines and the hemlocks,...

Henry Wadsworth Longfellow, in *Evangeline,* used *forest* to suggest the huge uncultivated country where his poem was laid.

Edgar Lee Masters writes in "The Lost Orchard":[1]

> A lost orchard is the memory of a friend
> Wronged by life, to death, who lies
> Lifelike, but with unseeing eyes.

An *orchard* has been planted by man, and carries the suggestion that there were once people associated with it.

---

[1]From *Invisible Landscapes,* by Edgar Lee Masters, Macmillan (1935, 1963).

Robert Frost writes, in "Stopping by Woods on a Snowy Evening":[1]

> Whose woods these are I think I know,
> His house is in the village though;
> He will not see me stopping here
> To watch his woods fill up with snow.

He describes a quiet experience, brief and solitary. *Forest* is too big a word. *Orchard* is too carefully spaced and planted. *Woods* is the right word both by denotation and connotation.

As you look up the meaning of unfamiliar words, check the pronunciation carefully. You must not only understand every one but speak it so that the audience understands it too. If you do not already know them, learn to follow the markings for pronunciation in the dictionary.

Investigation of Author's Method of Organization

Now read the whole selection again to be sure you see the relationship between the words and the overall effect. Then consider the way the thoughts and ideas are organized. Apply all you have learned in your speech and English classes to your analysis. The author has already organized the material. But you must know how he has done it.

List each point he makes and see how he makes it. Is the organization a sequence of events in the order of their happening? Or does he use flashbacks to tell you facts you need to know?

---

[1]From COMPLETE POEMS OF ROBERT FROST. Copyright 1916, 1921, 1923, 1928 by Holt, Rinehart and Winston, Inc. Copyright renewed 1944, 1951, © 1956 by Robert Frost. Reprinted by permission of Holt, Rinehart and Winston, Inc.

Be sure that you know the exact denotation, connotation, and pronunciation of every word in the selection you have chosen to interpret.

How does the author move from his introduction to the heart of the matter? Where and how does he make his points? Does he make statements and then use examples to prove his point, or does he use the illustrations first and then draw conclusions? Look carefully for connectives like *however* or *in addition*. In a story, look for indications of the passage of time or change of place.

After the climax is reached, how does the author handle the ending? What kind of conclusion is used? Does it sum up all the facts, or is it a surprise conclusion?

How to Put the Selection Together

Do not be afraid to take good literature apart. This will not spoil it for you. The more you analyze it, the more you will learn to respect the author's skill and the more confidence you will have in it when you present it to your audience. After each step in analysis put the piece back together, so you can see how everything works toward the overall effect.

After you take a careful look at the connotation of all the words the author uses, go back and reconsider the title to find the relationship between the two elements. Then examine the organization and re-read the entire selection to see how the word choice and organization work together. After each step in analysis re-read the selection, keeping in mind that the audience does not want a performance of bits and pieces. They want the whole experience. The whole is more than the sum of its parts. It is the interaction of all the parts working together to create the whole. No detail or aspect can be emphasized for its own sake. Keep your attention on the total effect and use everything you learn in your analysis to achieve it.

Later we will develop all the steps of analysis so you may become aware of every detail and the purpose it serves. It is impossible to communicate something you do not fully know. For your first assignment be content to know what every word means, how the material is organized, the mood to be established, and the overall effect you want your audience to experience.

PREPARING YOUR PERFORMANCE

As an interpreter, you keep the book with you while you re-create the selection. You may hold the book or put it on a stand. It does not matter whether you memorize the material or not. If you want to memorize, the book still serves as a center around which you work and reminds the listeners that you are a middleman between the author and them. Be careful to keep your concentration on communication and not on the act of memorization.

If you do not memorize, you must have mastered the material so well that you need not keep looking at the book for every word. An occasional glance should be enough. You must keep your eyes up and on the audience to hold their attention and gain directness of communication.

If you hold the book, learn to hold it low and casually in one hand so that you do not seem to hide behind it. The book should be tipped away from the audience so the white pages do not flash and distract their attention.

Practice Reading Aloud

You must begin at once to read aloud. The sound of the words as they are used together often helps you capture mood and control pace. Only after you are sure you know what effect the selection is to create do you begin to work *consciously* to perfect your vocal and physical techniques. *These techniques must always serve the material, not vice versa.*

The interpreter communicates with his voice and body, just as any speaker does. His responsibility to be heard and understood is the same as a public speaker's or a discussion leader's. But the interpreter often needs greater vocal control and flexibility than does the public speaker, because he is dealing with a wide variety of styles and of subject matter. He needs more breath control to make the most of some authors' styles.

For instance, the following line does not allow for a full breath within it, and the connotation and close relationship of the words indicate that the pace must be slower than that of ordinary conversation. Try it as a problem in breath control.

> Ceaselessly musing, venturing, throwing,
> seeking the spheres to connect them.

Poetry often requires exceptional vocal control to bring out the sound pattern that is so essential a part of its effect. Suspense in ghost stories, characterization in drama, and conversation between characters in a story all make demands on handling your voice effectively. You can only gain this type of control as a result of many hours of reading aloud.

The particular requirements of these different types of writing will be dealt with separately in their appropriate chapters. Now it is important to remember that your voice must be capable of doing everything that needs to be done to convey the full purpose of the author. But the voice, like other techniques, must never call attention to itself. The interpreter trains his voice to serve the varied demands of the literature he wishes to read.

Voice alone cannot do the whole job. Your listeners see you before they hear you. The way you walk to the platform can set a mood. As an interpreter, you must have a flexible, controlled body so that you look at ease and so no personal mannerisms distract the audience from the experience you are sharing with them. The better your technique, the less obvious it is. They must have their attention free to concentrate on *what* you are saying, not on *how* you are saying it.

Respond with Your Emotions

As you understand your selection more fully, you will find yourself responding not just to the ideas but to the emotions they call up as well. This is an important part of your understanding. As you allow the selection to play on your emotions, you will be aware that there are accompanying muscle responses: a tightening or relaxing of the muscles of the neck, back, hands, and arms, and certainly of the facial muscles. Emotional response and physical response are interrelated.

Don't be afraid of this emotional response. Without it, you cannot do full justice to the writing. If it is an honest response to the literature and a sincere desire to share with your audience, it will never become arty or theatrical. But do not try to assume an emotion you do not feel. Strive always for a genuine emotional response.

After each period of working on the details and techniques, be sure you go back and consider the selection as a unit. Put it back together. It is wise to do this at the beginning and end of every one of your practice sessions.

Finally, give careful thought to the overall impression you wish your audience to receive. It is a good idea to try to put this desired reaction into a single sentence, such as "I want them to be amused" or "I want them to understand the conflict within the character." This will help focus your attention on how the parts are related, and guide you when you prepare your introduction.

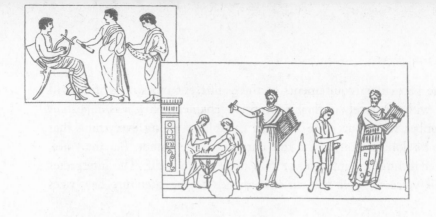

PERFORMANCE

When you perform, remember you have done all the preparation you can. Performance is not preparation. If you have prepared carefully, you know exactly what you want to achieve with your reading. Keep your mind on sharing this experience with your audience and getting the response you know the author wanted. Forget about yourself, except as the middleman between the author and the audience. This is not so easy as it sounds, but it is important. You have worked on your preparation. Now you must trust the author to hold the audience's interest, trust yourself to do justice to his work, and trust the audience to give their attention and interest. The audience want to enjoy a reading. They will follow you if you give them the chance.

Purpose of an Introduction

Use a brief introduction to your reading. It helps you and the audience. Do not tell them what the selection will say. The author will do that. If you present the selection properly, you will not need to explain it. Be as direct as in public speaking. Keep the introduction short and well organized. Introductions often serve as transition from one selection to another, and the tone should always be consistent with the reading that will follow. No humor before tragedy.

If your passage does not come at the beginning, you may need to explain what action has gone before. An introduction should accomplish three things for you and your audience. First, it gives you a chance to size up your audience. It allows you to test your voice so you are sure you are reaching the back row. It permits you to control and relax your body.

At the same time, it allows the audience to look at you. They will spend the first few seconds looking at you anyway. Don't risk wasting

260

the opening while they are satisfying their curiosity. The introduction gives them a focus of attention while they adjust so that they can see you easily.

Second, an introduction helps you organize your thoughts so you are thinking along the lines your selection demands. It does the same thing for your audience. In a room full of people there are as many trains of thought as there are people. Your introduction will channel their attention so they are ready to start with you on the literature.

Third, the introduction helps you arrive at the mood you need for what you are going to do. You may follow a reader whose selection was extremely funny, and you may be reading something that deals with death. Your introduction should lead you and your audience from laughter into the more serious mood necessary for your selection.

Adapting to Your Audience

In order to accomplish these three aims, you must consider your audience. How much do they know about your author or the selection? How much do they need to know to be prepared for it? What will appeal to them and help them into the proper mood? What experiences have they had that will help them identify with the experience the author has recorded? Many suggestions for effective public speaking can be used to make your introduction fit the material *and* the audience.

Your audience sees you as well as hears you. Earlier we mentioned the relation between emotional response and muscle response and suggested that the body plays an important role in communicating the emotional force of the piece. Your posture and carriage help set the mood for your material. The audience will quickly take on your degree of relaxation or tension.

The interplay of emotions and muscles begins with the interpreter's response to the selection. From the first time you read it, through every

261

step in preparation and performance, let yourself get excited about it. If it is worth working on and sharing with an audience, it should move you. This does not mean you indulge in an emotional display. It means you let the author have his way! One of the steps literature takes beyond facts is its appeal to the emotions. Emotional response of whatever degree is reflected in muscle response and bodily action. The audience respond by unconscious imitation of the interpreter's muscle tone so they are physically ready for whatever emotions or changes the piece requires.

Have you ever watched the facial expression and bodily tension of the spectators at a movie or a play? If you want your audience to be relaxed, you must practice controlled relaxation. If you want them to be tense for a climax, you must give the clue.

The interpreter's voice and body work together, under control of an alert and informed mind, to serve the author's purpose. Remember the audience sees you and hears you but what they are interested in are the author's ideas and thoughts and the way he expresses them. It is your job to interpret all these things for the audience so they share the experience with you.

MATERIAL FOR PERFORMANCE

A few selections are offered for you to interpret orally. They are only a sampling of the whole world of material available to you. You will enjoy finding additional selections for yourself from prose and poetry. You will find that sometimes there are two selections that treat the same wish or fear, but differ from each other in the method of handling the subject.

After you decide what to use, review the chapter for help in preparation. Analyze *all* the elements, and then put them together in a unit so you can share both meaning and experience with your audience.

Suggestions for Preparation

1. Read the following selection several times for the total effect.
2. What do you know about the author? Find out something about her life; then you should be able to analyze the selection better because it is autobiographical. Information about Jean Kerr will give you material for an introduction. Look at the selection in light of your information. Does the selection have more meaning? Notice the difference it would

make in your interpretation if you were unaware of the meaning of *rumor*.
3. What does the title suggest? Does it produce a humorous atmosphere in which to begin?
4. Look carefully at the organization of this excerpt from *Please Don't Eat the Daisies*,[1] by Jean Kerr. Put the selection together.

The twins are four now, and for several years we have had galvanized iron fencing lashed onto the outside of their bedroom windows. This gives the front of the house a rather institutional look and contributes to unnecessary rumors about my mental health, but it does keep them off the roof, which is what we had in mind.

For twins, they are very dissimilar. Colin is tall and active and Johnny is short and middle-aged. Johnny doesn't kick off his shoes, he doesn't swallow beer caps or tear pages out of the telephone book. I don't think he ever draws pictures with my best lipstick. In fact, he has none of the charming light-hearted "boy" qualities that precipitate so many scenes of violence in the home. On the other hand, he has a feeling for order and a passion for system that would be trying to a head nurse. If his pajamas are hung on the third hook in the closet instead of on the second hook, it causes him real pain. If one slat in the Venetian blind is tipped in the wrong direction he can't have a moment's peace until somebody fixes it. Indeed, if one of the beans on his plate is slightly longer than the others he can scarcely bear to eat it. It's hard for him to live with the rest of us. And vice versa.

Colin is completely different. He has a lightness of touch and a dexterity that will certainly put him on top of the heap if he ever takes up safe-cracking. Equipped with only a spoon and an old emery board, he can take a door off its hinges in seven minutes and remove all the towel racks from the bathroom in five.

Gilbert is only seventeen months old, and it's too early to tell about him. (As a matter of fact, we can tell, all right, but we're just not ready to face it.) Once upon a time we might have been taken in by smiles and gurgles and round blue eyes, but no more. We know he is just biding his time. Today he can't do much more than eat his shoelaces and suck off an occasional button. Tomorrow, the world.

My real problem with children is that I haven't any imagination. I'm always warning them against the commonplace defections while they are planning the bizarre and unusual. Christopher gets up ahead of the rest of us on Sunday mornings and he has long since been given a list of clear directions: "Don't wake the baby," "Don't go outside in your pajamas," "Don't eat cookies before breakfast." But I never told him, "Don't make flour paste and glue together all the pages of the magazine section of the Sunday TIMES." Now I tell him, of course.

And then last week I had a dinner party and told the twins and Christopher not to go into the living room, not to use the guest towels in the bathroom, and not to leave the bicycles on the front steps. However, I neglected to tell them not to eat the daisies on the dining-room table. This was a serious omission, as I discovered when I came upon my centerpiece—a charming three-point arrangement of green stems.

The thing is, I'm going to a psychiatrist and find out why I have this feeling of persecution . . . this sense of being continually surrounded. . . .

The wish to be somewhere else, to escape from noise and pressures, is a universal one. Here a poet remembers his home in Ireland and only in his closing lines does he hint at where he now lives.

THE LAKE ISLE OF INNISFREE[1]
by William Butler Yeats

I will arise and go now, and go to Innisfree,
And a small cabin build there, of clay and wattles made;
Nine bean rows will I have there, a hive for the honey bee,
And live alone in the bee-loud glade.

And I shall have some peace there, for peace comes dropping slow,
Dropping from the veils of the morning to where the cricket sings;
There midnight's all a glimmer, and noon a purple glow,
And evening full of the linnet's wings.

I will arise and go now, for always night and day
I hear lake water lapping with low sounds by the shore;
While I stand on the roadway, or on the pavements gray,
I hear it in the deep heart's core.

John Masefield expresses almost the same wish, but the life he longs for is different from Yeats' "bee-loud glade."

A WANDERER'S SONG[2]
by John Masefield

A wind's in the heart of me, a fire's in my heels,
I am tired of brick and stone and rumbling wagon-wheels;
I hunger for the sea's edge, the limits of the land,
Where the wild old Atlantic is shouting on the sand.

Oh I'll be going, leaving the noises of the street,
To where a lifting foresail-foot is yanking at the sheet;
To a windy, tossing anchorage where yawls and ketches ride,
Oh I'll be going, going, until I meet the tide.

And first I'll hear the sea-wind, the mewing of the gulls,
The clucking, sucking of the sea about the rusty hulls,
The songs at the capstan in the hooker warping out,
And then the heart of me'll know I'm there or thereabout.

Oh I am tired of brick and stone, the heart of me is sick,
For windy green, unquiet sea, the realm of Moby Dick;
And I'll be going, going, from the roaring of the wheels,
For a wind's in the heart of me, a fire's in my heels.

The following sonnet was written over a century ago but it still has much to say about material gain and about pride and ambition. Compare it with "Four Preludes on Playthings of the Wind," by Carl Sandburg.

OZYMANDIAS
by Percy Bysshe Shelley

I met a traveler from an antique land
Who said: Two vast and trunkless legs of stone
Stand in the desert. Near them, on the sand,
Half sunk, a shattered visage lies, whose frown,
And wrinkled lip, and sneer of cold command,
Tell that its sculptor well those passions read
Which yet survive, stamped on these lifeless things,
The hand that mocked them and the heart that fed;
And on the pedestal these words appear:
"My name is Ozymandias, king of kings:
Look on my works, ye Mighty, and despair!"
Nothing beside remains. Round the decay
Of that colossal wreck, boundless and bare
The lone and level sands stretch far away.

FOUR PRELUDES ON PLAYTHINGS OF THE WIND[1]
by Carl Sandburg

1

The woman named Tomorrow
sits with a hairpin in her teeth
and takes her time
and does her hair the way she wants it
and fastens at last the last braid and coil
and puts the hairpin where it belongs
and turns and drawls: Well, what of it?
My grandmother, Yesterday, is gone.
What of it? Let the dead be dead.

[1]From SMOKE AND STEEL by Carl Sandburg, copyright, 1920, by Harcourt, Brace & World, Inc.; renewed, 1948, by Carl Sandburg. Reprinted by permission of the publishers.

265

2

The doors were cedar
and the panels strips of gold
and the panels read and the girls chanted:
 We are the greatest city,
 and the greatest nation;
 nothing like us ever was.

The doors are twisted on broken hinges,
Sheets of rain swish through on the wind
 where the golden girls ran and the panels read:
 We are the greatest city,
 the greatest nation,
 nothing like us ever was.

3

It has happened before.
Strong men put up a city and got
 a nation together,
And paid singers to sing and women
 to warble: We are the greatest city
 the greatest nation,
 nothing like us ever was.

And while the singers sang
and the strong men listened
and paid the singers well,
 there were rats and lizards who listened
 ...and the only listeners left now
 ...are...the rats...and the lizards.
 And there are black crows
 crying, "Caw, caw,"
 bringing mud and sticks
 building a nest
 over the words carved
 on the doors where the panels were cedar
 and the strips on the panels were gold
 and the golden girls came singing:
  We are the greatest city,
  the greatest nation:
  nothing like us ever was.

The only singers now are crows crying, "Caw, caw,"
And the sheets of rain whine in the wind and doorways.
And the only listeners now are...the rats...and the lizards.

4

The feet of the rats
scribble on the doorsills;
the hieroglyphs of the rat footprints
chatter the pedigrees of the rats
and babble of the blood
and gabble of the breed
of the grandfathers and the great-grandfathers
of the rats.

And the wind shifts
and the dust on a doorsill shifts
and even the writing of the rat footprints
tells us nothing at all
    about the greatest city, the greatest nation
    where the strong men listened
    and the women warbled: Nothing like us ever was.

Some of us spend a good deal of time thinking about what kind of people we are. These three selections are on this theme. Two are humorous, and one is serious. Much of the humor comes from the selection of details and the organization that holds them together.

IF THE TABLES WERE TURNED[1]
by John Mason Brown

    The eight weeks were almost up. The summer camp to which we had sent our boys was just about over. They would soon have taken their farewell dips in the lake. They would soon have gone on their last picnics; ridden around the ring for the last time on a docile pony; scaled their last mountains, woven their last rugs, fashioned their last clay ash trays; and sung their parting songs. Within another two days the train bearing them back from the Adirondacks was due to arrive—at daybreak, of course. In other words, the moment had come when my wife and I were to receive the final reports on our boys.
    . . . We discovered a lot about our boys that neither we nor they had known before, and that we had never even suspected.
    But, on the night I had read these reports, an icicle of fear pierced my heart. My wife and I were just about to go away for a two-week vacation at a summer hotel.
    "Suppose," thought I in the dark stretches before the dawn, "suppose the tables were to be reversed! Suppose—oh perish the possibility!—that, at the end of our stay, the proprietress, a most observant woman, as experienced in the ways of adults as camp counselors are in those of the young, should send

[1]"If the Tables Were Turned" by John Mason Brown from *Morning Faces*, published in 1949 by McGraw-Hill Book Company. Reprinted by permission of the author.

our boys a report of similar frankness on our behavior during out visit!"

l had to switch on the light to rid myself of the nightmare. Because I can see my own report now. In fact, I haven't slept well since first I became haunted by the idea of how it would read.

"Although your father has shown decided growth in some areas since last summer, he still needs to develop a group consciousness. He does not seem to want to play with the other guests. He does not quite enter into the spirit of the lounge, for example. He is particularly reluctant in making friends with the girls in the older group, and avoids bridge, mahjong, and even solitaire, with undisguised stubbornness.

"...He is not as prompt at table as he might be. Instead of joining the circle at the door before lunch or dinner, he often comes in late, apparently having been some place else first. When he is reminded that the doors close at two and seven, because the waitresses have other dates, his reaction is not as sympathetic as might be hoped.

"...I am sorry to report that his is not a tidy duffel bag and that he does not keep his alcove as neat as he should. The presence of the clothes closet has been pointed out to him daily. Even so he shows no concentration in remembering either its whereabouts or its uses."

...In some such fashion, my conscience warned me, the proprietress of our summer hotel would have to report on me to my young, if she undertook the counselor's role. I was alarmed, as I have confessed, for several sleepless nights by the dread that such a report might come. Then a great reassuring calm possessed me. I suddenly remembered that the proprietress had never answered any of the letters I had sent her during the three months before our visit. Her disinclination to writing was my only safeguard.

We see very clearly what Ogden Nash envies in his fellow men. Enjoy the deliberate reaching for rhymes which adds to the humor.

A STITCH TOO LATE IS MY FATE[1]
by Ogden Nash

There are some people of whom I would certainly like to be one,
Who are the people who get things done.
They never forget to send their evening shirts to the laundry and then when
      they need them can't find anything but a lot of shirts without any
      starch,
And they always file their income tax return by the fourteenth of March.
They balance their checkbooks every month and their figures always agree
      with the bank's,
And they are prompt in writing letters of condolence or thanks.
They never leave anything to chance,
But always make reservations in advance.

---

[1]From VERSES FROM 1929 ON by Ogden Nash, by permission of Little, Brown and Co. Copyright 1936 by Ogden Nash.

When they get out of bed they never neglect to don slippers so they never pick up athlete's foot or a cold or a splinter,

And they hang their clothes up on hangers every night and put their winter clothes away every summer and their summer clothes away every winter.

Before spending any money they insist on getting an estimate or a sample,

And if they lose anything from a shoelace to a diamond ring it is covered by insurance more than ample.

They have budgets and what is more they live inside of them,

Even though it means eating things made by recipes clipped from the Sunday paper that you'd think they would have died of them.

They serve on committees

And improve their cities.

They are modern knight errants

Who remember their godchildren's birthdays and the anniversaries of their godchildren's parents,

And in cold weather they remember the birds and supply them with sunflower seed and suet,

And whatever they decide to do, whether it's to save twenty-five per cent of their salary or learn Italian or write a musical comedy or touch their toes a hundred times every morning before breakfast, why they go ahead and do it.

People who get things done lead contented lives, or at least I guess so,

And I certainly wish that either I were more like them or they were less so.

Only one person speaks in this poem of great loneliness . . . or perhaps they are the unspoken thoughts that she cannot bring herself to share. Remember, the title tells us it is an *effort* at speech.

EFFORT AT SPEECH BETWEEN TWO PEOPLE[1]
by Muriel Rukeyser

Speak to me. Take my hand. What are you now?
I will tell you all. I will conceal nothing.
When I was three, a little child read a story about
a rabbit who died, in the story, and I crawled
under a chair: a pink rabbit: It was my birthday,
and a candle burnt a sore spot on my finger, and I
was told to be happy.

Oh, grow to know me. I am not happy. I will be open:
Now I am thinking of white sails against a sky like
music, like glad horns blowing, and birds tilting,
and an arm about me. There was one I loved, who
wanted to live, sailing.

Speak to me. Take my hand. What are you now?
When I was nine, I was fruitily sentimental,
fluid: and my widowed aunt played Chopin,
and I bent my head on the painted woodwork, and wept.
I want now to be close to you. I would
link the minutes of my days close, somehow, to your days.

I am not happy. I will be open.
I have liked lamps in evening corners, and quiet poems.
There has been fear in my life. Sometimes I speculate
on what a tragedy his life was, really.

Take my hand. Fist my mind in your hand. What are you now?
When I was fourteen, I had dreams of suicide,
and I stood at a steep window, at sunset, hoping
toward death: If the light had not melted clouds
and plains to beauty, if light had not transformed
that day, I would have leapt.
I am unhappy. I am lonely. Speak to me.

I will be open. I think he never loved me:
he loved the bright beaches, the little lips of foam
that ride small waves, he loved the veer of gulls:
he said with a gay mouth: I love you. Grow to know me.

What are you now? If we could touch one another,
if these our separate entities could come to grips,
clenched like a Chinese puzzle... yesterday
I stood in a crowded street that was live with people,
and no one spoke a word, and the morning shone.
Everyone silent, moving.... Take my hand. Speak to me.

Anyone who knows the satisfaction of planting seeds and seeing them grow will understand this poet's attitude toward the wheat fields of Kansas.

THE SEED IN A MAN'S HAND[1]
by Geraldine Hammond

The seed in a man's hand—
    like water—like sand—like gold.
Life, one seed,
    a fact so simple that it is a dream,
And a dream so real that it is all truth.

For this seed alone,
    here in a man's hand,
Is the miracle of sun,
    of wide days,
And the turning earth.

Drop the seed, fling and scatter.
Space in rows precisely
    by machines man builds
To stretch his faith wide on the fields.
Now tumble earth and gentle it
    while sun lies golden on the trees
And strikes the river bright below,
And birds sing "Amen" to a planter's faith.

---

[1]Reprinted by permission of the author.

At this point you have probably de-cided that if you must examine every word in a reading you are to communi-cate, you had better limit yourself to a simple story. You'll find after the first few times the process becomes easier, and you have a sense of real satisfaction and confidence because you know ex-actly how it is constructed.

This method of analysis is basic for all types of literature. Now we will con-sider the special problems found in a narrative.

A narrative is a story. It tells what happens to whom, and how, why, when, and where. A narrative may be either prose or poetry.

PLOT

WHAT happens and HOW it happens provides the plot. It is made of a series

INTERPRETATION OF NARRATIVES

of events. Sometimes these events come about because of outside forces. This is true of "The Prairie." Sometimes they are the result of the kind of person involved as in ... *And Now Miguel.* You begin to work on a story by reading it through and asking "What happened to whom?"

Read the selections at the end of the chapter, then ask, "How did it happen in this particular way?" You will find the answers involve you in consideration of the setting and the characters. But first study the method of organization the author has used to introduce his story, achieve a climax, and conclude.

Organization

An author may organize his plot in many different ways. The paragraph which the author uses to open "The Prairie," a short story by Walter J. Muilenburg, does not mention the characters, but gives a description of the land. The author then introduces his characters with a flashback. Only after he has so "set the stage" does he start his narration.

The section from "The Hill Wife," a poem by Robert Frost, focuses immediately on the character and her relation to the setting. Then the poet proceeds to tell his story in direct chronological order.

The man in "Lux et Veritas," by Morton White, explains what reminded him of the story and then uses the flashback.

In "The Creation," by James Weldon Johnson, the various steps

273

coincide with the Biblical account. The poet gives very clear clues of plot progression by his repeated use of *then*.

There are many ways to organize the progress of a story because a writer may make his clocks and calendars go backward or forward or at any speed that suits his purpose.

Whatever organization the author uses, there will be minor events or small details as the story moves along that become important to the outcome. These are called *key situations* or *key speeches*. They are signposts that keep the story moving along the road it takes. They give us the *how* of the plot.

Climaxes, Key Situations, Speeches, and Sentences

Key situations, key speeches, and sentences are more numerous and more important in long narratives. But even in short selections they keep the story moving. Look for examples in the cutting from . . . *And Now Miguel.* The first key is when we learn that all the hired hands have gone to round up the sheep and Miguel is asked to do an important job he has never done before. If he had done it before, he would not have made a mistake. His uncle throws up the fleeces until the sack is full and Miguel tries to stamp them down with a result that surprises him. Then they discover that Miguel is missing. His father rescues him and drops him ignominiously in the dust for the climax. It could not have turned out this way without the clues.

A climax is the culmination of a series of events. It may be a point of emotional pitch, the outcome of character development, or as in . . . *And Now Miguel,* the inevitable result of circumstances or actions. In "The Hill Wife" the climax builds steadily to the moment when she "ran and hid in the fern." In "The Creation" it begins with God's decision to create a man and reaches its high point when He blows "the breath of life." The section that follows is the conclusion in which the results are clarified.

The title often gives you an important clue to the organization and location of the climaxes. "Lux et Veritas"[1] is the motto on the university seal and suggests the emotional climax comes in response to "belonging," although the action climax comes when the race is won.

There may be several climaxes in a selection, with one more intense

---

[1]Light and Truth, Yale University.

Here, and on following pages, Charles Laughton interprets a narrative. Note the variety he achieves with facial expression and gesture.

than the others. This is the *major climax.* The others are *minor climaxes.* In analyzing the organization of the plot, the interpreter must pay close attention to all key situations and key speeches so that his audience can follow the plot as it evolves and be ready to respond to major and minor climaxes. He must know where these climaxes are, and what purpose each serves, so he can use his vocal and physical techniques in performance to achieve the proper effect for the audience.

POINT OF VIEW

In a narrative there is a narrator who tells the story. The position the narrator takes in revealing plot and character is called *point of view.*

The point of view may be objective and the narrator merely reporting events as Frost does in "The Hill Wife." Or the narrator may be subjective and reveal things that are going on in the minds of the characters. Or perhaps he tells things that happen that the characters themselves could not possibly know. Or again, he may be one of the characters involved in the plot, as in the excerpt from ... *And Now Miguel*. In this case you need to suggest his age, sex, and mental state as he tells the story.

STYLE

As you look at these differences in point of view you will be aware that the selections differ also in style. *Style* is a term used to describe an individual way of writing. An author's style helps the interpreter discover mood and attitude in a reading and gives important clues for performance. Style includes the choice of words an author uses, the way he puts them together, and the length and grammatical complexity of paragraphs. Part of the humor in Saroyan's writing comes from the matter-of-fact way in which he tells perfectly ridiculous incidents. This provides the interpreter with an important guide. He, too, "plays it straight" as if it were the most ordinary kind of situation. The simple sentences and short paragraphs in ... *And Now Miguel* are right for the character telling the story, as is the less personal style of the outside narrator in "The Prairie." Notice how the short sentences give a feeling of speed to the action of "Lux et Veritas." The style of "The Creation" is particularly interesting when the poet uses a combination of Biblical and folk language. Contrast for example the line

> And God walked, and where he trod

with the closing line of the same stanza

> And bulged the mountains up.

Style can indicate the education, background, degree of emotional tension, and general attitude of the characters as well as that of the author. It helps produce a rhythm in the stress and flow of thought. Style is important in giving clues to many details in a story.

CHARACTERS

When something happens, it must happen to someone or something, so there are characters in every story. Much of the interest centers around the characters, and the interpreter must know everything there is to know about the people in the story in order to present them clearly to his audience.

There are two sides to every character, the outside and the inside, and one affects and influences the other. The outside is the physical aspect of the person. It includes age, sex, and any physical characteristics that may affect his attitudes and behavior.

The inside of a character is more complex. It includes attitudes and values that the person holds, emotional responses, psychological factors, and the state of tension or relaxation in which we find him.

How Character Is Revealed

Character is revealed in many ways and often we have to add all the clues in description, dialogue, and style to discover the complete character. The style that a character uses to speak and think indicates a great deal about him. The choice of words indicates attitudes and background. The sentence length and continuity of thought show the emotional state. You can check this by recalling your own speech when you are excited and contrast it with the meandering manner of a daydream.

The narrator often tells the reader what he wants him to know. This method is used in "The Prairie." Emily Dickinson, in her poem, gives us a picture of a situation. Sometimes there are stage directions telling us how a thing was done. You find these all through "Lux et Veritas."

277

The title sometimes helps with character clues. Another important element is what the character says about himself, others, and the setting, and we learn a great deal from what other characters say about him. If the interpreter needs to cut some of the character description or stage directions in order to stay within his time limit, he must remember everything so he can properly suggest the character to his listeners.

DIRECT DISCOURSE

Direct discourse is the exact quotation of a character's words. It is enclosed in quotation marks. Direct discourse demands sharp physical and mental focus. A speech is being said directly to someone. When a character speaks directly to someone else, his mind and usually his eyes go directly to that person.

The French have a way of indicating directness that is useful for an interpreter to remember. When they mean think of someone, they use the phrase *penser à* meaning "think to" or "think at." When they use *penser de,* "think of," they mean they have an opinion about something. If the interpreter remembers to "think to" his listeners, he will have no trouble with directness. When you are speaking to someone, the focus of your mind and eyes increases with the force of your thought.

To illustrate this, let's try an exercise in degrees of directness. A person has something that belongs to you that you value highly. He is not handling it carefully, and you are concerned about getting it back in good condition. You watch him for a moment and then think: *I wish he would give it back to me.*

Then—*In a minute I'm going to ask him to give it back to me.*

Soon you speak directly to him. "May I have it back now?"

He pays no attention to you, so you speak more firmly: "Please, give it to me."

If it is quite clear that he is in no hurry, you may lose patience and say, "Give it to me."

Notice how your mind and eyes focus more sharply on the person to whom you are speaking as you become more direct.

Direct discourse is a speech said directly to someone. The audience must know without question who is speaking. They must be able to identify the character at once so they don't misunderstand what he says. They must know what the character is thinking and feeling about what he says.

278

Handling Direct Discourse

When characters in a story are having a conversation, the interpreter suggests this directness. First, he assumes the degree of mental directness appropriate for the speech. Then, he indicates by direct eye focus that someone else is present. He places the one being addressed, at a convenient spot on the back wall very slightly above the heads of his audience. This enables him to give the character physical and mental directness.

The insertion of direct discourse in a story requires the interpreter to be able instantly to adjust his mental and emotional state, his vocal characteristics, and his bodily tension to whichever character is speaking.

Use of the Body in Direct Discourse

Facial expression will reflect what the character is thinking and feeling as the interpreter speaks the lines. Gestures are appropriate and helpful in direct discourse. But the gesture must suit the character and the situation. All these physical aspects are the result of what is going on inside the character. They must never be put on from the outside. They must always stem from the demands of the selection and reflect what is going on in the mind and body of the character speaking. It is the inside of the character that motivates the outside. The interpreter takes his clue from this fact and responds inside himself before he tries to assume any exterior manifestations of emotion. During performance he concentrates on sharing the experience with his audience—not on his bodily actions.

Use of Voice in Direct Discourse

Complete response to the character in the situation will be reflected in vocal quality and pace. Point of view and the style in which the character speaks will help you. Look at the difference between the style of the coach and the freshman in "Lux et Veritas." Consider the total character of Richard Cory before deciding how to read his "Good morning." The authors have given you many clues in the style of the speeches.

The exterior characteristics of age, sex, and physical condition will be given more specific attention in the next chapter. Now it is enough to concentrate on interior characteristics. Remember you are only *suggesting* the exterior characteristics. The individual differences within the broad classifications of age, sex, and condition are much more important.

If you have your characters identified in the mind of your audience, you can cut the "he saids" and "she saids." Just be sure each character is identified by name in his first speech. If the author has given stage directions, such as "he said gently" or "she shouted," you may cut them and simply follow them in your manner of delivery.

INDIRECT DISCOURSE

Indirect discourse is reported conversation, and is not enclosed in quotation marks. It includes thoughts not spoken aloud by the characters. Such phrases as "he hoped that," "I was afraid that," "we wanted to say that," and "you prayed that it would not happen" are indirect discourse. The interpreter needs to pay close attention to indirect discourse, because it reveals the characters' mental and emotional states.

In indirect discourse the interpreter uses whatever character and emotional and mental state are indicated, so his audience will know who the character is, what kind of person he is, and what his attitude and degree of tension are at the moment.

280

All of these matters are closely related to the why of the plot. Why the events take place as they do is called motivation. In most of our selections the motivation is clear as soon as we understand the characters involved. Miguel wants to be grown up. The motivation in "The Prairie" is first a desire for a change and later the wish to defeat the prairie.

Often motivation is subtly revealed as the characters develop. The interpreter must discover the *why* of the characters' responses and actions if he is to make the plot believable. What is perfectly acceptable for one character is not believable in another.

CUTTING

In cutting a story, look first for the major climax. You may wish to use only the major climax for your reading. Or you may choose a unit with a minor climax. In either case, find the key situations that explain the climax and make it believable. Then evaluate the descriptions to see which you can eliminate or condense without destroying the effect. You may

281

need to tell the audience some of the key situations that lead up to your selection. You will find that a few characters can sometimes be eliminated.

When you decide what to cut in the story, if the book is yours, mark the omissions clearly so you can easily follow them. Mark in pencil —never in ink—because you may later change your mind. Never put marks in a book that doesn't belong to you. The next person using the book may not want to use your cutting. If it is a library book, put small pieces of blank paper fastened with paper clips over the places you want to cut.

If you skip several pages, fasten them together with a paper clip so they all turn at once. Transitions may be typed on pieces of paper and clipped to the pages where you need them. No one can tell you what to cut and what to leave in. You will find more satisfaction in making your own cutting and using everything you feel must be included to preserve the author's intention.

People always love a good storyteller. You will find gratification in learning to tell stories so that what happens to whom, how, where, when, and why is absorbing to your listeners.

SETTING

Usually a narrative includes where and when the action takes place. The *where* and *when* together provide the *setting*. The specific place and time are sometimes relatively unimportant. But the period of history often makes the plot possible. And the *where* may also be important.

The setting is given by means of description. Descriptions are important. Some immature readers feel they can all be skipped because they think they don't have much to do with what happens. Do not underestimate the author. If description is there, it is there for a reason.

A common fault with untrained readers is to decrease their mental alertness and concentration when they come to a descriptive passage. The descriptions should be presented to the audience with the same attention that is used in other parts of the story. The audience must know where and when the events take place. Moreover, a description helps you set the mood. Look at all descriptions to see what purpose they serve. Then use them as important parts of the whole.

You may wish to cut some descriptions to stay within your time limit, but you must know what they contribute to the story before you do so. You may be able to condense somewhat and perhaps include important information in your introduction. If the time or place, or any detail of either, is significant in the selection you have made, you must tell your audience about it so they will find the plot believable.

MATERIAL FOR PERFORMANCE

ONE OF OUR FUTURE POETS, YOU MIGHT SAY[1]
by William Saroyan

When I was the fourteenth brightest pupil in the class of fifteen third-graders at Emerson School, the Board of Education took a day off one day to think things over.

This was years ago.

I was eight going on nine or at the most nine going on ten, and good-natured.

[1]Abridged from MY NAME IS ARAM, copyright, 1937, 1938, 1939, 1940, by William Saroyan. Reprinted by permission of Harcourt, Brace & World, Inc.

In those days the average Board of Education didn't make a fuss over the children of a small town and if some of the children seemed to be doltish, the average Board of Education assumed this was natural and let it go at that.

Certain Presbyterian ministers, however, sometimes looked into a sea of young faces and said: You are the future leaders of America, the future captains of industry, the future statesmen, and, I might say, the future poets. This sort of talk always pleased me because I liked to imagine what sort of future captains of industry pals of mine like Jimmy Volta and Frankie Sousa were going to make.

I knew these boys.

They were great baseball players, but by nature idiots, . . . healthy, strong, and spirited . . .

Ordinarily, however, our Board of Education had no such glorious faith as this in the young hoodlums it was trying to teach to read and write.

Nevertheless, one day our Board of Education took a day off to think things over quietly and after seven hours of steady thinking decided to put every public school pupil through a thorough physical examination to solve, if possible, the mystery of health in the young inhabitants of the slums.

According to documentary proof, published and tabulated, all the inhabitants of my neighborhood should have had badly shaped heads, sunken chests, faulty bone structure, hollow voices, no energy, distemper, and six or seven other minor organic defects.

According to the evidence before each public school teacher, however, these ruffians from the slums had well-shaped heads, sound chests, handsome figures, loud voices, too much energy, and a continuous compulsion to behave mischievously.

Something was wrong somewhere.

Our Board of Education decided to try to find out what.

They *did* find out.

They found out that the published and tabulated documentary proof was wrong.

It was at this time that I first learned with joy and fury that I was a poet. I remember being in the Civic Auditorium of my home town at high noon with six hundred other future statesmen, and I remember hearing my name sung out by old Miss Ogilvie in a clear hysterical soprano.

The time had arrived for me to climb the seventeen steps to the stage, walk to the center of the stage, strip to the waist, inhale, exhale, and be measured all over.

There was a moment of confusion and indecision, followed quickly by a superhuman impulse to behave with style, which I did, to the horror and bewilderment of the whole Board of Education, three elderly doctors, a half-dozen registered nurses, and six hundred future captains of industry.

Instead of climbing the seventeen steps to the stage, I *leaped*.

I remember old Miss Ogilvie turning to Mr. Rickenbacker, Superintendent of Public Schools, and whispering fearfully: This is Garoghlanian—one of our future poets, I might say.

Mr. Rickenbacker took one quick look at me and said: Oh, I see. Who's he sore at?

284

Society, old Miss Ogilvie said.

Oh, I see, Mr. Rickenbacker said. So am I, but I can't jump like that. Let's say no more about it.

I flung off my shirt and stood stripped to the waist, a good deal of hair bristling on my chest.

You see? Miss Ogilvie said. A writer.

Inhale, Mr. Rickenbacker said.

For how long? I asked.

As long as possible, Mr. Rickenbacker said.

I began to inhale. Four minutes later I was still doing so. Naturally, the examining staff was a little amazed. They called a speedy meeting while I continued to inhale. After two minutes of heated debate the staff decided to ask me to stop inhaling. Miss Ogilvie explained that unless they *asked* me to stop I would be apt to go on inhaling all afternoon.

That will be enough for the present, Mr. Rickenbacker said.

Already? I said. I'm not even started.

Now exhale, he said.

For how long? I said.

Oh, my! Mr. Rickenbacker said.

You'd better tell him, Miss Ogilvie said. Otherwise he'll exhale all afternoon.

Three or four minutes, Mr. Rickenbacker said.

I exhaled four minutes and then was asked to put on my shirt and go away.

How are things? I asked the staff. Am I in pretty good shape?

Let's say no more about it, Mr. Rickenbacker said. Please go away.

The following year our Board of Education decided to give no more physical examinations. The examinations went along all right as far as future captains of industry were concerned, and future statesmen, but when it came to future poets the examinations ran helter-skelter and amuck, and nobody knew what to do or think.

Here is a story of two lives told entirely by description. It is not a happy story. Basically it is the story of man's conflict with nature. The setting is important as the story builds to its climax and conclusion.

THE PRAIRIE[1]
by Walter J. Muilenburg

The prairie lay dreaming in the warmth of early summer. Level, monotonous, it stretched away until its green became drab in the far distance. It was alive, and yet lifeless; full of color, yet colorless; intangible mystery lurked in its contrast, a mystery of light and shadow and tints. Strange, dreaming, lovely, it lay beneath the intense blue sky. Underfoot the ground was bright with young grass and flowers, through which the light wind rippled

---

[1]By Walter J. Muilenburg from *The Midland*, copyright 1917 by Walter J. Muilenburg.

soundlessly. It was only when earth and sky met and their colors merged that one caught the hint of the wild power of the prairie, its sweep, its changelessness, its passive cruelty and callousness.

But John Barrett and his wife, newly-married and filled with the sense of dominant power which animate life feels over inanimate life, had thrown the challenge to the prairie. Even now, on that summer morning, their sod house stood out bravely in the silent sunshine. About it lay a wide circle of vivid green, half-grown crops of grain which were to supply the necessities of their pioneer life.

They had come from the East. The village where they were born had early labelled Barrett a "ne'er-do-well" and when he married Lizzie Delton it had passed final and irrevocable judgment on both. He was shiftless, a rolling stone, while she—oh, she was only one of the Deltons—a colorless, undersized woman with lackluster eyes.

After his sudden marriage, Barrett was seized again with the desire of change. His wife agreed, unquestioning, devoted as a faithful dog. Married life seemed stimulating to Barrett. They would emigrate into the prairie and win an easy life from the unplowed soil....

A week later they were on the way in an old, canvas-covered wagon. As they went out of civilization, the woman's face changed; a hint of color came into her cheeks and an occasional smile touched her face with a twisted beauty.

They reached the prairie in early spring. It invited them in its soft, wandering colors. The woman, as she breathed the mellow air, heavy with the odor of earth, grew more alive; sometimes she laughed at her husband's dry humor. The prairie lay before them, unscarred by trails, and they rambled leisurely over the soft grass, finding a pleasant excitement in the fact that their home might be just past the next swell of ground. To wander about the prairie was mysterious, romantic. The days were dreamily warm, the sky deep-blue, the meadow lark's song quivered continually; and beyond this was the lure of the tinted horizon, most mysterious when night came on. It came slowly always; the air dimmed and the immensity of the earth gained emphasis by sweeping breeze and twinkling vastness of the dark sky.

Late one afternoon they came to a small river. After camping there, they decided to make a home on its banks. A few days' hard work, the woman helping, and the sod house was complete. Next, they turned up the black prairie soil and sowed their grain. Everything promised success. Some impulse of life seemed to come to them from the depths of the earth. It was a paradise for the man and the woman....

Then over the prairie two months passed. The softness of spring widened into the fiercer heat of summer. Not a drop of rain had fallen for two weeks; the man's face shadowed as he watched his crops. And slowly the heat became more intense. The man began to curse under his breath. Then, as the heat of midsummer grew, the iron soul of the prairie bared itself to them. Grim, silent, it seemed waiting, with torturing patience, to achieve some masterstroke of tragedy. The man, longing for rain to save his crops, became morose with helpless anger. The crops withered slowly, drooping for the water which the soil could not give. Beauty brooded over the prairie. The sky was blue in the early morning, white at noon, and brilliant at sunset. But no clouds.

As time passed, a change came in the man and woman. They began to give themselves up to sudden, heavy silences, their talk was listless: when they smiled there was no spontaneity. The grip of the prairie seemed to close upon their souls. During the day, the man worked with sullen determination. The woman remained indoors, hands often idle, eyes vacantly on the horizon. In the evening, and after supper, they sat in front of the shack, facing the West, and watched the sun go down under the level line at the end of the world. It was then that the menace of the prairie stood out strongest. The last light was never a benediction, but always something ominous. Its beauty was savage, overpowering. There was nothing to hide the fierce, red light. The earth stretched, level and unmarked except for a single, twisted scrub oak by the dry creek bed—an empty horror of unobstructed space that grew indistinct in the red dimness of approaching darkness....

The hot, dry weather continued. The sky was always bright. The crops lay dead on the fevered soil. All animal life, too, had vanished from the plains. One morning, the woman saw a crow flapping heavily toward the shack. She watched in hope to see the bird alight—there had been so many birds in the spring—but it wavered only a moment above her and then swept its low flight on toward the East. She looked at the gray universe about her, and her face, also gray, hardened into quivering defiance. It seemed as if eternity lay about them; the past was dead, the future did not exist. They were living in an eternal present, a void that would endure forever. And always the heat, the quivering heat, and the gray menace of the horizon.

Summer merged into early autumn. The nights grew chilly, though the noon sun still burned. All the green life of the spring was yellow and dry as tinder. From sun-rising to sun-setting, the man and the woman hardly spoke. Helpless in the midst of a power before which their strength was nothing, they waited. Yet, dulled as they were, body and soul, they defied the prairie, passive, yet unconquered....

One night, as they sat at supper, the man burst out with the bitterness of his heart. The woman listened, immovable. Her stolid silence and her brooding calmness filled him with sudden rage and he swore at her. His fingers gripped the edge of the table as though to keep him from striking her. She said nothing, but the wild anger of something at bay flashed in her eyes. When the tension relaxed, both felt a horror of the primitive animal each had seen in the other.

Next morning, as the man stood in the doorway, he noticed a haze at the north. Then he sniffed at the sharp morning air. Turning, he spoke to his wife and went out. A little later, the horses were plowing furrows around the little shack. Toward the north, a deeper haze was growing. The horizon had a white, transparent color, as though a film of cloud were being drawn across the blue. The cloud-film grew rapidly. Then came the faint odor of smoke. The woman stopped a cry in her throat and stood, white-faced, hair awry in the morning wind. Had they not suffered enough? Then she started after her husband. He did not stop plowing or even look up at her.

The cloud in the north thickened. It became veined with streaks of dull

287

red. As it climbed in the sky, its outline broke into ragged, grotesque peaks, standing black and tempestuous against the pale blue sky. Then the wind strengthened and the acrid heat swept toward them....

From the north came a vibrating hum; the man looked up. Then his hands clenched slowly. Sweeping toward them, a distant wall of fire shone red through the growing smoke, its flames darting in pointed, wavering spires. It was moving with incredible swiftness toward the shack.

Then the fire caught them. Burning bits of grass, carried over the plowed strip, started small fires in the thatch roof of the shack. The two fought the flames with wet sacks, their faces showing hard and wild through the eddies of smoke. The thin, blank face of the woman was transformed; the cheeks, drawn into taut lines, were livid with hate.

Several times flames caught the shack, but each time they were beaten out. The barn caught and the man unloosed the horses. A shrill scream as they bolted directly into the wall of fire, and then the flames hid them. There, with the fire roaring above, in the vortex of a blind, insensate force, the naked force of the prairie, they still fought, beating out the flames upon the shack. The woman fell several times. At last she lay quiet on the hot ground, and the man fought the fire alone. It seemed to eat into his lungs, his head roared with it. Then he, too, gave up. He drew the woman close to him and putting a wet sack over her face, he crouched close to the ground, breathing in big, rasping gasps.

It seemed an eternity. When it was over, the man got up. Far to the south the fire still retreated. All around lay the blackened face of the prairie, with the mockery of the blue sky crouching above. The man stopped to uncover the face of his wife. She lay unconscious. He carried her into the shack. When she opened her eyes, they were so bright and hard that the man shrank from them.

But, as he saw the thin, white cheeks and the swollen veins on her forehead, he knew that the remnant of life would not last long. And for this he was glad. A few hours later, with the fierce heat of noon beating in at the door, she died. She had not the harsh strength to live. Life had not played fair with her. Dry-eyed and staring, the man sat beside the bed. All that afternoon he sat there. His face had fallen into long, hard lines, and was grim yet with defiance. Outside, the prairie smoked in the hazy afternoon.

That night, as the sun painted the west, he buried her. Then, staring across the blackened land, he watched the dimming sky. The glow grew fainter in the west. The angry red burned down to softer orange and yellow. Gray light closed over it. The man stood there a long time, watching the night deepen, the only living creature in all the blackened waste.

The next morning was gray with rain. The sky hovered near the earth and bound it in. The man came out of the shack with a bundle on his shoulders. Head bent, eyes to the ground, he walked away into the west, into the mysterious part of the horizon. His figure became vague as the mists hemmed him in. The rain ceased for a moment. In the distance his figure stood black against the bank of fog on the horizon. Then the rain commenced again and he was lost behind the gray clouds. All about, the prairie stretched away—cold, dreary, lifeless.

288

This poem also tells the story of a life by description until the last line climax. The point of view, however, is that of the "people on the pavement" rather than of an outside narrator.

RICHARD CORY

by Edwin Arlington Robinson

> Whenever Richard Cory went down town,
>   We people on the pavement looked at him:
> He was a gentleman from sole to crown,
>   Clean favored, and imperially slim.
>
> And he was always quietly arrayed,
>   And he was always human when he talked;
> But still he fluttered pulses when he said,
>   "Good morning," and he glittered when he walked.
>
> And he was rich—yes, richer than a king,
>   And admirably schooled in every grace:
> In fine, we thought that he was everything
>   To make us wish that we were in his place.
>
> So on we worked, and waited for the light,
>   And went without the meat, and cursed the bread;
> And Richard Cory, one calm summer night,
>   Went home and put a bullet through his head.

Although this poem is called "A Negro sermon" you will notice that it is *not* done in dialect. The mixture of folk simplicity and Biblical style is particularly effective, as was mentioned within the chapter. Each stanza has its own minor climax.

THE CREATION[1] (A NEGRO SERMON)
by James Weldon Johnson

And God stepped out on space,
And he looked around and said:
I'm lonely—
I'll make me a world.

And far as the eye of God could see
Darkness covered everything,
Blacker than a hundred midnights
Down in a cypress swamp.
Then God smiled,
And the light broke,
And the darkness rolled up on one side,
And the light stood shining on the other,
And God said: That's good!

Then God reached out and took the light in his hands
And God rolled the light around in his hands
Until he made the sun;
And he set that sun a-blazing in the heavens.
And the light was left from making the sun
God gathered it up in a shining ball
And flung it against the darkness,
Spangling the night with the moon and stars.
Then down between
The darkness and the light
He hurled the world;
And God said: That's good!

Then God himself stepped down—
And the sun was on his right hand,
And the moon was on his left;
The stars were clustered about his head,
And the earth was under his feet.
And God walked, and where he trod
His footsteps hollowed the valleys out
And bulged the mountains up.

Then he stopped and looked and saw
That the earth was hot and barren.
So God stepped over to the edge of the world
And he spat out the seven seas—
He batted his eyes, and the lightnings flashed—
He clapped his hands, and the thunders rolled—
And the waters above the earth came down,
The cooling waters came down.

Then the green grass sprouted,
And the little red flowers blossomed,
The pine-tree pointed his finger to the sky,
And the oak spread out his arms,
The lakes cuddled down in the hollows of the ground,
And the rivers ran down to the sea;
And God smiled again,
And the rainbow appeared,
And curled itself around his shoulder.

Then God raised his arm and he waved his hand
Over the sea and over the land,
And he said: Bring forth! Bring forth!
And quicker than God could drop his hand,
Fishes and fowls
And beasts and birds
Swam the rivers and the seas,
Roamed the forests and the woods,
And split the air with their wings.
And God said: That's good!

Then God walked around,
And God looked around
On all that he had made.
He looked at his sun,
And he looked at his moon,
And he looked at his little stars;
He looked on his world
With all its living things,
And God said: I'm lonely still.

Then God sat down—
On the side of a hill where he could think;
By a deep, wide river he sat down;
With his head in his hands,
God thought and thought,
Till he thought: I'll make me a man!

Up from the bed of the river
God scooped the clay;
And by the bank of the river
He kneeled him down;
And there the great God Almighty
Who lit the sun and fixed it in the sky,
Who flung the stars to the most far corner of the night,
Who rounded the earth in the middle of his hand;
This Great God,
Like a mammy bending over her baby,
Kneeled down in the dust
Toiling over a lump of clay
Till he shaped it in his own image;
Then into it he blew the breath of life,
And man became a living soul.
Amen. Amen.

This section from a full length book has a kind of warm humor. Its climax is a gentle one which depends for its effectiveness on full comprehension of the young boy who is too old to cry and too young to be able to laugh at the situation into which he got himself.

...AND NOW MIGUEL[1]
by Joseph Krumgold

Just to look at, the morning was all right. Or even, to tell the truth, it was a nice morning. The sun was shining and the shadows were long and heavy when we came out of the house. The sky was blue and big like there was more of it around than usual, more clear sky thin as deep water all around. Over the mountains there was clouds looking like a flock of clouds grazing up there, big and little ones. And over the house, there was a couple of little ones, tramp clouds, like orphans. The Sangre de Cristo,[2] they looked closer than I ever saw them before. Or maybe that was just because of the way I felt.

I felt good that morning when we all went out to finish the shearing. I could still almost taste last night's supper in my mouth, the food and the jokes and everything. When we all walked out together, the others finishing their cigarettes after breakfast, my grandfather told me to hang up the bag for the wool. The rest of the unshorn sheep had to be herded from the fields, where they had grazed all night, into the corral. All the other hands had to go out to round them up and bring them in. So it was up to me, my grandfather said, to hang up the big sack. Me, that is, and Uncle Eli.

I was glad to do this because hanging the sack, after all, is an important job which you don't ask anyone at all to do and which I had never been

[1]From ...AND NOW MIGUEL, copyright 1953 by the author, Joseph Krumgold. Thomas Y. Crowell Company, New York, publishers.
[2]A range of mountains in New Mexico.

asked to do before. I knew how it worked, though, from watching.

First, Uncle Eli and I, we got this iron hoop, like a hoop off a barrel only thick and solid, and this hoop we put around the top outside the opening of the sack. Then we turned over the cloth of the sack, which is burlap, we turned it over the hoop all the way around. All that's left is to take some nails, which you use like they were pins, to fasten the turned-over burlap to the rest of the sack so that the hoop is all covered over and it can't fall off.

Once you do this, it's very easy to hang the sack. All you do then is to go up on the wall of the shed where is nailed this square wooden frame and drop the bottom of the empty sack through the frame. But the opening of the sack can't go through because the hoop is bigger than the wooden square and it rests on the square letting the sack hang down its full length, six or seven feet. That's all there is to it.

But once we got the sack hung up, Uncle Eli said, "Stay up there, Miguelito. We'll get started and sack up these fleeces from yesterday."

So there I was up on top. Fleeces flying up from Uncle Eli. Everybody as busy and working as fast as they could, like on the day before. And soon the woolly fleeces filled up the sack to the very top. I stepped in the middle to stamp them down. And it was like the whole world gave way from right under my feet.

I dropped slowly down to the bottom of the sack. One long drop, and then a soft bump. There had not been enough fleeces to hold me up, not enough soft wool. I just went down, slow, and there was nothing to do. The sides of the bag, the burlap, was hard and rough with nothing to catch, not even with fingernails. Like going down a smooth tunnel standing straight up. There was no way to save myself. And yell, I couldn't yell. How could I yell and tell everyone what a fool I was to be falling that second into the bag which was for the wool?

I didn't yell.

I didn't breathe.

I looked up. As if I was climbing the rough cloth with my eyes, I looked up all the little crisscrosses of the cloth, and at the end I reached the top. Way up, high above me, I saw the sky, still blue like this morning but no longer big and wide. An eye, a round eye it was, way up at the end of the tunnel, still blue and with one tramp cloud, an orphan cloud.

I breathed. And then, *Madre Dios*,[1] a shadow went past the eye. It was a fleece. And right away another. Eli, without looking, he was still throwing fleeces up to me and I wasn't there. The fleeces were going right over the top of the bag. Another came and another. And no one to catch them....

Someone yelled. "What are you doing with the fleeces, Eli? Throwing them away?"

"Eli!"

"What?" That was Eli. "What's wrong? Well, what do you know! Miguel! Where is he? Miguel!"

The fleeces stopped. And everywhere shouts. For me, Miguel.

---

[1]Literally translated "Mother of God" but used as a fairly common exclamation of serious surprise by the Spanish Americans.

I didn't say anything. I wished only that my name was something different from Miguel. Alexander, Joe, Babaloo—anyone, except me.

It was my big brother Blasito who thought of it first. "Maybe he fell into the bag?"

They screamed and yelled and laughed at how funny this was. There were also other jokes. When I looked up again it was just in time to see the face of my father come into the round blue hole way up there, above my head.

"Is this any time to start playing games, hide and seek, like you were a little boy?"

When he said this I stopped breathing again.

He put down his hand. It hung there, big fingers and a big thumb, right in front of my nose.

The big finger, upside down, shook at me. I put up my hands and took the hand hanging there in front of my nose. As soon as I did my father grabbed me by the wrist.

"Games," he said. "At a time like this."

He lifted me up into the bright day. He dropped me over the side. I fell into the dirt at the bottom of the bag....I sat there in the dirt without moving because there was nowhere I could think of to go. When I fell I picked up a handful of dirt and now I let the dirt go out of my hand, a little bit at a time.

Whatever dirt there was left in my hand, I threw it away.

I made myself small and I got up. I walked away from the shearing shed across the yard, without looking back. No one called me to look back and there was no one I wanted to see. And in this way I was able to reach the gate which led to the path that went to the house.

That's the way it was on the second day of the shearing.

294

BECAUSE I COULD NOT STOP FOR DEATH[1]
by Emily Dickinson

> Because I could not stop for Death,
> He kindly stopped for me;
> The carriage held but just ourselves
> And Immortality.
>
> We slowly drove, he knew no haste,
> And I had put away
> My labor, and my leisure too,
> For his civility.
>
> We passed the school where children played
> At wrestling in a ring;
> We passed the fields of grazing grain,
> We passed the setting sun.
>
> We paused before a house that seemed
> A swelling of the ground;
> The roof was scarcely visible,
> The cornice but a mound.
>
> Since then 'tis centuries; but each
> Feels shorter than the day
> I first surmised the horses' heads
> Were toward eternity.

LUX ET VERITAS[2]
by Milton White

I've been looking through the Yale Class of 1936 Twenty-Five-Year Book—issued for the twenty-fifth reunion—and I've come to the conclusion that probably my chief claim to fame is the fact I went to school with John Hersey, Stewart Alsop, John Crosby, and August Heckscher, among others. Not that any of those people would remember me—I left Yale in March of my freshman year, after my father died. I see by the directory, too, that Mike Sayles is now "president and treasurer of Sayles, Inc., department stores, southwestern Ohio." Mike would remember me; we were roommates.

Still, the whole thing has started me thinking, and it may be that after all I have my *own* claim to fame: I'm the only freshman in Yale history ever thrown into a shell as coxswain to the Yale varsity crew less than twenty-four hours after his arrival in New Haven. Maybe Mike Sayles would even remember that.

The first evening, just at dusk, the Whiffenpoofs appeared in the Oval.

I knew they were the Whiffenpoofs because I heard someone call out their name, and I leaned out the window and listened to them. When the Whiffenpoofs had finished, all the fellows leaning out the dormitory windows applauded. I did, too. I thought "The Whiffenpoof Song" was the saddest, most beautiful song I'd ever heard.

The Payne Whitney Gymnasium was brand-new that year. The building, even inside, looked like a cathedral to me, and I felt there was something almost irreverent about the line of freshmen, all wearing nothing but shorts, waiting to be checked and weighed and assigned to something in Phys. Ed. Bright sunshine poured through the tall windows. My turn came at last. I stepped on the scale.

The Physical Education man in charge of weighing us wrote down my name, address, and birth date as I answered his questions; then, half glancing at the scale, he said to me, "Both feet on the scale."

"I've got both feet on the scale," I said.

He stopped writing. "Huh?" he said. He tapped the side of the scale and looked at me objectively for the first time. The indicator had returned to eighty-nine.

"That's what I weigh," I said, pushing back my glasses.

"How tall are you?" The Physical Education man grabbed my arm and pushed me against the measuring rod at the back of the scale.

"I'm five-five and a half," I said.

The metal bar of the measuring rod came down smack on the top of my head. "You're five-five," the Physical Education man said. He stepped back and stared at me. Then he reached out and grabbed my arm again. "Come on," he said.

He led me into the main corridor and pressed a button to signal the elevator. Horrified, pointing to my shorts, I said, "I'll get my clothes on first."

"You don't need clothes," he said. The elevator door opened and he pushed me inside. "Rowing tanks," he said to the operator. "Have you ever been a coxswain?" he asked me. "What was your prep school?"

"Coxswain?" I said. And I added, "I didn't go to prep school. I went to Springfield Central High School."

"Oh," he said.

"Coxswain?" I repeated shakily.

We stepped out of the elevator and he led me down a corridor and into a large, overheated room that echoed with the sound of shouts and splashing oars and running water. The room smelled of chlorine. In one of the practice tanks, eight men rowed like mad while the fellow sitting in the coxswain's seat beat against the sides of the "boat" with blocks of wood and cried, "Hip! Hip! Hip! Hip!"

The Physical Education man beckoned triumphantly to a man who carried a megaphone. "Look what I've got!" he yelled, raising my arm. "Eighty-nine pounds, five-five. Where's the coach?"

The crew stopped rowing. The man with the megaphone shouted that the coach had already left for the boathouse. He hurried over to us and stopped short in front of me. The words "Assistant Coach" were printed on his T shirt. "Eighty-nine pounds?" he cried.

I pushed back my glasses and realized my hand was shaking. He tapped me on the chest with the megaphone. "The bus'll be along in half an hour," he said. "Go on upstairs and get dressed, then come back down here. Before we go, I'll give you a few pointers about what a coxswain has to do."

"Coxswain?" I said.

"Coxswain," he said. "The varsity cox has an appointment with the Dean this morning, and anyway, we need a substitute. We always have trouble finding enough coxswains."

Standing in the corner of the elevator, still in my shorts, I tried to summon the courage to protest. The Physical Education man had never once let go of my arm. "I don't even know how to steer a boat," I said.

"Not a boat. A *shell*," he said.

"Good heavens," I said.

In the bus, on the way to the boathouse, I sat alone in the back seat, my hands clenched; as I listened to the other men in the bus chattering and laughing, it suddenly came to me that they must actually be the Yale varsity crew. Desperately, I went over and over what the assistant coach had told me about tiller ropes and feathering oars and "Way enough," which was the command to stop. I said to myself, looking down at my hands, "Port, left hand. Starboard, right hand..."

One of the fellows sitting in front of me turned. "Did you say something?" he asked.

I shook my head. The bus was crossing a bridge, and at the far end, off to the left, stood a large red brick building with a wide dock in front of it. Some oarsmen were lowering a shell into the river. I felt my heart pound, and the pounding continued when I shook hands with the coach on the dock and listened to the assistant coach explain me: "Freshman...eighty-nine pounds, five-five..."

The coach looked at me with narrowed eyes. "Take off your jacket," he said, nodding toward the boathouse. When I returned, he led me firmly to a motorboat. He told me to get in, and he climbed in after me. The man at the wheel raced the motor. The boat sped away from the dock and headed in the direction of two shells skimming along the river. "Just watch," the coach said to me. Then he raised his megaphone and shouted instructions to the crews. All at once, I was aware of the smell of wet mud and marsh grass in the air.

The spray from the motorboat wet my glasses, so that most of the time I could see very little. But as we followed the shells up and down the river, I tried to keep my eyes on the coxswains. They sat perched on the edge of their seats, confident, beating out the stroke with wooden blocks, urging the shells on with the movement of their bodies, and shouting "Hip! Hip!" through megaphones that hung close to their lips. The oars moved in unison.

"Catching on?" the coach shouted at me. He added something I couldn't hear.

"What?" I said, drying my glasses.

The man at the wheel called out, "Varsity's ready." He pointed to a shell and a crew waiting at the edge of the dock.

"Let's go in," the coach said.

The motorboat swerved, and a few moments later we pulled up to the dock and stopped. The coach turned to me. "O.K.," he said. "Take them out on the river."

I felt myself turn pale. "What?" I said. "Me?"

The coach picked up a coxswain's megaphone from under the back seat of the motorboat. "Here, put this on." He half lifted me out of the boat and onto the dock. "Snap it up. Let's go," he said. "You'll do all right."

I approached the shell, terrified. The coxswain's seat seemed incredibly inadequate. Suddenly the oarsman sitting nearest me said, "It's O.K. I'm the stroke."

"You're what? I thought the stroke was the time—the beat."

"I know," he said, with a grin. "Confusing. But don't let that worry you. You take the count from me." He reached up and helped me climb into the shell. I clung to the sides, not breathing. The stroke had taken the megaphone from me. Still grinning, he adjusted the headband so that the megaphone fit me. "All set now?" he said.

One of the crew in the back of the shell called out, "Pray, everybody."

"O.K. Shove off!" the stroke called.

The crewmen dipped their oars into the water and started to pull the shell away from the dock. The stroke yelled at me, "The rudder!" I jerked the tiller ropes, each of which ended in a wooden block. The shell swayed. I shouted frantically, "I've never been—"

"Straighten 'er!" the stroke yelled.

I drew the tiller ropes straight. The shell steadied, but my hands were shaking. The stroke grinned again. He said to me quietly, "Easy does it. Head her toward the other shells."

The crew began to row rhythmically. I clutched the tiller ropes and kept my eyes glued on the two shells waiting for us in the middle of the river. The shell skimmed over the water. The long oars dipped, pulled, emerged, glistening in the morning sunlight, and dipped again. I found myself watching them, fascinated.

Too late I noticed that we were passing the other shells. The stroke yelled at me, "Give us the order to stop!"

"Stop!" I yelled through the megaphone.

The crew burst into laughter. The stroke murmured to me, "Way enough."

I remembered. "Way enough!" I shouted.

The crew stopped rowing. They trailed their oars to slow us down, and I sat tense as they turned the shell around. We drifted into position between the two other shells. The motorboat drew alongside us. The coach called out, "We'll race to the bridge. You!" he said, pointing to me. "Head for the center arch." He waved his megaphone in the direction of the bridge, far down the river.

The coxswains in the other shells leaned forward, alert. "Ready all!" they shouted to their crews.

I felt my throat tighten. I swallowed, then I shouted to the varsity crew, "Ready all!"

The coach raised his hand. A pistol shot cracked. "Gosh!" I cried.

"Hip...Hip!...Hip!" I began to shout.

"Hip! Hip! Hip!" I yelled. I leaned forward almost double, to keep the wind from slowing us. The crew moved back and forth in their seats with superb precision. The oars glistened in the sun. The bridge loomed closer. "Hip! Hip! Hip!" I cried.

Out of the corner of my eye I glanced at the other shells. They seemed to be about half a length behind me. My heart pounded. The shell flew over the water. My megaphone had slipped to one side. "Hip! Hip! Hip!" I yelled hoarsely, afraid the crew could not hear me. Perspiration trickled down my glasses. I felt a wide, cold shadow pass over me as the shell swept under the bridge. "Hip! Hip! Hip!" I continued yelling.

The stroke grinned at me. "O.K. We've won."

"We've won!" I yelled exultantly. "Stop!" Then quickly I corrected myself. "Way enough!" And, sitting upright in the coxswain's seat, I shouted, "Wonderful, wonderful!"

I repeated the words to myself as I clambered off the bus at the corner of College and Elm and started to run toward Berkeley Oval. The sky was clear blue.

Outside in the bright sunlight, humming "The Whiffenpoof Song," I ran across Berkeley Oval toward the Commons. Trees threw sharp shadows over the sidewalk. The bells in Harkness Tower tolled the half hour. Suddenly I slowed down, because the sidewalk had become a blur. I couldn't tell exactly what was making me cry, if I was crying, except that it was everything.

Drama presents a character or characters in a situation *without* a narrator intervening between the action and the audience. The plot is revealed by dialogue and action. Everything the listeners know they learn from what the characters say and do. Dramatic literature includes monologues, soliloquies, and plays.

In a dramatic monologue and a soliloquy, we hear from only one character. Monologue comes from *mono* meaning "single" and the Greek verb meaning "to speak." Thus in a monologue there is a single speaker who addresses other characters who do not speak. Soliloquy comes from the Latin words *solus* meaning "alone" and the verb *loqui* meaning "to speak." In a soliloquy there are no other characters present.

A play is written to be presented on a stage with all the visual aids that scenery and costumes can give and with a full cast of characters. Consequently, it presents some special problems to the single interpreter.

INTERPRETATION

OF DRAMATIC LITERATURE

FIRST STEPS IN PREPARATION

Both the interpreter of drama and the actor start with the author's words, and both are instruments through whom the author's play is transmitted to an audience. Both must be true to the author's intention. Both use physical and vocal techniques to communicate all the elements of the play to the audience. Both study the complete play so the author's full intention is perfectly clear. The steps in preparation for the actor and the interpreter are almost identical up to final preparation for performance.

We discussed this type of analysis when we were concerned with direct and indirect discourse. In a play, the complete understanding of a character is sometimes more difficult because there is no narrator to step in and explain matters to us. Nor does the audience have any narrative to tell them what is in a character's mind. The interpreter must communicate all these with his voice and body. Changes from one speaker to another are likely to be rapid. You must look for and find every possible clue for motivation, and pay particular attention to all stage directions, whether you intend to speak them aloud or use them as a guide to your own preparation and performance.

A play is constructed with acts and sometimes scenes within the acts. It is important to know how the plot of a play is developed. In the analysis of narratives you should locate all key situations and climaxes. In a drama the key situations are called key scenes, but they have the same function. They are signposts along the road of the plot.

Key speeches are of two kinds: a speech may be a key to the plot development, or it may be a key to character. There are also key actions.

Often these are best handled as narration and given to the audience direct.

Just as narration may be organized in many different ways, a play may move right along in steady chronological order, or it may have flash-back scenes, or quiet scenes in which a previous episode is recalled, or any combination of these. There may be several subplots which you may or may not wish to touch in your cutting. Many times when there are one or more subplots, the scenes will alternate with those that move the main plot forward.

As soon as you are sure how the plot is organized, move to the study of the characters. First decide what each character contributes to the play. Whose play is it? Around whom does the plot revolve? The answer to the latter question will often include several characters. Each character in every scene is there for a reason.

After you have examined the separate parts, look at the play as a whole again. Reread it to be sure you know how the plot moves and how it achieves its point, both in relation to key scenes and climaxes and to the function of the characters and their speeches. After you have reëxamined the relationship of the parts to the whole, you may wish to do some cutting. In the case of the actor, this will be done for him by the director. As an interpreter, you may select a key scene or scenes for your performance or, as your experience increases, you may do a cutting of an entire play. The same general rules for cutting a narrative apply to cutting a play. You eliminate the characters' names before each speech, because it is the duty of the interpreter to make those characters clear by sugges-tion without having to identify them each time.

HANDLING STAGE DIRECTIONS

You will cut most of the stage directions except for entrances and exits, the rise and fall of the curtain, and bits of business that bear directly on the plot. These can be paraphrased, put into appropriate style and then used as narrative inserts, when you speak directly to the audience in your own person.

Sometimes the playwright will phrase his stage directions so they may be used almost as an introduction or to close a scene or explain a piece of action. Usually they will need to be put in somewhat less abbre-viated style. Remember that an introduction helps establish the mood and can be accomplished by a description of the setting.

VOCAL AND PHYSICAL TECHNIQUES

Both actor and interpreter turn next to vocal and physical techniques so everything they do with voice and body helps make the character vivid to the audience. In this phase of preparation, both practice "walking through" the business or bits of physical action of the character portrayed. Both pay particular attention to the style of dress, age, and physical condition that affect the way the character sits down and gets up, enters and leaves the room, and handles objects within the room. The interpreter, who may be concerned with several characters in his final performance, is wise to take them one at a time, until the mental, physical, and vocal pattern is set for each one.

Establishing Muscle Memory

As an interpreter, as well as an actor, you must go through this physical phase of preparation, even though you may not take a step in your actual performance. There is no reason why you shouldn't move about in performance as well as in preparation, for such movement helps communicate the author's intention. But actually moving about during preparation, as the character would on stage, adds vitality to the real performance.

Let your muscles get the feel of each big overt action until they are accustomed to it. Then try the scene with no action at all, standing in one place but recalling what you did in the previous stage of preparation. Your muscles will respond to the memory of the big action and have an important effect on the pace and emotional impact of the entire performance. This is called muscle memory. Do not neglect this important physical aspect. It is not acting, but *preparation* for vital interpretation.

FINAL STEPS IN PREPARATION

Up to this point the interpreter and the actor follow almost identical steps in analysis and preparation. Each is now ready to apply the principles of his art to a performance. It is only at this point that the differences between acting and interpretation become sharply apparent.

It is in the exterior aspects that the differences appear. It may be said that the actor begins to add exterior details to make his characterization physically explicit. The interpreter now begins to eliminate physical explicitness, refining the gestures to suggest the tensions that underlie them.

303

The actor works to convince the audience that he *IS* the character both mentally and physically. He has memorized his lines. He uses real properties. He enters and leaves the stage, opening and closing doors on the set. He is fitted for a costume which helps create the illusion of a period. He practices with make-up so he no longer looks like himself, but like an old man or a bearded soldier or whatever person he is playing. He does everything he can to be the character physically. He responds as the character mentally and emotionally.

The interpreter begins to work toward suggestion at this point. You may or may not memorize your material. You will find, however, that you need to have it more nearly memorized than when you are working with other forms of literature, because you must be able to handle the suggestion of character and direct dialogue without interrupting the scene to refer to the book. An occasional glance is all you can manage. You must work out all the physical and mental aspects of each character with as much care and attention to detail as the actor does. You know everything about the characters—how every one of them thinks, feels, reacts, speaks, and moves.

To help the actor achieve explicitness, an actual set is constructed, in which he plays his part. But as an interpreter you have only a book, which you always take with you—whether you have memorized the material or not—an empty stage, and sometimes a reading stand. You will not have the help of properties, scenery, lighting, costumes, and make-up. Nor will you have the actual presence of other people on the stage. You are the sole middleman between the script and the audience and are intent on sharing the characters' experiences, not demonstrating them. You must be technician, property man, curtain puller, costumer, director, and the entire cast of actors all by yourself. It is not an easy assignment, but it is by no means impossible. The interpretation of dramatic literature requires conscientious work on techniques. It demands steady concentration on many details at once during performance. But when the interpreter is successful, the play becomes a clear and moving experience to his audience.

Establishing the Setting

How do you fill all these requirements? First, the significant parts of the setting must be told to the audience so they will know where and when the events take place. You need not give every little detail. Judge what is important and establish it clearly for your listeners.

304

The important thing to remember is that the scene being set is *not* on any stage. It does not surround the interpreter. The stage must be set *in the minds of the audience.* Therefore, you do not indicate a fireplace behind you when describing the setting. It is not behind you on the stage. The fireplace is in the room you are helping the audience create in their minds. You simply tell them what they need to know, as a narrator would do in a story. They will establish the room, the garden, or whatever setting is needed, in their imaginations.

Introducing the Characters

Having created the "visual aspects" of the setting in your listeners' minds, you introduce the character or characters in your reading. This can be done quite simply. It is helpful to establish the relationship of the characters to each other with a phrase such as "his wife," or "their daughter." Remember the audience has no program to consult to keep the names straight. Study the selections at the end of this chapter and see how simply and straightforwardly the characters are introduced. You need not tell the audience very much about them as they develop. Your performance will take care of that. If there have been some important developments in plot before the scene you are to use, include this information in your introduction, as you did in introducing a cutting from a narrative.

Once the setting is established and the cast of characters assembled in the minds of the audience, you may simply say, "As the curtain rises, so-and-so is speaking." There are many ways to phrase this information. Make sure that you understand the mood and thought of the scene; then use whatever seems suitable.

Establishing Characters' Attitudes, Emotions, and Actions

Now comes the interpreter's most important function—that of establishing the characters' attitudes, emotions, and actions clearly. By this time you are accustomed to projecting the mental attitude and emotional response, and all the aspects of interior characterization from the script to the audience. You know how effective the reader's physical response is in eliciting emotional response from the audience. It is of special importance in the interpretation of drama. Whatever is going on in the mind, muscles, and emotions of the character speaking must also be going on in your mind, muscles, and emotions as you say the speech. An interpretation that does not carry this full response is not a good job.

But do not confuse full response with uncontrolled response. The actor *or* the interpreter who becomes so worked up that he forgets his responsibility to the audience is not a successful performer. Nor is the actor who is so wrapped up in what the character is experiencing that he forgets an important piece of business likely to be popular with his director and his fellow players. The interpreter who is so carried away that his eyes fill with tears and his voice becomes unmanageable calls attention to himself and away from the character and action in which the audience is most interested.

SOME SUGGESTIONS ON TECHNIQUES

Drama requires more physical and vocal suggestion than a narrative, because everything the audience learns comes only through the characters. There is no narrator to step in and fill in the necessary description and explanation.

The audience must always know who is speaking. Therefore, vocal and physical techniques must be sharply defined to make clear sex, age, and physical attributes of the character, as well as their interior aspects. The following suggestions are very general and must, of course, be varied to suit individual plans and characters.

Indicating the Sex of a Character

A male interpreter is often at a loss as to how he should suggest the voice and actions of a female character, just as a woman may have difficulty suggesting those of a masculine speaker.

It is not usually necessary to do more than shift the weight ever so slightly to differentiate between the sexes. You need not put your feet far apart for a man or bring them together for a woman. Such a performance would distract the audience, who will become fascinated by your footwork and forget all about what you are saying.

Men usually distribute their weight fairly evenly on the centers or heels of both feet. Women tend to balance forward on the balls of their feet with more pressure on the toes than the heels. Frequently one foot is slightly forward to bear most of the weight. You need not shift your feet to do this. Any movement should be imperceptible to the audience. They will only be aware of firmer muscle tone when the men speak. A feeling of broad shoulders and heavy muscles in the upper arms will help

306

In the history of the theater, many fine actresses have demonstrated their versatility by playing male roles. Here, Siobhan McKenna, following the precedent of Sarah Bernhardt, plays *Hamlet*.

establish strength when a woman is suggesting a male character, while a man need only feel smaller-boned and finer-muscled, and the suggestion in posture will probably be enough for his audience. Here is a place where muscle memory is most helpful.

Vocally the watchword is to underplay rather than be specific. The audience will accept the slightest change of voice if the interpreter is consistent.

A woman using the lowest octave of her voice to suggest a man speaking succeeds only in limiting her range and straining her throat, so the audience will clear theirs in sympathy. She need only relax her throat so all the overtones and undertones are given a richer quality. If she takes a good, full breath so there is strength in her voice, the attitude of the character will dictate any other vocal variations. A man need only lighten his voice and use less vigorous projection to allow his tone to come primarily from the top of the throat. He need not lift his voice above its natural pitch. He just lightens the quality.

Remember you are only *suggesting* the sex of the character speaking. The individual differences within the sexes are more important to the character.

Indicating Age

Age is one of the most relative of all exterior aspects of character. Too often the interpreter who has not done a careful job of analysis will jump to the conclusion that anyone who isn't young is on the verge of senility. Fortunately, that is a fallacy! All old people do not have hunched backs and cracked voices. If you observe older people carefully, you will see that many of them carry themselves erect and speak firmly. Let the degree of feebleness be dictated by what the author tells you about the vigor and vitality of the character. If you make the character too feeble, you may not be able to build a convincing climax that requires strength and energy. The style of the speeches is the important clue.

As a rule older people move more slowly than younger ones. They use smaller gestures with more importance attached to the hand than to the upper arms and shoulders. They often keep their hands close to their bodies instead of reaching out vigorously in wide arm movements. Try getting the feeling of weakened muscles in your arms and shoulders. Practice handling articles with this feeling until you are used to it. Your muscles will carry the memory into performance.

Older people are often less sure of their sight and balance than younger people. Their legs do not have the vigor they once had.

They tend to keep their feet close to the ground when they walk and to shorten their steps. They often sit still a great deal, and their muscles go slack. Train your muscles specifically in rehearsal, and the suggestion will come through in performance without any acrobatics of stooping and straightening for characters of different ages.

Vocal technique will help in suggesting age. Older people tend to use a narrower range of inflection than young persons. They do not become so actively excited, and the pace of their speech is slower and the rhythm less staccato than when they were young. This can also be true of people who are not physically vibrant or who are bored or very tired. Notice the contrasts and quick changes in vitality in *The Member of the Wedding*. (See page 313.)

Remember that the exterior characteristics need only be suggested. As an interpreter you are not asking the audience to believe *you are* the lonely girl in *The Member of The Wedding*. You are asking them to believe that there is such a person. It is the effect of these interior qualities on attitude that is basic to the audience's sharing of the experience.

Using More Than One Character

Frequently the interpreter is required to suggest several characters within a scene. Whereas an actor has the other actors on stage with him, the interpreter must handle the entire cast as it moves on the stage he has created in the audience's minds.

Once you have managed to get one character thoroughly in hand, it is not a difficult matter to add the others. In preparation you will find it wise to establish each character fully before going on to the next. In the process of analysis you will have decided which characters are important. Take the most important character first and thoroughly develop him, mentally, emotionally, and physically. Then add the next character, developing him with the same care. Then put the two together. This process may be followed, no matter how many characters you wish to suggest.

Angle of Focus

There are a few additional suggestions for technique that may help you and the audience avoid confusion. One of these is the matter of eye focus. You will recall the suggestion that in direct discourse you select a section of the back wall to serve as an area of focus. When you are handling two or more characters, you simply select a separate area toward which *each* addresses his speeches. It simplifies the problem for both audience and interpreter if each specific character speaks in the same direction no matter whom he is addressing.

This technique can be clarified graphically. When you are speaking as a narrator, you look at and speak to the audience. When you are speaking as a character you look at a specific area behind the audience and *slightly* above their heads.

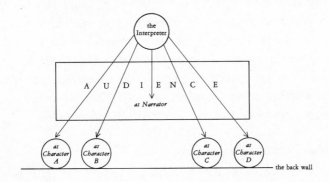

Be careful to keep the areas you assign to the various characters as close together as possible. Then the continued change of direction does not become obtrusive. The angle widens as it goes away from you. To place two characters at the outside edges of the triangle causes you to look so far from side to side that you behave like a spectator at a tennis match. Keep the angle as narrow as possible. A shift of the eyes with a slight turn of the head are all that is needed to indicate that another character is speaking if you use your voice and muscles to project the mental and emotional differences between the characters at the same time. Remember that shuffling your feet, or any other mannerism, will distract your audience from concentration on the drama.

It is a known fact that an actor must not only learn his own lines but also learn to hear what the other characters say so that he can respond properly. Otherwise his speeches plod along with no relation to the scene as a whole. As an interpreter handling more than one character, you must learn to "have heard." Be sure each character has heard, and is replying to the preceding speech with the motivation that causes that character to react as he does. This requires you to pick up the thread of the thought development in the person of the character who has heard the speech. It requires split-second response that includes mental and emotional reaction and vocal technique.

There is no short cut to developing this ability. It takes thorough preparation of each character and the reconstruction of the situation so that each character is in proper relation to every other one.

No character can be allowed to drop out of the scene. He must emerge complete and vivid the moment he picks up his cue. Remember a cue can be picked up by a glance or a facial expression. You need not race breathlessly from one speech to the next. A pause can be effective in indicating reaction. However, the pause must be within the character's thinking, and be so indicated by his picking up the cue physically and mentally. There must not be a sag between characters. As soon as one character finishes his speech and action, the other character picks up immediately, whether or not he starts to speak. This is important in keeping the scene moving smoothly and in establishing interplay.

Suggesting Certain Properties

One other problem sometimes puzzles the interpreter. This is what to do about handling properties and physical contact between characters.

310

Remember that suggestion, not explicit demonstration, is the interpreter's goal. An action is the exterior manifestation of an inner motivation. Why and how a character acts is often more important than what he does. Practice the action fully in preparation, just as you do any action. Then concentrate on suggesting the tension behind the action rather than performing the action itself.

If one character hands another a letter to read, it will make a difference whether he gives it eagerly or tentatively. The empathy involved is important. A slight reaching out of the hand toward the area of address should be enough. When the second character takes the letter, let your audience see the manner in which he takes it rather than try to make them believe that you have grasped a piece of paper out of thin air. Does the character snatch it quickly or does he hesitate? Is he eager to read it, or is he doing so against his will? The answers to these and other related questions will affect facial expressions and muscle tone of the body as well as the speed of the action itself. It is the purpose served by the exchange of the letter, and not merely the actual exchange, that is important to the audience.

Likewise, an interpreter does not sit down as one character and leap to his feet to answer himself as another character. The sitting down is unimportant. The muscle tone that suggests the reason for sitting down is the important factor. Does the character sink wearily into the chair or sit nervously on its edge or preside over a formal meeting? The audience will respond with empathy if the interpreter has made use of muscle memory throughout the last phases of his preparation.

Even more specific physical action, such as a blow, can be suggested. An interpreter who clenches his fist and strikes at empty air is quite likely to look a little odd, to say the least. It is safer to tell the audience what is taking place. If this cannot be accomplished without breaking the scene, let the interpreter remember that a blow is an outward manifestation of an inner motivation. A sharper directness of eye focus, a general tensing of all the muscles and appropriate empathy, with only a slight, quick thrust of the clenched fist to point the action, will take care of the situation. The interpreter is not delivering or receiving the blow. The characters in the audience's minds are performing the action. If the emotional response is carefully suggested, the action will be clear. Moreover, the lines will refer to the action, so there is little chance that the audience will miss the point.

THE ACTOR AND THE INTERPRETER OF DRAMA

Early
Preparation

Study of the author's play
Analysis of complete play
    organization of plot
    key scenes
    key speeches
    climaxes
    relationship of parts to whole
Analysis of characters
    relationship to plot
    relationship to setting
    relationship to each other
Analysis of individual character
    interior characteristics
    change or development of interior aspects
    exterior characteristics
    practice physical actions
Reëxamination of above in relation to whole play
Full response to character in situation

	THE ACTOR *Explicitness*	THE INTERPRETER *Suggestion*
Final Preparation for Performance	Memorizes lines completely Plays within physical setting Perfects make-up and costumes Perfects entrances and exits and all stage business	May or may not memorize Works out narration in appropriate style to establish setting in audience's minds Uses muscle memory to suggest degree of tension or relaxation in the physical actions
Performance	Does not carry his script Takes his place in visible scene set up around him Is explicit in outer characteristics Has full inner response Asks audience to believe he *is* the character and that events are happening before their eyes *Demonstrates* the experience *before* the audience's eyes	Takes script to platform Sets scene in minds of audience by narration Suggests outer characteristics Has full inner response Asks audience to believe there is such a character and events do take place in the imagined setting *Shares* the experience *with* the audience

MATERIAL FOR PERFORMANCE

In this scene from the first act of *The Member of the Wedding*,[1] by Carson McCullers, we meet three characters: Berenice, the cook; Frankie Addams; and Frankie's seven-year-old cousin, John Henry West, who lives next door. Berenice has been with the Addamses for many years. Frankie is twelve years old, unattractive, and motherless.

The setting is the kitchen and part of a Southern yard. It is late August. In the scene preceding this one Jarvis, Frankie's older brother, has just introduced his fiancée to the family. Frankie and John Henry listen in awe to the plans for the wedding, and now Janet and Jarvis have allowed them to go to the kitchen and join Berenice in a game of three-handed bridge. Frankie is restless and distracted and soon gives up all pretense of playing to wander aimlessly about the room.

FRANKIE [*standing with one foot on the seat of the chair, leaning over the chair back and laughing*]. Did you hear what Jarvis said?

BERENICE. What?

FRANKIE [*after laughing more*]. They were talking about whether to vote for C. P. MacDonald. And Jarvis said, "Why I wouldn't vote for that scoundrel if he was running to be dogcatcher." I never heard anything so witty in my life. [*There is a silence during which* BERENICE *watches* FRANKIE, *but does not smile*]. And you know what Janice remarked. When Jarvis mentioned about how much I've grown, she said she didn't think I looked so terribly big. She said she got the major portion of growth before she was thirteen. She said I was the right height and had acting talent and ought to go to Hollywood. She did, Berenice.

BERENICE. O.K. All right! She did!

FRANKIE. She said she thought I was a lovely size and would probably not grow any taller. She said all fashion models and movie stars...

BERENICE. She did not. I heard her from the window. She only remarked that you probably had already got your growth. But she didn't go on and on like that or mention Hollywood.

FRANKIE. She said to me...

BERENICE. She said to you! This is a serious fault with you, Frankie. Somebody just makes a loose remark and then you cozen it in your mind until noboby would recognize it. Your Aunt Pet happened to mention to Clorina that you had sweet manners and Clorina passed it on to you. For what it was worth. Then next thing I know you are going all around and bragging how Mrs. West thought you had the finest manners in town and ought to go to Hollywood, and I don't know what-all you didn't say. And that is a serious fault.

[1]From "The Member of the Wedding" by Carson McCullers. Copyright 1951 by Carson McCullers. Reprinted by permission of New Directions, Publishers.

FRANKIE. Aw, quit preaching at me.

BERENICE. I ain't preaching. It's the solemn truth and you know it.

FRANKIE. I admit it a little. [*She sits down at the table and puts her fore-head on the palms of her hands. There is a pause, and then she speaks softly.*] What I need to know is this. Do you think I made a good impression?

BERENICE. Impression?

FRANKIE. Yes.

BERENICE. Well, how would I know?

FRANKIE. I mean, how did I act? What did I do?

BERENICE. Why, you didn't do anything to speak of.

FRANKIE. Nothing?

BERENICE. No. You just watched the pair of them like they was ghosts. Then, when they talked about the wedding, them ears of yours stiffened out the size of cabbage leaves...

FRANKIE [*raising her hand to her ears*]. They didn't!

BERENICE. They did.

FRANKIE. Some day you going to look down and find that big fat tongue of yours pulled out by the roots and laying there before you on the table.

BERENICE. Quit talking so rude.

FRANKIE [*after a pause*]. I'm so scared I didn't make a good impression.

BERENICE. What of it? I got a date with T. T. and he's supposed to pick me up here. I wish him and Honey would come on. You make me nervous.

[FRANKIE *sits miserably, her shoulders hunched. Then with a sudden gesture she bangs her forehead on the table. Her fists are clenched and she is sobbing.*]

BERENICE. Come on. Don't act like that.

FRANKIE [*her voice muffled*]. They were so pretty. They must have such a good time. And they went away and left me.

BERENICE. Sit up. Behave yourself.

FRANKIE. They came and went away, and left me with this feeling.

BERENICE. Hosee! I bet I know something. [*She begins tapping with her heel: one, two, three—bang! After a pause, in which the rhythm is estab-lished, she begins singing.*] Frankie's got a crush! Frankie's got a crush! Frankie's got a crush on the *wedding!*

FRANKIE. Quit!

BERENICE. Frankie's got a crush! Frankie's got a crush!

FRANKIE. You better quit! [*She rises suddenly and snatches up the carving knife.*]

BERENICE. You lay down that knife.

FRANKIE. Make me. [*She bends the blade slowly.*]

BERENICE. Lay it down, *Devil*. [*There is a silence.*] throw it! You just!

[*After a pause* FRANKIE *aims the knife carefully at the closed door leading to the bedroom and throws it. The knife does not stick in the wall.*]

FRANKIE. I used to be the best knife thrower in this town.

BERENICE. Frances Addams, you goin' to try that stunt once too often.

FRANKIE. I warned you to quit pickin' with me.

BERENICE. You are not fit to live in a house.

314

FRANKIE. I won't be living in this one much longer; I'm going to run away from home.

BERENICE. And good riddance to a big old bag of rubbage.

FRANKIE. You wait and see. I'm leavin' town.

BERENICE. And where do you think you are going?

FRANKIE [gazing around the walls]. I don't know.

BERENICE. You're going crazy. That's where you going.

FRANKIE. No. [Solemnly.] This coming Sunday after the wedding, I'm leaving town. And I swear to Jesus by my two eyes I'm never coming back here any more.

BERENICE [going to FRANKIE and pushing her damp bangs back from her forehead]. Sugar? You serious?

FRANKIE [exasperated]. Of course! Do you think I would stand here and say that swear and tell a story? Sometimes, Berenice, I think it takes you longer to realize a fact than it does anybody who ever lived.

BERENICE. But you say you don't know where you going. You going, but you don't know where. That don't make no sense to me.

FRANKIE [after a long pause in which she again gazes around the walls of the room]. I feel just exactly like somebody has peeled all the skin off me. I wish I had some good cold peach ice cream. [FRANKIE goes out into the back yard and BERENICE finishes her work and leaves for her own home. FRANKIE watches her go and observes:] Seems like everybody goes off and leaves me. [She walks toward the Wests' yard, calling, with cupped hands.] John Henry. John Henry.

JOHN HENRY'S VOICE. What do you want, Frankie?

FRANKIE. Come over and spend the night with me.

JOHN HENRY'S VOICE. I can't.

FRANKIE. Why?

JOHN HENRY. Just because.

FRANKIE. Because why? [JOHN HENRY does not answer.] I thought maybe me and you could put up my Indian tepee and sleep out here in the yard. And have a good time. [There is still no answer.] Sure enough. Why don't you stay and spend the night?

JOHN HENRY [quite loudly]. Because, Frankie. I don't want to.

FRANKIE [angrily]. Fool Jackass! Suit yourself! I only asked you because you looked so ugly and so lonesome.

JOHN HENRY [skipping toward the arbor]. Why, I'm not a bit lonesome.

FRANKIE [looking at the house]. I wonder when that Papa of mine is coming home. He always comes home by dark. I don't want to go into that empty, ugly house all by myself.

JOHN HENRY. Me neither.

FRANKIE [standing with outstretched arms, and looking around her]. I think something is wrong. It is too quiet. I have a peculiar warning in my bones. I bet you a hundred dollars it's going to storm.

JOHN HENRY. I don't want to spend the night with you.

FRANKIE. A terrible, terrible dog-day storm. Or maybe even a cyclone.

JOHN HENRY. Huh.

FRANKIE. I bet Jarvis and Janice are now at Winter Hill. I see them just

315

plain as I see you. Plainer. Something is wrong. It is too quiet.

JOHN HENRY. I'll stay and spend the night with you.

FRANKIE [*suddenly stopping her turning*]. No. I just now thought of something.

JOHN HENRY. You just a little while ago was begging me.

FRANKIE. I know where I'm going.

[*There are sounds of* CHILDREN *playing in the distance.*]

JOHN HENRY. Let's go play with the children, Frankie.

FRANKIE. I tell you I know where I'm going. It's like I've known it all my life. Tomorrow I will tell everybody.

JOHN HENRY. Where?

FRANKIE. [*dreamily*]. After the wedding I'm going with them to Winter Hill. I'm going off with them after the wedding.

JOHN HENRY. You serious?

FRANKIE. Shush, just now I realized something. The trouble with me is that for a long time I have been just an "I" person. All other people can say "we." When Berenice says "we" she means her lodge and church and colored people. Soldiers can say "we" and mean the army. All people belong to a "we" except me.

JOHN HENRY. What are we going to do?

FRANKIE. Not to belong to a "we" makes you too lonesome. Until this afternoon I didn't have a "we," but now after seeing Janice and Jarvis I suddenly realize something.

JOHN HENRY. What?

FRANKIE. I know that the bride and my brother are the "we" of me. So I'm going with them, and joining with the wedding. This coming Sunday when my brother and the bride leave this town, I'm going with the two of them to Winter Hill. And after that to whatever place that they will ever go. [*There is a pause.*] I love the two of them so much and we belong to be together. I love the two of them so much because they are the *we* of me.

THE CURTAIN FALLS.

Fredric March discusses his interpretation of a rôle in *Long Day's Journey into Night.*

These speeches from Shakespeare's *King Henry The Fifth* offer an interesting comparison. The first is delivered by the King at the beginning of the attack on the French forces in the Battle of Agincourt in 1415.

KING. Once more unto the breach, dear friends, once more;
    Or close the wall up with our English dead.
    In peace there's nothing so becomes a man
    As modest stillness and humility:
    But when the blast of war blows in our ears,
    Then imitate the action of the tiger;
    Stiffen the sinews, summon up the blood,
    Disguise fair nature with hard-favored rage;
    Then lend the eye a terrible aspect;
    Let it cry through the portage[1] of the head
    Like the brass cannon; let the brow o'erwhelm it
    As fearfully as doth a gallèd rock
    O'erhang and jutty his confounded base,[2]
    Swilled with the wild and wasteful ocean.
    Now set the teeth and stretch the nostril wide,
    Hold hard the breath and bend up every spirit
    To his full height. On, on, you noble English,
    Whose blood is fed from fathers of war-proof![3]
    Fathers that, like so many Alexanders,
    Have in these parts from morn till even fought
    And sheathed their swords for lack of argument:
    Dishonor not your mothers; now attest
    That those whom you called fathers did beget you.
    Be copy now to men of grosser blood,
    And teach them how to war. And you, good yeomen,
    Whose limbs were made in England, show us here
    The mettle of your pasture; let us swear
    That you are worth your breeding; which I doubt not;
    For there is none of you so mean and base,
    That hath not noble lustre in your eyes.
    I see you stand like greyhounds in the slips,[4]
    Straining upon the start. The game's afoot:
    Follow your spirit, and upon this charge
    Cry 'God for Harry, England and Saint George!'

The second speech is from Act IV, scene III later in the siege. The English forces are weary and outnumbered by the French. Gloucester, Bedford, Westmoreland, Exeter and Salisbury come to the King's tent but he has not yet returned from scouting the French lines. They talk and

---

[1]Portholes.
[2]Jut over worn rocks below.
[3]Derived from fathers of proven valor.
[4]Leashed.

their anxiety is obvious. They are all seasoned warriors and their experience tells them that victory will be hard won.

GLOUCESTER. Where is the king?

BEDFORD. The king himself is rode to view their battle.

WESTMORELAND. Of fighting men they have full three-score thousand.

EXETER. There's five to one; besides, they all are fresh.

SALISBURY. God's arm strike us! 'tis a fearful odds.
    God be wi' you, princes all; I'll to my charge:
    If we no more meet till we meet in heaven,
    Then joyfully, my noble Lord of Bedford,
    My dear Lord Gloucester, and my good Lord Exeter,
    And my kind kinsman, warriors all, adieu!

BEDFORD. Farewell, good Salisbury, and good luck go with thee!

EXETER. Farewell, kind lord; fight valiantly to-day;
    And yet I do thee wrong to mind thee of it,
    For thou art framed of the firm truth of valor.
                                        {Exit Salisbury.}

BEDFORD. He is as full of valor as of kindness,
    Princely in both. *{Enter the King.}*

WESTMORELAND. O that we now had here
    But one ten thousand of those men in England
    That do no work to-day!

KING.   What's he that wishes so?
    My cousin Westmoreland? No, my fair cousin:
    If we are marked to die, we are enow
    To do our country loss; and if to live,
    The fewer men, the greater share of honor.
    God's will! I pray thee wish not one man more.
    By Jove, I am not covetous for gold,
    Nor care I who doth feed upon my cost;
    It yearns me not if men my garments wear;
    Such outward things dwell not in my desires:
    But if it be a sin to covet honor,
    I am the most offending soul alive.
    No, faith, my coz, wish not a man from England:
    God's peace! I would not lose so great an honor
    As one man more, methinks, would share from me
    For the best hope I have. O, do not wish one more!
    Rather proclaim it, Westmoreland, through my host,
    That he which hath no stomach to this fight,
    Let him depart; his passport shall be made
    And crowns for convoy put into his purse:
    We would not die in that man's company
    That fears his fellowship to die with us.
    This day is called the Feast of Crispian:
    He that outlives this day, and comes safe home,

318

Will stand a tip-toe when this day is named,
And rouse him at the name of Crispian.
He that shall see this day, and live old age,
Will yearly on the vigil feast his neighbors,
And say, 'To-morrow is Saint Crispian:'
Then will he strip his sleeve and show his scars,
And say, 'These wounds I had on Crispin's day.'
Old men forget; yet all shall be forgot,
But he'll remember, with advantages
What feats he did that day: then shall our names,
Familiar in his mouth as household words,
Harry the King, Bedford and Exeter,
Warwick and Talbot, Salisbury and Gloucester,
Be in their flowing cups freshly rememb'red.
This story shall the good man teach his son;
And Crispin Crispian shall ne'er go by,
From this day to the ending of the world,
But we in it shall be remembered—
We few, we happy few, we band of brothers;
For he to-day that sheds his blood with me
Shall be my brother. Be he ne'er so vile,
This day shall gentle his condition.[1]
And gentlemen in England now abed
Shall think themselves accurs'd they were not here,
And hold their manhoods cheap whiles any speak
That fought with us upon Saint Crispin's day.

{*Enter Salisbury*}

SALISBURY. My sovereign lord, bestow yourself with speed.
The French are bravely in their battles set[2]
And will with all experience charge on us.
KING. All things are ready if our minds be so.
WESTMORELAND. Perish the man whose mind is backward now!
KING. Thou dost not wish more help from England, coz?
WESTMORELAND. God's will, my liege! Would you and I alone,
Without more help, could fight this royal battle!
KING. Why, now thou hast unwished five thousand men,
Which likes me better than to wish us one.
You know your places. God be with you all!

---

[1]give him the rank of a gentleman.
[2]in their battle positions.

This amusing satire depends for some of its humor on sharp contrast between the directors and Mrs. Partridge. Their attitudes will help dictate pace and muscle tone.

From THE SOLID GOLD CADILLAC[1]

The time is the present. The scene is a large room somewhere in downtown New York. An annual stockholders' meeting is in progress and the directors have been carrying on routine business with lightning speed, depending on the stack of proxies to eliminate any comment or opposition from the stockholders who are sitting on folding chairs in the meeting room. Mr. Blessington, the chairman of the board, is presiding. Beside him at the directors' table are Mr. Metcalfe, the company President, Mr. Snell, the Treasurer, and Mr. Gillie, the Secretary of the company.

As our scene opens, Mr. Gillie has just read the roster of officers, and Blessington rises to say:

BLESSINGTON. Thank you, Mr. Gillie. Do I hear a motion to accept Mr. Gillie's report?

SNELL. Moved.

METCALFE. Second.

SNELL. 750,000 proxies vote aye.

BLESSINGTON. Opposed? Carried. And now the report of the man you're really waiting to hear from, your Treasurer, Mr. Clifford Snell.

SNELL. Thank you, Jack. [*The big smile*] Well, folks, I'm the fellow you either like or dislike. Depending on the size of the dividend check, eh? ...And here's the report on how we did this year. I'm sure all of you have found it on your chairs, alongside of Mr. Gillie's little booklet. It isn't as compact as Warren's report, but then you can't do things with figures the way you can with words.... Anyway, suppose you and I kind of thumb through it together.... Let's see. Page 11—just one example. Page 11. Assets—26 billion, one million, seven hundred and ninety-two thousand, eight hundred and ninety-one dollars and seventy-two cents. Now, I think that's pretty good, don't you?

BLESSINGTON. Fine, Clifford. Just fine.

GILLIE. Fine.

[*He continues to flip the pages idly touching ever so lightly on billions in assets and making no mention of debits or expenses.* BLESSINGTON *calls for a motion of approval of the treasurer's report, and the directors respond with their shotgun-quick "Moved—second—proxies vote aye." But before* BLESSINGTON *can call for a unanimous approval from the stockholders, a dumpy little woman has got to her feet. She is* MRS. LAURA PARTRIDGE, *owner of ten shares of stock, who is attending her first stockholders' meeting.*]

---

[1]Condensed from THE SOLID GOLD CADILLAC, by Howard Teichmann and George S. Kaufman. Copyright as an unpublished work 1953 by Howard Teichmann and George S. Kaufman. Copyright 1954 by Howard Teichmann and George S. Kaufman. Reprinted by permission of Random House, Inc.

BLESSINGTON. Yes, Madam?

MRS. PARTRIDGE. Oh! Well, I'm sorry— it's nothing, really.

BLESSINGTON. Then you don't wish the chair to recognize you?

MRS. PARTRIDGE. The—chair?

BLESSINGTON. I am the chair, Madam.

MRS. PARTRIDGE. Oh. I didn't quite—

BLESSINGTON. Do you wish the chair to recognize you?

MRS. PARTRIDGE. I did have something I wanted to ask, but—

BLESSINGTON. Certainly, Madam. What was it you wanted to know?

MRS. PARTRIDGE. Well, it's not really something I want to know, exactly—it's —kind of something I don't like.

SNELL. Can't we get ahead with this, Jack?

BLESSINGTON. Something you don't like? What is it?

MRS. PARTRIDGE. Well, it's—this. [*she holds up the blue book*]

BLESSINGTON. You don't like Mr. Snell's report? All of it?

MRS. PARTRIDGE. No. I don't mean all of it. I—I like the color.

SNELL. Isn't this a little ridiculous?

MRS. PARTRIDGE. I'm sorry, I—I've never attended a stockholders' meeting before. Maybe I'd better sit down.

BLESSINGTON. Just as you wish, Madam.

MRS. PARTRIDGE. Thank you.

BLESSINGTON. Now, there is a motion—

MRS. PARTRIDGE. On the other hand—it says here that the salary for the Chairman of the Board next year will be $175,000. [*Gossipy*] Tell me—is that true?

BLESSINGTON. Well—uh—wherever did you get a notion like that, Miss—uh—

MRS. PARTRIDGE. *Mrs.* Mrs. Partridge. It's on Page 96. Right here.

BLESSINGTON. I see. Uh—Mr. Snell, as Treasurer, would you care to answer that question?

SNELL. Yes, indeed! Happy to oblige... The—uh—could I hear the question again, please?

MRS. PARTRIDGE. I don't want anyone to think I'm nosy but is it true that the Chairman will get $175,000 next year? It seems such a lot of money.

SNELL. Why—Madam. In a company of this size that is not considered a large salary. Not a large salary at all. I believe that answers the question.

BLESSINGTON. Yes. There is a motion—

MRS. PARTRIDGE. Well, would it be just awful if I asked another question? What does the Chairman of the Board do?

SNELL. My dear lady, as an attorney, I can assure you that the office of Chairman of the Board is one prescribed by law. New York State Corporation Code, Section 23. We have very little to say about it—we're just obeying the law.

MRS. PARTRIDGE. Oh I'm sure of that. Only—what does he do?

BLESSINGTON. He presides over the board. The Chairman of the Board presides over the board of directors.

MRS. PARTRIDGE. Now I understand. Thank you so much.

BLESSINGTON. Not at all. We are always happy to—

MRS. PARTRIDGE. How often does he do that?

BLESSINGTON. I beg your pardon?

MRS. PARTRIDGE. How often does he preside over the board?

BLESSINGTON. Why—uh—how often *is* that, Mr. Gillie?

GILLIE. How's that?

BLESSINGTON. How often does the Board meet?

GILLIE. Why—four times a year, isn't it? [*firmly, to Mrs. Partridge.*] Four times a year.

SNELL. That is also prescribed by law.

MRS. PARTRIDGE. Now I know I'm asking a lot of questions, but—how long do the meetings last?

BLESSINGTON. Oh, several hours. At least several hours.

MRS. PARTRIDGE. *Two* hours, would you say?

BLESSINGTON. Yes. Yes, indeed. And then there's the annual stockholders' meeting.

MRS. PARTRIDGE. So that makes five times? ... Well, five meetings a year—that's ten hours in all—you mean he gets $175,000 for just working ten hours?

BLESSINGTON. It's a big job, Mrs. Partridge ....

MRS. PARTRIDGE. Ye-es—still ... it says you used to get $75,000 and now it's going to be $175,000—that's $100,000 more—now, how much did *you* used to get, Mr. Snell?

SNELL. Madam, that is not the point.

MRS. PARTRIDGE. Goodness, I know it isn't, but let's add up, just for fun. Shall we? May I borrow your pencil? Thank you. Now, how much did you say you used to get, Mr. Snell?

SNELL. You'll find everything in the report. I don't recall that—

MRS. PARTRIDGE. Oh, here it is. Fifty thousand dollars. Of course, to the ordinary person, fifty thousand dollars—gracious!

SNELL. This seems to me hardly a matter for—

MRS. PARTRIDGE. Well, I don't mean to be a nuisance, but—can just anybody make a motion?

BLESSINGTON. Certainly, Madam.

MRS. PARTRIDGE. Oh, good. Well, I move the salaries are too big.

BLESSINGTON. It is not quite the proper form for a motion, Mrs. Partridge—however, if someone seconds it—do I hear a second to Mrs. Partridge's motion?

MRS. PARTRIDGE. *I* second it. [*brightly*]

SNELL. Madam, you cannot second your own motion.

MRS. PARTRIDGE. Why not? I'm for it.

SNELL. It's a matter of parliamentary law.

MRS. PARTRIDGE. I don't care what they do in Parliament—I think the salaries are too big, and that some of us here ought to form a stockholders' committee.

BLESSINGTON. A committee?

GILLIE. Committee?

MRS. PARTRIDGE. To look into the salaries of our company's directors. And until we come back with our report—

BLESSINGTON [*a panicky look at his fellows*]. Mrs. Partridge, the chair has

322

decided not to act on the matter of salaries today. The meeting is adjourned, if someone will so move.

SNELL [*lightning-fast*]. Moved.

METCALFE. Second.

BLESSINGTON. It's moved and seconded that we adjourn—opposed? Carried. The meeting is adjourned. The meeting is adjourned for six weeks.

MRS. PARTRIDGE. Six weeks! I can come.

BLESSINGTON. That's splendid.

[*And the stockholders begin to move about the room, as the directors retire for a council of war.*]

Your introduction may be used to "set the stage" for your dramatic interpretation.

The Barretts of Wimpole Street[1] by Rudolf Besier is the story of the courtship and marriage of the poets Elizabeth Barrett and Robert Browning. This scene represents their first meeting although they have corresponded and known each other's poems for some time. Elizabeth Barrett has been an invalid all her life, a condition accepted by her family and friends and encouraged by her tyrannical father. This must be remembered in communicating her attitude during this scene.

The formality of speech is part of the Victorian era in which they lived. They are both mature and intelligent people.

[1]From THE BARRETTS OF WIMPOLE STREET by Rudolf Besier, by permission of Little, Brown and Co. Copyright, 1930, 1958 by Rudolf Besier.

The scene is Elizabeth Barrett's bed-sitting room at Number 50 Wimpole Street, London. The year is 1845. The maid has just announced Mr. Robert Browning, who, after months of pleading, has finally been invited to call.

Robert Browning enters. He is a dark, handsome man in the middle thirties. His manner is sincere and ardent.

BROWNING [*pausing for a moment a few steps beyond the threshold*]. Miss Barrett?

ELIZABETH [*stretching out her hand*]. How-do-you-do, Mr. Browning?

BROWNING [*crosses to the sofa and takes her hand in both of his*]. Dear Miss Barrett—at last! [*raises her hand to his lips*] At last!

ELIZABETH [*still all nerves, and rather overcome by the ardor and unconventionality of his manner*]. I—I've had to put off the pleasure of meeting you much longer than I wished....

BROWNING [*still holding her hand*]. Would you ever have received me if I hadn't been so tiresomely insistent?

ELIZABETH. As you know from my letters, I have not been at all well during the winter, and I—[*Realizing her hand is still in his she gently withdraws it*]. But won't you take off your cape?

BROWNING. Thank you.

ELIZABETH. I—I hope you don't find the room very close, Mr. Browning?

BROWNING. No, no...

ELIZABETH. My doctor obliges me to live in what I am afraid must be to you a—a hot-house temperature....

BROWNING [*throwing a quick glance around the room*]. Wonderful! You may think, Miss Barrett, that this is the first time I've been here. You're quite wrong, you know!

ELIZABETH. But—

BROWNING. Quite wrong. I have seen this room more times than I can remember. It's as familiar to me as my own little study at home! Before I came in, I knew just how your books were arranged, just how that tendril of ivy slanted across the window-panes—and those busts of Homer and Chaucer are quite old friends, and have looked down on me often before!

ELIZABETH [*smilingly protesting*]. No, really—!

BROWNING. But I never could make out who the other fellows were on top of the wardrobe, and—

ELIZABETH [*laughing, and now quite at her ease*]. Oh, come, Mr. Browning! I know that dear Mr. Kenyon is never tired of talking about his friends; but I can't believe that he described my poor little room to you in detail!

BROWNING. I dragged all the details I possibly could out of him—and my imagination supplied the rest. Directly after I had read your brave and lovely verses I was greedy for anything and everything I could get about you.

ELIZABETH [*smilingly*]. You frighten me, Mr. Browning!

BROWNING. Why?

ELIZABETH. Well, you know how Mr. Kenyon's enthusiasms run away with his tongue? He and I are the dearest of friends. What he told you about poor me I quite blush to imagine!

324

BROWNING. You mean, Miss Barrett, about you—you *yourself?*

ELIZABETH. I feel it would be hopeless for me to try to live up to his description.

BROWNING. He never told me anything about you—personally—which had the slightest interest for me.

ELIZABETH [*puzzled*]. Oh?

BROWNING. Everything he could give me about your surroundings and the circumstances of your life I snatched at with avidity. But all he said about *you* was quite beside the point, because I knew it already—and better than Mr. Kenyon, old friend of yours though he is!

ELIZABETH. But—Oh, Mr. Browning, do my poor writings give me so hopelessly away?

BROWNING. Hopelessly—utterly—entirely—to *me!* . . . I can't speak for the rest of the world.

ELIZABETH [*smilingly*]. You frighten me again!

Their conversation turns to poetry and to the admiration they hold for each other's work. Elizabeth, schooled all her life to defeat and weakness cannot rise to Browning's level of exuberance. At last he takes her hands in his and says

BROWNING. I've more life than is good for one man—it seethes and races in me. Up to now I've spent a little of all that surplus energy in creating imaginary men and women. But there's still so much that I've no use for but to give! Mayn't I give it to you? Don't you feel new life tingling and prickling up to your fingers and arms right into your heart and brain?

ELIZABETH [*rather frightened and shaken*]. Oh, please . . . Mr. Browning, let go of my hands. . . . [*He opens his hands; but she still leaves hers lying on his palms for a moment. Then she withdraws them, and clasping her cheeks, looks at him with wide, disturbed eyes.*]

BROWNING [*softly*]. Well?

ELIZABETH [*a little shakily, with forced lightness*]. You—you are really rather an overwhelming person, and in sober truth, I'm—

BROWNING. No—don't tell me again that you are afraid of me! You're not. It's life you're afraid of—and that shouldn't be.

ELIZABETH. Life?

BROWNING. Yes.

ELIZABETH. Well, when life becomes a series of electric shocks!

BROWNING [*smilingly*]. Was it as bad as all that?

ELIZABETH [*smilingly*]. Indeed, yes! Do you affect other people in the same way?

BROWNING. They've often told me so.

ELIZABETH [*lightly*]. No wonder I hesitated about meeting you, much as I wanted to! Something of your disturbing vitality must have come to me from your letters and poems. . . . You'll laugh at me, Mr. Browning, but do you know we very nearly didn't meet today after all! When my maid told me you had arrived I was so panic-stricken that I all but sent down a message that I was too unwell to receive you. And it was a big effort to pull myself together, and behave like a sensible woman, when you came into the room!

BROWNING. I think I must have been quite as nervous as you at that moment.

ELIZABETH. You, Mr. Browning!

BROWNING. Yes—and I'm anything but a nervous man as a rule. But that moment was the climax of my life—up to now.... Miss Barrett, do you remember the first letter I wrote you?

ELIZABETH. Yes, indeed! It was a wonderful letter.

BROWNING. You may have thought I dashed it off in a fit of white-hot enthusiasm over your poems. I didn't. I weighed every word of every sentence. And of one sentence in particular—this sentence: *"I love your books with all my heart—and I love you too."* You remember?

ELIZABETH [*lightly*]. Yes—and I thought it charmingly impulsive of you!

BROWNING [*almost with irritation*]. But I tell you there was nothing impulsive about it. That sentence was as deeply felt and anxiously thought over as any sentence I've ever written.

ELIZABETH. I hope I have many readers like you! It's wonderful to think I may have good friends all the world over whom I have never seen or heard of.

BROWNING. I am not speaking of friendship, but of love. [*Elizabeth is about to make a smiling rejoinder*] No, it's quite useless your trying to put aside the word with a smile and a jest. I said love—and I mean love—

ELIZABETH. But, really, Mr. Browning, I must ask you—

BROWNING [*swiftly interrupting her*]. I'm neither mad nor morbidly impressionable—I'm as sane and level-headed as any man alive. Yet all these months, since first I read your poems, I've been haunted by you. And today you are the center of my life.

ELIZABETH [*very gravely*]. If I were to take you seriously, Mr. Browning, it would, of course, mean the quick finish of a friendship which promises to be very pleasant to both of us.

BROWNING. Why?

ELIZABETH. You know very well that love—in the sense you, apparently, use the word—has no place and can have no place, in my life.

BROWNING. Why?

ELIZABETH. For many reasons— but let this suffice. As I told you before, I am a dying woman.

BROWNING [*passionately*]. I refuse to believe it! For if that were so, God would be callous, and I *know* that He's compassionate—and life would be dark and evil, and I *know* that it's good. You must never say such a thing again. I forbid you to.

ELIZABETH. Forbid, Mr. Browning? ...

BROWNING. Yes—forbid. Isn't it only fair that if you forbid me to speak of you as I feel, and I accept your orders, as I must, that I should be allowed a little forbidding as well?

ELIZABETH. Yes, but ...

BROWNING [*breaking in with sudden gaiety*]. Dear Miss Barrett, what a splendid beginning to our friendship! We have known each other a bare half hour and yet we've talked intimately of art and life and death and love, and we've ordered each other about, and we've almost quarreled! Could anything be happier and more promising? ... With your permission, I'm going now. Mr. Kenyon impressed upon me to make my first visit as short as possible, as strangers tire you. Not that I'm a stranger!— Still I can see that you are tired ... When may I call again?

ELIZABETH [*a little dazed*]. I don't quite know ... I—

BROWNING. Will next Wednesday suit you?

ELIZABETH [*as before*]. Yes, I—I think so. But perhaps it would be better—

BROWING. Next Wednesday then.

ELIZABETH. But—

BROWNING. At half-past three again?

ELIZABETH. Yes—but I—

BROWNING [*bowing over her hand*]. *Au revoir* then.

ELIZABETH. Good-bye.

BROWNING [*gently masterful, retaining her hand*]. *Au revoir.*

ELIZABETH [*a little breathless, after a slight pause*]. *Au revoir.*

BROWNING. Thank you. [*He kisses her hand, turns and picks up his cape, hat, etc. and goes out. The moment after the door has closed behind him Elizabeth sits up and clasps her face with both hands. Then she slips off the sofa and unsteadily gets on to her feet. With the help of the table and the chairs, she manages to cross the room to the window. Grasping the curtain to support herself, she stands looking down into the street after the departing Browning, her face as alive with excitement and joy as though she were a young girl. And the scene slowly closes.*]

Analyze your selection thoroughly before presenting it.

Poetry differs from prose in three general ways. The first difference is the importance of the sound pattern in poetry. Sounds are often important in prose, but they are a basic and integral part of poetry. *The sound pattern of a poem dictates, and is dictated by, all the elements of its structure.*

As you become acquainted with the study of poetry, you learn that the study of its structure is called *prosody* and it is an extremely complex art. For our purpose we will limit the consideration of prosody to the arrangement of light and heavy stresses within the lines, length of line, rhyme (if the poet uses it), and the contribution to the sound pattern of vowels and consonants in adjacent words.

Second is the poet's intention. When an author creates a work in poetry instead of prose, he does so because he is interested in the emotional impact of the ideas. This does not mean poetry

THE INTERPRETATION OF POETRY

never deals with concrete facts. It means that the poet, in his work, uses the sound pattern and connotative elements of his poem to go beyond the facts to an emotional experience.

Third is the high degree of condensation characteristic of poetry. The prose writer might use an entire novel to tell the story of "Richard Cory." To achieve this condensation, the poet makes every word count, not only for denotation but for connotation as well, and whatever added suggestion the sound of the words can carry.

Poetry is of particular interest to the oral interpreter. Its extreme condensation requires close analysis and careful control of emphasis, inflection, pace, and pause. The emotional impact is best served by the interpreter's knowledge of how mind and body can work together to share an experience with an audience. The sound pattern cannot be effective until it is heard. The interpreter's voice is as essential to a poem as a musical instrument is to a musical score. Words on the printed page carry a meaning whether they are read aloud or silently, but poetry depends for its *full impact on the blending of sound and sense.*

TYPES OF POETRY

There are many different types of poetry. Sometimes classification is made on the basis of the structure, as with the sonnet. For our purpose, we will classify poetry on the basis of characteristics of content, as *narrative, dramatic,* or *lyric.*

It is very important to remember that content and structure cannot be separated when considering a poem. The sense and sound work together. What the poem says is only a part; and the sound pattern is another part. They must be used together before you have a poem.

When the content is basically narrative, as in "The Creation" (see page 290), you begin your analysis as you would for any narrative. Then you analyze the sound pattern, or the structure, to see how and where it advances the story.

Poetry may be dramatic. Some plays are written in poetry. Aside from these, a poem is dramatic when it presents a character in a situation without an intervening narrator to tell us what is happening. "Effort at Speech Between Two People" (see page 270) is a good example of this type. In dramatic poetry you must be aware of what kind of character is speaking and why he says what he does.

Lyric poetry shares a highly personal emotional experience of the poet with others. It is comparable to a personal essay or a mood piece. It does not present a story. It is an emotional experience, rather than a series of events, and the one who has the experience is the poet. The time and place in which it happens and the poet's physical characteristics are less important than they are in a narrative, because the experience is of inner emotional response rather than an exterior activity.

FIRST STEPS IN UNDERSTANDING POETRY

Some people don't like poetry. They complain they can't understand it, that it has nothing to do with practical matters, and it doesn't really make sense. That depends on what kind of sense you are asking it to make. A poem need not give facts. Literature goes beyond facts. It is the writer's interpretation and evaluation of facts that are important. We learn to let the writer have his way about what he is trying to say and the way he says it. This approach is doubly important to the poet, since the experience the author shares is a highly personal one. All emotional experiences are not limited to flowers, swooning ladies, and stars. Find a poem about something that interests you. There is no subject in the world about which poets have not written.

If you don't like poetry or feel you don't understand it, try reading a poem aloud, paying close attention to the sound patterns. It is meant to be read aloud. You may find you have been looking at poetry the wrong way. You may even find you've never heard it read well. Poetry need not jog and jingle. But the way the words sound helps the mood and meaning.

Read the poem aloud over and over until the sounds catch your ear. It is always wise to let a poem work on you before you begin working on it. Remember poetry demands a great deal of the reader, just as music does of the musician and the listener. Respond to it from your own experience, and let the poet have his way. Let the poem express what the author wants to say in the way he has written it.

FINDING THE POET'S CLUES

If each reader responds according to his own memories and experience, may not the poem mean completely opposite things to different people? The answer is no. A poem means what the poet intended it to. Then how do we know what he intended if the associations are so personal for both him and us?

The answer to this question is in our earlier discussion of universal experiences. A poet must choose a reference that will produce a comparable memory in the minds of his readers. Notice that we have not said identical. We used the word *comparable.* Poetry moves on various levels. The best poetry grows with us. A poem may mean one thing to you when you are ten, and a great deal more when you are fifteen. A poem about rural life may mean more to one who knows the country than to one who has never seen an apple orchard or a wheat field.

However, if one reader finds a poem sad and another finds it happy, someone is obviously wrong. Perhaps the poet has failed to make his connotations clear and universal. But more likely, one of the readers has taken one line or one image and let it twist the entire poem, ignoring everything else the poet wrote. You must use *all* the clues the poet gives you.

CONSIDERATION OF MEANINGS

One very important clue a writer gives is a well-chosen title. Some poems do not have titles, but when they do, the titles are chosen to direct our minds and support the condensation of the poetry.

An example of the importance of a title is in this sonnet by Archi-

bald MacLeish.[1] Read the poem first without the title.

Quite unexpectedly as Vasserot
The armless ambidextrian was lighting
A match between his great and second toe
And Ralph the lion was engaged in biting
The neck of Madame Sossman while the drum
Pointed, and Teeny was about to cough
In waltz-time swinging Jocko by the thumb—
Quite unexpectedly the top blew off:

And there, there overhead, there, there, hung over
Those thousands of white faces, those dazed eyes,
There in the starless dark, the poise, the hover,
There with vast wings across the canceled skies,
There in the sudden blackness, the black pall
Of nothing, nothing, nothing—nothing at all.

At first glance, this poem seems to be about a circus. We do not know
who Vasserot and Madame Sossman, or Teeny and Jocko, are. Ralph is
identified as a lion, Jocko is the classic name for a trained monkey, and
Teeny may be assumed to be an elephant. The acts are in full swing
when, quite unexpectedly, the top blows off, and overhead there is the
terrible blackness of nothing—nothing at all. This would be a frightening
poem if it were about a circus—but when we look at the title, "The End

[1]The selection from Archibald MacLeish, *Poems 1924-1933*, 1933, is reprinted by permission of and arrangement with Houghton Mifflin Company, the authorized publishers.

of the World," the poem takes on more meaning. Read it now with the title in mind. You will see the irony of the circus theme.

Some aspects of any title are not apparent until study has been given to other aspects of the reading. Do not neglect the author's "label." He used it for a purpose.

Discovering the Poet's Style: Word Choice

Moving from the title to the selection itself, study some details in "The End of the World." Your first task is to be sure of the denotation and connotation of the words. "Ambidextrian" must be identified. After you define it and combine it with "armless" you may be puzzled until you put it back into the side-show atmosphere of the poem's first stanza. You may need to look up "pall" in a dictionary to get the full implication of its use.

There are many other words that bear close inspection. "Quite unexpectedly" carries a load of implication. So do "pointed," "dazed," "poise," "hover," and "canceled." Try reading the poem aloud and let the sounds and the associations of the words help you with the mood. If you rewrote the poem using almost the same words, you would be acutely aware of the importance of the position of each word.

Grammatical Structure

As soon as you are sure you understand the denotation and the connotation of the words, notice how the author used them. It may sometimes be necessary to look at the grammar of an involved sentence to under-stand the relationship of the various parts.

"The End of the World" is one long sentence. When it is reduced to its grammatical core we have "The top blew off, and there (was) nothing," although the poet has omitted the "was." All the rest of the words, phrases, and clauses modify and depend on "the top blew off, and there (was) nothing." Even though "quite unexpectedly," is not part of the subject and predicate, strictly speaking, it must be included in the "core." The poet has indicated it's important by his repeated use of it. So we have "Quite unexpectedly the top blew off, and there (was) nothing."

Notice how this single statement is developed. In the first stanza attention is focused on specific people and animals. There are physical references in "armless," "great and second toe," "the neck of Madame Sossman," "cough in waltz-time" and "thumb." These are small, familiar things that keep our attention on the performance so we are shocked by the unexpectedness of "the top blew off."

See how skillfully the poet goes from names-plus-identification, such as Vasserot, the armless ambidextrian, and Ralph the lion, to just names for Madame Sossman, Teeny, and Jocko.

A close look at the second stanza is equally rewarding. After "the top blew off," there is no further mention of individuals. Instead there are "those thousands of white faces, those dazed eyes," all reflecting the same shock and horror. This is followed by nonhuman references to "wings," "skies," and "blackness," then "pall," and "nothing," repeated like a bell of doom.

Compare the references in the two stanzas, look at the adjectives that modify and color the nouns in each. The only adjectives in the first stanza are *armless* and *great* and *second.* In the second stanza we have many adjectives. There are *"white* faces," *"dazed* eyes," *"starless* dark," *"vast* wings," *"canceled* skies," *"sudden* blackness," and *"black* pall."

The second stanza is a sharp contrast in almost every aspect. It has no connectives, almost no verb forms, and no identifications. There is focus on place, which is described as "there," "overhead," and "over." After place is established, the "overhead" references shift to the more subtle words, "starless," "poise," "hover," "wings," "skies," "blackness," and "pall," and then "nothing." The poem starts with attention to specific things, shifts from the specific to the abstract, and then into nothing. It pounds the repetition of both "there" and "nothing."

The way in which the words are put together into phrases and clauses within the sentence, and introduced by "as," "and," and "while" gives the effect of many things going on at once in the first stanza. We have:

> As Vasserot was lighting
> And Ralph was engaged in biting
> While the drum pointed
> And Teeny was about to cough
> swinging Jocko

The underlined verb forms add to the feeling that things are happening, or about to happen, as in a three-ring circus. This contrasts sharply with the sudden suspension of all action in the second stanza. Then the poet uses the simple past tense of "blew." "Blew off" is the last verb in the poem. We have already noted that the poet left out "was" in the last stanza; and "hung," in its first line, is used as a participial adjective.

IMAGERY

Because poetry is so condensed, poets make appeal to the senses. You know the relationship between bodily response and emotional response. The way we receive impressions of things and store up memories is through our senses. You can check this from your own experience. Recall a carnival, for instance. You will remember the color, the people, the lights on the rides, and sideshow tents. You recall the music of the merry-go-round, the shouts of the barkers, and the squeals of the people on the sky rides. You remember the smell of hamburgers, popcorn, and even the dust-filled air. The taste of cotton candy, the excitement and tension of a ferris-wheel ride, the heat inside the tents may all be part of your memory.

Poets appeal to the senses to stir memories and aid connotation. We see, hear, taste, smell, feel the weight or texture, or warmth or chill of our memories, and our muscles respond. The emotional associations we have with these senses come to our help. The poet can suggest a wealth of connotation when he uses imagery that appeals to our senses.

There are six kinds of imagery that appeal directly to the senses: visual, that appeals to our sense of sight; auditory, to our sense of hearing; olfactory, to our sense of smell; gustatory, to our sense of taste; tactile, to our sense of touch; and thermal, to our response to heat and cold.

There are two kinds of imagery that appeal to the muscles. One is kinetic and indicates physical activity. It is closely related to the theory of muscle memory. The second is called kinesthetic and refers to tension and relaxation of the muscles.

An appeal to one sense usually calls up accompanying appeals to others. As you let yourself see, in your mind's eye, the activities in "The End of the World," you will hear the noise, smell the peanuts and cotton candy, see all the glitter and pageantry that make a circus so exciting. By allowing all your senses to respond you draw on your experience and make the poem richer for yourself and for your audience.

A chart of the various appeals to senses in "The End of the World" would make an interesting study, but it is enough for now that you recognize how these appeals work and allow yourself to let the whole experience flow through your senses, into your muscles.

Figures of Speech

Appeal to the senses is the purpose of figures of speech. Three of the most common literary figures of speech are: the simile, the metaphor, and personification. All imply comparison.

The *simile* states that something is like something else. It may look, move, sound, smell, taste, or feel like something else. The sense appeals established by the first object are transferred to the second object or person. Let us take the beginning of the poem, "A Lady," by Amy Lowell.

> You are beautiful and faded,
> Like an old opera tune
> Played upon a harpsichord;

These lines combine appeal to visual and auditory senses. There is a difference between "an old opera tune played upon a harpsichord;" and "an old folk ballad played on a banjo"! Instead of taking ten lines to tell us what the lady looked like and how she suggested the delicate elegance of past centuries the poet has used a simile. She follows this with another:

> Or like the sun-flooded silks
> Of an eighteenth-century boudoir.

A *metaphor* is like a simile in that it uses qualities of one object to describe another object. The difference is that while a simile says something is like something else, a metaphor says something *is* something else. This same poem has a metaphor in its last stanza.

> My vigor is a new-minted penny,
> Which I cast at your feet.

Personification is used when a writer takes an object or an abstraction, such as love or death, and endows it with human qualities. Carl Sandburg uses personification in his poem "Grass." Emily Dickinson personifies death in the poem, "Because I Could Not Stop for Death." Personification is a metaphor because a nonhuman object or abstraction is said *to be* a person, so that its appearance, action, and other qualities can be described in terms of sense imagery.

Apostrophe is closely related to personification. It is direct address to a personification, or to someone who is absent, or to an abstraction. A poet's use of apostrophe helps you get a clear image and firm mental focus.

Another literary figure of speech is *allusion.* The use of allusions may be a stumbling block to an easy comprehension of some poems. Use the reference works suggested in the appendix and be sure you know the person, place, or thing referred to. Literature is full of allusions to mythology, to historic people, events, and places. It is important to understand why Sandburg used the place names he did in "Grass."

SCANSION

The first element we will consider in the sound pattern is the arrangement of light and heavier stresses within a line of poetry. The grouping of light and heavier stresses into feet is called *scansion.* It has been of interest to poets and scholars for centuries. The interpreter goes a step further than the scholar. He scans as a guide to reading the poem. He combines what he finds in the arrangement of light and heavier stresses with all the other elements of content and sound pattern that he discovers by analysis.

Within each line of traditional poetry there is a pattern of light and heavier stresses. These for centuries have been grouped as units, and have been known as feet. The most common is the *iamb,* a lightly stressed syllable followed by one with a heavier stress, as in the word *within.* The iamb is indicated ⌣ ⁄ . The combination of light and heavier stress need not be within a single word, as you can see from these lines from "Abraham Lincoln Walks at Midnight."

He cannot rest until a spirit-dawn

Shall come:—the shining hope of Europe free:

Other types of poetic feet, used within iambic poems, or that may pre-
dominate are:

> Trochee, marked / ◡, as in *Bringing* long peace...
> Anapest, marked ◡◡ /, which is combined with iambs in:
>
> Two roads diverged in a yellow wood,
>
> Dactyl, marked / ◡◡, as in:
>
> Wonder is not precisely knowing,

You will notice that in this line from Miss Dickinson's poem she combines dactyls with trochees. Two other types, not so common but often
used in modern poetry, are the pyrrhic, marked ◡ ◡, which has only two
light stresses, and the spondee, which is two heavy stresses and is marked
/ /. "Two roads" and "long peace" are spondee feet in the examples above.

The interpreter scans a poem to find what feet the poet used. He does
not force the poem into a pattern which cannot be achieved when the
poem is read aloud. He lets the poet have his way and studies the poem.

It is important for the interpreter to consider the degree of stress.
All syllables marked with / will not have the same weight of stress. For
the interpreter, stress is influenced by the connotation and tone color of
each word in its relation to the whole poem.

The interpreter scans because he must read the poem aloud. He is less
interested in traditional feet than in the arrangement of light and heavier
stresses to increase tone color and to support emotional impact. The important thing for him to discover is where the poet has broken the accepted pattern and what this indicates about climaxes.

Scansion of Sonnet xxx

The easiest way to discover the variations within the pattern is to group
the stresses into traditional feet. Here is a copy of a sonnet with the stresses
marked, as the poem might be read, to develop some of the aspects discussed in relation to content and emotional impact. We have grouped the
stresses into traditional feet. Wherever there is a variation of the iambic
foot, we have underlined it. You may disagree with the marking of one
or several feet. Remember, for the interpreter the problem is one of degree.

338

If you change the marked stresses in an occasional place, the chances are there will be little to alter in the general conclusion we have reached.

SONNET XXX[1]
Love Is Not All
by Edna St. Vincent Millay

> Love is | not all: | it is | not meat | nor drink |
> Nor slum | ber nor | a roof | against | the rain; |
> Nor yet | a float | ing spar | to men | that sink |
> And rise | and sink | and rise | and sink | again; |
> Love can | not fill | the thick | ened lung | with breath, |
> Nor clean | the blood, | nor set | the frac | tured bone; |
> Yet ma | ny a man | is mak | ing friends | with death |
> Even | as I speak, | for lack | of love | alone. |
> It well | may be | that in | a diff | icult hour, |
> Pinned down | by pain | and moan | ing for | release, |
> Or nagged | by want | past re | solu | tion's power, |
> I might | be driv | en to sell | your love | for peace, |
> Or trade | the mem | ory of | this night | for food. |
> It well | may be. | I do | not think | I would. |

Someone interested only in scansion for its own sake might mark each of the following lines, for instance, with five iambic feet to the line.

> Love is | not all: | it is | not meat | nor drink ...
> Love can | not fill | the thick | ened lung | with breath ...
> Pinned down | by pain | and moan | ing for | release ...

This is correct. The poem is a sonnet, and five iambic feet per line is a characteristic of the sonnet structure. But the interpreter does not read

[1]From COLLECTED POEMS, Harper & Brothers. Copyright 1927-1955 by Edna St. Vincent Millay and Norma Millay Ellis.

the lines that way. He stresses "love" rather than "is," as the poem opens to catch and hold his audience's attention on this important word.

The imagery and the tone color of "Pinned down by pain" would be weakened by insisting on the iambic foot. In the thirteenth line above, it is the memory of *this* night that is important, so the poem becomes a more specific experience when we allow the spondee foot on "this night."

LENGTH OF LINES

In traditional poetry, line length is measured by the number of feet, as we noted when we discussed the Sonnet by Miss Millay. When a poet is consistent in the lengths of his lines, it provides a strong unifying element to the sound pattern. But when he varies a single line in a stanza, the interpreter must assume he did it on purpose and look for the effect it has on pace or change of emotional tone.

In free verse, scansion is often erratic and may not fall into a predominant type of foot. We must then look elsewhere for the rhythmic basis. In free verse it is usually found in the number of syllables, not feet, in the lines, or in the number of stresses per line whether or not they are traditional feet. The line is a basic rhythmic unit within the sound pattern of the poem and must not be ignored.

A poet ends his lines where he does for a reason. This is particularly true of modern verse where the poet can make his lines any length because he is not holding himself within a traditional form. Even in traditional poetry, line lengths are important.

The interpreter takes his cue from the poet. He always uses some kind of a pause at the end of every line of poetry. But a word of caution before you take this rule at its face value. There are all kinds and lengths of pauses. Most poets indicate by punctuation what kind of pause should interrupt the flow of thought. This is not always a perfect guide because some poets have nearly as much trouble with commas as you and I.

The whole unit of thought may not be complete in each line. It is not completed until the end of the sentence. The interpreter will not use a terminal, end-of-the-thought pause until he *reaches* the end of the thought. Often the second line is a separate clause, as in:

> My vigor is a new-minted penny,
> Which I cast at your feet.

340

The interpreter handles the pause after *penny* as he would in prose. The poet has given him a visual clue with the comma.

Straddling Lines

There is not always such a clear indication as a comma. Take the lines:

> Like an old opera tune
> Played upon a harpsichord.

The lady is not just *like an old opera tune,* but *like an old opera tune* (that is) *played upon a harpsichord.* There is no punctuation at the end of the first line. This is an *enjambment* line. The word is French, meaning "straddling." The thought straddles the line end. It is also called a run-on line, but that term indicates the interpreter runs full speed into the next line. Straddling is a more exact word for our purpose.

A well-written poem gives the interpreter a chance for a slight pause where the thought straddles the lines. Sometimes the opportunity comes when a new characteristic is being added, as *played upon a harpsichord.* Sometimes it comes from the need to stress tone color or emphasize sense appeals. As in this second line:

> And the perfume of your soul
> is vague and suffusing,
> With the pungence of sealed spice-jars.

These three lines provide two different pause lengths before the thought is completed. Attention to line lengths gives the poem an underlying pulse from the flow of sounds and pauses. This is important in unrhymed poetry and free verse.

Handling straddling lines requires a delicate touch, a sensitive mind, and a trained ear. These are the requisites of a skilled interpreter, and your ability to control the line-end pauses will increase as you practice. The audience should never be conscious of the divisions into lines as you read. They are not interested in how it is arranged.

TONE COLOR

Before we take a look at the third element of the sound pattern, that is, rhyme, let us consider the contribution of the vowel and consonant sounds within adjacent words that produce tone color.

You may read that certain combinations of sounds have specific associational effects on the hearer. This is not entirely true. You need only compare *sleep* and *slap* to be aware that the vowel change does not account for the whole difference in your response. Nevertheless, the way sounds are combined can be very helpful in bringing out all levels of association. Most authorities agree it is practically impossible to separate sound from connotation.

The manipulation of vowels and consonants to achieve a sound effect is called tone color. Tone color is a large term that embraces such technical matters as alliteration (the repetition of the initial sound in two or more adjacent words, as *big, black bug*), onomatopoeia (a word whose sound imitates the object or action it refers to, as *sizzle*), assonance (agreement of vowel sounds), and consonance (agreement of consonant sounds). We are concerned with how sounds blend within the poem rather than with labeling each type.

Attention to tone color is of great help in varying the pace of your performance and giving you and your audience time to savor the sounds and understand the connotations of the appeal to the senses. Tone color is part of the sound pattern, and its effect on the emotions is deliberate. Make full use of all combinations of sounds when you read the poem aloud.

In general, poetry should be read slower than other forms of writing, because it is condensed and dependent on sound reinforcement for its full impact. Your diction must be especially good to read poetry aloud. Notice how the sounds help the imagery and the shock of the eighth line of "The End of the World," when you are careful to bring out the *p* and *b* of "top blew off." In "A Lady," if instead of "Smolder the fallen roses of outlived minutes," one said "Smoder the fawn rose of oulived mints" one would not only have a peculiar meaning but would lose all value of the *l*, *m*, and *n* sounds in the line. Poetry should feel good in the mouth as you say it. Take the time to pronounce all the sounds the poet used.

In our discussion of scansion we mentioned "Pinned down by pain," which is a subtle example of tone color. The need to pronounce the *d* of "pinned" before "down" and the repetition of the *p* and *n* in "pain" create a tight-jawed feeling that it connotes.

Tone color is a vital part of content and contributes to connotation and structure in its relation to the sound pattern. Content and structure cannot be separated; they must work together. For analysis they are treated

342

individually, but they must always be put together and considered for their mutual effect. Otherwise you do not have the poem.

RHYME

Rhyme is the correspondence of sounds in the final syllables of two or more lines of poetry. The pattern of rhyme sounds makes up the rhyme scheme.

In rhyme scheme the sounds are especially prominent because they are repeated at regular intervals. Their position at the line-end where there is a pause, be it ever so slight, gives the sound added emphasis. When a poet uses rhyme, he does so to bind the poem together. Sometimes he will use rhymes within the line and at the end, as Tennyson does in "The Lotos-Eaters" when he says:

> Sun-steeped at *noon*, and in the *moon*
> Nightly dew fed.

Even "dew" is very close to "moon" and "noon." Modern poets do not often use inner rhyme, but they frequently take a rhyme sound on the final syllable of a line, even when there is no formal rhyme scheme, and repeat or approximate it *within* the lines that follow. This is not strictly rhyme, but it produces a subtle sound pattern.

Free verse can also rhyme and the poet often inserts rhyme in a section of a long poem. Whenever you encounter rhyme, use it as a unifying device. You will find it helps the mood. Examine this use of rhyme in Robert Frost's poem "The Road Not Taken." This is a disarming but brilliantly constructed poem. Look at the rhyme words:

wood	fair	lay	sigh
both	claim	black	hence
stood	wear	day	I
could	there	way	by
undergrowth	same	back	difference

Turn to the poem and note how many of the sounds are repeated or approximated throughout it. The shifting from one type of *o* sound to another within the first stanza is a strong contribution to the mood of gentle remembering. How much farther "far" seems placed among the *o* sounds in the fourth line!

MATERIAL FOR PERFORMANCE

The following poems offer a wide variety of ideas, mood, and sound patterns. Whichever one you choose, remember to let the poet have his way. Make full use of all imagery and all elements of the sound pattern. Pay particular attention to the line lengths.

Here is a witty, yet serious, comment on the definable and indefinable in modern poetry.

POETRY[1]
by Marianne Moore

I, too, dislike it: there are things that are important beyond all this fiddle.
  Reading it, however, with a perfect contempt for it, one discovers in
    it after all, a place for the genuine.
      Hands that can grasp, eyes
        that can dilate, hair that can rise
          if it must, these things are important not because a

high-sounding interpretation can be put upon them but because they are
  useful. When they become so derivative as to become unintelligible,
    the same thing may be said for all of us, that we
      do not admire what
        we cannot understand: the bat
          holding on upside down or in quest of something to

eat, elephants pushing, a wild horse taking a roll, a tireless wolf under
  a tree, the immovable critic twitching his skin like a horse that feels a flea, the
  baseball fan, the statistician—
      nor is it valid
        to discriminate against "business documents and

school-books"; all these phenomena are important. One must make a distinction
  however: when dragged into prominence by half poets, the result is not poetry,
  nor till the poets among us can be
      "literalists of
        the imagination"—above
          insolence and triviality and can present

for inspection, "imaginary gardens with real toads in them," shall we have
  it. In the meantime, if you demand on the one hand,
    the raw material of poetry in
      all its rawness and
        that which is on the other hand
          genuine, you are interested in poetry.

[1]Reprinted with permission of the publisher from *Selected Poems* by Marianne Moore. Copyright 1935 by Marianne Moore.

ABRAHAM LINCOLN WALKS AT MIDNIGHT[1]
(IN SPRINGFIELD, ILLINOIS)
by Vachel Lindsay

It is portentous, and a thing of state
That here at midnight, in our little town
A mourning figure walks, and will not rest,
Near the old court-house pacing up and down,

Or by his homestead, or in shadowed yards
He lingers where his children used to play,
Or through the market, on the well-worn stones
He stalks until the dawn-stars burn away.

A bronzed, lank man! His suit of ancient black,
A famous high top-hat and plain worn shawl
Make him the quaint·great figure that men love,
The prairie-lawyer, master of us all.

He cannot sleep upon his hillside now.
He is among us:—as in times before!
And we who toss and lie awake for long,
Breathe deep, and start, to see him pass the door.

His head is bowed. He thinks of men and kings.
Yea, when the sick world cries, how can he sleep?
Too many peasants fight, they know not why;
Too many homesteads in black terror weep.

The sins of all the war-lords burn his heart.
He sees the dreadnaughts scouring every main.
He carries on his shawl-wrapped shoulders now
The bitterness, the folly and the pain.

He cannot rest until a spirit-dawn
Shall come;—the shining hope of Europe free:
A league of sober folk, the workers' Earth,
Bringing long peace to Cornland, Alp and Sea.

It breaks his heart that kings must murder still,
That all his hours of travail here for men
Seem yet in vain. And who will bring white peace
That he may sleep upon his hill again?

GRASS[1]
by Carl Sandburg

Pile the bodies high at Austerlitz and Waterloo.
Shovel them under and let me work—
      I am the grass; I cover all.

And pile them high at Gettysburg
And pile them high at Ypres and Verdun.
Shovel them under and let me work.
Two years, ten years, and passengers ask the conductor:
      What place is this?
      Where are we now?
      I am the grass. Let me work.

Emily Dickinson did not write any long poems, but she was able to achieve great condensation within a few lines.[2]

Wonder—is not precisely Knowing
And not precisely Knowing not—
A beautiful but bleak condition
He has not lived who has not felt—

Suspense—is his maturer Sister—
Whether Adult Delight is Pain
Or of itself a new misgiving—
That is the Gnat that mangles men—

---

[1]From CORNHUSKERS by Carl Sandburg. Copyright 1918 by Holt, Rinehart and Winston, Inc. Copyright renewed 1946 by Carl Sandburg. Reprinted by permission of Holt, Rinehart and Winston, Inc.
[2]Poem #581 "Wonder Is Not Precisely Knowing" from BOLTS OF MELODY, New Poems of Emily Dickinson, edited by Mabel Loomis Todd and Millicent Todd Bingham. Copyright 1945 by Millicent Todd Bingham. Reprinted by permission of Harper & Row, Publishers, Incorporated.

This free verse poem is especially rich in imagery. Make full use of the contrast in the last stanza.

A LADY[1]
by Amy Lowell

You are beautiful and faded
Like an old opera tune
Played upon a harpsichord;
Or like the sun-flooded silks
Of an eighteenth-century boudoir.
In your eyes
Smolder the fallen roses of out-lived minutes,
And the perfume of your soul
Is vague and suffusing,
With the pungence of sealed spice-jars.
Your half-tones delight me,
And I grow mad with gazing
At your blent colors.

My vigor is a new-minted penny,
Which I cast at your feet.
Gather it up from the dust,
That its sparkle may amuse you.

Here is a selection from a poem that seems at first glance to be only a listing of images. On closer observation, however, it reveals the poet's philosophy of life and death. The kinds of silences are grouped into those that are easily associated with each other, a device that helps retain the unity.

SILENCE[2]
by Edgar Lee Masters

I have known the silence of the stars and of the sea,
And the silence of the city when it pauses,
And the silence of a man and a maid,
And the silence for which music alone finds the word,
And the silence of the woods before the winds of spring begin,
And the silence of the sick
When their eyes roam about the room.
And I ask: For the depths
Of what use is language?
A beast of the field moans a few times

[1]The selection from Amy Lowell, SWORD BLADES AND POPPY SEED, 1914, is reprinted by permission of and arrangement with Houghton Mifflin Company, the authorized publishers.
[2]From *Songs and Satires,* by Edgar Lee Masters, Macmillan (1916, 1944).

347

When death takes its young:
And we are voiceless in the presence of realities—
We cannot speak.
A curious boy asks an old soldier
Sitting in front of the grocery store,
"How did you lose your leg?"
And the old soldier is struck with silence,
Or his mind flies away
Because he cannot concentrate it on Gettysburg.
It comes back jocosely
And he says, "A bear bit it off."
And the boy wonders, while the old soldier
Dumbly, feebly, lives over
The flashes of guns, the thunder of cannon,
The shrieks of the slain,
And himself lying on the ground,
And the hospital surgeons, the knives,
And the long days in bed.
But if he could describe it all
He would be an artist.
But if he were an artist there would be deeper wounds
Which he could not describe.

The formality of the structure helps give this poem affirmation, strength, and dignity. Use the repeated lines carefully to express this affirmation.

AND DEATH SHALL HAVE NO DOMINION[1]
by Dylan Thomas

And death shall have no dominion.
Dead men naked they shall be one
With the man in the wind and the west moon;
When their bones are picked clean and the clean bones gone,
They shall have stars at elbow and foot;
Though they go mad they shall be sane,
Though they sink through the sea they shall rise again;
Though lovers be lost love shall not;
And death shall have no dominion.

And death shall have no dominion.
Under the windings of the sea
They lying long shall not die windily;
Twisting on racks when sinews give way,
Strapped to a wheel, yet they shall not break;

Faith in their hands shall snap in two,
And the unicorn evils run them through;
Split all ends up they shan't crack;
And death shall have no dominion.

And death shall have no dominion.
No more may gulls cry at their ears
Or waves break loud on the seashores;
Where blew a flower may a flower no more
Lift its head to the blows of the rain;
Though they be mad and dead as nails,
Heads of the characters hammer through the daisies;
Break in the sun till the sun breaks down,
And death shall have no dominion.

THURSDAY[1]
by Edna St. Vincent Millay

And if I loved you Wednesday,
    Well, what is that to you?
I do not love you Thursday—
    So much is true.

And why you come complaining
    Is more than I can see.
I loved you Wednesday,—yes—but what
    Is that to me?

This grim and starkly realistic poem of the witnesses at an auto accident contains some difficult words you will need to look up, but it asks a very modern and moving question.

AUTO WRECK[2]
by Karl Shapiro

Its quick soft silver bell beating, beating,
And down the dark one ruby flare
Pulsing out red light like an artery,
The ambulance at top speed floating down
Past beacons and illuminated clocks
Wings in a heavy curve, dips down,
And brakes speed, entering the crowd.
The doors leap open, emptying light;
Stretchers are laid out, the mangled lifted
And stowed into the little hospital.

[1]From COLLECTED POEMS, Harper & Brothers. Copyright 1927-1955 by Edna St. Vincent Millay and Norma Millay Ellis.
[2]Copyright 1941 by Karl Shapiro. Reprinted from POEMS 1940-1953, by Karl Shapiro, by permission of Random House, Inc.

Then the bell, breaking the hush, tolls once,
And the ambulance with its terrible cargo
Rocking, slightly rocking, moves away,
As the doors, an afterthought, are closed.

We are deranged, walking among the cops
Who sweep glass and are large and composed.
One is still making notes under the light.
One with a bucket douches ponds of blood
Into the street and gutter.
One hangs lanterns on the wrecks that cling,
Empty husks of locusts, to iron poles.

Our throats were tight as tourniquets,
Our feet were bound with splints, but now,
Like convalescents intimate and gauche,
We speak through sickly smiles and warn
With the stubborn saw of common sense,
The grim joke and the banal resolution.
The traffic moves around with care,
But we remain, touching a wound
That opens to our richest horror.

Already old, the question Who shall die?
Becomes unspoken Who is innocent?
For death in war is done by hands;
Suicide has cause and stillbirth, logic;
And cancer, simple as a flower, blooms.
But this invites the occult mind,
Cancels our physics with a sneer,
And spatters all we knew of denouement
Across the expedient and wicked stones.

The two lines just below the title are from Joseph Conrad's *Heart of Darkness*, and a phrase used by English children on Guy Fawkes' Day. Find out about both sources. The three kingdoms are: actual death but accepted with faith, which Kingdom has a capital "K"; sleep or unconsciousness in which the subconscious may plague those who doubt and fear; and physical life which is merely existence without will or moral life. Notice what builds to climaxes are almost immediately canceled and come to nothing. Make careful use of line-lengths to help achieve this hesitant, negative quality.

THE HOLLOW MEN[1]
by T. S. Eliot

Mistah Kurtz—he dead,
A penny for the old guy.

I

We are the hollow men
We are the stuffed men
Leaning together
Headpiece filled with straw. Alas!
Our dried voices, when
We whisper together
Are quiet and meaningless
As wind in dry grass
Or rats' feet over broken glass
In our dry cellar

Shape without form, shade without colour,
Paralysed force, gesture without motion;

Those who have crossed
With direct eyes, to death's other Kingdom
Remember us—if at all—not as lost
Violent souls, but only
As the hollow men
The stuffed men.

II

Eyes I dare not meet in dreams
In death's dream kingdom
These do not appear:
There, the eyes are
Sunlight on a broken column
There, is a tree swinging
And voices are
In the wind's singing
More distant and more solemn
Than a fading star.

Let me be no nearer
In death's dream kingdom
Let me also wear
Such deliberate disguises
Rat's coat, crowskin, crossed staves

In a field
Behaving as the wind behaves
No nearer—

Not that final meeting
In the twilight kingdom

III

This is the dead land
This is cactus land
Here the stony images
Are raised, here they receive
The supplication of a dead man's hand
Under the twinkle of a fading star.

Is it like this
In death's other kingdom
Waking alone
At the hour when we are
Trembling with tenderness
Lips that would kiss
Form prayers to broken stone.

IV

The eyes are not here
There are no eyes here
In this valley of dying stars
In this hollow valley
This broken jaw of our lost kingdoms

In this last of meeting places
We grope together
And avoid speech
Gathered on this beach of the tumid river

Sightless, unless
The eyes reappear
As the perpetual star
Multifoliate rose
Of death's twilight kingdom
The hope only
Of empty men.

V

*Here we go round the prickly pear
Prickly pear prickly pear
Here we go round the prickly pear
At five o'clock in the morning.*

Between this idea
And the reality
Between the motion
And the act
Falls the Shadow

                      For Thine is the Kingdom

Between the conception
And the creation
Between the emotion
And the response
Falls the Shadow

                      For Thine is the Kingdom

For Thine is
Life is
For Thine is the
This is the way the world ends
This is the way the world ends
This is the way the world ends
Not with a bang but a whimper.

THE ROAD NOT TAKEN[1]
by Robert Frost

Two roads diverged in a yellow wood,
And sorry I could not travel both
And be one traveler, long I stood
And looked down one as far as I could
To where it bent in the undergrowth;

Then took the other, as just as fair,
And having perhaps the better claim,
Because it was grassy and wanted wear;
Though as for that the passing there
Had worn them really about the same,

And both that morning equally lay
In leaves no step had trodden black.
Oh, I kept the first for another day!
Yet knowing how way leads on to way,
I doubted if I should ever come back.

I shall be telling this with a sigh
Somewhere ages and ages hence:
Two roads diverged in a wood, and I—
I took the one less travelled by,
And that has made all the difference.

[1]From COMPLETE POEMS OF ROBERT FROST. Copyright 1916, 1921, 1923, 1928 by Holt, Rinehart and Winston, Inc. Copyright renewed 1944, 1951, © 1956 by Robert Frost. Reprinted by permission of Holt, Rinehart and Winston, Inc.

In this chapter we are interested in studying a method of group interpretation: choric interpretation.

Choric interpretation is not a separate art. It is a part of interpretation and is governed by the same rules and methods as individual interpretation. The difference lies in the use of many voices, bodies, and minds, working together. Good choric interpretation is more than just a group of people saying the same words at the same time and starting and stopping together. Precision is important because without it the audience cannot understand what is being said. However, the techniques of choric interpretation are always a means to an end, never an end in themselves.

You may wish to try group interpretation in the classroom or more formally for an assembly program or public performance. Your attention to technical details will vary with the purpose for which you are going to use choric work.

CHORIC INTERPRETATION

RESPONSIBILITIES OF THE INDIVIDUAL IN A CHORIC GROUP

Your director will divide the material into various units, and the voice group you are in will not speak the entire selection in performance. Nevertheless, *you are responsible for the whole selection* so you and your unit will fit smoothly into the total effect. That is why your early rehearsals will be done in unison.

Follow the same general process of analysis you use when you are going to perform alone. You must discover each separate element in the selection so you know what you have to work with. Then put the material together again. Much of this will be done during discussion with the group, but you must know from individual study the meaning, the denotation, and the connotation of each word, the method of organization, and all the details you have learned to study.

Critics of choric interpretation often claim that the individual must give up his own ideas to work with a group. Sometimes this happens, but we know that good writing gives unmistakable clues to all who do a thorough job of analysis. If there is disagreement as to meaning, the group must reëxamine the piece together and arrive at a common response. If you *let the author have his way,* you are almost certain to work toward the same effect. Until the entire group reaches agreement, you will discuss and analyze, because the audience must receive a unified effect.

Individual analysis remains the first step in choric interpretation. After you have completed this analysis, you work on your techniques of voice and body to achieve the best possible communication of all the parts that make up the whole. A group is only as effective as each individual member working in it. You will soon learn to hear the others in relation to yourself and blend your techniques with theirs. Don't be afraid to speak out and make use of all you have learned. Your director would rather tone down a group than try to force life into one that is tentative, with everyone waiting for someone else to speak out. How much you work alone between group rehearsals will make all the difference.

As you begin to work aloud on the selection, pay particular attention to your enunciation. Each word must be clear and distinct. This is even more important with a group than with a single reader because a slurred vowel or muffled consonant, multiplied by the number in the group, makes the reading unintelligible to the audience. Remember controlled volume and a good firm tone are the result of proper breathing. Vocal energy is of the utmost importance in choric interpretation.

BODILY ACTION IN CHORIC INTERPRETATION

It is a common error to think of choric interpretation in terms of voices alone. The voice and body must work together to communicate what the mind has learned. Whenever the audience sees the choir of interpreters, bodily action must be considered, because it can add or detract from the effect of the communication. Posture and muscle tone must be as alert and vital for group work as for an individual performance. Be sure you respond to all the imagery and emotional elements during your rehearsals and use this response when you are with the group.

A choir may use gestures just as an individual interpreter does. It is a safe rule that gestures *do not describe* an object. A group of adults with their arms stretched out to look like trees is distracting, to put it mildly. Gestures should come from the way the object *makes you feel.*

SELECTION OF MATERIAL

The range of material suitable for choric interpretation is far wider than is sometimes supposed. The first consideration is the author's intent. If the writing is intended to share an extremely individual and private experience it is probably better for a single interpreter. If the selection speaks for many people, even though expressed in the single voice of the writer, it is suitable for a choir. "The End of the World," for instance, would be

At rehearsals, the director leads the chorus; at the performance, the director does not appear onstage.

appropriate, and T. S. Eliot's "The Hollow Men" is very effective as a choric piece. A love sonnet that implies one person speaking to or of another person would be less safe. But all literature that uses the personal pronoun *I* need not be avoided. You will find some first person singular suggestions at the end of this chapter.

The stronger a work is, the more suitable it is for performance by many voices. This is true of patriotic selections and subjects that have great dignity and depth. The presence of strong masculine voices in a choir is especially helpful in these cases.

Another factor in selecting material is the kind of climaxes the reading contains and the way they are achieved. Material that depends on sharp contrasts or on accumulation for the climaxes often is most effective with many voices.

The richness and importance of the sound pattern are important considerations. Tone color and all the subtle aspects of rhythm often can be brought out more effectively by a group with different voice qualities and levels of pitch than by a single interpreter.

VOICE DIVISIONS

Some material may be divided into units, with various voice groups speaking only specific parts of the whole selection. This may be the result of the director's decision or the outgrowth of group discussions.

There are many ways of arranging any selection. The decision will depend on the size of the group and the quality of the available voices, so it is never satisfactory to try to use someone else's arrangements. What worked for ten people may not do for thirty.

The clues for the voice arrangement will come from the demands of the material. There may be lines or sections that call for strong voices, while others will need a lighter touch. The decision will be based on tone color and connotation and on the senses you wish to arouse.

The type of climax may be a determining factor in the arrangement. Climaxes are built in numerous ways. If you build a cumulative one, your director may wish to add voices as the tension builds. This is the arrangement suggested for "The Negro Speaks of Rivers" at the end of this chapter. Or he may prefer to use the effect of unison and ask you to increase volume as the tension builds. If the climax is sudden and depends on sharp contrast, he may use an abrupt change in voices to emphasize it. If the selection diminishes after the climax, as in the last line of "Stage Directions," he may want to decrease the number of voices to enhance this effect.

Ask yourself how a particular unit was meant to sound. Then decide whether the effect can best be attained by a single voice, by unison, by two, three, or any number of voices blended for a particular quality, or by a clear division between light and dark voices.

LIGHT AND DARK VOICES

The term *light and dark voices* may need some explanation. The difference is not of pitch but of resonance. Light does not mean high, but refers to a voice having fewer overtones and undertones than a dark, or lower, voice. The difference is like that between a violin and a cello. Both can produce the same note on the scale, but the resonance is different.

The classification of voices within any group càn only be relative. There may not be any voice that is undeniably light or dark within your choir. But by comparison some are darker than others. Never push your voice up or down from its natural range for a humorous effect. If you do, the result will be artificial and violates one of the basic rules of good interpretation by calling attention to the performers and away from the reading.

REHEARSAL SUGGESTIONS

After preliminary discussions you begin to work aloud in group rehearsals. If all of you have done a thorough job in your individual analyses, you will soon move from unison to whatever voice division you decided on.

Mark your manuscript clearly so you remember all directions. The simplest method is to mark each selection as you go along, using *LV* for light voices, *DV* for dark voices, and *U* for unison. You will find this method used at the end of the chapter. It will help keep the unity of the selection if you know which group is to speak which unit. Underline those units you will speak. When you work alone, read the entire selection several times, and then work in detail on your assigned units.

KEEP THE SELECTION TOGETHER

Whenever a selection is divided into separate voice divisions there is danger of losing the unity. It is your responsibility to see that this does not happen. When you are not speaking, continue to concentrate on the whole reading. Your unit or units must fit into the plan and become a functioning part of the total effect. Your body and mind must remain alert and responsive, and you must be ready to pick up your cue without breaking the pace. If you think about the poem even when you are not speaking, you will be ready when your cue comes. Take a good breath before you begin and then speak the words cleanly and clearly. You must project to the back of the room just as you would when you perform alone. This does not mean you should shout, but that your tones should be sustained and firm.

Vocal monotony shows up more in a choir than in an individual performance. A group tends to drop to the lowest common denominator, and the pace gets slower and slower if each waits for somebody else. If you feel that the selection is dragging during rehearsal, either in pace or inflection, take the responsibility for picking it up. By the time you are ready to perform you will have established the habit of trusting each other and thus keep the material moving without rushing it or slighting the pauses.

A problem that sometimes develops during rehearsals is that undue attention is given to the quality of the sound at the expense of the content. This may result in overemphasis of the rhythm. Or the tone color may be so tempting the choir soars into an orchestration of beautiful sounds signifying nothing. If this happens, recall the first steps in your analysis, especially of the organization of content and the location of climaxes. Every detail must relate to every other detail for the total effect, and no one aspect of your interpretation should call attention to itself.

THE TIMING OF GESTURES

When your group uses gestures, they must be carefully worked out so their timing is perfect. Hands flying up and down at various intervals are totally ineffective. All the palms should be turned the same way, and the pace and extent of each gesture should be the same for every member of the group. It is better to understate than overstate any big gesture, but don't be afraid to use one when it is appropriate and adds strength to communication and emotional response.

Bodily action may range from a subtle change in muscle tone to dance movements, depending on the requirements of the selection and the ability of the group.

The arrangement of the choir on stage can suggest the mood of the selection. There are many ways of grouping people so they present an interesting and appropriate picture. At the end of the chapter are some suggested groupings for poems. They are only suggestions and may need to be changed, depending on the size of the group and the purpose of the choric interpretation. For informal classroom work this aspect can be eliminated.

SUGGESTIONS FOR PERFORMANCE

You have the same responsibilties during a group performance as in a single performance, but, in addition, you must blend your voice to achieve the effect needed for the sound patterns, and discipline and time your bodily actions so they are in harmony with the others and do not break the total effect.

It is the responsibility of each member of the choir to keep constant mental contact with the audience. Just because there are twenty-nine other people is no reason for one to drift off into his own little dream world. A choir is only as effective as each member chooses to make it.

The Director's Role

If a director stands in front of the choir during performance, the attention of the group is focused on him and never reaches the audience. This results in loss of mental contact and lack of directness because the attention of the audience is held by the director. The physical presence of the director during performance violates two basic rules of good interpretation. First, it calls attention to the mechanics of the art and detracts from the reading of the selection. Second, it interferes with directness and hinders communication.

Your group will need direction during rehearsals. It is a wise director, however, who works as far back in the room as possible so the group becomes accustomed to projecting past the edge of the platform. As you get used to working together, keeping your attention concentrated on the material, and sharing it with the audience, the director can step aside. In the last phases of rehearsal he should not need to do more than give an occasional corrective signal. The most he needs to do during performance is to give an unobtrusive starting signal from wherever he is seated in the auditorium.

Miscellaneous Suggestions

Whether or not you memorize your selections depends on personal preference and some practical considerations. A group often feels more secure with manuscripts, especially if rehearsal time has been limited. If typed papers are used, they should be uniformly bound for appearance and ease in handling.

Black loose-leaf notebooks are practical. Every member of the group must be sufficiently free of dependence on the page to ensure directness and holding the attention of the audience. If your group uses large gestures, a manuscript will be awkward.

Depending on the mood and degree of dramatic elements in the material, a choir may stand or sit or assume varying positions on the stage. Steps and platforms are effective for grouping a large choir in a limited amount of space.

It is often effective to change the grouping during a single selection when it is long enough to sustain such a variation. When a change of position is used within a selection, the timing and extent of the movement must be in harmony with the mood and emotional tone of the lines. Remember that the positions of your hands and feet, as well as general posture, can be important.

If your group is giving a public performance, you will need to rehearse coming on and off stage. It is important that you look as if you know where you are going and are ready for the performance. If there are changes of grouping between numbers, this, too, must be rehearsed so there are no traffic jams.

All changes should be accomplished as quickly and quietly as possible. Remember everything your audience can see or hear is a part of the performance.

Costumes

In general, the simpler the dress, the less obtrusive the individual members of the choir will be and the more easily the audience will accept them as a single instrument. Many groups use dark trousers and white shirts open at the neck for the men, and dark skirts and long-sleeved white blouses for the women. Black and white gives enough contrast to look interesting, and the uniformity is pleasing. Choir robes or academic gowns are effective, although they may not be easy to obtain. It is wise to keep the clothing nondescript so it will be appropriate for a wide variety of selections.

The decision not to use specific, theatrical costumes is a practical and

an aesthetic one. If the program includes several selections, there is danger that costume changes may take longer than the performance. More important is the aesthetic consideration. All members of a choir should blend into a single unit. The choir, like the individual interpreter, is not asking the audience to believe they are a specific group of characters. They are trying to create images in the minds of the listeners by suggestion. An exception is when a choir is part of a staged play, as in Greek tragedies or T. S. Eliot's *Murder in the Cathedral*.

The same reasoning should govern the use of make-up. Enough make-up to highlight the eyes and mouth is helpful. The amount depends on the stage lighting and the size of the auditorium.

Descriptive make-up is dangerous and unnecessary unless the choir is part of a play cast.

The use of special lighting effects must be dictated by the material. An elaborate sky-drop set with a throne for "Stage Directions" would overshadow the brief poem. It would rob the audience of their majestic throne room by putting it on stage where they can only watch it—not share it. At times mood lighting may be appropriate if the selection is long and dramatic enough for such effects to be helpful rather than obtrusive. In general, a choir group does not use extensive lighting because, like the individual interpreter, they wish to suggest—not be specific—in setting and exterior details.

MATERIAL FOR PERFORMANCE

This poem tells the history of the Negro race very effectively when done in unison. Division into voices tends to emphasize the separate sentences in the second stanza and break the unity. However, if great care is used the unity can be preserved. Two arrangements using different voice divisions are suggested below.

```
    x     x               x     x

    x     x               x     x
                DUET
             ⌒
    x     x   x     x     x     x

    x     x     x         x     x
       DV       SOLO         LV
```

THE NEGRO SPEAKS OF RIVERS[1]
by Langston Hughes

I	II		
Unison	Unison	I've known rivers:	This opening statement should be made by the group, *not* an individual, to help the audience know it is a race speaking.
Lv	Dv	I've known rivers ancient as the world and older than the flow of human blood in human veins.	This line should not be broken since the "and" does not really add a new idea but reinforces, the "ancient" by adding "human."
Dv	Unison	My soul has grown deep like the rivers.	
Lv	Lv	I bathed in the Euphrates when dawns were young.	
Dv	Dv	I built my hut near the Congo and it lulled me to sleep.	Great care must be taken to keep these separate "phases of history" building to the "Mississippi" which is the climax.
½ Lv + ½ Dv	Lv	I looked upon the Nile and raised the pyramids above it.	
Unison	Dv	I heard the singing of the Mississippi When Abe Lincoln went down to New Orleans,	
Unison	Unison	and I've seen its muddy bosom turn all golden in the sunset.	
Unison	Unison	I've known rivers:	Be sure to let muscle tone suggest the tension or relaxation implied in the verbs of the four phases.
Unison	Lv	Ancient	
Unison	Dv	dusky rivers.	
Unison	Unison	My soul has grown deep like the rivers.	

This ridiculous love story is patterned on the old ballads. Part of its humor comes from the close attention to rhyme. You will notice there are no enjambment lines to lessen the effect. The arrangement suggested below is one of many that would be effective.

THE BALLAD OF THE OYSTERMAN
by Oliver Wendell Holmes

[UNISON] It was a tall young oysterman lived by the riverside,
[Lv] His shop was just upon the bank, [Dv] his boat was on the tide;
[UNISON] The daughter of a fisherman, that was so straight and slim,
Lived over on the other bank, [Dv] right opposite of him.

[Dv] It was the pensive oysterman that saw a lovely maid,
Upon a moonlight evening, a sitting in the shade;
[UNISON] He saw her wave her handkerchief, as much as if to say,
[Lv] "I'm wide awake, young oysterman, and all the folks away."

[UNISON] Then up arose the oysterman, and to himself said he,
[Dv] "I guess I'll leave the skiff at home, for fear that folks should see;
I read it in the story-book, that, for to kiss his dear,
Leander swam the Hellespont,—and I will swim this here."

[UNISON] And he has leaped into the waves, [Lv] and crossed the
    shining stream,
[Dv] And he has clambered up the bank, [UNISON] all in the
    moonlight's gleam;
[Dv] O there were kisses sweet as dew, [Lv] and words as soft as
    rain,—
[UNISON] But they have heard her father's step, and in he leaps again!

[UNISON] Out spoke the ancient fisherman,—[Dv] "O what was that,
    my daughter?"
[Lv] " 'Twas nothing but a pebble, sir, I threw into the water."
[Dv] "And what is that, pray tell me, love, that paddles off so fast?"
[Lv] "It's nothing but a porpoise, sir, that's been swimming past."

[UNISON] Out spoke the ancient fisherman,— [Dv] "Now bring me
    my harpoon!
I'll get into my fishing boat, and fix the fellow soon."
[UNISON] Down fell that pretty innocent, [Lv] as falls a snow-white
    lamb,
[UNISON] Her hair drooped round her pallid cheeks, [Dv] like
    seaweed on a clam.

[UNISON] Alas for those two loving ones! [Lv] She waked not
    from her sound.
[Dv] And he was taken with a cramp, and in the waves was drowned;
[UNISON] But Fate has metamorphosed them, in pity of their woe,
And now they keep an oyster-shop for mermaids down below.

This is one of the most popular selections for choric interpretation.
There are many ways to arrange it. You may want to try several different

ones. Solo voices are very effective, if they are strong enough. Watch the line lengths even when voice divisions come within the lines. Allow the tone color to come through and change the rhythm as the poet changes it. Volume control is important in the handling of this poem.

JAZZ FANTASIA[1]
by Carl Sandburg

> {Dv} Drum on your drums, {Lv} batter on your banjoes,
> {MIXED GROUP} sob on the long cool winding saxophones.
> {UNISON} Go to it, O jazzmen.
>
> {UNISON} Sling your knuckles on the bottoms of the happy tin pans,
> {Lv} let your trombones ooze, {Dv} and go husha-husha-hush with
> the slippery sand-paper.
>
> {Dv} Moan like an autumn wind high in the lonesome treetops, {Lv}
> moan soft like you wanted somebody terrible, {MIXED GROUP} cry
> like a racing car slipping away from a motorcycle cop, {UNISON}
> bang-bang! you jazzmen, bang together {SOLOS OR SELECTED GROUPS}
> drums, traps, banjoes, horns, tin cans—
> {Dv} make two people fight on the
> top of a stairway and scratch each other's eyes in a clinch tumbling
> down the stairs.
>
> {UNISON} Can the rough stuff ... {Dv} now a Mississippi steamboat
> pushes up the night river with a hoo-hoo-hoo-oo ... {Lv} and the green
> lanterns calling to the high soft stars ... {MIXED GROUP} a red moon
> rides on the humps of the low river hills ... {UNISON} Go to it,
> O jazzmen.

The exaggerated assurance and smugness of "The Disagreeable Man" is suggested by vocal inflection and a rather pompous posture. This is a poem that might well profit from the use of gestures.

THE DISAGREEABLE MAN
by William S. Gilbert

> {UNISON} If you give me your attention, I will tell you what I am.
> I'm a genuine philanthropist ...
> {Dv} All other kinds are sham.
> {UNISON} Each little fault of temper and each social defect
> In my erring fellow creatures, I endeavor to correct;

---

[1]From SMOKE AND STEEL by Carl Sandburg, copyright, 1920, by Harcourt, Brace & World, Inc.; renewed, 1948, by Carl Sandburg. Reprinted by permission of the publishers.

366

To all their little weaknesses, I open people's eyes;
And little plans to snub the self-sufficient I devise;
{Lv} I love my fellow creatures—
{UNISON} Yet, everybody says, I'm such a disagreeable man!
And I can't think why!

{Lv} To compliments inflated I've a withering reply;
{Dv} And vanity, I always do my best to mortify;
{Lv} A charitable action I can skillfully dissect;
{Dv} And interested motives I'm delighted to detect.
{UNISON} I know everybody's income and what everybody earns,
And I carefully compare it with the income tax returns;
But to benefit humanity however much I plan,
Yet everybody says, I'm such a disagreeable man!
And I can't think why!

{UNISON} I'm sure I'm no ascetic; I'm as pleasant as can be;
You'll always find me ready with a crushing repartee;
{Lv} I've an irritating chuckle;
{Dv} I've a celebrated sneer;
{Lv} I've an entertaining snigger;
{Dv} I've a fascinating leer;
{UNISON} To everybody's prejudice I know a thing or two;
I can tell a woman's age in half a minute—and I do—
But although I try to make myself as pleasant as I can,
Yet, everybody says, I'm such a disagreeable man!
And I can't think why!

Enjoy the obvious rhymes in this poem. It allows for considerable
muscle response to implement the "agony" of the experience.

WAITING FOR THE BIRDIE[1]
by Ogden Nash

{½ GROUP} Some hate broccoli, {½ GROUP} some hate bacon,
{UNISON} I hate having my picture taken.
How can your family claim to love you
And then demand a picture of you?
The electric chair is a comfortless chair,
But I know an equally comfortless pair;
{½ GROUP} One is the dentist's, my good sirs,
{½ GROUP} And the other is the photographer's.
{UNISON} Oh, the fly in all domestic ointments
Is affectionate people who make appointments
To have your teeth filled left and right.

[1]From I'M A STRANGER HERE MYSELF by Ogden Nash, by permission of Little, Brown
and Company. Copyright 1935, 1936, 1937, 1938, by Ogden Nash.

Or your face reproduced in black and white.
You open the door and you enter the studio,
And you feel less cheerio than nudio.
The hard light shines like seventy suns,
And you know your features are foolish ones.
The photographer says, Natural, please,
[½ GROUP] And you cross your knees [½ GROUP] and uncross your
    knees.
[UNISON] Like a duke in a high society chronicle
The camera glares at you through its monocle
And you feel ashamed of your best attire,
[⅓ GROUP] Your nose itches, [⅓ GROUP] your palms perspire,
[⅓ GROUP] Your muscles stiffen, [UNISON] and all the while
[UNISON] You smile and smile and smile and smile.
It's over; [½ GROUP] you weakly grope for the door;
[UNISON] It's not; [½ GROUP] the photographer wants one more.
And if this experience you survive,
Wait, just wait till the proofs arrive.
You look like a drawing by Thurber or Bab,
Or a gangster stretched on a marble slab.
And all your dear ones, including your wife,
Say There he is, that's him to the life!
[½ GROUP] Some hate broccoli, [½ GROUP] some hate bacon,
[UNISON] But I hate having my picture taken.

This highly dramatic impressionistic poem will support a great deal
of action. A group might be arranged in many different ways.

STAGE DIRECTIONS[1]
by William Rose Benét

[UNISON] Trumpets. [Dv] Enter a King, in the sunset glare.
[Lv] He sits in an antique chair. [Dv] He fingers an antique ring.
[UNISON] The heavy cloak on his back is gold and black.

[DUET] The hall is tall with gloom. [DUET plus Lv] A window
    stands
Full of scarlet sky. [DUET plus Dv] The hands of trees entreat the
    room,
Plucking and plucking the pane. [UNISON] An oblong stain

[UNISON] Of scarlet is flat on the floor. The projected flare
Slants to the foot of the chair. [DUET plus Dv] The chamber's
    farther door
Slowly advances its edge. [DUET plus Lv] A smoky wedge

[1]Reprinted by permission of DODD, MEAD & COMPANY from GOLDEN FLEECE by
William Rose Benet. Copyright 1933, 1935 by Dodd, Mead & Company.

368

Of thick blue mist, growing wider as the door swings
Noiseless, twitches the king's hands. {DUET} He is crouched like a
  spider.
{DUET plus Lv} His eyes are green as glass. {UNISON} Shudderings
  pass

{UNISON} That shrink him in his cloak. The door is wide.
The doorway, from side to side, is packed with mist like smoke.
The dreadful scarlet dies from the windowed skies.

{SOLO} Silence crosses the room. {SOLO plus DUET} Nothing more.
{SOLO, DUET plus Lv} Silence crowds from the door, {UNISON}
  gathers, gathers in gloom.
His fluttering fingers rise to cover his eyes.

{SOLO} Silence says nothing at all. {UNISON} It is thickly pressed,
Like a multitude obsessed with terror, from wall to wall.
{SOLO} Silence, {SOLO plus DUET} deep with dread, {UNISON} is
  the weight of lead

{UNISON} That slowly constricts his breast. Fingers fight
At the throat, in fierce despite of death, as the drowned resist
Green gulfs that roar and ring...
                    {SOLO plus DUET}
                    Exit the King.

This poem by Robert Frost tells an entire life story in an individual
way. The suggested arrangement takes advantage of the dialogue in the
early lines. Notice the narrator's lines that are not in quotation marks.
The groups suggested in the long stanza may be solos, trios, quartets, or
any size group of light and dark voices that works out for your choir.

THE LOVELY SHALL BE CHOOSERS[1]
by Robert Frost

{UNISON} The Voice said, {Dv} 'Hurl her down!'
{UNISON} The Voices, {Lv} 'How far down?'
{Dv} 'Seven levels of the world.'
{Lv} 'How much time have we?'
{Dv} 'Take twenty years.
{½ Dv} She *would* refuse love save with wealth and honor!
{½ Dv} The lovely shall be choosers, shall they?
{Dv} Then let them choose!'
{Lv} 'Then we shall let her choose?'

[Dv] 'Yes, let her choose.
Take up the task beyond her choosing.'

[UNISON] Invisible hands crowded on her shoulder
In readiness to weigh upon her.
But she stood straight still,
In broad round ear-rings, gold and jet with pearls
And broad round suchlike brooch,
Her cheeks high colored,
Proud and the pride of friends.

[UNISON] The Voice asked, [Dv] 'You can let her choose?'
[Lv] 'Yes, we can let her and still triumph.'

[Dv] 'Do it by joys, and leave her always blameless.
[GROUP I] Be her first joy her wedding,
That though a wedding,
Is yet—well something they know, he and she.
[GROUP II] And after that her next joy
That though she grieves, her grief is secret:
Those friends know nothing of her grief to make it shameful.
[GROUP III] Her third joy that though now they cannot help but know,
They move in pleasure too far off
To think much or much care.
[Lv] Give her a child at either knee for fourth joy
To tell once and once only, for them never to forget,
How once she walked in brightness,
And make them see it in the winter firelight.
[Dv] But give her friends for them she dare not tell
For their foregone incredulousness.
[GROUP IV] And be her next joy this:
Her never having deigned to tell them.
Make her among the humblest even
Seem to them less than they are.
[Lv] Hopeless of being known for what she has been,
[Dv] Failing of being loved for what she is,
[UNISON] Give her the comfort for her sixth of knowing
She fails from strangeness to a way of life
She came to from too high too late to learn.
[Lv] Then send some *one* with eyes to see
And wonder at her where she is,
[Dv] And words to wonder in her hearing how she came there,
But without time to linger for her story.
[Lv] Be her last joy her heart's going out to this one
So that she almost speaks.
[UNISON] You know them—seven in all.'

'Trust us,' the Voices said.

The poems included here are a small sampling of the almost limitless material useful for choric interpretation. They were chosen for their variety of mood. In addition you might be interested in trying some of the material in other chapters of this book, especially *The Lady* by Amy Lowell, *The Creation* by James Weldon Johnson, and *The Hollow Men* by T. S. Eliot.

A few of the many others you will enjoy are:

Robin-a-Thrush..a traditional ballad
Gifts Without Season..Joseph Auslander
The Walrus and The Carpenter..Lewis Carroll
Jabberwocky..Lewis Carroll
Western Star..by Stephen Vincent Benét
The People, Yes..by Carl Sandburg
Daniel and *Ghosts of the Buffalos*..Vachel Lindsay
Jesse James..by William Rose Benét
Squaw Dance and *Weeng*..by Lew Sarett
The Forsaken Merman..by Matthew Arnold
Up at a Villa, Down in the City..by Robert Browning
Morning Song from *Senlin*..by Conrad Aiken
The Guest of the Ribaud..by Arthur Guiterman
The Twelve Days of Christmas..A traditional ballad

Play production is the glamour child of speech. It is colorful, rewarding, exciting, and often hectic. The audience comes in a gala mood, and for a period of about two and a half hours may be moved to laughter or tears, or both. All the emotions of a lifetime can be crowded into a play, as in Wilder's *Our Town.* That brief experience represents weeks of preparation, not only by the cast, but by all the production crews. A play is always a coöperative effort. No play will be successful unless everybody understands his responsibilities and fulfills them without any hesitation.

SELECTING A PLAY

The first thing to consider in choosing a play is the purpose for which the play is to be given. It may be for maximum participation, as in a class play, for experimental purposes in a series of plays, or for financial gain for a fund

CHOOSING AND CASTING THE PLAY

or project. The second consideration is of the year's program. Serious plays, comedies, and some pre-modern drama make a season more rewarding.

The first problem is where to start looking. There are numerous play publishers who send on request complete catalogues with brief descriptions of all the plays they publish. Some such publishers are listed at the end of this section. The catalogues should be ordered *at least* ten to twelve weeks prior to production date.

Some directors appoint a reading committee to make a list of plays for consideration. The director will make the final choice, but much of the preliminary weeding out can be done by capable students.

When the play catalogues arrive, they are divided among the committee members, and the treasure hunt begins. There are several ways of listing plays in these catalogues, and it takes some practice to read the lists intelligently.

If you want to use as large a cast as possible, the commercial catalogues are helpful because they list the number of men and women required for each play. Some even list plays by the number in the cast. This number may often be adjusted by combining parts, adding to crowd scenes, or dividing parts to make more speaking parts. The proportion of men to women can be varied by changing a butler to a maid.

If the production is to be experimental, you will find period plays, costume plays—many of foreign origin—and one-act plays which can often be put on together to make an interesting evening. Don't overlook anthologies of plays or books on theater history, because there you will find more variety than any commercial company stocks. Many such plays are out of copyright and may be used without royalty.

The date of copyright appears on each play. Copyrights run twenty-eight years and may be renewed once. After that period the play is in public domain, and anyone can use it without paying a royalty. Adaptations and translations are copyrighted. A copyrighted play may not be used for public performance without permission from the copyright holder. This is obtained by writing the publisher or author whose name appears in the copyright notice.

In selecting a play for profit, first consider your audience. You will succeed with a play that appeals to your own community. If you live in an urban area, try to avoid plays recently done by groups near you.

Plays are listed as royalty, nonroyalty, or budget. A nonroyalty play is an old one or one designed for a specific occasion, such as Christmas, and you pay only for the scripts. Budget plays have a small royalty fee that is often adjusted according to the size of the audience.

Royalties

New plays are royalty plays. This means a fee, clearly stated in the catalogue, must be paid for each performance. The full fee must be paid promptly, sometimes before, but usually immediately after, production. It is illegal and unethical to use a play without payment of royalty. In addition to the royalty, copies of the script for the full cast must be bought, because copying a royalty-protected play is illegal.

Some publishers will reduce the royalty for second or third performances. Others have a system whereby you pay a percentage of the receipts up to a stated amount. Such an arrangement can be helpful if you are concerned about profits. If you select a play for a contest and do it a dozen times, you are still liable for royalty on each performance. Some publishers will adjust the fee when you explain your situation.

Catalogues list the number of sets required and whether they are interior or exterior. Adjustments can sometimes be made in the number of sets. It is better to choose a good play and skimp on set changes than to sacrifice a suitable script because you have only one set. Scene changes can be suggested with a few set pieces used against curtains.

There is a notation about costumes, such as mod., for modern, or 1788, uniforms.

374

Each play listing includes a brief description of the plot and sometimes a critical comment by former directors. The summaries have been prepared to explain the story line and the general tone of the play. Be careful of such phrases as "a laugh a minute," "you'll howl," and similar overstatements. No play is that funny for three acts. If it were, neither audience nor actors could bear up under the strain.

After the committee has examined the catalogues and marked likely titles, they meet to select a dozen or so for closer examination. A single copy of each title should be ordered so you may study the actual text. One publisher has a system whereby you may order single copies of ten or more royalty plays and return those you do not use for credit on copies of your selected plays. The returned copies must be in good condition.

Making Your Final Selection

There are many things to consider in selecting a suitable script. The acceptability of the plot and characters for your community is of first importance. If a play offends your community, it is a poor choice no matter how great its literary merit. The next consideration is the language. Undue profanity, illiteracy, vulgarity, or dialect that ridicules any race or country have no place in a high-school play.

A good script should be dramatic. Drama is based on conflict and action. There should be enough action onstage to hold the interest of the audience and challenge the actors. Action should not merely be discussed. The play must "move" and have enough climactic moments to make its points.

John Dietrich, in *Play Direction*, listed in the bibliography at the end of this section, suggests that you read each play five times. The first reading may be rapid for a general impression of its type and suitability. The second is much more carefully done with particular attention to the story line and the situations on which the conflict is built. Here the matter of taste and community acceptance is important. The third reading is to clarify the structure of the whole script in terms of climaxes, major units of development, balance between acts, and general "playability." The fourth permits you to concentrate on characterization and test the credibility of the dialogue and the interrelationship of characters. The final reading is devoted to solving production problems. A realistic but optimistic evaluation of your own stage is important here.

A study in versatility: Sir Laurence Olivier in three contrasting roles. At left, he plays an aging actor in *The Entertainer*, with Joan Plowright. In the middle photograph, he plays Henry II in *Becket*, with Arthur Kennedy in the title role. On the right, he plays Becket to Anthony Quinn's Henry II in the same play.

Three Important Questions

When you are ready to make your final recommendation to the committee, ask yourself three questions. First, "Can we cast it?" (Macbeth is a magnificent play but not a good choice if you have no one who can play Macbeth.) The ideal high-school play has several good-sized rôles and is not a one-star show. Do you have the proper balance of men and women to cast it? The short parts can often cause the real trouble. Have you someone who can play a grandfather or a ten-year-old so the part will be convincing?

Second, "Can we stage it?" Most settings can be simplified and suggested. However, if the believability of the play depends on three realistic sets and you have only one set, you may be putting too much strain on the audience. Costumes, too, may be simplified. An elaborately costumed show may make heavy demands on your budget.

Third, "Can we afford it?" The royalty must be paid and the copies bought. If the school budget will not permit a fifty-dollar fee, face the fact realistically.

If these three questions are answered affirmatively and you like the play, recommend it to the director, who makes the final decision.

TRYOUTS

The method of holding tryouts that your director uses depends on how many students want to participate and on the amount of time he has before the play must go into production. Tryouts are held a week or ten days before rehearsals are scheduled.

A director may have in mind one or two people who might carry the important rôles, but he will not precast the show. A play is cast from those who appear at tryouts. If a student is not interested enough to come to a tryout, he will not be a very coöperative member of the cast, despite his ability. Do not expect an invitation to a tryout. It is your responsibility to get a copy of the play and be at the tryout sessions.

There is at least a week's notice of tryouts, and there is more than one session. This gives you time to arrange your schedule so you can be present. If it is impossible for you to attend, speak to the director, and he may find another time when you can meet with others in similar predicaments.

Tryouts should move as quickly as possible. They are time-consuming and wearing, but careful planning can make them less so.

Tryout Scripts

The play reading committee can be of great assistance during the period before tryouts. It is impractical to give the complete script for tryouts because there are never enough to go around. The scripts get hard use during rehearsals and should not have added wear before they are given to the cast. The director selects a few scenes for tryouts, each one lasting a few minutes. The committee members help with selecting these scenes. Copies of these scenes can be typed or dittoed. This does not violate the law, since these excerpts are small units, not substitutes, and are not for public performances.

There should be different scenes for a wide variety of characters, although each scene should not need more than three actors. It is difficult to evaluate more than three people in a tryout period. If there are several similar characters, such as three or four teen-agers, they need not each be represented. The director will choose the most challenging scene and/or character for use as tryout material and cast the other characters of the same type from that test.

In addition to the excerpts, a few copies of the play may be available in the director's office so that those who wish to try out may read it and decide which character interests them. They may then ask for the scene in which that character appears and take it home to study before tryouts. If this practice is followed, the tryout notice will state that scripts are available.

Here again the committee can help in staffing the room where the scripts are kept and in making sure that none are lost.

Information Sheets

Before tryouts the director will have made as many information sheets as will be needed. Many directors who do several shows during a year make a whole season's supply at once. You will be asked to fill out this sheet at tryouts or when you pick up the script. The form asks for name, address, and telephone number. Address and telephone number are important in case of emergency or changes in rehearsal time. You may be asked for your class schedule so special rehearsals of small scenes can be arranged.

Most sheets ask about previous experience. Do not be disturbed if you have had none, because this information is to help the director in regard to new students he may not know. There will be a space for your other commitments. This includes all other activities, athletics, glee club, and student council, with a notation of the days and hours of each activity. It includes regular medical or dental appointments, music lessons, and part-time employment. This record is invaluable in arranging rehearsal schedules.

Some sheets include the question, "Will you accept a small part?" A small part can turn out to be a greater challenge and more fun than the lead. An old theater adage says, "There are no small parts; there are only small actors." Don't let the number of lines fool you. However, if you do not wish a small part, say so. Perhaps you are involved in so many activities that unless you can play the part you really want, it is not practical for you to take *any* part. It is better for the director to know this in advance than to have to recast later on.

The director will collect the information sheet from each applicant before hearing him read. The committee can help to see that every applicant has completely filled out the form before it is given to the director.

Types of Tryouts

There are two general types of tryouts—general and screening. Each varies according to the situation and the individual director's preferences. The general tryout is used when scripts or excerpts are available in advance. Everyone who wishes to try out can do so. Each applicant names the part or parts he is interested in, and is allowed to read all his choices. He may come back as often as he wishes during the tryouts.

The screening process is more useful when the applicants have no opportunity to become acquainted with the entire play and do not know what part they want to read. The director tells the group the story of the play and sketches the essential qualities of each rôle. He makes clear that some students may not be cast for the rôles they read in tryouts. He passes out scripts and asks specific people to read several parts, both large and small. The director knows what he is looking for and casts from general adaptability, making notes that certain people might fill one or more parts whether or not they read them.

The most common method of casting is a combination of screening and general tryouts. A time is set and anyone who wishes to take part in the production meets with the director. The director reviews the plot and sketches the general type of characters needed. If the number of people at the session is large, numbers may be given applicants as they arrive so

379

they may be heard in turn. Typed excerpts are handed out, and each student has a chance to read before the entire group.

If copies are available before the tryout the director may ask each applicant for his preference in rôles. The director's knowledge of the relations between the characters enables him to put two or three applicants in a significant scene and still attend to personal preferences. If a student wishes to read several parts, the director will probably permit it.

Call-Backs

Immediately after each tryout, the director goes over the information sheets of the students and adds appropriate remarks for his own use in final casting. After everyone has a chance to read for all the parts he is interested in, the director may post a call-back sheet. This is a list of those the director would like to hear again and from whom he selects his cast. Call-back tryouts concentrate on specific parts, and each is told the part he is being considered for. If you are not interested, say so. Call-backs give you some time to study that part.

After call-back tryouts, the director makes his final decision. He appoints his assistant director, stage manager, and all crews. He posts this list with the cast list because technical personnel are equally important; without them actors would be helpless. The director is aware of this, and anyone who wants work on the technical staff should make his wishes known.

Remember, tryouts are just that. If scripts are available, make a thorough job of analysis and then do your best to bring out the qualities you have discovered in the character. Do not try for spectacular effects and original characterizations. The director will develop what is needed as the rehearsals progress. He is more interested in your posture and your stage presence, in your ability to project a flexible voice, concentrate on the job at hand, and to respond to the other characters than in extreme vocal and physical techniques or emotional displays. Respond to the situation in your scene in the way you think your character would respond. Speak clearly and in full voice and be mentally alert. The rest is up to the director.

Casting

When the director is ready to cast the play, he considers many things. If you do not receive a rôle, it does not indicate you are not as good an actor

The director and cast of *Camelot* on the first day of rehearsal.

as someone else. There are many factors in getting a smoothly working cast to project an entire show.

The director evaluates three separate steps. First he assesses the rôle and the essential qualities each character must have to be true to the play. His choice may hinge on physical characteristics such as height, weight, and coloring, matters over which you have no control. Most parts do not call for specific characteristics, but there is a general range that must be suggested so the audience believes the plot and the relationships among the characters.

He takes into consideration the vocal characteristics of each part. Pitch, quality, rate, and ability to handle dialect may be items of importance. He considers the degree of emotional reaction each part must encompass.

He will study tryout sheets and review his comments in light of the character requirements, attempting to fit the actor to the rôle physically, vocally, and in his/her capacity for response. He considers dependability and coöperation, based on his past experience with an applicant. The most difficult element to evaluate is that indefinable "sense of performance," or stage presence, that some people possess. It is not a magic trick, especially on the amateur level.

It results from concentration on the job and a desire to project the character, with all its levels, to the audience. It requires a mixture of seriousness and enjoyment, of humility and self-confidence, and it develops with experience.

Special Considerations in Casting

After the tentative cast is chosen, the director may reëxamine it in terms of contrasts. These may be physical, vocal, or both. Some directors cast by type. Others go to the other extreme and use what is called educational casting, that is, they give a part to a student unsuited to the rôle to give him a chance to learn from the experience. Both methods have advantages and disadvantages. Most directors try to avoid the extremes. If the director's decision does not agree with your opinion, remember that the show as a whole is his main concern.

Some directors use double casting. This is practical only when the production is given more than once. He may double cast the longest rôles and allow those selected alternate performances. When the system of double casting is used, more people are given a chance to participate, but it is difficult to bring both casts to a high degree of polish.

He must allow at least thirty per cent more time for rehearsals. Both casts should be present at most rehearsals so the directions need not be repeated. One cast watches the other work and learns from observation. Then the casts change places, either in part or as a whole, and rehearsals move ahead.

Understudies

A wise director plans ahead for emergencies. Most plays allow understudy assignments. This does not mean a duplicate cast. Usually a person with a short part understudies a longer part. It is not necessary to have more than the three or four long parts so protected. When the understudy moves in as a replacement, the assistant director steps in and takes the shorter part. If you are cast as an understudy, you must be present at the rehearsals of the scenes you are understudying, and you will have a few opportunities to rehearse onstage.

A few days after the call-back sessions, the director posts a list of the cast, understudy assignments, and technical personnel. This is your official notice to report for your script and rehearsal schedule. You are then responsible for the script, for learning your lines, and for attending conferences with the director regarding technical matters. You will arrange your schedule to be present at every rehearsal and/or crew call to which you are summoned.

382

ACTIVITIES

1. Play reading. Read five one-act plays of as many types as possible: farces, fantasies, character comedies, problem plays, tragedies, and satires.

    a. Write outline play reports, using the form recommended by your teacher.

    b. Make charts of the plays with a separate column for each of the following: *Name of play, Playwright, Source, Kind of play, Cast requirements, Set requirements, Recommendations as to use* (P.T.A., variety show, class, church).

2. Casting.

    a. Select casts for the above plays, using movie stars you know.

    b. Select casts for the plays, using members of your class.

    c. As a class, conduct tryout exercises. Have a number of students read parts from plays they all know. Discuss the factors to look for in judging suitability for a part.

    d. Make an information or rating sheet to use as a guide in casting.

3. Program planning.

    a. Plan a program of three one-act plays, all of different types, suitable for a school matinee, an evening performance, or both. Mention the type of play and the set requirements for each. If you know your class well, suggest a tentative cast and a production staff.

    b. Make a list of plays suitable for a young people's church group to present during the year; for example,

        1. A religious play for presentation in the sanctuary.

        2. A play with a strong ethical theme for presentation in the church auditorium or assembly hall.

        3. A humorous, but worth-while play, for a social occasion or a money-raising project.

    c. Do the same for club use; e.g., Hi-Y, Y-Teens, Junior Red Cross, Thespians.

4. Definite play plans.

    a. Cast and give a one-act play for your class. (If you have no guests, you do not have to pay royalty.)

    b. If your P.T.A. has a meeting devoted to programs presented in the classrooms, prepare a short play on a youth problem, such as dropouts, and one with a funny family situation for light entertainment.

    c. Plan to give a children's theater play.

        1. Select a play that will run about an hour.

        2. Label it *Fantasy* or *Historical play* or *Realistic play* or *Musical*.

        3. Label it for the age level of interest.

        4. Cast it from your class. Double cast the longest parts. Select your production staff.

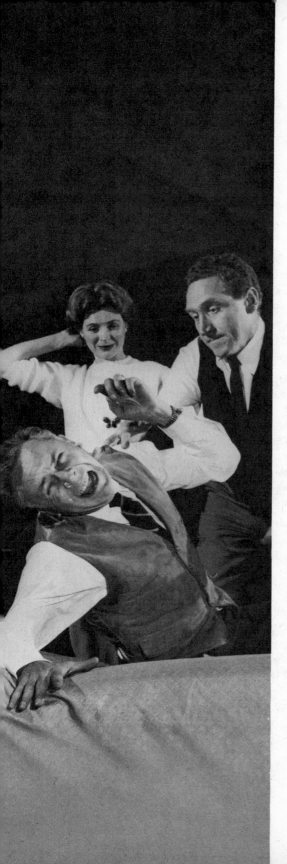

With the first rehearsal the director takes the responsibility of blending and developing all aspects of production to build a unified play. He will spend hours before rehearsal making lists to coördinate plot, character, language, background, climaxes; and planning the most effective way to project them for one unified effect on the audience. He knows what he wants and his instructions will be based on long-range plans. If you do not understand what he wants, ask him. If you don't understand why, ask him privately after rehearsal.

The director needs to work as efficiently as possible and will use traditional stage terms you will be expected to understand. The most common terms are listed here with brief definitions, so you may respond intelligently to his instructions.

REHEARSAL PROCEDURES

Ad lib: to speak lines not in the script. This is allowed only when called for by the director, as in crowd scenes. It never takes the place of a required line. When called on to *ad lib,* decide what you will say in keeping with the scene and your purpose in it. There may be a sudden lull, and the audience will hear what you say. Be sure the words make sense.

Apron: the part of the stage in front of the curtain.

Blocking a scene: setting the movement and business (see below).

Build: increase tension in a scene or speech.

Business: all visual activity that doesn't involve movement from one place to another. (See also stage movement.)

Call: an announcement of the time actors and crew are to report for rehearsal or performance.

Clear stage: command to all actors and crew members to leave the stage.

Cross: move from one place to another; indicated by X on scripts.

Cue: a word, movement, sound, or action that signals you to perform the next action or speak the next line.

Curtain: signal that the curtain is going up or coming down.

Curtain call: raising the curtain at the end of the play so the actors may acknowledge the applause. Nobody misses a curtain call!

Cut: command to stop the scene. Also, to eliminate a line or action from the play.

Downstage: the part of the stage toward the audience. (See chart on page 393 for stage positions.)

Heads up: warning that something is falling or being let down. Look up and get out of the way!

Lines: speeches of the actors.

Motivation: the total of forces and reasons behind a speech or action.

Pick up: accelerate.

Places: command to actors and technicians to take performance places for the scene.

Properties: usually called "props." All furniture and objects used in the play. Large pieces are "set props," and small pieces are "hand props." Things carried onstage by actors are "personal props."

Proscenium: the wall containing the arch framing the stage.

Run-through: go straight through an act or scene without interruption for corrections.

Set: the scenery, and larger properties.

Stage movement: movement from one place onstage to another.

Take stage: assume a dominant position and attitude.

Timing: the use of pause and pace to achieve an effect; emphasizing a line or action so it becomes more climactic than the preceding one.

Topping: to gain emphasis by abrupt increase in intensity, volume, or speed.

Walk-through: performs the actions indicated in the blocking.

The director watches rehearsals from out in the house and interrupts from time to time to give directions. That is what he is there for. He is the only one who can tell whether or not your work is effective. He lets you know whether what you are doing projects across the footlights. In a performance the audience is not concerned with how you feel, but with how you make *them* feel. If you are playing the part honestly and with intelligence and have profited by the director's help, the audience will feel exactly what you want them to. Rehearsals establish patterns of technique so you can be sure you're accomplishing the playwright's purpose.

Some people can correct a flaw immediately, while others need to work it out slowly by themselves. The director knows this. Correction in public is never pleasant, but only a rank amateur resists direction. Keep a pencil with you to mark every suggestion in your script.

SOME FUNDAMENTAL RULES

There are a few fundamental rules for rehearsal demeanor which are never violated by anyone interested in "getting the show on the road." The first is promptness. Be in the theater a few minutes before each call so you are ready to get to work at once. There is no excuse for absence from rehearsal. If you cannot be at a rehearsal let the director know in time so he can contact the others and arrange another time. Only an emergency suspends these rules, and you had better come with your leg in a cast to prove the emergency.

When you are onstage or backstage waiting for your cue, tend strictly to business. There may be a delay while a detail is worked out. This is not a rehearsal break. Spend the time working on your lines. Never indulge in chit-chat during a rehearsal. Your cue will come faster than you expect, and the next delay may be your fault.

When you are not needed for a scene do not leave without the permission of the assistant director. If you want to go off to study your lines tell him exactly where you will be so he may call you when you are needed. The director may decide to repeat your scene, and you may be needed at once.

It is permissible for actors to watch rehearsals from the back of the theater when they are offstage, except at dress rehearsals. But it is immature and unprofessional to engage in conversation with others while the rehearsal is going on. A whisper can be distracting.

Allow time to go backstage and make your entrance properly. An entrance over the footlights destroys the scene the actors are building.

An actor never appears out front in costume and make-up. This rule is in effect at first dress rehearsal unless the director suspends it. Never, never does an actor join the audience at any performance. He stays in the dressing room and waits until the curtain calls. Then he removes his make-up and changes into street clothes before going out.

Rehearsal Schedule

The amount of time you spend rehearsing depends on many things. If rehearsals are scheduled for two or three hours every day of the week, a modern three-act comedy can be ready in four or five weeks. A difficult play takes six to eight weeks. You may not be called to every rehearsal, but it is wise to allow this amount of time. A director often breaks the acts into small scenes and rehearses them separately. He may start with the large scenes and then keep only certain actors to work on smaller scenes in the last part of rehearsal periods. He plans the rehearsal schedule so you will know when you will be needed. It is difficult to plan more than a week in advance because some scenes progress slower than the director anticipated, while others develop more rapidly.

Your director will give you a tentative schedule for the entire rehearsal period at the first reading. It will be subject to change but gives you an idea of deadlines. You can estimate what you need to work on as the weeks go by. They go by faster than you expect.

A SAMPLE REHEARSAL SCHEDULE

A schedule for a three-act modern comedy might look like the one below. Unless otherwise indicated, all rehearsals are for two hours.

1st Week

Monday	3:30	Read through entire play...all cast and technical personnel
Tuesday	3:30	Act I, pp. 2-17 blocking and walk-through
Wednesday	3:30	Act I, pp. 17-29 blocking and walk-through
Thursday	3:30	Act I entire ... set business and movement
Friday	3:30	Act I entire ... characterization

2nd Week

Monday	3:30	Act II, pp. 30-42 blocking and walk-through
Tuesday	3:30	Act II, pp. 42-54 blocking and walk-through
Wednesday	3:30	Act II entire ... set business and movement
	4:30	Act I entire ... LINES ... NO BOOKS
Thursday	3:30	Act I entire
	4:15	Act II entire ... characterization
Friday	3:30	Act II entire

3rd Week

Monday	3:30	Act III, pp. 55-66 blocking and walk-through
Tuesday	3:30	Act III, pp. 66-end blocking and walk-through
	4:30	Act III entire
Wednesday	3:30	Act II entire ... LINES ... NO BOOKS
	4:30	Act III set movement and business
Thursday	3:30	Act I entire
	4:30	Act II entire

| Friday | 3:30 | Act II entire |
| | 4:30 | Act III entire |

4th Week

Monday	3:30	Act III entire ... LINES ... NO BOOKS
Tuesday	3:30	Act I entire
	4:30	Act II entire
Wednesday	3:30	Entire play in sequence
Thursday	3:30	Entire play in sequence
Friday	3:30	Entire play in sequence or special call as needed

5th Week

Monday	7-9	Entire play in sequence ... All cast and technical personnel
Tuesday	7-9	Entire play in sequence
Wednesday	6:30-9:30	DRESS REHEARSAL ... sets, props, costumes, sound
Thursday	6:30-10:00	DRESS REHEARSAL ... above plus make-up, lights, dressing, PICTURES
Friday	6:30-9:30	FINAL DRESS
Saturday	8:00	PERFORMANCE
	Cast Call ... 6:30	

HOW TO BEGIN YOUR PREPARATION

Before the first rehearsal, underline or otherwise mark each of your speeches in your script. Do not bother with the stage directions, except for entrances and exits, because they may be changed. Write your name, address, telephone number on the script and the name of your character.

After each rehearsal concentrate on suggested corrections. Then work on details of the next scheduled scene. This includes character analysis for that scene, plus business and stage movements. If you have any questions, make notes of them so you can ask your director about them.

After the first rehearsal, begin to learn your lines. People memorize so differently that it is foolish to make hard and fast rules. Sometimes it is better to read a whole scene many times and try to memorize it as a unit. Sometimes you learn a speech at a time. As soon as possible, get your eyes up from your book during rehearsals. If you think you know a page or two, try it without using the book. You'll find stage movement and business helps you remember the lines. The polishing of your memorization is done at rehearsals, but the spade work is done between rehearsals.

Left, Richard Rodgers and Samuel Taylor, who wrote *No Strings*; right, George Kaufman with Hildegarde Neff in *Silk Stockings*.

Get someone to cue you by reading the ends of speeches before yours so you learn the cues. Some find it helps to take the plot line and recast in their own words, as "Then he comes in and he says ... and I say ... etc." This helps put the speeches in their proper progression so when you return to the words of the playwright, they are not isolated sentences.

Draw a rough sketch of the stage arrangement, so that you know which folding chairs represent the davenport, and which frame the doorway. You will not have an actual set and props to help you until the last week of rehearsal.

What to Do Between Rehearsals

What you do between rehearsals makes all the difference between a worth-while session where you accomplish a great deal and a dull two hours reading lines.

As soon as you get your script, read the whole play at least three times. After the first reading, analyze the plot and locate the climaxes and key scenes. Then begin character analysis of your character. After the second reading, consider how your part fits the whole, what it contributes to the climaxes and key scenes. With the third reading, start the detailed character analysis that continues until the last week of rehearsals and grows with each reading.

Every time you go over a scene at home or in rehearsal, remind yourself of the kind of person your character is. How does he feel about

Director Joshua Logan with William Shatner and France Nuyen, of the cast of *The World of Suzy Wong.*

the situation in each scene? What does he contribute to it, and how is he changed by it?

Listen, in character, to each speech, know what the speaker means, how he means it, and how your character feels about what is said. This will make it easier to remember your lines and pick up your cues properly and with the necessary promptness.

The director has indicated on the schedule when your lines are to be fully memorized. When he says "no books," he means it. Leave your book offstage. You may need to be prompted at first. Review those places before the next rehearsal. There is absolutely no excuse for not knowing lines. That is part of your contract when you accept the part. Lines must be delivered exactly as written because the next speaker is expecting them, and, if you don't give them exactly, he may not be able to reply in a way that makes sense. If you find a speech awkward, discuss it with your director, so the others will become accustomed to any changes he may permit you to make.

Picking up Cues

Rehearsals are usually slow for the first few weeks. But the week before dress rehearsals, the pace begins to approximate that of a performance. The assistant director times each scene and act, and you become all too familiar with the demand "Pick it up!" (explained on p. 385, this chapter). It does not mean everyone is to speak faster. It means to tighten the

391

texture of the scene. When scenes drag it's because actors don't pick up their cues fast enough. A cue does not always need to be picked up by speech. It may be picked up by action, facial expression, quick focus of eyes and attention, a laugh, or a sob. But there must not be a split second of *meaningless* pause. Every second contributes to the play.

You will be ready for your cue if you listen, in character, to the speech before yours. You do not take turns doing speeches and acts but do them in response to what has just happened. This does not mean you do not use pauses. A pause may be necessary and effective, but only if something is happening in the character's mind. Your director will help you time necessary pauses and set the pace. The point is not how long it takes *you* to answer or react, but how long the audience thinks it would take the character you are playing. Your director is seeing it from out front and is in a position to know. Your character and his reactions are important only as they relate to the scene. Keep *that* moving.

Stage Movement

In a fully staged play it is necessary to distinguish between large movements, such as crossing a stage, and small actions like opening a letter. In the list of terms on page 385, *business* is defined as all visual activity that does not involve movement from one place to another. Movement from one place to another is *stage movement*.

The director works out stage movement on paper before the first rehearsal. This is blocking a scene, and involves many crosses, entrances, and exits. He will tell you at an early rehearsal where and when he wants you to cross within a scene. Mark these directions in your script and do them at every rehearsal. Their purpose may be to illuminate character, or suggest a degree of emotional tension. They may add variety or contrast to the stage picture, or for psychological relationship during a scene. He tells you how to sit, on the arm of a chair, on a table edge, in a low chair, or on a foot stool. Carry the instruction out exactly as planned, because what each actor does contributes to the whole. If you forget a cross, you break the pattern of movement and throw the stage picture out of balance.

Marking Stage Movement

Let us consider the basic problem of your position onstage at the opening of your scene, and the crosses from one area to another which you make during the scene. Mark every one of these in your script. Your director will use the terms *downstage, upstage, right, left,* and *center*. These are easy to keep straight, if you remember two facts: *stage right* and *stage left* refer to the *actor's* right and left as he stands center stage facing the audience. This is practical, since it is the actor who moves right or left. *Cross right* means you cross to your right.

Upstage and *downstage* are not so simple, unless you know the history of the terms. You are accustomed to a theater with a sloping floor so the front seats are lower than the ones in back. This permits the audience to see over the heads of those in front. Once the theater floor was flat and the stage sloped. The back part of the stage was higher than the front, so the actors in back could be seen. The back of the stage was called upstage, and the front near the curtain was called downstage. This was practical when stages were in large halls, or public squares, but the modern theater with its sloping rows of seats is more pleasant for actors, who no longer need the agility of a mountain goat for a quick exit.

Stage Areas

Study the chart below, so you learn the stage areas and their abbreviations. All the areas on the chart below are behind the curtain line. The stage in front of the curtain is the *apron*. Few plays use this area.

	UR *Up* *Right*	URC *Up* *Right* *Center*	UC *Up* *Center*	ULC *Up* *Left* *Center*	UL *Up* *Left*	
OFFSTAGE	R *Right*	RC *Right* *Center*	C *Center*	LC *Left* *Center*	L *Left*	OFFSTAGE
	DR *Down* *Right*	DRC *Down* *Right* *Center*	DC *Down* *Center*	DLC *Down* *Left* *Center*	DL *Down* *Left*	

THE APRON   Curtain Line   PROSCENIUM WALL

OUT FRONT

Go to center stage and face front. Divide the stage into upstage, downstage, and middle section. Remember right and left, refer to your right and left. Get the diagram in mind, and practice moving from one area to another until it is easy to remember the designations. When your director says "Cross to the chair down right," mark your script X *to chair DR.*

How the director works in rehearsal: for *The Desperate Hours,* Robert Montgomery, in the picture at left, demonstrates an action for an actress, who then performs it according to his direction.

Often the stage movement your director gives will not be the same as that in your printed script. No two productions are alike, and what worked for the original set may not work on your stage. Ignore the printed directions and follow the director's instructions.

General Suggestions on Stage Movement and Business

It is dangerous to establish rules for stage movement, because no two characters, or scenes, or plays are alike. However, here are some standard suggestions that are helpful.

How you perform an action is as important as what you do. Every physical action must be right for the character you are playing. It must be in harmony with the scene. It must be motivated by how the character feels, what he is thinking, what kind of person he is in the current situation. Posture, muscle tone, speed of movement, grace, poise, deliberate awkwardness, facial expression, and many other outward signs are all a part of any physical action.

Your ability to satisfy the above requirements depends in large part on your comprehension of the character and the scene. A stage movement has three parts: a beginning, a focal point, and an ending. Don't ooze into a cross. Start the stage movement all in one piece, and in character. Go where you are supposed to go, in the way you are supposed to move. When you get there, stand still.

One of the surest signs of an amateur is the actor who shuffles his feet and seeps behind a piece of furniture. Move in a room onstage as you would offstage. Don't hide behind the furniture, shuffle, or disappear into the back wall.

394

Rehearse stage movements carefully, so that you will time your crosses correctly.

(1) Start a cross before a speech, but you should be where you are going before it is finished.

(2) Move in your own lane, not in that of another character, except in unusual cases.

(3) Cross downstage of other characters and in front of furniture.

(4) Do not move with, or in the same direction as, another character, except for comic effects.

(5) Your cross may be direct, or in a round-about route, and you need to time the pauses in your speech so that you finish the cross before you stop speaking.

(6) When you move to the right, step out with your right foot; when to the left, with your left foot. This keeps you from twisting your feet as you turn.

(7) When you stop, keep the upstage foot ahead of the downstage foot, so when you turn your body toward center stage, you pivot easily and don't have to untangle your feet or turn your back to the audience. Practice until it becomes second nature.

(8) On exits, open doors with your upstage hand, so you are turned toward the audience.

(9) On an entrance, turn toward the audience and reach back to close the door with the downstage hand.

Entrances and Exits

Entrances and exits deserve attention. They are often important climaxes. A badly executed entrance can ruin a scene, and a weak exit makes the scene fizzle out like a defective skyrocket.

At least two pages before each entrance, write in large letters—*warn entrance*. You need that long to get ready. There is an old saying that an entrance involves two minutes and six paces. The two minutes are spent getting into character and fixing the situation in mind.

Before you enter, remind yourself of what has happened onstage and what your character has been doing offstage. Where has he been? How long has he been gone? What has he been doing? What does he feel about where he has been and what he has been doing? What situation does he expect to find onstage? Is this the actual situation? Does he

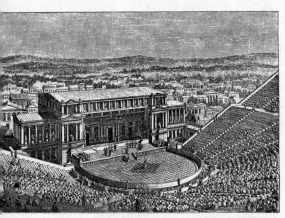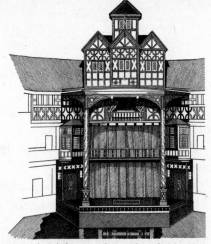

Some historic theaters: the Theater of Dionysus in Athens, where the classic Greek plays were performed in contest; an Elizabethan theater, where Shakespeare's plays were produced; the Drury Lane Theater in London, where the famous Garrick performed; the theater in the French royal palace at Versailles.

know what has been going on, or will it surprise him? Why has he arrived at this particular moment?

Where does he go, and what will he do after he enters? Why? How? If this is his first entrance, he must establish his relationship with the other characters. If this is a second, third, or fourth entrance that the character has made, it must underscore character development and relationships.

The six paces mean you start your entrance six steps away from the door you will come through. This gives you time to establish muscle tone and pace. It creates the illusion that you have been somewhere, not just lurking backstage ready to leap on at your cue. This makes a difference in the effect of your entrance.

An entrance serves to establish what is to come; an exit sustains what has taken place. You must keep in mind where your character is going, what he is going to do, why he is going to do it if it is a result of what has been said or done. How does he feel about leaving? How do the others feel about it? The answers to these questions help you understand why the director wants the exit fast or slow, direct and forceful, or broken with a pause at the door and a last look at the room; whether it should be executed with a speech or in a moment of silence following a speech such as a farewell. The *how* can often be answered by the *why*. When you exit, continue at least six steps offstage before you drop character. You can still be seen by the audience on the far sides of the house. Don't break the illusion by letting the audience see the "machinery" behind the play.

396

Details of Business

It is impossible to offer suggestions on how to handle every piece of business you might need in all the plays in the world. However, a few of the more common ones may be of interest. When you talk on a telephone onstage, keep the mouthpiece below your lips, so your voice will carry to the back of the auditorium and so the audience can watch your facial expressions. Hold the mouthpiece well below the chin and drop the head a little to speak into it. The same rule is applicable when reading letters, newspapers, or books. They should never, except for special effects, hide the mouth and chin. Remember the front row is lower than the stage. Be sure you can see the footlights over what you are reading. It is a temptation not to memorize the letter, poem, or newspaper article you are to read. Resist that temptation! Learn those lines. The letter may be misplaced, and another subsituted by the prop crew, and you will be left with no lines.

Scenes of eating or drinking should be rehearsed carefully. Food should be used during rehearsals, even though it is only crackers and water. Actors must become accustomed to spacing bites and swallows so they can continue their speeches without having their mouths full. Small bites, a long time spent in cutting, salting, spreading bread, and other activities will preserve the illusion of eating without interfering with the scene's progress.

Love scenes are often staged so the actual kiss is hidden from the audience. Embraces and kisses are rehearsed until both participants feel easy. An awkward position of the arms, hands, or feet can ruin a good

397

scene. If the participants stand facing each other in profile to the audience, the man can turn slightly so the back of his head is between the woman's face and the audience. The kiss may be faked to preserve make-up.

Duels, fights, and murders are handled in the same way. The recipient of the fatal blow can face upstage, or be blocked by the other character, so the sword thrust, or upper cut, and a gunshot is faked. This takes perfect timing on the part of both aggressor and victim and must be rehearsed as carefully as a dance routine.

Falls and faints are easily mastered. The arms hang limp, so that the shoulders are relaxed. Keep the torso straight and allow the body to sag sideways, so you fall on your side. First the ankle and side of the lower leg hit the floor, with the rest of the body serving as a balance, then the thigh and hip.

Then the torso turns and pulls the body face down, or up, as the director demands, with the head drooping forward to continue the movement. When the body is down, the head rolls into position. The secret is to control relaxation and balance.

Do not catch yourself with your knees or your hands. After a few practices, you can execute this smoothly and convincingly. If you relax and go down slowly, you will not hurt yourself. The same process is followed in falling downstairs. Use the hand rail to steady yourself until you can break the fall.

Final Rehearsals

The last week before dress rehearsal is devoted to doing the play in sequence, so everyone can work to build the total effect. This is a trying week for both actors and director. The novelty has worn off, energy is running low, and tempers are jumpy. Don't be discouraged. Spend the time perfecting your contribution in terms of the whole play, and you will find a real challenge.

There should be three dress rehearsals. It is difficult for a director to check everything in one rehearsal. The first dress might be devoted to seeing that the set stays up, the doors open, the furniture is right, and sound effects work. The set and props, with the exception of flowers and dressing, should be complete. This is the time to check the fit of costumes, ease of handling, and practice quick changes. The actors may expect to be neglected at this rehearsal. They should have their lines and characters

On the left, opening night of a production of Shakespeare's *As You Like It*; on the right, director Moss Hart with the stars of *Camelot,* Julie Andrews and Richard Burton.

so controlled they are not distracted by the technical personnel, for whom this rehearsal is intended. The actors must be ready to carry on a scene despite a prop man moving a table, or the stage manager ringing phone bells, and the costume crew changing a piece of jewelry. Every member of the cast remains for the entire rehearsal, because the director will have final instructions. It will be necessary to rehearse the curtain calls. This should be done at each dress rehearsal.

The second dress checks all the things that went wrong the first time. This time the director will attend to lights and make-up. These must be done together. Make-up must not be left to the final rehearsal, because colored lights change tones and shadows, and you'll need another rehearsal to check the corrections. You will not need to make up your neck and arms for the second dress, if your make-up is dark and the costume fragile.

Final dress rehearsal is exactly like a performance. There are no interruptions or delays. A small audience is invited to help the actors get the feel of the performance. It must go smoothly. The old adage, "a bad dress rehearsal makes a good performance," is not true. Certainly an error in a final rehearsal will alert everyone for performance, but a bad dress rehearsal only causes stage fright and makes the director worry.

ACTIVITIES

1. A counting-out game for stage directions. Divide the stage into fifteen hypothetical areas by putting chairs and/or actors in each area. (Some actors must be on stage.) One person serves as director, who points at each actor in rapid succession and gives stage directions. For example, "Make a downstage cross to Down Right," or "XDC to left of chair." If there is one step in the wrong direction, the actor is out!

2. Exercises for foot and hand technique. Follow carefully the directions in Chapter 7.

a. Enter as an important person through door DL.

b. Cross to Center and pantomime a conversation addressed to person at RC.

c. Turn and exit again DL, giving a parting line in pantomime just before you go out.

d. Repeat the above directions, except exit by door DR.

e. Repeat the above, but add two spoken lines, one at Center and one near the door.

Reminder: Be sure to begin your lines before you reach Center.

3. Stage business. Develop a scene in which stage business plays an important part. For example, a demonstration beginning: "Here, that isn't the way to use a bat. Let me show you. You...."

4. Gait. Develop a scene in which there is significance in the way you walk; from *The Barretts of Wimpole Street,* try Papa Barrett's ominous entrances and exits. Or show Elizabeth's first shaky steps as Robert Browning leads her from the couch. Note that she nearly falls. Use lines, if possible.

5. Faints and falls. Portray each of the following, observing the suggestions in the text, but work toward character discrimination:

a. Fall as Elizabeth's sister Henrietta does when struck by her father.

b. Fall as someone stabbed, tragically, as Macbeth; humorously, as the guards in Act I of *The Romancers.*

c. Begin to faint as Lady Macbeth when she says, "Help me hence, ho!"

d. From a sitting position, drop to the couch or the floor as Juliet does when she drinks the potion and says, "Romeo, I come. This do I drink to thee!"

e. Portray a realistic death as Cyrano after his final line, "My white plume!" Or try a humorous one as the Conspirator after his final line in Act I of *The Romancers.*

6. Fencing. Stage a dueling scene, using blunted fencing foils. Try the one from *Cyrano de Bergerac* or the one from *The Romancers.* Remember that the footwork and swordplay must be worked out as neatly as a dance.

7. Tempo. Select a scene in which the tempo builds up to a crisis; for example:

a. Lady Macbeth waits for her husband while he murders King Duncan. Build increasing tension after he staggers onstage with bloody hands until the end of the scene. The knocking at the gate increases the tension at the end.

b. Petruchio, in *The Taming of the Shrew,* is left alone with Katharina. He begins by saying, "Good morrow, Kate; for that's your name, I hear." Build tempo gradually, with slapstick abandon, until his line, "I must and will have Katharina to my wife!"

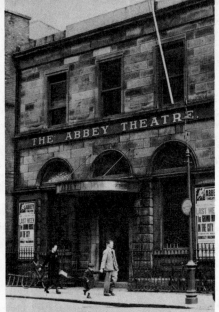

Where talent grows: on the left, an "off-Broadway" theater in Greenwich Village; on the right, Dublin's Abbey Theatre, where many fine actors and playwrights started.

8. Eating and drinking. Plan a dining scene, either of your own invention or from a play. For example, act out first, without props, scenes from *Our Town* or *The Happy Journey*.

a. Emily and George in the drugstore

b. Dr. Gibbs at breakfast

c. Mr. Webb and George on the wedding morning

Then try a scene in which actual food or beverage is needed as in *Why the Chimes Rang* or *Life with Father* or *You Can't Take It with You*. Time your lines and your business carefully.

9. Ad libbing. Plan to direct a scene of your own invention or one from a play in which there are more than three characters who make an entrance or an exit as a group, ad libbing as they do. For example, have them react and leave, ad libbing, after this line: "What are you all doing? Will you get out of here?!" Or try the end of the banquet scene in *Macbeth* or the entrance of the teen-agers in one of the scenes from *Bye, Bye, Birdie.*

10. Character analysis. In essay or outline form, write a character analysis of a part you have played, will play, or would like to play. Include the following matters:

a. a description of the physical aspects;

b. the mental and emotional characteristics;

c. educational background;

d. family; and

e. motivation and what lengths the character would go to to achieve his end.

Include the importance of the character to the development of the plot, and the relationships and attitudes to other characters in the play.

401

Aside from the director the most important people in any production are the assistant director, stage manager, house manager, and crew heads and members. Without them the actors couldn't get the show on the road. They are selected for efficiency, dependability, maturity of judgment, ability to work with others and follow instructions while working independently.

Many high-school plays do not require as elaborate a chain of command as the one discussed here. How many people will be on the technical staff depends on the director's wishes. Often a modern play requires fewer staff members than one with complex sets and costumes. The number of people interested in such positions and the ability and experience of each will be a deciding factor. No one except your director can tell how many people are needed. There are many different ways to produce a play, and the following discus-

TECHNICAL PERSONNEL

sion needs to be adapted for each play and director.

The chart on p. 404 is a version of the professional theater setup and may be simplified or expanded according to need.

This arrangement holds good until dress rehearsals. Then and during performances, the director is out front and the stage manager is in charge onstage and backstage. He supersedes the assistant director. The house manager takes his cue from the stage manager to signal the audience that intermissions are over and to close the auditorium doors.

It cannot be overemphasized that all the duties and privileges of the technical staff carry with them heavy responsibilities for tact, good nature, and steady nerves. Temperament or a show of authority are signs of insecurity and immaturity. Each one must know his job, plan it carefully, and work with everyone to get the show together. Any questions of policy or problems of personality are taken to the director in private conference and are not discussed before the cast and crews.

THE ASSISTANT DIRECTOR

If you are named assistant director, you attend all rehearsals unless excused by the director. You sit with the director and write down everything he says during rehearsal—except private mutterings!

The assistant director needs at least two copies of the play script. One is used at rehearsals and marked as the play progresses. This is his work script. The other is kept as a permanent prompt book. It is valu-

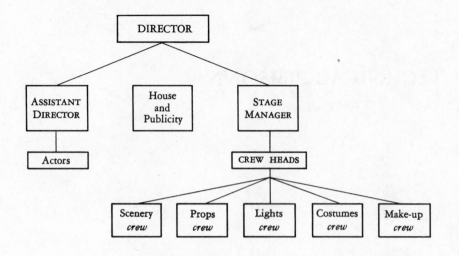

able to have a complete, permanent record of the show. This prompt
book is made by the assistant director, after the show is over, from the
notes on his work script.

THE WORK SCRIPT AND THE PROMPT SCRIPT

One method of preparing work and prompt scripts is to measure the size
of the pages in the script and mark off a space one-fourth inch smaller
in the center of twice the pages of plain notebook paper. With a razor
blade, cut out the center section. You can do quite a stack at once. Take
the pages of the printed script and insert one between two pages of paper
so the printed page can be read through the opening. Paste the insertion
in place. If you use two scripts, you simply paste the pages directly on
the paper. For this method you need two copies because one side is pasted
down. This is an easier method, but it is more costly because you use
four scripts before the permanent prompt book is completed.

It is best to put the pages on large sheets of paper in a loose-leaf
notebook. This allows wide margins for notes.

The work script is needed at every rehearsal. You need a clip board
and paper or a large clip on the front cover of the work script to make
notes. Don't forget a pencil. You will need several because the actors
borrow them and forget to return them. A pen is not wise because there
will be many changes.

If the director wishes the actors' copies of the script returned after the show, the responsibilities of the assistant director begin when the cast and technical list are posted. You number each script and keep a record of the person to whom it was given so you can check them back at the end of the run. A simple form on a single card is sufficient.

Copy	*Character*	*Returned*
#6	Mary	5/25/65
#768	Stage Manager	Work Script and Prompt Book

Use the character name rather than the name of the person playing the part. It helps avoid confusion. A copy of the final program is in the completed prompt book to refer to if needed.

CAST INFORMATION

As assistant director you take charge of the information sheets filled out at tryouts, or make your own list. The director may write comments on the originals that are confidential. If so, make your own list with the name, address, telephone number, character name, class schedule, and commitments of each cast member. It is helpful to list the scenes and/or pages in which each character appears. The information sheet looks something like this:

NAME: Sue Smith
ADDRESS: 1213 Maple
PHONE: 4-9321

CHARACTER: Mary

	MON.	TUES.	WED.	THURS.	FRI.
1st Period	Eng.	Eng.	Eng.	Eng.	Eng.
	Latin	Latin	Latin	Latin	Latin
3rd Period	Study	Study	Band	Study	Band
	Etc.				
3:30	. . . . . .	. . . . . .	. . . . . .	Dentist	. . . . . .
4:30	Lesson	. . . . . .	. . . . . .	. . . . . .	. . . . . .

Act I, sc. 2, 3, 4 or pp. 6-9, 11—15
Act II, entire
Act III, sc. 3, 4 or pp. 29—end

Such a record enables the director to tell at a glance who would be available for an extra rehearsal or a changed schedule.

Rehearsal Responsibilities

The assistant director posts rehearsal calls and informs everyone of any changes. He keeps a copy of the tentative schedule for the entire rehearsal period so the director can consult it.

You arrive a few minutes before each session and see the stage is set for the next scene. Next, check the characters needed for that scene and tell the director when everyone arrives. If the director is delayed, and you are instructed to, start the rehearsal at the appointed time.

You are responsible for seeing that all actors are in the rehearsal room in time for their entrances. If they leave the room, go out quietly and get them. All actors should check with you before leaving. Do not act as truant officer. Merely tell the actor "You're on" and return to the side of the director. Answer all questions about future rehearsals, but you have no authority to excuse anyone. Work with individual characters on cues and troublesome spots whenever they or the director ask for it.

USING YOUR WORK SCRIPT

During rehearsals hold a work script with all cuts and changes marked. If an actor misses a cut, go to him later to be sure he has it marked. Do not offer corrections or suggestions until told to do so by the director.

Make a sketch of the stage and furniture so you can use it in marking all business and stage movement. Number or letter chairs so you know which of two chairs, DR, an actor sits on. You must know all the terms listed on page 385.

You may work out your own system of marking the work script. But it saves time and trouble if you use the same code used in the permanent prompt book. There are many ways of marking a script. A notation of *John X UC, to window* in the margin is enough. If the cross is a circular one, draw a diagram like this:

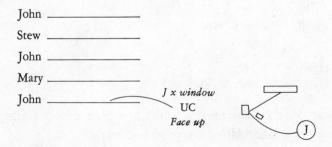

John ——————

Stew ——————

John ——————

Mary ——————

John —————— *J x window*
UC
Face up

If John turns and faces front, the notation will be *face down*. If he pauses at the fireplace, it might be drawn:

Do not write between the lines of the script, because it will be difficult to read. Cross out all printed stage directions not used and repeat in the margin, or underline in color, those that are retained.

At the end of each rehearsal, remind the cast of the next call and wait to see if the director has any additional comments. Pick up any debris, and see that the windows are closed and the hall left in good order.

Last Rehearsals and Performance

When the actors begin to work without scripts, it is your job to prompt when necessary. In the first few rehearsals, wait until the actor asks to be prompted. Then give the first few words of the speech. By the last rehearsals, prompt as soon as it is apparent the actor needs it. You will learn to sense this. At dress rehearsal prompting is done from offstage, loud enough for the actor to hear, but not loud enough to carry to the audience. You time scenes and acts and keep a record of the time.

After each dress rehearsal and performance, gather up strayed scripts and return them to their owners. After the last performance, indicate when and where the scripts are to be turned in. Keep reminding people to get them back. Here the check list of the numbered copies comes in handy. After the last performance, turn in the completed prompt book to the director.

The job of assistant director is a demanding one, but it is most rewarding because of the opportunity to learn all the details of production and watch a director at work with his cast.

STAGE MANAGER

The stage manager assumes direct responsibility for everything backstage during rehearsals, dress rehearsals, and performances. He is responsible for everything onstage except the acting and the lines. This assignment requires a person of emotional stability, even temper, a high degree of efficiency, and dependability. It is a position of executive authority second only to the director's. Handle your co-workers with respect, and a collection of accurate lists.

You use the vocabulary of the actor and assistant director, but you need to know several additional terms.

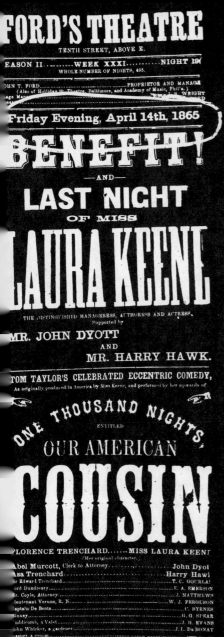

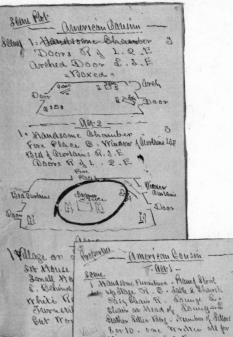

At a performance of "Our American Cousin," at Ford's Theater, Abraham Lincoln was assassinated. Shown here, on the left, is a playbill for the evening of the assassination, April 14, 1865. On the right are a set diagram and a prop list that were used in the performance of the play. The set diagram shows the scene onstage at the time of the shooting, and the prop list shows (in the third listing from the last for Act 2) the gun that fired the shot.

Act curtain: the main curtain across the front of the stage.

Asbestos: the fireproof curtain hung between the proscenium and the act curtain.

Backdrop: a large hanging at the back of the stage setting.

Backing: a drop or flat behind an opening to mask the backstage area from the audience's view.

Batten: a pipe or strip of wood on which scenery or drops are hung.

Blackout: sudden elimination of all stage lights.

Curtain line: where the act curtain meets the floor. Also the last line before the curtain is lowered.

Cyclorama: usually called a "cyc." Any set of curtains or draperies enclosing the playing area on three sides.

Dim out: smooth, gradual elimination of lights.

Dress the set: add flowers and other decorative details.

Flat: a wooden frame covered with canvas and painted. A door flat contains a door frame, a window flat has an opening for a window, etc. Flats lashed together form a set.

Flies: overhead area where scenery is hung for storage.

Floor cloth: material, usually canvas, covering stage floor to deaden sound.

Floor plan: line drawing of set and furniture as seen from above.

House lights: all lights in the audience area.

Kill: eliminate, as a light or an unwanted property.

Level: a platform.

Prompt book: the permanent record of technical details of a production.

Ramp: a sloping platform used instead of steps.

Strike: remove from playing area. Strike the set or lights, means put them away in proper storage places after a performance.

Work lights: large lights used for the crew's work but not during performance.

Rehearsal Responsibilities

As stage manager you report to the assistant director after your appointment and pick up two copies of the script. You make a work script of one, and keep the other for the permanent prompt book to be filed with the director after the last performance. Although this prompt book contains slightly different information, the general procedure is the same for both assistant director and stage manager. Your prompt book contains a floor plan of each act with all furniture marked. Get a complete list of costumes used from the costume crew head and record when they were obtained. Make a similar list of properties, and include both in your prompt book.

Attend all early rehearsals where cuts, movement, and business are given. Consult the tentative rehearsal schedule for dates, and check with the assistant director a day or two before to be sure there are no changes. You are welcome at all rehearsals, and may feel free to attend whenever you wish to clarify any details or double check the work script.

Meetings with Crew Heads

How many meetings and hours of work will be required depends on the elaborateness of the production and the number of crews you have. Stage managers have been known to do everything but act and dress the actors. However, you should have an assistant stage manager, a lighting man, and someone to handle costumes and make-up.

Assuming that you have an assistant and a crew head for each phase of production, the plans need to be carefully prepared so everyone feels useful, and there is no undue pressure because of things that should have been started earlier. Set up a production schedule and get it approved by the director.

Often you will be helped by the art or shop teacher who is in charge of the set. Whatever procedure he wishes to follow, you adopt it. There are many ways of doing a job, and you can help only if you follow instructions.

If you are given full responsibility, consult with the director during the first week and make drawings of the sets required. Consult the scenery crew head so the work gets under way when the stage is not being used for a rehearsal. The crew head checks available flats, drops, and incidental pieces such as fireplaces and bookcases to see what needs repair and repainting and what must be constructed.

Next have a conference with the head of the prop crew and make sure he understands the director's wishes. The head of the prop crew makes a prop plot, listing all furniture, hand props, and personal props with the scenes in which they are needed and their location, whether onstage or offstage. Discuss the props with the director to find his prefer-

410

The crew heads do their jobs: props are checked and costumes repaired for the next performance.

ences in style, color, size, or any special demand the script may make, such as a chair that collapses or a vase that breaks as it falls.

The next conference is with the heads of the costume and make-up crews about the director's plans for renting, borrowing, or making costumes. The crew head notes any peculiar demand for make-up, checks available supplies and sources of costumes and make-up, and reports back to the director.

Finally, have a conference with the light crew head to discuss the director's plans for lighting. It is improbable that any new lighting equipment will be ordered for an individual show, because it is expensive. The crew head gets all the lighting equipment out of storage and makes necessary repairs. He checks all gelatine and, after consultation with the director, reorders what is needed.

About the middle of the third week, there should be a meeting of all crew heads to check progress and coordinate the general plan. You and all crew heads attend the first run-through rehearsal, and make careful check lists.

411

If there is an assistant stage manager, he makes a cue sheet for all sound effects and curtain cues. All cues must be marked so he has two minutes' warning before each cue. One of you must be in a position to see the stage, so a telephone does not go on ringing after it has been picked up, or the final curtain cut an exit that is a second slower than it should be.

Dress Rehearsals and Performances

At dress rehearsals and performances, the stage manager needs three eyes, four hands, several sets of legs and perhaps two heads! Since this is impractical, make an organized work script, marked so you can read it in the semidarkness backstage. A small flashlight that clips to your work script is a most valuable possession.

Suggested Schedule

You trust your crew heads, but it is wise to make a last-minute check to see they are all ready in time. Crews and crew heads must be in the theater well ahead of performance. You will need to arrive at least forty-five minutes before curtain time. On arrival, check with all crew heads to see they are on schedule. You are not concerned with whether or not the actors arrive. That is the business of the assistant director. Go to your dark corner, get out the work script, and watch the clock. Thirty minutes before curtain time send your assistant to the dressing rooms to announce, "Half-hour." Notify all crew heads and check with the light crew head to be sure the house lights are on.

After the call "Half-hour," you and the scenery crew head recheck the set. Try all the doors to be sure they work. Check draperies, floor covering, and every detail on the scenery plot. Next, the prop crew head goes over his list with you, and every item is checked for position, whether onstage or off. Such items as tea in the teapot and openers for bottles must not be overlooked.

While you are checking the set and props, your assistant should try all sound effects, and make sure the curtain ropes are not tangled. He keeps track of the time so he may make the next call, "Fifteen minutes."

By "Fifteen minutes" the audience will begin to arrive. Make a final check with the light crew head who, meanwhile, has tested every switch and checked his plot.

At the call "Five minutes," check to see that all technical personnel

412

are in their places. The actors will come up from the dressing rooms and take their places on stage. Those who come onstage early in the play will take positions offstage. As soon as the actors enter the backstage area, they are your responsibility. To keep track of things, you can make a quick and accurate check list as follows:

At Rise..On....Mary, John, Fred
　　Ready Off...R...Sue
　　　　　L...Bob

The prop crew head checks all actors to see they have their personal props. You may need to remind the actors to keep quiet because of the audience out front.

At "Two Minutes," call for quiet onstage and backstage. Check that the assistant director is in his place and is ready to prompt. Make sure all crew members are offstage and that no actors have wandered off. Then announce, "Asbestos going up," and signal the assistant stage manager to raise the fire curtain.

Standard Cues

At curtain time, you need to give the following cues. Write them down because if you forget one, a crew member will not act but wait for it. This is when you need four hands. The signals must be given quietly, because only the act curtain is between you and the audience.

Work lights out.
Stage lights set.
House lights to half (hold it
　　a second for the audience
　　to settle in their seats.)
House lights out.
Ready on stage.
Curtain going up.
Curtain.

During the scene, watch for warnings of sound effects, light changes, character entrances, and all other details. You need not run about and give the cues for these, because the crew members and actors should handle them. However, glance around to be sure everything is ready.

413

At the close of the scene, the order of the commands is reversed. They become:

Curtain.
Work lights.
House lights.
Stage lights off.
Clear stage.
Strike.

At the command "Strike," the crews change scenery, properties, and lighting effects as rapidly as possible. The scene changes should be carefully rehearsed. The size of your backstage area dictates the method of storage. The most efficient method is a separate area for each act and a convenient table or cupboard for props, where they can be divided by acts.

If this is not possible, arrange two areas for temporary storage during performance. Props and set for the third act are stacked behind those for the second act. When articles or flats are taken offstage at the close of the first act, they are taken to a separate area out of the way. Props go off first and then flats. When the second act is over, the articles struck are placed in front of the first-act articles. When the performance is over, the crews strike the third-act set and props and store them in their original storage area. The second-act articles are then moved in front of them, and the first act is set up onstage. This leaves the second area free, so that the next night the process can be repeated.

While the crew members are striking and stacking, you are busy clock watching, so before the end of intermission your assistant can warn the cast and crews, "Three minutes." They then take their places for the

414

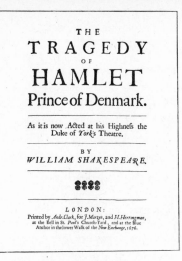

next act. The house manager warns the audience the intermission is over. Check all lists for the second act, and the routine begins again.

At the end of the performance there are curtain calls. Your assistant gives the call "Onstage" and you give the command "Curtain." The curtain should be open briefly for curtain calls. Rehearse it at every dress rehearsal. It is your job to judge the applause and terminate the calls by calling for house lights.

The Stage Manager's Prompt Script

After the performance, you and your assistant are the last to leave. See that all lights are out and everything is put away. Crew heads are responsible for their equipment, but the final check is your responsibility.

Your final prompt script is turned in after the last performance. It contains a sketch of each set and the furniture as it was located in the set. Include all crew plots, with every detail needed to repeat the show exactly as it was. You are responsible for getting these plots from the crew heads. The script shows all cuts, entrances, exits, and any significant use or change of position of properties. You include the playing time of each act and the length of intermissions.

The job of stage manager requires, and develops, flexibility and efficiency. He is the most important and the busiest man in the house at dress rehearsals and at performances. He makes everything click so unobtrusively the cast can concentrate on presenting the play to the audience, confident that all the mechanical details are in good hands. Without a good stage manager the opening curtain would never go up, and the final curtain would never come down.

HOUSE MANAGER

Most school production staffs combine the responsibilities of house manager and publicity manager. This is because the house manager has few duties until the actual performance, and by that time the publicity is all delivered. Publicity requires a person who meets people well, is persuasive, and can meet deadlines.

Publicity Schedule

Most newspapers give more space to a story that reaches them well in advance of the performance date. It is better to type a separate letter to each paper than to send carbon copies. Address it to the drama editor by name. The first story to be sent out is the announcement of the title of the play and the names of the cast and technical personnel. This goes out when the list is posted. Newspapers may not use all the names, but they should be included. This notice contains the date of production and the place and time of performances. It gives the name of the school and of the director. Be sure the release contains the "who-what-where-when" of goods news writing. If there is a benefit, mention the "why." A similar story is given to the school paper. This is the time to get help from the art department in making posters.

At least three weeks before production, a second release goes out, repeating the vital information and a paragraph or two about the play. Some publishers furnish suggestions for publicity with the scripts. Check to see whether such help is available.

Photographs

In addition to stories, newspapers often use pictures if they reach the editor well before production. It is your responsibility to consult with your director, contact a photographer, and make an appointment. Sometimes newspapers send their own photographer. You then notify the director and assistant director so the cast will be told at least a week before the appointment. You are present when pictures are taken to provide names and other information.

The usual time for pictures is during the second dress rehearsal, but this is too late for publicity purposes. Publicity pictures must be at the newspaper offices not less than two weeks, and preferably three, before performance. The papers will want clear, sharp, close-up, black-and-white,

416

glossy prints. Since the play will not be ready three weeks ahead of performance, the most interesting pictures are action shots of a rehearsal. If any costumes are available, use them.

In addition to scenes from the play, backstage pictures are always interesting. A costume fitting, the prop crew moving furniture, or the scenery crew painting a set give people the feeling of being in the glamorous backstage area. A shot of the director and cast in action is interesting to newspaper readers.

Newspaper and professional photographers are busy people. Have everything ready at the appointed time. You should have some ideas for pictures that you have discussed with the director. The photographer may not use these ideas, but they are welcome.

At the same time the second notices are sent to the newspapers, releases are sent to radio and television stations. Repeat these about a week before performance. If a television appearance can be arranged, remember the royalty and permission do not cover your using a scene from the play.

Posters are effective if they are eye-catching. At least one publisher furnishes posters with all royalty plays. Or the school art department may make them. Posters contain the name of the play, the name of the group giving it, the time, place, date, cost of tickets, and where they may be obtained. Local stores and businessmen are gracious about displaying posters, but permission must be obtained before putting one anywhere. Pick them up after the performance. Then give them to the cast as souvenirs, keeping one for the director's office.

House Duties

The house manager works with the business manager of the school, who orders and distributes the tickets. This is done early so they can be on sale at least three weeks before performance. You keep accurate records of how many tickets each person takes, because the books must balance after the performance.

It is customary to send two complimentary tickets to all newspapers and radio and television stations where publicity has been sent. It is not necessary to give complimentary tickets where posters are put up, unless they are requested.

It is wise to check with the program printer at least three weeks before performance, so he will schedule your job and advise you of the deadline. The program copy should go to the printer a week or more before performance. Check with all cast members so that their names are spelled correctly and show the copy to the director for final approval. When the proofs are ready, pick them up. Check with the director for errors. When the programs are delivered the day before performance, you are in charge of them until you turn them over to the ushers.

In conference with the director, make a list of ushers, two for each aisle and different ones for each performance. Ask them to serve far enough in advance so they have no other plans. They report for duty thirty minutes before performance time. When they arrive, give them the programs, and check to see they understand the rows and seat numbers. Each usher has a small flashlight for seating latecomers. It is customary to give some programs to the cast and the director, taking them down to the dressing rooms.

If tickets are sold at the door, you may be in charge of the box office. In this case, you need about twenty dollars in small change, which the school business manager gives you in a cash box and which is returned with the receipts.

Your Duties at Performance

During performance stay near the door to prevent interruptions. When the house lights go up for intermission, open the doors to the lobby, and check the exact time. Three minutes before the intermission is over, ring a bell or flick the lights in the hall, and take your place at the door. When the house lights are lowered, close the doors.

After performance, if the school business manager is not present, gather up the money and take it to the business office, or give it to the director before he leaves. Check to see that all windows are closed and the house is in good shape. Pick up forgotten umbrellas and lost articles and take them to the box office or to the lost and found office.

The publicity and house manager is a public relations man. He is the official host and his courtesy and calmness never vary. He plans carefully for the comfort and convenience of his guests.

ACTIVITIES

1. Divide the class, by drawing lots or by using volunteers, into crews for a technical staff and stimulate the work involved in planning a production. For your imaginary production, choose a play with which the whole class is

familiar. Meet by crews (scenery, props, lights, costumes, make-up). Then report to the class as a whole, in panel discussion or symposium style, the work of your crew, giving all the specific problems peculiar to your play.

2. Select a play with which you are familiar, and develop one of the following projects:

a. Draw costume plates for the characters (or at least the main characters, if the cast is very large). Color them, keeping in mind the harmony and contrasts needed for characters onstage together.

b. Draw sketches of scenery for one or more sets.

c. Draw floor plans for all sets, preferably to scale.

d. Draw diagrams or sketches of make-up for all character parts. Indicate grease paint numbers, colors of liners, and all special treatment.

3. If you cannot draw, make a small scrapbook of pictures cut from magazines to provide ideas for each of the projects described above—sets, costumes, furniture arrangement, window treatment.

4. When your class plans a production, indicate your choice of crew (see above) or committee (house and publicity) and outline the work involved. Include a time schedule and deadlines.

5. Plan a style show of costumes made either from your backstage wardrobe or of varicolored school clothes. Darken the classroom and turn colored lights on the models, studying the effects of various colored gelatines on costume colors.

6. Volunteer to work backstage in a nearby community playhouse and then give a report on your duties and experiences during the run of the show.

7. Make an inventory of the flats, drops, and incidental pieces available in your school's scene dock. What color is predominant in each? What size is each?

8. Select a scene from a play and prepare a sample prompt script, working according to the directions in Chapter 8.

The scenery and property crews are often combined under one crew head. He is responsible to the stage manager and checks with him before the curtain goes up for each act to report all properties are in place. He and his crew assist the stage manager, construct, assemble, and store scenery and gather, store, and return borrowed properties.

If you are appointed head of this crew, you and your crew will work on construction before dress rehearsals. Usually you will not have to construct an entire set. You will call a crew meeting after casting to study what is available and check scenery for repairs. You may find you have to add a flat or two or repaint a set.

Remember it is impossible for your crew to work onstage during rehearsals. Each crew member needs pencils, pads of paper, and work clothes with pockets for nails, hammers, and screwdrivers.

SCENERY AND PROPERTIES

The director provides you with floor plans showing the way he wants the set, drawn to scale, and considers the width and height of the proscenium. It shows the outline of the set, the position of doorways, windows, the location and direction of stairways, and fireplaces, bookcases, and window seats. Sometimes a director gives you only a rough sketch. Then you need to make your own scale drawing. You work from the scale drawing and, with the director and stage manager, draw up plans for adding whatever else you need. If the art or shop teacher supervises the construction you will work directly with him.

The floor plan you work from should be large. Use ½ inch to the foot. The floor plan you make from the stage manager's prompt book will be either ¼ inch or ⅛ inch to the foot, depending on the size of your stage. A floor plan looks something like Figure I. It includes all backings and marking pieces and indicates the wall of the backstage area, the proscenium base, and all windows, doors, and immovable objects.

As soon as you and the stage manager have had a conference with the director and become familiar with the floor plan, issue your crew call. Spend some time going over the floor plan with them. Next examine everything available for use and make repairs where needed. Make a list of all the materials that will be necessary, and be sure to check paint supplies to see that paint is still usable. List all properties that will be needed, and sources where they may be obtained. With the authorization of the proper school authority, order material for the new construction.

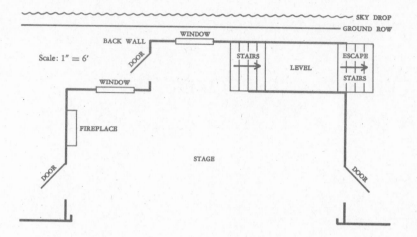

TYPES OF SCENERY

STANDING PIECES are called flats. There are also window, door, and fireplace flats. These are large wall-type frames that windows, doors, or fireplaces fit into. There are also wing flats. These are two flats hinged together so they fold face in. They are useful for backing behind open archways and behind doors to block the view backstage, and to indicate a room offstage. Flats are a little higher than the proscenium, and they are built to a maximum of 5′ 9″ wide, so that they can be carried by one crew member.

HANGING UNITS are cycloramas, backdrops, and borders. Borders hide the tops of upstage flats and the battens and ropes above stage. They are plain or cut out and painted to suggest foliage if it is an outdoor scene.

BUILT-UP UNITS are steps, platforms, window seats, trees, rocks, and mounds of earth.

SET UNITS stand independently on the floor: a fence, wall, or row of bushes seen through a low window. These are braced and weighted with small sandbags.

You may combine the above types to get variety in your set. However, construction of scenery takes time and money. It must be designed for most rapid construction, must be economical, strong enough to be safe, and easy to handle.

It is planned for quick and silent shifting between scenes and must be accurately fitted for easy assembling. It must be designed so it can be compactly stored.

SCENERY CONSTRUCTION

You need lumber, canvas, hardware, tools, plywood (sometimes called profile board) for corner and keystone blocks and set pieces, and paint to build a flat. If your town is small and you are building a complete set, you need time to order and receive some of these things.

Lumber

The best lumber for scenery is white pine. You need a supply of 1″ x 3″ boards for flats and 1″ x 4″ boards for doors. You may order these in lengths long enough to cut into useful pieces. But if you are not an experienced carpenter you'd better have the lumber yard cut them to length. At any rate, have the lumber dressed and surfaced at the yard. This removes about ⅛″ from the thickness and about ¼″ from the width of each piece.

Try to impress on your dealer your need for lumber that is not warped, because the edges of the flats must fit smoothly together.

Canvas

Canvas is the best material to use to cover flats to be stored for future use. Duck canvas is cheaper than scene linen. Heavy unbleached muslin is least expensive and easier to find in department stores. Be sure, however, that it is a very heavy quality because the finer weaves are not as durable.

Measure the height of your flats, multiply by the number you need, and order the canvas, adding three inches to the length of each flat. Check the width for the most advantageous size to buy. You need the width of each flat plus three inches.

Let us say your flats are 12′ high by 5′ 9″ wide. You will need 12′ 3″ (flat height plus three inches) or 4 yd. 3″ of material 72″ wide. If you cannot get 72″ canvas, you need to allow for a seam. It would be safer to get 39″ material and use two widths, or 8 yd. 6″ for a single flat. Multiply this by the number of flats you need.

Hardware

The first five of these items will have to be ordered from a theatrical supply house. The rest can be found in any well-stocked hardware store. You may be unfamiliar with those illustrated on page 424.

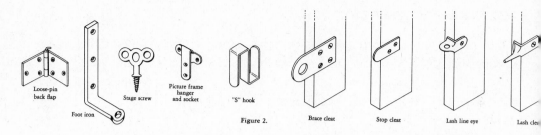

Loose-pin
back flap

Foot iron

Stage screw

Picture frame
hanger
and socket

"S" hook

Figure 2.

Brace cleat

Stop cleat

Lash line eye

Lash cleat

Brace cleats: if you plan to use special propping by stage braces on isolated sections or at the ends of a long, flat wall where foot irons are not used, use one brace cleat for each flat.

Lash cleats: at least four for a 12′ flat.

Lash line eye: one for each flat.

Foot irons: to screw scenery to floor, one per flat.

Stage screws: one for each foot iron.

Screws: No. 8 wood screws (⅞″ and 1½″). No. 9 wood screws (1½″).

Corrugated fasteners: No. 5 (¾″).

Nails: wire nails (4, 6, and 10 penny), finishing nails (assorted), lath nails (1¼″), clout nails (1¼″).

Carpet tacks: Nos. 4 and 6.

Hinges: loose-pin back flaps, each flap 2″.

Strap hinges: each flap 6″.

Soft steel strips: (³⁄₁₆″ x ⅞″) for saddle irons.

A flat piece of iron: for clinching or flattening nail points of blocks.

Sash cord: No. 8 for lash liner, one length for each flat. It should reach from the top to within 3″ of the bottom of the flat. It is knotted at one end to prevent its slipping through the line eye (see Figure 3).

Tools

Each crew member has his own screwdriver, folding ruler, and pencils. There should be several hammers, a metal square for truing corners, a small hand plane, a sharp saw, and a sharp knife or single-edged razor blade.

424

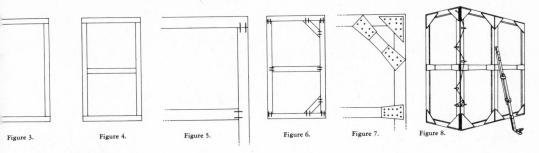

Figure 3.   Figure 4.   Figure 5.   Figure 6.   Figure 7.   Figure 8.

Paint Supplies

Flake or ground gelatin glue.
Scene paint (pigment powder).
Whiting.
Four good quality paint brushes (8″, 4″, 2″, and a ½″ liner).
Yardstick.
Charcoal stick.
Chalk.
Snap line (about 30 feet of heavy cotton cord).
Several 2 or 3 gallon pails and smaller pans.
Metal or wooden paddles to stir the paint.
Two-burner hot plate to cook the glue.
Rags.
Sponges.
Newspapers or drop cloths to protect the floor.

CONSTRUCTING A FLAT

The first step in making a flat is to clear a large floor space and assemble your equipment where it is handy. Check the floor plan so you are sure of all dimensions. Measure each board and label it in pencil so you are certain of its exact length. If it has not been cut at the lumber yard, mark it as you cut it.

A flat is constructed so it can be moved without catching on the floor and wrenching out of shape, so the bottom and top boards are fastened to the side boards as shown in Figure 3.

The side pieces for a 12′ flat are 11′ 6″ long, because 3″ is added by each top and bottom piece, by the top and bottom rails.

Each flat is braced by one or more cross braces, called toggle rails. They are put no less than 6′ apart, so a flat more than 12′ high would need two toggle rails. The toggle rail is set inside the frame and is 6″ shorter than the width of the flat. Other braces 3′ 6″ long with mitered ends are set across the upper and lower right-hand corners of the flat.

Thus for each 12' x 5' 9" flat you need:

> 2 pieces: 1" x 3" x 5' 9" (top and bottom rails).
> 2 pieces: 1" x 3" x 11' 6" (sides).
> 1 piece: 1" x 3" x 5' 3" (toggle rail).
> 2 pieces: 1" x 3" x 3' 6" mitered (corner braces).
> 4 triangles: 8" x 8" of $\frac{3}{16}$" profile board (corner blocks).
> 6 rectangles: 6" x 3" of $\frac{3}{16}$" profile board (keystone blocks).

Assemble the entire frame on the floor before you start to nail. Be sure the top and bottom rails are correctly placed. Use a metal square to true all the corners. The frame should look like Figure 4.

Drive in two corrugated fasteners flush across the seam. Do this at all four corners and at the toggle rail. Check each corner after it is fastened to be sure it is still true. The fasteners will look like Figure 5.

Next put the corner braces against the side pieces and the bottom and top rails and nail them with corrugated fasteners, making sure they fit tight. Both bottom and top corner braces should be on the right side. Your frame then looks like Figure 6.

Take the four corner blocks you cut from $\frac{3}{16}$" plywood into 8" x 8" triangles and the six keystones that are the 6" x 3" rectangles. Place these $\frac{1}{4}$" from the outside edge of the frame and attach them with a number of $1\frac{1}{4}$" nails, as in Figure 7. You need a clinching iron under each block to flatten the nail points so they don't stick out. If your school makes a practice of reusing lumber, use screws instead of clinch nails. Screws are easier to remove when you dismantle the flat to remake it for another show.

Applying Hardware

You may apply the hardware before or after the canvas is put on. But it must be done before the flat is painted to prevent damage to the paint. If it is done after the frame is finished you eliminate one turning of the frame, since it is already face down.

Place a lash line eye with the eye toward the inside of the frame in the upper right-hand corner, so it fits snugly. Put a lash cleat just above the toggle rail on the same side, with the point toward the inside of the frame. Put another lash cleat on the left side halfway between the two which are on the right side. Add two more, one on each side, with the lower one 3' 6" from the bottom. If the flat is more than 12' you will need more lash cleats. Secure them to the frame with screws. The

426

frame will then look like Figure 8. The lash cleats allow you to lash the frames together with the sash cord. For the method of securing them, see the illustration in Figure 2.

If you make a wing flat, omit the lash line eye and lash cleats and use hinges, placing them so the flats fold face to face. Paste a strip of canvas the full length of the flat on the back side of the frame over the hinges. It must be loose enough to permit the fold. This prevents light leaking through the crack when the flats are opened for use.

Covering the Frame

Now you are ready to cover the frame. If the flat is to be permanent, use canvas. If you plan to reconstruct the flat for the next show, muslin is more practical.

Turn the frame over so that the side with the braces and hardware is down. Cut a length of fabric 3″ longer than the length of the frame. If you are using canvas less than 72″ wide, the seaming should be done by machine to bring the overall width to at least 72″. Lay the canvas over the frame so about 1½″ extends over the edge on all sides. If it is seamed, the rough side of the seam is on the underside. Use No. 6 carpet tacks driven part way to fasten the canvas to each of the four corners. The material should be kept straight and smooth but not stretched tight.

After the four corners are tacked, tack the canvas at about 6″ intervals all around the frame, but not across the toggle rail or corner braces. Keep the tacks no farther than a half inch from the inside edge of the frame. It is best to tack one end, then tack the other end, and the sides last.

Remove the four temporary tacks from the corners and fold back the loose edge of the material so the frame is exposed. You are now ready to paste.

The agent can be prepared by one of the crew while the frame is being made. Use a large bucket and mix one pound of flake glue in two quarts of water. Heat it until it is thoroughly dissolved. Stir from time to time so it does not burn. When the glue is dissolved one pound of whiting is added.

Using a two- or three-inch brush, apply the hot mixture generously to the frame. Press the cloth onto the frame, being careful not to pull it out of shape. With a smooth piece of wood or a clean dry rag, press down on the canvas to be sure it is stuck everywhere. Drive a couple of tacks halfway into each corner and, with a sharp knife, trim the canvas

Sets, at least the essentials, should be ready for use in rehearsal. Shown here, at the top, is a completed set for the Broadway production of "The Desperate Hours." The cast uses a skeleton set for rehearsal. Note that a set of this kind allows action to be portrayed in various parts of the house pictured and allows the action to be transferred from one room to another without losing the continuity of the play.

about ¼" inside the outer edge. This drives the cut edge into the wood, where it stays after the glue is dry. Be careful because canvas tends to stretch when it is wet. Allow the glue to dry for several hours or overnight before proceeding. Meanwhile, go ahead with constructing and covering another flat; keep the glue warm.

Painting the Flat

Size is used to prepare new canvas for painting. It is made by using three or four pounds of the glue used in construction. The glue is put in water and allowed to soak overnight. Then it is cooked, just as the glue was. When it is hot, it is diluted so that it is very thin. Four pounds of glue make twelve to eighteen gallons of size. It is best to make plenty because it takes time to prepare. It can be kept for a day or two, or reheated and diluted.

You may add some of the pigment you will use in painting or use whiting to seal the pores of new canvas and prepare the working surface. Size is applied generously with a wide brush so every bit is covered. Allow the size to dry overnight. The next day the canvas will have shrunk so it is tight. You are now ready to start painting.

The first coat is the prime coat. It isn't necessary for a flat that is being repainted. If you use heavy, new canvas you can combine the sizing

429

and prime coats by making the size thicker and adding pigment of the color you wish. If you use unbleached muslin or very porous canvas it is better to use two coats.

Scene paint is made from dry pigment, glue, and water. Prepared calcimine or cold-water paints tend to turn chalky-looking under stage lights and often rub off. It is much wiser to make your own. Paint stores have a wide variety of colors and you can select the ones you want from a color chart or mix your own. Rarely will you find exactly the tone you want, so you need to do some experimenting. Your paint dealer can help you select colors if you show him what you want. But you must do your own mixing and testing.

The dry pigment is added to glue and water exactly the way you made size. It should be warm when you stir in the pigment. Stir until it is all dissolved and the mixture has the consistency of heavy cream. It is best to add a little at a time because once it's in, you can't get it out. Remember paint looks darker when it's wet than when it's dry and that colored lights will change it. It is wise to try a little paint on a piece of wood and, when it is dry, check it under the stage lights you expect to use.

Make as much paint as you will need since it is difficult to match. Two three-gallon pails should cover seven flats 12' high and 5' 9" wide. Use an 8" brush and cover the surface evenly. If you cannot finish all the flats in one day, save the paint and reheat it. But it must be stirred again.

One coat of paint must be completely dry before a second is put on. If the second coat does not hide the first, it was too thin. If the first coat was completely dry and still "bleeds through," the paint of the second coat is too hot or the first coat needed more glue. If this happens you will need a third coat to hide the bleeding. There is no way to tell how many coats you will need. One coat over the primer should do a new flat. One or more will be needed to cover old flats, depending on the color to be hidden.

Textured Surfaces

Most scene designers prefer a broken surface to a flat color. This can be achieved by using a different tone of the same color or by adding another color after the basic color is dry. One method is to use a fairly dry brush lightly, with long, free strokes in various directions over the surface. See that the brush is not too full of paint and that the strokes are even and light. A word of caution! Try the new colors under the stage lights before

Long-handled brushes such as these help set-painters do their jobs quickly and efficiently.

you start to paint. Wait for the paint on the samples to dry. Test under colored lights so the effect will be the same as at performance. Look at it from the back of the auditorium.

Another method of varying surface texture is "dragging," used to suggest wood grain. The brush is even drier than for the above process, and the strokes are all made in the same direction.

A large sponge dipped in the paint, squeezed dry, and patted gently over the canvas breaks a too-smooth surface. Look at the results frequently from a distance to avoid bunching or unattractive spacing.

"Spattering" uses a brush full of paint spattered over the canvas in small drops. This takes considerable practice and can be combined with the other methods. Always judge the effect of your textures from a distance. This is the way the audience sees it. Take it easy, you can add more, but you can't take off an excess. Consult the books listed in the bibliography (see page 496) for more involved and decorative painting processes.

PROPERTIES

The prop crew works with the stage crew during construction. If the stage crew is responsible for both stage and properties and there are scene changes, it is wise to appoint an assistant as prop-crew head to be sure everything will be in place for rehearsals and performances. All properties are assembled and ready for use by the first dress rehearsal.

The prop crew divide the list so one person is responsible for checking furniture, another, for hand props, and a third, for personal props the characters carry on or offstage. Each keeps a careful list, not only of the property but of its position on or offstage, who brings on what personal props, and what he does with them when he is onstage.

The prop crew spends much time finding the proper articles. Props, like scenery, must be right for the mood of the play, the demands of the script, and the characters who use them. In period plays they must be in keeping with the era. There are books on period furniture and costumes you can consult.

Color, size, and artistic suitability must be considered. If the script calls for a heavily furnished room and your stage is small, the director may suggest some pieces be eliminated. Or if they are all necessary to the action, they can be scaled down. A small love seat can take the place of a large sofa, or a winged chair substituted for an overstuffed one.

When arranging furniture onstage, keep it two feet back of the curtain line so the actors don't have to play behind it. The backs of chairs and sofas should be low, and tables sturdy enough to lean on. When the director approves the arrangement, usually after each scene at the first dress rehearsal, the position of all furniture is marked. This is done with chalk marks on the floor where the legs of furniture are placed. White adhesive tape is also used unless there is a rug. Local firms sometimes lend furniture. If they do, be sure to give them a credit on the program. Anything you borrow, whether from a firm or an individual, is your responsibility. It *must* be returned clean and unmarred immediately after the last performance. Borrowed furniture must be placed offstage and covered between rehearsals and performances. Small articles are put away. *Never* leave the props onstage where actors and crew may lean on them.

The prop crew takes charge of all properties after the scene is over, even though the actor provided the prop. That is your job. You must know the next night where the prop is.

The prop crew head keeps a master list of all props including where they were obtained, by whom, when, where, and by whom they are returned. There should be enough description so it is clear what article is referred to.

The prop crew head makes a floor plan with all furniture arranged and labeled. He needs a plan for each scene. On the same sheet is a list of every article needed, stating whether it is on at the opening. There are separate lists for each scene, with notations of all changes to be made between scenes. In addition to the plan, there are notations such as:

Act I

On	*Off R*	*Off L*
Davenport, LC	Suitcase (Mary)	Tea tray (Anne)
Draperies, URC	Coat (Mary)	Teapot
(drawn)	Book (Mary)	Tea
Table, DR		Cups
Vase, on table DR		Saucers
Flowers (roses) in		
vase, DR		
Letter in envelope		
in drawer desk DL		
Curtain—strike tea tray, etc.		

The list must be checked each night before curtain. After dress rehearsals and performances, it is rechecked to be sure everything is put away and a notation made of what is to be replaced, such as the tea and a new envelope for the letter. Each crew member has an individual list of his responsibilities.

Here are a few hints about props that may be useful. If several days have passed between scenes, remember to change the flowers. If the flowers are not to be handled, artificial ones are traditional. If they are to be handled, they had better be real so they won't rattle. Your local florist often has day-old flowers that are cheaper than fresh ones.

If food is served, put an old blanket under the tablecloth to prevent clatter of dishes. If the food is not to be eaten, you can mold it from paper towels soaked to a pulp, shaped, and painted. Colored water is substituted for all beverages. It is easy to swallow and does not coat the actor's throat.

Mirrors are placed so they do not reflect in the eyes of the audience. A thin coating of Bon Ami cuts the glare. Glass is removed from pictures for the same reason; it also decreases their weight. Eyeglasses can be bought at the ten-cent store and the lenses removed.

Envelopes should have pointed flaps with only the point pasted. Letters are authentic, not just lines of scribble, because the audience may see them when they are laid down. Check all pens and cigarette lighters before each performance to see that they work. Put a little bit of water in the bottoms of the ash trays so any cigarettes go out easily.

Props to be broken, such as vases or glasses, can be broken and then glued very lightly. This has to be done after each use. Often it is simpler to get cheap replacements. Be very sure they are fragile enough to break. Cheap glass is often the toughest. Buy an extra piece and test it.

A prop man must have ingenuity, imagination, steady nerves, a sense of responsibility for other people's property, and a foolproof list he checks constantly.

ACTIVITIES

1. a. Assume you are constructing a flat 11′6″ high and 4′6″ wide. List the number of lumber pieces needed with the dimensions of each.

   b. How much canvas would you order to cover two of these flat frames?

2. Draw a floor plan, arranging and labeling furniture for a dinette scene at breakfast time. Use three characters: mother, father, and son. Enter son midway through scene.

3. Make a list of properties (furniture, hand props, and personal props) for the plan in question.

4. Make a miniature, unpainted flat from materials you can assemble or your teacher provides, using string for lash line and small nails for cleats.

5. Plan a guided tour of your school stage to check on materials and equipment on hand. Take note of all items described in this chapter: flats, hanging units, cyclorama, built-up units.

6. Make a field trip to a nearby community playhouse. How does their equipment compare with yours? Ask questions about the construction of unusual pieces such as rocks, trees, archways, stained-glass windows.

7. Divide the class into groups and make illustrated reports on period furniture, window treatment, and interior decorating, useful in planning period plays.

8. If you are an art student, or interested in art, plan an illustrated talk on moods created by

    a. Line arrangement (lofty archways or bizarre, angular motifs)

    b. Color effects

Discuss their use on stage in scenery and props.

9. Select one of the plays you have read. Using appropriate columns for the names of the props and their position on or off stage, chart them, dividing them as follows:

    a. Stage props

    b. Hand props

    c. Personal props

The work of the costume and make-up crew will depend upon many factors, such as the size of the cast, the number of changes required, the size of the budget, and whether there is a costume room where old costumes are stored and current costumes are kept. The crews work together until nearly time for dress rehearsals. About a week before dress rehearsals they are divided into costume personnel and make-up personnel, with an assistant crew head to supervise one of the divisions.

COSTUMES

As soon as you are named crew head, report to the assistant director to get a copy of the script. You may not need to keep it permanently, but you need it for a few days to make preliminary plans.

It is the duty of your crew to locate, assemble, repair, and/or construct everything that is worn in the show.

COSTUME AND MAKE-UP

During dress rehearsals and performances you help dress the actors when they need it, keep check of all articles, see that costumes are pressed before the next night, and make whatever repairs or adjustments are needed. After the last performance, you return everything borrowed or rented, and store what you have room to keep.

Before you call your crew, begin to make your lists. Read through the play, making notes on the characters' ages, financial condition, social position, and any details that may be relevant to the clothes they will wear. Make a note of all costume changes indicated in the script, and of over-coats, gloves, hats, umbrellas, scarfs, and special jewelry called for.

Plan to attend an early run-through rehearsal so you can consider the play as a unit. Then make an appointment to discuss the costumes with the director.

The director may have only a general idea of the costumes he wants the actors to wear. He may tell you he wants a particular color for a char-acter, or a type of material, such as organdy, for a party dress, or a suit or tuxedo. Note all suggestions and start to make your plans. These need to be checked with the director for his approval, but after the first con-ference you can work without him until everything is assembled.

Costumes reinforce a play. It is not a fashion parade. A costume's purpose is to add visual emphasis to the actor as an integral part of the play. Costumes reflect character and character changes identify position and relationship, as with royalty or members of the clergy. Costumes help the actor submerge his personality into that of the character.

Burt Lancaster, in "Birdman of Alcatraz," is made up to look progressively older. Here he is shown being made up, and with his makeup complete at the beginning and end of the picture.

Sometimes an actor objects to the costume the director has in mind. An actor may want to look glamorous or sophisticated when the part calls for simplicity. Turn the matter over to the director. He has the final word.

Costumes are modern, period, or stylized. The script often dictates the classification, although period plays have been done in modern costumes. Your director decides which he wants to do.

Costume Sources

Modern costumes seem the simplest to get, but this is not always the case. The best way to start is to ask each actor what he has that is suitable for his rôle. Ask him to bring it well in advance so the director may approve it. Set a date two weeks before dress rehearsal for actors to bring their costumes so you and the director may check on color and general compatibility. Let the director make the request, but it is your responsibility to remind him. You and your crew will be present to make notes of all approved costumes.

If the actor has nothing suitable, you try to borrow what you need. Exhaust every other possibility before resorting to borrowing, because you are responsible for seeing the clothes are returned clean and in perfect condition.

Period and stylized costumes may be rented, borrowed, made, or improvised. Renting costumes is the most satisfactory way, but it is expen-

438

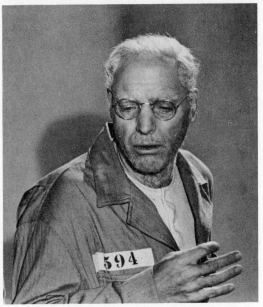

sive. A list of costume-rental houses appears at the end of this chapter. If you are giving a popular play, such houses have several sets of costumes made for that script. They have three different qualities that differ in material, in trimming, and in price.

If you plan to rent from a professional costume house, write immediately after your first conference with the director, giving them the name of the play, the date of production, and requesting prices, express charges, and charts for measurements. The costumes will come in large trunks, with each character's garments and accessories listed. Keep the list to check when you repack them. They must be sent back the day after the final performance to avoid extra rental charges.

If you have parents who sew, or a coöperative home economics department, you may want to make the costumes. This can be as expensive as renting, and requires time and effort. One advantage, however, in making the costumes is that you have them to restyle for other plays. If you have a costume room to store them you will find that a simple, basic period costume can be redraped into a bustle, padded for Elizabethan plays, or put over hoops. Old, discarded formals and negligees are useful if you have room to store them.

Line and Color

In making new costumes or restyling old ones, remember that line and color are the most important considerations. Line is significant in period costumes. Line includes length and cut of skirts or trousers, sleeve styles, necklines, jacket and coat lengths and styles. These are indicated in the silhouettes of all the important eras in most of the costume books listed in the bibliography (see page 493).

The texture and draping quality of a fabric often makes or breaks a period costume. Fabrics are either stiff, like brocade, velveteen, heavy muslin, or crinoline, or they drape easily, like soft wool and loosely woven synthetics, or they float, like chiffon or extremely sheer silk. The weave of inexpensive fabric is often faulty and it is difficult to drape.

There are costume fabric houses listed at the end of this chapter, who send samples and have a far wider range of textures and colors at more reasonable prices than department stores. If you are experienced, you can find wonderful bargains in bolt ends. Check the material carefully to be sure it drapes or gathers the way you want it to. If you are planning period costumes, consult the books for details of color, line, and fabric.

Color is much too involved to discuss in detail. A good costume book will tell you whether a given period was characterized by dark, rich colors, pastels, or prints. The most important thing to remember in selecting colors is that stage lights change or intensify them. Therefore, lighting plans and scenery need to be taken into consideration.

Solid colors with contrasting trim are more useful than figured material. They are less obtrusive and better adapted for restyling. Texture affects colors under stage lights. Corduroy and velveteen absorb light and are intensified, while satin reflects light and looks paler and shinier.

Crew Responsibilities

You need a separate sheet for each character in the play. It lists everything worn by that character and all changes and notes, such as *wet* for a coat or umbrella if the plan requires it. About a week before dress rehearsal the sheets are given to the crew members, and each concentrates on the costumes assigned to him. A sample costume sheet looks something like this:

440

CHARACTER NAME_____BOB_____   PLAYED BY_____JOHN SMITH_____

ACT I.   On at opening, *list of garments.*

    1. Black shoes
    2. Black sox
    3. Navy blue trousers
    4. Navy blue suit coat
    5. White shirt
    6. Red tie
    7. Raincoat (wet)
    8. Striped red and navy cap (wet)

    Accessories

    1. Black umbrella (wet)
    2. White handkerchief (breast pocket)
    3. Wrist watch

ACT II.   Enter page 34, from off R.

    Garments as above

    Strike   1. Raincoat
               2. Cap
               3. Red tie
    Add   1. Bow tie

    Accessories as above

    Strike   1. Umbrella
    Add   1. White carnation (buttonhole)

ACT III.   On at opening, *garments*

    1. Tennis shoes
    2. Red socks
    3. Blue jeans (dirty)
    4. Red shirt (right shoulder torn)

    Accessories

    Strike   1. Wrist watch

Each crew member keeps his own sheets and checks them before each performance to see that the costumes are arranged for easy handling between acts. Anything which is worn in a play is a costume. The actors should leave at the theater anything of theirs that is being used in performance. If there is no place to keep the costumes, each actor is provided with a list of the items he needs and for which he is responsible. Before each performance, check the list as a safeguard against a substitution in case something is forgotten.

It is not unheard of for an actor to decide to add a decorative touch to his costume or even to substitute a more becoming garment. When or if this happens, take the matter to the director at once. You are appointed to carry out his plans. You have no authority to approve or reject any change.

After the last performance, you and your crew check every item so you know it is returned to its proper owner. Everything except the most fragile things should be sent to be cleaned. The cleaner may return the borrowed garments to their owners. Then you should call the owner in a few days to make sure that everything is satisfactory. This makes it easier to borrow the next time.

Here are a few hints you may find helpful. If dress collars or clerical collars are used, have an extra supply. Make-up is difficult to remove from starched surfaces.

If a costume is to be torn, soiled, or stained while a character is off-stage or between acts, it is simpler to get a duplicate costume than to damage and repair for each performance.

Tights are rinsed after each wearing so they fit smoothly.

It is better to press costumes as soon as they are taken off, than be

For her role in "Pocketful of Miracles," actress Bette Davis had to play the part of a poor, ill-kempt street vendor, Apple Annie, who is transformed into a "lady." These

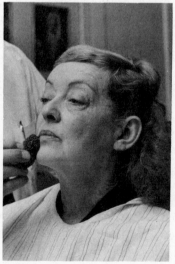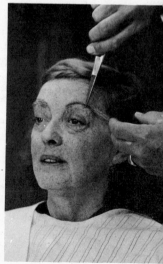

442

photographs show, step by step, the difficult makeup job that was necessary for the movie.

443

rushed before performance the following night.

Name tags with the character name and the scene in which it is needed are attached with clip clothes-pins, and all a character's costumes are kept together and hung in the order they will be needed.

You need a supply of straight pins and a variety of small, black safety pins that will not catch the light. You need black and white thread and needles. A pair of scissors is useful for snipping threads and frayed edges. Keep a can of noninflammable spot remover and a stiff clothes brush handy to remove make-up stains from lapels and collars.

If hoops, robes, and heavy capes are to be used, the actors should rehearse in them for at least a week so they learn to handle them easily. These need not be the exact garments used for the performance but as near the same size and weight as possible.

MAKE-UP

Two weeks before dress rehearsals, the make-up crew should check supplies on hand and order replacements.

Most actors do their own basic make-up, but they need help and supervision. There is one crew member for every three actors if there are no special problems. If the make-up is complicated, a crew member is assigned to this job.

If the cast is large, as for a pageant, a make-up line is used, with one crew member for each make-up step. He moves down the line applying this one process and is followed by others doing eye shadow, etc.

As crew head you may take on your share of cast members, but you need to check that everything is moving. Watch the clock so everyone is ready ten minutes before curtain time. This includes a last-minute check of ears, backs of necks, hands (including nail polish), hair-line blending, and body make-up.

Make-up is completed before costumes are put on and then is smoothed and touched up. Hair styles are part of your job and should be inspected after the costumes are on. Actors are reminded to bring smocks, large towels, or old sheets to protect their clothing and costumes.

Kinds of Make-Up

Make-up materials are divided into paint, powder, and applicators. Paint is grease or greaseless and comes in sticks, tubes, and liquid form. It in-

444

cludes base skin colors and the intense shades for shadowing and high lights. Powder is used to soften make-up, to set it and prevent smearing, and to tone down shine under the lights. Applicators are brushes, pencils, powder puffs; and cleansing tissues are for removing make-up.

In making plans and checking supplies, take into consideration the types of characters the script requires. Age, temperament, racial characteristics, health, and sex are reflected in basic skin tone and in the high lights and shadows needed. You need to consider the actor and his relationship to the rôle he is playing. You may need to darken or lighten his natural coloring.

Supplies

Most actors have their own make-up kits. Student kits can be obtained from Elizabeth Arden, New York, N.Y.; Max Factor and Co., Los Angeles, Calif., or the M. Stein Cosmetic Co., New York, N.Y. Drug stores often stock them or can get them in a reasonable length of time. Prices range from about $4.00 to $5.50, depending on whether old-age make-up is included. There are male and female kits that differ in base colors. The male kit is several degrees darker in tone.

These firms also have group make-up kits that sell for about $50.00. If you assemble your own, you will save some money, provided you do not need too many special effects. A large fishing-tackle box is excellent for group make-up.

You need the following supplies with one item for every three cast members.

Brushes: several ¼" flat sable brushes for character lines.

Cleansing creams: large jars of any standard brand will do.

Cleansing tissues for removing make-up.

Eyebrow pencils: black and brown, available at the dime store.

Face powder: used to set grease paint. Factor #12 and #22 or Stein #7 and #9.

Greaseless make-up for foundation color, solid cake for face and liquid for body make-up. Factor #2 and Cream Rose; Stein Cream Blush, #23, #7, #7a.

Grease paint, tubes or sticks. Factor #2½, #3, #5½, #6, #7 and #8; Stein #3, #3½, #5, #12, #13, and #24; Arden #5, #5x, #6x, and #12x.

Liners and shading colors (also called grease paint in intense colors. They come in small, round metal boxes and are applied with a fine-line brush).

Factor #9 (very dark red), #5 (light blue), #16 (medium blue), #4 (dark blue), #12 (white), and #1 black); Stein moist rouges, #2 (medium orange red), #3 (medium red), #6 (light red), and liners #12, #13 (very dark red), #14 (medium orange red), #8 (light blue), #11 (medium green blue), #9 (medium blue), #10 (dark blue), #15 (white), and #17 (black).

Mascara, black and brown, for accenting eyelashes and brows.

Powder puffs, any good brand that washes.

Rouge, for applying liquid or cake make-up.

If there are to be beards or sideburns, you will also need:

Crepe hair, usually wool crepe rather than real crepe. Should be dampened and stretched before applying to straighten it. Light, medium, and dark grey, light, medium, and dark brown, blonde, auburn, white, and black. It is sold by the yard.

Spirit gum, a liquid adhesive for attaching crepe hair. Apply it over complete make-up rather than directly on the skin.

Acetone, for removing spirit gum.

Scissors, for shaping beards.

In addition you need combs, hairpins, soap, smocks or large aprons to protect the costumes and the clothes of the crew, and a bottle of nail polish remover for the actress who forgot to remove her polish. Acetone may be used.

This list of materials may seem expensive, but good stage make-up is an important investment. Street make-up simply does not carry beyond the footlights. You will not use all the supplies for a single show. The rest can be stored and added to for the next production.

Application of Make-Up

If you use the stick type of grease paint, you need a thin layer of cold cream under it. Do not use cold cream under soft tube-type grease paint. Apply the base a little at a time. A dozen small dots scattered over the face and neck are enough. The thinner the base coat the less likely it is to smear and the less you'll be troubled by perspiration. Smooth the base coat well up to the hair line, onto the ears and behind them, down the neck, and the back of the neck to below the neckline of the costume. Blend and smooth with the whole hand, not just the finger tips, until there are no demarcation lines. When you have finished, rub a clean finger

446

across your face. If paint comes off or the finger leaves a mark, you have too much base. Pat it off with cleansing tissue and reblend.

Next apply the rouge. Start with a *small* dot of rouge on each cheek and blend with straight upward strokes. Be sure it is blended before you add more. If you put on too much you damage the base coat when you take it off.

Eye shadow is applied so it is heaviest at the lashes and shades to blend with the base as it reaches the eyebrow. It is heaviest at the center of the lid and shades off as it reaches the corner of the eye. After the eye shadow is smoothly blended, use a hair-line brush or eyebrow pencil to draw a thin line about a sixteenth of an inch from the edge of each upper lid, starting two thirds of the way toward the nose and ending slightly beyond the corner of the upper lid. On the lower lid draw a thin line about one third of the way in from the *outer* corner to meet the line on the upper lid. Pat it gently with a clean finger if it is too harsh.

Eyebrows are darkened with an eyebrow pencil or mascara. Follow the natural curve of the brow, except for character or comic make-up. Apply the color with short, light strokes. The brows may be extended but should not be exaggerated for straight make-up.

Men and women with light lashes will need to accent the lashes with mascara. This is done after the make-up has been powdered. Brush the lashes up, being careful not to get the mascara in the eye, as it burns.

The last step is the lipstick. The best procedure for straight make-up is to follow the natural line of the lips. Men need a light touch of lipstick. Apply it a little at a time with the finger or a brush and then blend it. After the shape and color has been attained, press a powder puff gently on the lips to set the color.

There are additional techniques for character make-up of all types. The safest method is to consult a good book and practice until you can get the effect you want.

Always try a make-up under the stage lights because the colors have a peculiar effect on what looks natural in the make-up room. That is one of the reasons for full make-up at dress rehearsal. After the make-up has been approved, make careful notes of what you used so it can be duplicated. If possible have a small spotlight attached in the make-up room with the color of the main lighting. Then you can test the make-up as it is applied. Squinting through your eyelashes helps you see how the make-up will look from a distance.

Here are a few rules about the effect of colored light on make-up.

1. White light tends to kill natural color in the face.

2. Amber light kills reds and reddish tones.

3. Pale-blue light turns flesh tones pale gray, while dark-blue light kills all colors in ordinary make-up.

4. Blue-green light, used for moonlight, turns red to black.

5. When most of the light is directly overhead, a little light carmine mixed with the base is applied to the eye sockets to eliminate heavy shadows.

When the actors have their own make-up kits, they are responsible for putting away their supplies. When a group kit is used, the make-up crew starts cleaning the tubes and reassembling the equipment as soon as the cast goes onstage. They leave a few cans of powder, some puffs, an eyebrow pencil, some rouge, and lipsticks for touch-up between acts. If there is a change in make-up between acts, all the necessary equipment is gathered together in a cleared space so no time will be lost.

When the show is over, all actors remove their make-up before leaving the dressing rooms. The make-up crew picks up all cleansing tissue, sees that wash bowls are clean, puts away the chairs, and leaves the room in perfect order. If the play is to be repeated the next night, the charts are gathered up and put in the make-up kit, ready for distribution again. All brushes are wiped clean, and powder puffs washed. Have a double supply of powder puffs because they may not dry overnight.

After everything is in order, the make-up crew head takes the kit and reports to the costume crew head.

The costume and make-up crew have an important, creative job. The audience's first impression of a character comes from seeing what he looks like and what he's wearing. Without costumes and make-up, theater would lose much of its appeal and excitement.

ACTIVITIES

1. Use a good reference book on the history of costumes, and draw (or find) costume plates for women's clothing for the following periods in theatrical history: Greek and Roman, Medieval, Shakespearian, Restoration, eighteenth century, nineteenth century. Plan a symposium, assigning one period to each member of the group, and report on style of costumes, materials, colors, and accessories.

These woodcuts by Toshusai Sharaku show three actors of the Japanese Kabuki theater.

2. Repeat the exercise above, but report on men's dress. Follow these reports with a discussion of the correlation between styles and the characteristics of the era, socially, economically, culturally, and ideologically.

3. Report on changes in costume styles in the twentieth century. Do you see any correlation between styles in costume and styles in architecture? between costumes and interior decorating? Explain and demonstrate.

4. In coöperation with the music department, plan a Christmas assembly program, presenting Christmas carols from many lands. By means of lighted and living tableaus, show a figure, or a group of figures, costumed in the national dress appropriate to each song.

5. On an assigned day, have several members of your class wear a shade of blue; several other members, a shade of red; and several others, green. Arrange with a member of your stage crew to provide colored lights to be directed on each of these groups on stage. Take notes on the different effects as the color of the groups changes. Reread the portion of the chapter dealing with colors and materials, and discuss the reasons for these effects.

6. Give a demonstration lecture on the history of hair styles.

7. Give a report on the history of stage make-up. Include the use of make-up for television.

8. Give a report on the use of masks in Oriental plays. The use of visual aids.

9. Obtain from Max Factor's Make-up Studio, Hollywood, California, a set of make-up booklets, or find pictures in other sources. Select one of the character types you might like to portray and draw an enlargement of the facial features, labeling as to the kind of make-up needed. Check with your teacher for accuracy and on the make-up materials available. Then, on an assigned day, when all the materials are ready, each student applies the special make-up and you have a make-up parade.

10. Working with a partner, decide on animal make-up for a children's play, and make up each other as that animal. Try a bear, a cat, a tiger, a mouse, a rabbit, a penguin, and a raven. You may need extra accessories such as bills, artificial cheeks, or blackened straws for whiskers. How would you costume that animal character?

The duties of the lighting crew vary, depending on the script and the amount and kind of lighting equipment available. The usual responsibilities are: preparation of equipment, including checking the condition of equipment, cleaning, and repairing; making a lighting plot to be filed in the permanent prompt script; mounting and focusing equipment; giving warnings and cues for all light changes within scenes; cleaning and storing equipment after the show is over; and helping with pre-performance planning.

In most cases, crew members do not operate the switchboard. It is dangerous to allow those who do not understand electricity to operate or connect any electrical equipment. Stage switchboards carry heavy loads and must be treated with respect. A custodian or faculty member takes over management of the

STAGE LIGHTING

board. It is important that no unauthorized person is allowed to operate it. A responsible person should be present to supervise every crew call.

If you have been instructed on how to work your switchboard, you, as crew head, may be allowed to take over the board under supervision. Remember, yours is a heavy responsibility. NEVER make any adjustments to the board or to the equipment without first cutting off the power. Pull the master switch for the entire board. NEVER touch metal, such as a screwdriver or wrench, to wiring or equipment when the power is on. NEVER place equipment so it touches scenery or hangings that are not fireproof. Stage lighting equipment generates heat. All crew members wear heavy cotton gloves to prevent burns while adjusting the units. Before turning on the switchboard be sure every crew member HEARS THE WARNING and is not handling wiring or connecting equipment. NEVER allow others to handle the switchboard. You are responsible for the prevention of fire and injury and for the care of expensive equipment—as well as the artistic aspects of the lighting.

As a member of the lighting crew, you need to be familiar with the terms listed in Chapters 7, 8, and 9. In addition you need the following vocabulary:

Dimmer: a device on the switchboard that permits the light to be reduced by degrees from full to almost out.

Down: reduce the light in a lighting instrument.

Full up: use the maximum amount of light.

Gelatines: semitransparent color medium called "gels."

House lights: the lights in the auditorium.

Lamp: what the layman calls a light bulb.

Mogul base: the large base of a lamp for spotlights.

Teaser position: directly above the top of the stage side of the proscenium arch.

Wattage: the amount of electric power in a given lamp.

Work lights: the bare, utilitarian lights on stage turned off for performance.

The names and types of various pieces of equipment such as borders, spots, floods, and strips are treated in the text.

PRELIMINARY PLANNING

When you are appointed head of the lighting crew, report to the assistant director for a copy of the play. You will make a prompt script similar to that prepared by the stage manager. If no copy is provided and you are to operate the board, you will have to depend on the stage manager for warnings and cues. Nevertheless, you must be familiar with the play.

After you read the play, consult the director, and make notes of his plans for the scenes. He may sketch only the general effects as they are called for. In that case, you go ahead with plans to achieve the effects he wants. All your plans must be checked with him before they go into operation. His is the final word.

Read through the play and make a list of the time of day for each scene, time changes within scenes, lamps to be turned on and off, fire in the fireplace, or any special lighting effect called for in the script.

Functions of Stage Lighting

The basic function of lighting is to improve visibility. The amount of light onstage permits the audience to see the actors without strain. Too much light makes a glare, and too little causes discomfort and reduces the effectiveness of the other aspects of the production. Your first consideration will be to ensure visibility.

A second function of stage lighting is to suggest time and place. The time of day and season of the year decide the use of equipment and color.

Late afternoon exteriors use more amber, and night scenes rely on blue. Interiors use an increase in amber as the day advances from morning to night. A morning room in a wealthy house has more warm color and overall light than a dingy room in a tenement. Your second consideration will be to suggest time and place.

The third function is to create or intensify mood. Your director will decide what effect he wants for certain scenes. It is your job to reinforce the mood of the scene, whether it be mysterious, fantastic, realistic, comic, or tragic. Realistic and comic scenes use more bright lighting, nearly white with a slight shade of amber. This varies with time of day. Mysterious and tragic scenes use less light and tend toward red and blue. Fantasy may be suggested in innumerable ways. Spot lighting in brilliant, unrealistic colors, producing exaggerated shadows, is sometimes useful.

The fourth function is to help emphasize by producing or eliminating shadows or by highlighting details of the stage picture. Leaf shadows on an exterior wall, spots of color, or sharp illumination of a statue or stairway to point up a detail of form or texture is included in this category. This use of light is interesting and useful, but it varies with the requirements of each script and the amount and kind of equipment you have. Books will give you added help in this. This is your *last* step in planning. Do not sacrifice visibility, setting, or mood. These four functions are often combined, and sometimes one piece of equipment can achieve all of them.

Lighting must not call attention to itself and distract from the total effect. It supports and is coördinated with every other aspect of the production, and does not steal the show.

The Light Plot

You now decide where you need light onstage and what kind it should be. This is what a light plot is designed to show.

Consult the stage manager and get a floor plan the director has approved for each scene. Read the play again, checking your notes on time of day, season, and general mood of each scene. Notice the areas to be seen through windows and doors. Pay attention to all changes within scenes, such as a gradual darkening to show time passing, turning on or extinguishing lamps, and other details relevant to your job.

Study the floor plan and make a copy for your own use. If there are set changes, you need a floor plan for each set. On the sample floor plan below, the heavy lines indicate scenery walls. There are three doors that are used and must open and close. The window allows a view of a ground row of bushes. The stairway shows two bottom steps. The first concern is in lighting the acting area for visibility. The acting area is that within the set and in view of the audience.

Using the floor plan as a guide, divide the stage into a series of overlapping elliptical areas 8' x 10' wide and 6' x 8' deep. Be sure the overlap is about two feet, so they blend. There is an uneven number of areas across the stage so no section falls between areas of proper intensity. Beginning down right, number each area with a Roman numeral. With a set 24' wide and 15' deep and a 4' depth for the hall, your plan looks like this.

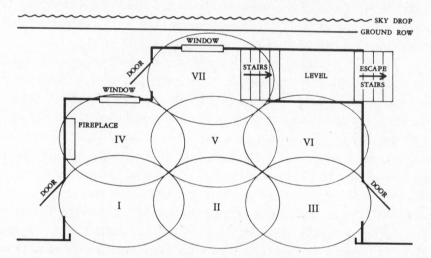

In the floor plan above, there are seven areas to be lighted for visibility. After you know how many areas you must light, check the equipment, and plan to make the best of what you have.

Your first concern is the spotlights. You need two spotlights for each of the areas. If you do not have fourteen spotlights, use the ones you have for the areas where most of the action occurs, and use borders, foots, and floods to light the rest of the stage. This is not a satisfactory substitute, but it may be a necessity.

Spotlights vary in the size of lens, casing, and lamp capacity. The smallest standard spotlight has a lens 4½" in diameter and a lamp of 250 to 400 watts. These are baby spots. Other spotlights have lenses 6" to 8" in diameter, and use mogul bases and lamps with wattage of 500 watts and up. They are designed to be mounted on a floor stand and/or overhead battens, ceiling beams, or the balcony edge out in the house. They

454

have yokes and suspension irons with heavy clamps for overhead mounting. They have focusing slides to permit the lamps to be moved forward or backward within the casing. Behind the lamp is a reflector to augment the light. All spotlights have color media frames made to fit just in front of the lens. These are of thin tin and open to hold the gelatines or other media.

Test all the instruments as you check the equipment so you are certain everything works, and can advise the director of exactly what is needed. Do this as soon as possible, as your local store may not carry everything you need, and some things will have to be ordered. Later, you and your crew can make a more careful inspection of the equipment, but this preliminary inspection is necessary.

In ordering lamps and planning the amount of light to be used, check the capacity of the switchboard. If you attach more lights than your switchboard is capable of handling, you will blow a fuse and risk a fire hazard. The custodian of your building will help you keep a balance between the capacity of the board and the number and size of your lamps. In buying lamps for spotlights, be sure to note the instructions on the back of the lamps. Some mogul base lamps burn base down, others burn base up. Check your equipment to be sure which kind you need.

Uncolored light onstage is harsh and uninteresting. All stage lights except work lights are used with a color medium of some type. The most widely used medium is gelatine. It is semitransparent and comes in sheets 20″ x 22″ and can be cut to fit any frame. It is inexpensive but not as durable as some other media because it is affected by heat and humidity. It comes in a range of more than a hundred colors. The Brigham Gelatin Company of Randolph, Vermont, will send a sample book and suggestions for combinations of colors. Gelatine must be stored flat to prevent its cracking.

Other semitransparent media are transoline and transpara, both similar to gelatine but more durable. They are more expensive and do not come in as wide a range of colors.

Strip, foot, and border lights often have detachable glass disks of different colors. These are the most durable of all color media and the most expensive, but the range of colors is limited. Red, blue, and green are basic colors and are sufficient for your purpose.

You need to check all gelatines to be sure there are enough in good condition. They are fragile and dry out and crack when stored. The most

The head of the lighting crew, if he is responsible, careful, and very competent, may take over the operation of the switchboard.

456

useful numbers from the Brigham list are #17, special lavender, used with #57, light amber; #29, special steel blue, used with #62, light scarlet; and #2, light flesh pink, used with #25, daylight blue. Either combination produces nearly white light, though the first pair provides more amber. For morning or early evening sunlight reflection, #2, light flesh pink, is useful. You will need a few sheets of medium blue, any of the light greens, a true scarlet, some gray to tone down the other colors, and some frosted that suffuses the light when placed in front of all colors. Check the frames for each light. Order enough gelatine for emergency replacements.

Lamps may be purchased in red, blue, amber, and green for use in strips, foots, and borders. You can dip regular white lamps and make them almost any color. This is done with lamps of the vacuum type. Lamps should be clean before dipping. Attach the lamp to an extension cord, light it, and lower it into a small can filled with dip. The lamp should be covered clear to the base. But do not get the socket wet! Leave it in the dip for a second or two, then draw it up, letting the excess drip back into the can and *not* into the socket. Absorb any bubbles with a paper towel and allow the lamp to dry. It will dry quickly if you leave it lighted. Dipping is not recommended except as a temporary measure, because the color burns off quickly if the lamp is more than 50 watts.

Allocating the Equipment

As soon as you take care of replacements and know exactly how much equipment you have, the next step is to make a plot showing the location of each instrument and the area it lights.

Let us assume that you have fourteen spots to light the seven areas in our plan above.

The downstage areas (I, II, and III in the floor plan) are best lighted from the auditorium. You need six spotlights of 1000 watts each for these three areas. Areas IV, V, and VI are lighted from the teaser position. The lamps in these spots may be of 500 watts each. Area VII may be lighted from a teaser position or from a pipe batten a little way upstage, depending on what best suits the size of the opening into the hallway.

The spotlights located in the house are called beam spots, shown on your light plot by the initials BS, and numbered from stage right to stage left. These beam spots should strike areas I, II, and III from positions separated by a horizontal angle of 45 degrees and from a vertical angle of 35 to 60 degrees. This will vary with your special setup.

457

The spotlights mounted above the stage are called teaser spots and designated on the plot by the initials TS, and numbered in the same way. They have a much wider horizontal angle, and you need to test them for focus according to the area of space you have to light.

BS 1 and 4 angle together to light area I, as indicated by the arrows in the diagram below; BS 2 and 5 focus on area II; and BS 3 and 6, on area III.

The plot has the teaser spots on a line drawn in front of the stage

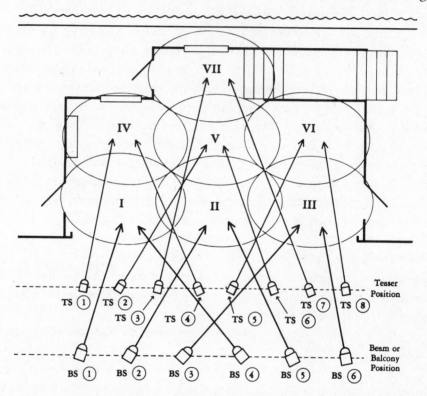

for greater clarity. The actual position for these spots is behind the top of the proscenium arch as indicated by the arrows. The same angling prevails for the teaser spots as for the beam spots. TS 1 and 4 cover area IV; TS 2 and 6 cover area V; TS 5 and 8 cover area VI; and TS 3 and 7 are angled back to focus on area VII.

Special Area Lighting

After you have allocated the equipment for visibility of the acting area, turn your attention to special requirements.

458

Some of the more usual lighting effects are fireplace glow, a beam of moonlight, and sunlight through a window. These are achieved by using baby spots with colored gelatines in the proper place and well masked, so the spot cannot be seen from out front, and high enough so the light will not shine into the audience or cut across an exit and cause shadows when actors move in front of it.

The ground row of bushes in our sample plot requires special lighting. Area lighting would not reach it. Moreover, it needs more green and amber than the area lighting. Strip lights are best for this area and for the backdrop behind the ground row, called a sky drop, which requires a predominance of blue light.

Strip lights are rows of ordinary low-wattage lamps. They are blue, amber, red, and sometimes green. They are wired in three or four circuits, with the colors evenly spaced. One circuit controls each color so it can be turned on or off with the others left burning. There are several models and various lengths of strips available. They are mounted in single rows, and can be hung from a batten or placed on the floor. The blue lamps are 100 watts, the others, 65 watts. You may vary the usual proportion of colors, or use all one color for a particular effect. In our sample plot there is more green and amber with few red and blue lamps per strip for the ground row, while the sky drop strips are predominantly blue lamps:

Blending or Tonal Lighting

Strip lights are sometimes useful for tonal lighting if they can be concealed and you have plenty of them. The more usual instruments for this purpose are borders, foots, and floods.

Border lights are hanging strip lights that extend across the entire acting area. They may hang in the teaser position or farther upstage, depending on the depth of your set. Sometimes there is a second row at midstage, which is useful if your set is very deep. They are tipped slightly upstage so their light helps illuminate the back wall.

Some directors object to the use of footlights, and others consider them essential. When footlights are installed across the front of the stage at the edge of the apron, they extend only three fourths of the width of the proscenium, so light will not spill outside the acting area. They are wired to three or four circuits, so each color may be turned on or off the full length of the strip. The lamps in the footlights are of low wattage, not more than 60 watts.

459

Floodlights are mounted on a pipe batten overhead or on heavy stands offstage. They use lamps of 750 or 1000 watts. When mounted on stands, they must be set high enough to prevent shadows when actors must move in front of them, and turned upstage so their light will not spill beyond the curtain line. Floodlights are used to light scenery, and never to light actors. They direct strong light onto large areas, and cannot be focused like spotlights.

It is important to check the total wattage of the light for tonal effects. The total wattage of tonal lighting is not more than 10 per cent of the total wattage of the area lighting. We use fourteen spotlights for area lighting in our sample plan. The six beam spots have lamps of 1000 watts, the eight teaser spots have 500 watts. The total area wattage is 10,000. There should not be more than 16 lamps of 60 watts each in borders and foots combined, and no floods are use for tonal lighting.

Preparation of the Equipment

Call your crew together and begin a careful inventory of instruments and accessories.

All spotlights are dusted inside and out, and the lenses cleaned. All lamps in strips, borders, and footlights are wiped clean of dust, tested, and replaced. All wiring is checked and repaired. This includes the wiring from the instruments themselves, and any additional stage cable to be used as extensions.

As soon as all equipment is cleaned and brought to working order, the crew begins mounting and angling the various pieces. You cannot do any focusing until the switchboard is set up, and fine focusing has to wait until the set is up.

While planning the best use of your equipment and where to locate it, you make general decisions that effect the operation of the switchboard. Some of the area spots are in the house in the beam positions or on the edge of the balcony, and some are in the teaser position. You have to decide which spots will be used together. Foots and borders have separate circuits for color, and you decide whether they are to be used together, or separately for special effects.

All these matters influence the way these instruments are connected to the separate circuits of the switchboard. Most switchboards are flexible, and careful planning saves confusion and mistakes during the pressure of performances. Make sure the two spotlights that cover each area are connected to the same circuit or to adjacent circuits so they can be worked together. The strip for the ground row is connected separately, so it does not suddenly come on with amber and green in the middle of a night scene. Recheck your floor-plan chart, and note which lights are needed together.

On a separate paper, draw the face of your switchboard and number each switch. Each switch controls a circuit, and there is a receptacle to connect the stage cable for individual instruments. If you do not have such connections at the board there will be cables attached leading to outlets in the house for the beam spots, on the stage floor, and in the teaser position.

If your board has three horizontal banks of six circuits each, your switchboard sketch looks like this, with the top bank labeled A, the second, B, and the bottom, C. The circuits are numbered from left to right as you face the board.

A 1	A 2	A 3	A 4	A 5	A 6
B 1	B 2	B 3	B 4	B 5	B 6
C 1	C 2	C 3	C 4	C 5	C 6

L 1	R 1
L 2	R 2
L 3	R 3
L 4	R 4
L 5	R 5
L 6	R 6

If the board has two vertical rows of switches, the sketch looks like the one on the right above, with L and R indicating left and right as you face the board.

In the space beside each switch insert the initials and numbers of the instruments connected to that circuit. Thus, if your beam spots are to be connected to circuits 1, 2, and 3 on the top bank, the chart will look like this:

A 1	A 2	A 3
BS ①	BS ②	BS ③
BS ④	BS ⑤	BS ⑥

Or, for a vertical board, it would be indicated like this:

L 1 - BS ①	BS ④
L 2 - BS ②	BS ⑤
L 3 - BS ③	BS ⑥

Continue to mark the positions for all pieces of equipment, and indicate in what scenes they are to be used.

Some of the members of your crew should be preparing and marking gelatine frames. Each frame is marked with a piece of tape with initials of the instrument for which it is intended. If changes are to be made during performance, the act and scene in which each frame is to be used is added. They should be stored in proper order, away from heat and moisture. Make a few extras in case of breakage.

As soon as the set is in place, the crew does the final focusing of all the lights that are mounted and angled. One member takes a position in the center of each area and assists in getting the focus accurate. Color media are used as soon as the lights are set, so adjustments in color can be tried before the pressure of dress rehearsals.

Controllable Properties of Light

There are three controllable properties of light: amount, distribution, and color. You consider all three in your final plans.

The amount or quantity of light depends first on the number of instruments you have. It depends on the wattage of the lamps you use. Wattage is marked on the lamp, and the higher the wattage the more light it gives. Most stage equipment has reflectors. They are concave disks of polished metal, or surfaces behind the lamp painted white or silver. The reflectors increase the amount of light from the lamp.

Many switchboards have dimmers in, or next to, the board. These allow you to dim or brighten the light from the various instruments, separately or in groups, by controlling the amount of power.

All the above methods may be used in combination to control the amount of light, or for spot or area illumination. As you look at the lighting from out front, you may want to increase or decrease the amount of light in some areas.

462

The second controllable property of light is distribution. With spotlights, distribution is controlled by changing the angle of the instrument and/or moving the lamp backward or forward within the casing. You can mask off part of the lens opening, so that the light does not cover a large area. Do this by placing a piece of tin in the color medium frame so the opening is large enough to permit light to fill the desired area. Check your lighting from out front, in a darkened auditorium, to be sure no light is spilling into areas where you don't want it.

The third controllable property of light is color. It would be impractical to cover all details of effective and exciting use of color in this discussion. If your equipment is extensive and you are interested in this phase of production, consult some available books. Color is useful in intensifying mood, in providing visibility and an interesting stage picture. It must never call attention to itself or distract from the total effect.

When the set is up and your color media are in place, go to the back of the auditorium and test it against the colors in the scenery. Certain combinations of colors emphasize or cancel certain tones in paint. If there is any difficulty with the scenery colors, you will have to change your lighting, since it is impractical to repaint a whole set. You will have consulted the stage manager and the costume and make-up crew heads well in advance to forestall any disagreement.

DRESS REHEARSALS AND PERFORMANCE

It is important to have the lights in place by dress rehearsal so the make-up can be checked and corrected. Make-up colors are not pure colors and lights can have a strange effect on them. The stage lights can cancel subtle make-up lines. If there is difficulty, the make-up should be adjusted. If some difficulty develops with the costumes, it is more practical to make adjustments in the lighting. You will then need to do some experimenting with combinations and intensities.

The lighting crew arrives ahead of dress rehearsal and performance time so they can make a complete check of all equipment. This means turning on each instrument and seeing that it is properly focused and contains the correct gelatine. All connections are checked for safety.

Crew members are assigned specific responsibilities, such as gelatine changes, connecting strip lights, and standing guard over floor plugs and cables to keep actors from falling over them in the dark. If dimmers are used, they require special rehearsal. If gradual, smooth transitions are required, they are carefully timed and done with almost unbelievable slowness. The pace is controlled by counting very slowly and recording the number when the pace is approved. You may have a dimmer changed only a few degrees and use a count of eight or ten. Any abrupt change calls attention to itself and distracts the audience.

When the stage manager gives the "Five-Minute" warning, all crew members are in their assigned places. After the actors are onstage and the stage manager has taken his position, he gives a cue to warn for the opening curtain. As soon as you receive this cue, turn on the stage lights, turn off the work lights, and be ready to dim the house lights. On the cue "House Lights," you start to dim the house lights, except the exit lights, which are left on all the time. The house lights are dimmed slowly and smoothly and, when three-fourths down, the beam spots and foot-lights begin to come up. This is done a few seconds before the curtain is opened. An audience grows nervous in a totally dark theater.

For changes within the scenes, the stage manager gives the warning and a cue that you have marked on your own cue sheet.

At the end of a scene, you wait for the cue "Curtain," and then turn up the house lights as the curtain starts to close. The house lights should be one-fourth up when the curtain comes together. Then bring them up to full quickly and smoothly. Turn on the work lights, and turn off the stage lights until the next scene is called.

After the final curtain, bring the stage lights up to full for the curtain calls, leave the house lights down until the stage manager signals the curtain calls are over, then bring the house lights up to full.

After the curtain is closed, turn on the work lights, cut the master switch that controls all stage lights, so the crew may set up for the open-ing scene. This saves time. Be careful in refocusing or changing gelatines, because the equipment is hot.

After the last performance, the crew strikes and stores all the equip-ment and accessories used during the show. This means removing and storing spotlights and gelatines, disconnecting and coiling cables, and removing and storing lamps from strips and foots.

The head of the lighting crew is responsible for the safety and good repair of all the equipment. One moment of carelessness may have serious results. A position on the lighting crew demands maturity, good judg-ment, technical know-how, a strong sense of order and responsibility.

464

ACTIVITIES

1. Arrange a guided tour backstage and make an inventory of all stage lighting equipment in your school. Draw a diagram of your switchboard.

2. Visit a community theater or another school in your vicinity, inspect their lighting equipment, and compare it with yours.

3. Make a study of "warm" and "cool" colors. Give a report demonstrating their effect, as used separately and in combination. What psychological or mood effect of each color should be considered?

4. Select a "problem scene" from a play and explain how you would achieve effective lighting.

   a. The ladder scene in *Our Town*, where Emily and George are looking at the moon from their respective windows.

   b. The flashback or dream sequences in John Steinbeck's *Molly Morgan*. (Use no change of set.)

   c. A fantasy dance of the trolls, invented for a Scandinavian pageant.

   d. A scene of your own invention, in which lighting will enhance the mood or the message.

5. Find information about "black light" and luminous paint. Give a report, using visual aids if possible. Get a copy of the children's play, *Greensleeves' Magic* or *Simple Simon* and show how black light would help in effecting magic. (Substitute any play requiring magic.)

6. Bring in examples of lighting a "disappearing act," as Mephistopheles in *Dr. Faustus* or of the Duchess in *Greensleeves*. How would you wire for an explosion on stage? What explosive would you use? What precautions would you take?

7. Do research on scrim curtains. How would a scrim curtain and appropriate lighting provide supernatural effects in pageantry or in "Why the Chimes Rang" or the witches' scenes in *Macbeth?*

8. In *Everyman*, presented without a front curtain, what would your lighting problems be?

   a. Area lighting

   b. Blackouts for prop changing

   c. Mood lighting

Try simulating a stained-glass window by means of small floodlight with various painted color slides behind a translucent "window."

9. Do research on projecting scenery by means of lights. Report to the class and illustrate your talk.

10. Show how lighting may be used to contrast a sunny day with night. Work out plans for both interior and exterior sets.

11. Enlist the help of your physics department in building a spectroscope.

We turn now to a recent innovation in producing plays or dramatic literature. Readers' Theater is a stylized art form that combines many features of traditional theater with those of interpretative reading, although it differs from both in some important ways. This form has several names, "Group Reading," "Concert Performance," or "Readers' Theater." We will use "Readers' Theater," but we are not so concerned with what it is called as with learning how it works.

Sometimes Readers' Theater is closer to conventional theater and sometimes it is almost pure interpretation, depending on the demands of the script and the preference of the director. We will begin to draw our parallels from our previous study of the interpretation of drama.

You know the method of analysis and the techniques a single reader uses to interpret a scene in which there are

READERS' THEATER

two or more characters. In Readers' Theater there is a separate interpreter for each part and he reads only the lines of his particular character, just as an actor presents only one character in a staged play. In this regard Readers' Theater most closely parallels a conventional production. The interpreter and the actor use all their skill to project the complete *inner* character to the audience. The difference lies in the interpreters' use of suggestion rather than in explicit *external* objects and physical characteristics.

The interpreters in a Readers' Theater production hold their scripts or put them on reading stands. But they play directly to the audience, not to each other, since they are placing the scene in the minds of the audience. They sit or stand, use reading stands or not, as their director wishes. They usually remain present onstage, even after their characters would have left the stage in a staged production. They wear their own clothes, though often in a prearranged style, and only enough make-up to emphasize their features under stage lights. We will study each of these elements in more detail later.

CHOOSING A PLAY FOR READERS' THEATER

Plays best for Readers' Theater are those where the action the audience must see to understand the play is kept to a minimum. If the plot depends on the secret entrance of a thief through a window, on a murder onstage, or on something that must be visible, the play would not be successful in Readers' Theater. But if the lines make clear what happens and to whom and how, or if a climactic action takes place offstage and is reported by a character, the play can be produced in Readers' Theater.

Since the audience receives all information through the ears and only visual suggestion through the eyes, the language must be of literary quality and build to climaxes that hold the audience's attention.

Some of Shakespeare's plays are more effective done in this manner than when staged with limited costumes and a small budget. Restoration comedies are delightful in this medium and classic Greek plays are perfect for it. Many of Shaw's plays can be used to advantage.

PREPARING A SCRIPT FOR READERS' THEATER PRODUCTION

Readers' Theater requires very few changes in a well-written play. The play can often be presented as written. Because there is no specific action for the audience to see, more concentration is required of them. It is wise to limit the playing time more than if there is visible action to hold their attention. A Readers' Theater play should not run over two hours' playing time. Your director will plan for intermissions at appropriate places to allow the audience and the interpreters to relax. These intermissions need not come at the places indicated by act conclusions, since there is no change in scenery or costumes. They may come after climactic moments that complete a cycle of events, or at a high point in the emotional development. A curtain may be drawn, or the cast may leave the stage and return after the intermission to their places in full view of the audience.

Divisions between scenes are eliminated when they merely indicate an entrance or exit of a character. This kind of division is found in Shakespeare and in many classic and foreign plays. The passage of time or change of place may be indicated on a printed program, or by the use of a narrator who remains in an inconspicuous place during the scenes and comes forward when needed to speak to the audience in the manner of an oriental stage manager.

Casting

The range of characters you can handle in Readers' Theater is much wider than in a stage performance. In the first place physical characteristics are less important. You need not look like the character you inter-pret. Height, weight, coloring, and hair style are of minor importance. The ability to make interior characteristics convincing is the main criterion. You may feel free to try out for any part you want, whether you fit the physical description or not. Incongruities place an added burden on both you and the audience, but a high-school student can suggest an old, dignified man if he is capable of transferring the mental and emotional characteristics to the audience.

The director is more interested in a good, flexible voice and stage presence than in whether you look the part.

Rehearsal Suggestions

A Readers' Theater production takes as much rehearsal time as a fully staged performance. The difference lies in the fact that more attention is given the actual script, and less to setting, lights, and costumes. The absence of explicit sets and realistic costumes means that the interpreters must suggest all these things to the audience, making it necessary that all techniques of performance are under complete control.

Rehearsal procedure for Readers' Theater differs in detail from that of a fully staged play. The first few rehearsals consist of an informal group reading the entire play. This is important so all members of the cast come to understand the director's concept of the play and the con-tribution each speech and scene make to the play. Even if you read only one speech, it is important for you to listen to read-through rehearsals.

During the first half-dozen rehearsals the director makes cuts and additions. He may alter these as the play progresses, so mark them in pencil, but clearly enough to be easily read. Each reader is concerned primarily with his own character and lines. Very soon each needs to develop the habit of listening to the other lines so that all begin to coör-dinate. This is extremely important. You must listen, react, and reply.

Memorize your lines because you must be free of the script by per-formance time. You have the script before you during performance, but you cannot risk looking down for every line. The scenes will be better paced if you know your lines and listen and respond to the others.

The second week of rehearsals, start rehearsing on your feet. At this point you become aware of one of the real problems of Readers' Theater. You have an irresistible desire to turn and address your lines to the character they are meant for. Until you've had some experience it

is extremely disconcerting to be directing your mind and voice to the audience and have the reply to your line come from a reader who is sitting beside you.

When the temptation is too great, the director will, perhaps, divide the cast in half and let them work across the room from each other. Then you will be projecting out front, mentally and physically, but you will have an area of focus to help you. After a few such sessions the habit of speaking, looking, and thinking out front will be easier. When you again take your place onstage, continue to visualize the characters you speak to as if they were still across the room. You need to remind yourself of this from time to time.

The rehearsal technique of *playing across the room* is useful to get a good mental focus, help you concentrate on what the other character is saying so your lines answer him properly, and move the action along. You "hear" what is said as if it came from out front. When you reply, your mind goes out across the audience to where you have placed the other characters, just as it does when you handle an entire scene alone.

470

If you turn and address another reader, you pull the scene out of the audience's mind and place it onstage. You ask the audience to believe the person next to you is really Queen Elizabeth and present them with an impossible task, since she neither dresses nor looks like good Queen Bess. In Readers' Theater you are still an interpreter and you use the same techniques for creating a scene that you learned to use in the interpretation of drama.

When you are speaking to other characters, it is not necessary to keep your eyes glued on a single spot on the back wall. Feel free to turn your eyes and body slightly as long as you keep the scene out front. Do not let the angle of your body, or the focus of your eyes, move inside the proscenium nor beyond the outside of the audience area.

When we discussed angle of focus for an individual interpreter, we indicated placement of characters in Figure 1. Assume that there are six characters in a Readers' Theater production: A, B, C, D, E, and F. Interpreter A uses the same technique suggested for the interpreter of drama, except that his position at the far right of the stage does not allow him so wide an angle at the right. But it is easier for the audience to know whom he is addressing if he indicates a general direction. Thus interpreter A adjusts his area of focus as illustrated in Figure 1. Interpreter F does the same thing to keep from going too far to his left. When characters address each other their lines of focus cross somewhere in the center of the audience area.

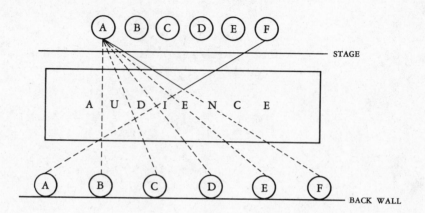

The lines of focus from A to B, C, D and E continue to the back wall for purposes of projection. Each member of the cast makes use of the entire back wall area, shifting his eyes *and* his mental directness within the width of the audience area.

Feel free to move about, but, for practical purposes, it is wise to indicate crosses by a few steps and to remain near your reading stand. Otherwise, the audience wonders where you are going and loses the character you have created in their mental picture of the scene.

During the middle period of rehearsals work to understand the "why" and "what" of everything your character says. The procedure is the same for Readers' Theater as for interpretation of drama, except that you concentrate on one character instead of all of them. But, you must know the relationship of your character to the others and make this relationship clear to the audience. Motivate each speech with appropriate mental, emotional, and physical reactions.

The final ten days of rehearsal you polish the details. One of these is pace. As you work on a play you become aware that some scenes have more suspense than others, while some scenes move faster than others. Your director helps you decide questions of pace, but you will want to take a good look at the structure of the play to see how the scenes fit so the plot moves in its proper rhythm.

472

Be sure that you are speaking loudly enough to be heard in the auditorium. If you cannot be heard, everything else is lost. During every rehearsal, keep your visualized characters placed against the back wall and project both your voice and your mind the full distance.

Entrances and Exits

Work on the timing of your entrances and exits, although you do not actually leave the stage at the end of your scenes. Entrances and exits are made in many ways. A technique frequently used is to stand for your scenes and to sit for your exits. This is effective if you use high stools. If the play is short, all readers may stand during the entire play. Then the exits may be handled with a step back, a general relaxing of muscle tone, and lowering the head. Sometimes you may leave the acting area, retire to the back of the stage, and sit with other readers whose characters are offstage.

Whatever technique your director adopts is carefully timed. Take your cue from the kind of exit you would make onstage and use your power of suggestion to make this clear to the audience. If the scene has been tense and your character exits rapidly, then time your sitting or crossing to the back of the stage fast, and relax abruptly. If the scene has a slow, dim-out closing, move smoothly, and hold your muscle tone for a second before lowering your head and eyes.

Entrances and exits in Readers' Theater depend for their effectiveness on mental control and carefully timed physical movement. Remember that when you are interpreting, your circle of concentration includes the entire audience. Reach out with your mind, and make sure your voice and bodily action, whether it is gesture, eye focus, facial expression, or muscle tone, is adequate for the size of the room in which you are working.

When your character enters, stand or move in quickly and firmly, or slowly and gently, as the scene demands. Stand with your muscles alert so you command attention. Widen your circle of concentration to include the entire room, place the characters to be addressed at the back of the room, and direct your thoughts, voice, and eyes to them. When your character exits, reverse the process at whatever pace is right for the character. Sit or move to the area designated as offstage, maintain muscle tone a few seconds, then relax, drop your eyes, and bring your circle of concentration to a small area around yourself. Do not turn your attention to the other characters, but keep alert for your next cue.

473

The way you sit "offstage" is important to the appearance of the entire production. You are not out of sight when your character leaves the scene. If you use a high stool, it is more comfortable to put one foot on the brace, and the other on the floor. Decide with the others which foot to keep up, so when several characters are offstage they present a picture that does not distract from the scene. You must sit still. Any movement will immediately call the attention of the audience away from the scene in progress. Only hams steal scenes. Real performers are interested in the play. This physical discipline is tiring. Start practicing it several weeks before performance.

Practice holding your manuscript. If you use typed pages, put them in a stiff notebook. When you are on, hold the script in one hand, with the other on the open book or notebook to keep your place, and be free for gestures. Keep the manuscript tipped toward you so the white pages won't catch the light. After you leave the scene, turn quickly and quietly to your next entrance. Then hold the manuscript in your lap. If you use a reading stand, the problem is simpler. With a reading stand, you turn to your next scene and leave the manuscript on the stand when you step back or sit down.

If there are several pages between your scenes, clip them together. You don't want to turn pages every few minutes when you are out of scene. Mark your entrances in large enough writing, so you can see them from a distance. Most professionals put a WARN mark several speeches before their entrances so they are ready for them. Keep your attention on the play so you do not cause a break in pace. But keep your eyes down and remain mentally out of scenes you are not in.

You do not need to memorize lines as completely as if you were not using a script, although you may wish to do so. You must be free of the book in order to keep the dialogue moving and the speeches focused, and to hold the attention of your audience.

474

SETTING

The most effective stage background for a Readers' Theater production is a simple neutral curtain. There should be no attempt to portray an actual period or location because the setting, like the action and characters, is in the minds of the audience, not on the stage. It is better to hang the background curtain at the center of the stage, so there is no expanse of empty stage behind the readers. Such space tends to swallow up the voices and spoil the symmetry of the stage picture. Readers' Theater may be presented before the front curtain if there is enough room for the interpreters to work. It is ideal for work in the classroom.

The interpreters stand near the front of the stage so their voices will carry readily. They may form a straight line, or a curve, or be grouped in twos or threes, depending on the area and the number of characters involved. There is no need to group them according to their relationship. This may be done in such a play as *Mary Stuart,* where Elizabeth might be at one side with her court and Mary at the other side with her attendants. If there are many short scenes and only a few characters, an attempt may be made to keep a balance of activity so that half the stage does not get too much play, leaving the other half without activity for long periods.

Readers' Theater may be used even when there is no stage or curtain. That is one of its advantages. The cast may enter together and take their places in the area used as a stage, in full view of the audience. When the play is finished, they leave. This should be rehearsed so everyone knows exactly where they are going, and they sit or rise to leave at the same time. If there is no backstage area, they may enter from the front row of the audience, or the back of the house, and return to that location when the play is over. Whatever is practical is effective, as long as it is done with decorum and dignity.

COSTUMES AND MAKE-UP

Since the picture the audience sees is fairly static, the use of color in the girls' dresses is often attractive. Full skirts are easier to manage than tight ones, especially if the reader is to sit. Cocktail-length dresses are more graceful onstage than street-length. Color is choosen for its harmonious-ness with the draperies, and with the clothes of the others. Solid colors are best, although this depends on the director's taste. Sequins and rhine-stones are distracting. Jewelry is kept at a minimum. Small earrings which will not catch the light and simple necklaces are permissible. Bracelets jingle against the reading stands and interfere with handling the script.

Men wear tuxedos, or dark suits with white shirts, and conservative neckties. If the play is not modern, corduroy sport shirts and dark trousers are effective. Corduroy looks rich under stage lights, and the colors are excellent. When the shirts are buttoned at neck and wrist and worn tucked in, they take on a surprising degree of formality that helps to suggest a period. A small strip of matching material placed over the buttons, and then buttoned through the buttonholes, will disguise its casual origin. Tie-clips and wrist watches catch the light and are removed before performance.

A light base of pancake make-up keeps you from looking anemic under the lights. The eyebrows are darkened and sometimes the outline of the eye accented by a pencil line and/or eye shadow. Men and women need this type of make-up if the lights are strong. Age lines, gray, or partly gray hair, or character make-up are not necessary, since you are not asking the audience to believe that you are the character.

Readers' Theater is an exacting technique, but experience will prove it satisfying to both cast and audience.

SUGGESTED PLAYS

Following is a list of some of the plays which have been produced in Readers' Theater technique. Some are adaptations but most of them can be used almost without change. There are hundreds of others which would work equally well.

Sophocles. *Antigone, Oedipus Rex, Oedipus at Colonus,* and *Electra.*
Euripides. *Alcestis, The Trojan Women, Ion,* and *Hippolytus.*
Shakespeare. *Measure for Measure, King John, King Lear,* and *Troilus and Cressida.*

476

Racine. *Phaedra,* and *Berenice.*

Friedrich Schiller. *Maria Stuart.*

William Congreve. *The Way of the World*

Henrik Ibsen. *A Doll's House, Hedda Gabler,* and *Ghosts.*

Thomas Sheridan. *The Rivals.*

Anton Chekhov. *The Boor.*

John Masefield. *Philip, the King.*

Molière. *Tartuffe.*

Robert Browning. *The Ring and the Book.*

G. B. Shaw. from *Back to Methuselah, Candida, Pygmalion, Bouyant Billions* and *Don Juan in Hell.*

Jean Giraudoux. *Amphitryon 38* and *Electra.*

Coffee and Cowan. *Family Portrait.*

Maxwell Anderson. *Elizabeth, the Queen,* and *Mary of Scotland.*

Tennessee Williams. *The Glass Menagerie.*

Goethe. *Faust,* Part 1.

Robinson Jeffers. *Medea.*

Maeterlinck. *Pelléas and Mélisande.*

Oscar Wilde. *Salome,* and *The Importance of Being Earnest.*

Stephen Vincent Benét. *Western Star, Listen to the People,* and *John Brown's Body.*

Archibald MacLeish. *The Fall of the City,* and *The Trojan Horse.*

Sidney Howard. *The Silver Cord.*

Laurence Housman. *Victoria Regina.*

Martin Flavin. *Children of the Moon,* and *The Enchanted.*

Edwin Arlington Robinson. *Tristram.*

Thornton Wilder. *The Bridge of San Luis Rey,* and *The Long Christmas Dinner.*

Christopher Fry. *The Lady's Not For Burning, The Boy With a Cart,* and *A Phoenix Too Frequent.*

Noel Coward. *Blithe Spirit.*

George Kelly. *Craig's Wife.*

W. H. Auden. *For The Time Being,* and *The Ascent of F6.*

John Milton. *Samson Agonistes.*

Lillian Hellman. *The Little Foxes.*

John Van Druten. *Young Woodley.*

T. S. Eliot. *The Cocktail Party.*

Marc Connelly. *The Green Pastures.*

Robert Frost. *A Masque of Reason.*

Dylan Thomas. *Under Milkwood.*

Robert Penn Warren. *Brother To Dragons.*

John Dos Passos. *U.S.A.*

A Readers' Theater performance of *As You Like it* by the Brooklyn Heights Players.

ACTIVITIES

1. Read a monologue, such as Robert Browning's "My Last Duchess." Practice addressing imaginary persons diagonally front. As in the Browning poem, you will occasionally look at props, or other characters in slightly different positions.

2. Select a play the class is familiar with, for example, Shakespeare's *Macbeth*. Volunteer in groups and demonstrate various techniques most acceptable in Readers' Theater productions. Study the following list for suggestions.

   a. Readers standing, stepping forward as they "enter." Experiment with the Witches' scenes. Use no lecterns.
   b. With readers standing at lecterns give the various scenes between Macbeth and Lady Macbeth.
   c. With readers seated on stools, with or without lecterns, enact any large group scene, such as Act II, scene 3.
   d. With the readers seated in student chairs, averting their bodies when "offstage," present the sleepwalking scene. When necessary you may use a narrator to lead into the action. If you do, remember that this member of the group speaks directly to the audience.

3. Demonstrate the techniques involved in building a scene to a climax. Use facial expression, build-up or vocabulary intensity, cue pick-up, and overlapping of lines as your principal devices. Here are some suggestions.

a. Katherine and Petruchio scene from *The Taming of the Shrew*. Emphasize increased volume, energy, inflection, and facial expression.

b. The Mephistopheles, Lucifer, and Faustus scene from *Dr. Faustus*. Add particularly, satanical laughter.

c. The final husband and wife scene from *A Doll's House*. Here you have an opportunity to increase the intensity, line by line.

4. Divide the class into five or more groups. Have each group select, rehearse, and present in Readers' Theater style, a cutting from a play of a different theatrical period. Study the examples below, and make your own selections.

a. Greek or Roman period, Sophocles' *Antigone*.

b. Medieval period, *Everyman*.

c. Elizabethan period, Shakespeare's *King Lear*, or Marlowe's *Dr. Faustus*.

d. Eighteenth century, Goldsmith's *She Stoops to Conquer*.

e. Nineteenth century or modern, Wilde's *The Importance of Being Earnest*.

Discuss the differences you discover in play structure, dialogue, and characterization.

5. Working in groups select plays of various types to demonstrate the differences in structure and emphasis. Make fifteen-minute cuttings, and present them to the class.

a. A folk play, Marc Connelly's *The Green Pastures*.

b. A fantasy, Alice Gerstenberg's "Overtones," and Paul Osborn's *On Borrowed Time*.

c. A satire, George Kaufman and Moss Hart's *Once in a Lifetime*.

d. A poetic play, Stephen Vincent Benét's *A Child Is Born*.

e. A character drama, George Bernard Shaw's *Saint Joan*.

f. A historical play, Friedrich Schiller's *Maria Stuart*.

6. Sift out two or more *contrasting* threads of plot from a Shakespearean play. Present a scene or two from each thread in Readers' Theater style, using a narrator to provide background and continuity.

a. *The Merchant of Venice*
   1. Romance of Bassanio and Portia
   2. Court procedure over the pound of flesh
   3. Elopement of Jessica and Lorenzo

b. *Henry V*
   1. War strategy and battlefield scenes
   2. Courtship of French-speaking Katherine by English-speaking Henry, using Alice as interpreter

c. *Hamlet*
   1. Hamlet, the ghost, and Hamlet's friends
   2. Hamlet and Ophelia
   3. The gravedigger's scene

7. Select three different types of plays suitable for P.T.A. meetings or community programs. Be sure you check the royalty situation before you begin work. Prepare a half-hour cutting of each, and cast and rehearse it thoroughly. Have them ready for public presentation whenever you may be called on. A possible repertoire might be: *The Dust of the Road* by Goodman; *Life with Father* by Clarence Day; *Cyrano de Bergerac* by Edmond Rostand.

In the preceding chapters we have been concerned with various face-to-face speech situations. In all of them an individual—the communicator—speaks, reads, or acts before a group and is both seen and heard. He works in full view of the audience. He has the advantage of seeing his audience. He is conscious of their reactions to what he says or does. Both audience and the *communicator* react to one another.

To examine how the communicator must adapt to the different situation in radio and television, we must define the term *electronic media* in relation to communication. Both radio and television depend on electronic devices to pick up, amplify, transmit, and reproduce sound and pictures. Electronics, rather than the physical presence of the speaker, is the media of communication.

With the use of these *electronic media* the communicator is removed from his audience. He cannot see them

RADIO AND TELEVISION

or hear them, and so cannot react to them. He knows nothing about them except that they have turned on the switch of a radio or television set. There may be only a few hundred people in the audience (in the case of a small, local station) or there may be millions for a national network program. It is not the size of the audience that is important but its distribution. The audience consists of many small home groups with not more than three or four persons in each group.

In radio the communicator is not seen by the audience; only his voice is heard. In television he is seen and heard. In both cases he comes as a guest and not as an intruder. The communicator who fails to visualize and adapt to this intimate relationship will find himself unwelcome.

There is a further difference between the small groups that make up this audience and the single large group that gathers in an auditorium. The home audience is easily distracted and can move at will, leave the room or turn off the program. They often talk to each other while the program is on. In an auditorium or theatre there are fewer distractions. It is not easy to get up and walk out nor is it socially acceptable to talk during the performance. The communicator who depends on electronic media must use all his skill to gain and hold his audience's attention.

RADIO

Your first appearance in a radio studio can be an exciting but unsettling experience. Usually you get the impression you are in a deserted room in which there are no chairs at all, or many folding chairs scattered in disordered groups. There may be a table with a microphone and several standing microphones, and a bewildering number of cables to trip over. Everyone but you seems to know what to do.

Remember this is an electronic medium. The engineers, the director and the station personnel are there to handle the technical details and you need not concern yourself with them. Your responsibility is to stand or sit where you are told, and concentrate on what you are going to say and watch for a few simple signals.

Few radio studios are much bigger than the average living room, and most are smaller. The physical conditions are not important. The microphone is the communicator's sole contact with his audience. Sometimes there is a small audience in the studio, but it is only incidental and should be disregarded by the communicator unless it is there to provide reactions such as laughter in a comedy program. The studio is separated from the control room by a soundproof glass window. In large radio stations an engineer and a director (or studio announcer) may be in the control room. In smaller stations one man will function as announcer-director-engineer. The communicator is briefed by a control-room director before broadcast time. He describes visual cues or signals that will be used. There will be the raising of the right arm, a few seconds before air time and the abrupt dropping of the arm as the "You're On Now" cue. There may be a two-handed signal: arms held out, fingers meeting and slowly pulling away to denote "slow down"; and for "speed up," two hands again, held in front and rolling over and over one another. They are graphic and their meaning cannot easily be misunderstood; the radio speaker learns to keep his eyes on the control room. He must remember that in radio, all directions are given visually, since the microphone would broadcast all vocal directions.

Once you have been briefed by the director, he returns to the control room and speaks to you through a talk-back speaker in the studio. He will ask you to say a few words into the microphone. Say something you expect to use in performance. If you plan a wide variation in intensity and/or volume, mention it so he will be ready for it. Don't try to outguess him. He will tell you if you are not coming over satisfactorily and suggest you move closer to or farther away from the microphone. Try to remember the distance. If it is not right he will signal you to move.

If there is theme music, or musical selections, within the show, you

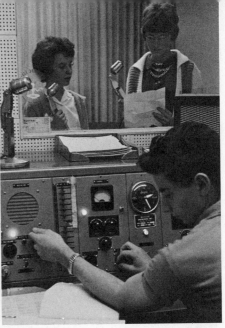

will hear them through the same speaker. But you are still "on the air," and all unnecessary foot shuffling, paper shuffling (even face scratching) must be avoided.

In speaking on radio, you may be talking to one or more people in the studio, as in an interview or discussion, or you may be alone with your radio audience. (Which one famous announcer once called the "audio radiance.")

Let us suppose the program on which you take part is a discussion with one other person who stands on the other side of the microphone. Talking directly to the person, you express yourself facially and with gestures to help your voice become free and natural and encourage him to react. The microphone cannot smile, shake its head, or answer a question; the person can and will. If you are alone in the studio, imagine the microphone is your friend. It can be, in your mind, a specific person to whom you speak naturally or it can be "mike," as it is to many professionals.

Although the radio speaker is not seen by his audience and communicates by his voice alone, he should never forget that bodily response is important and adds variety and vitality to his voice. Response to imagery affects the muscle tone of the whole body and so affects the voice and all vocal techniques. Use your body and voice together as you do in any other speaking situation. But be careful not to move out of the area where the microphone picks up your voice.

The radio speaker uses imagery exactly as an interpreter does when it is in the material he presents.

But you may not talk about something that makes an appeal to the senses. You may talk with another person about a political matter, but you are really talking to your unseen audience. How do you do it? The answer is in the word "talk." Arthur Godfrey, once said that his *real* audience consisted of only one person, and that was the only one he talked to. This belief lies at the heart of all communication in radio or television. Your audience is really just one person to whom you direct your performance. It is this *conversational tone* that appeals to the "one listener." Conversational tone is the result of many factors but the most important are mental directness, a strong desire to communicate, and an awareness of the one-listener-and-you relationship. If a script is needed for exact timing, you handle it as an interpreter does. Whether you use a script or not, you are reaching out with your mind to one listener, but you do not need to project vocally or physically in order to reach a back row.

While all speakers should develop the ability to listen critically to themselves, the radio speaker must depend almost entirely on his own ear to correct any errors in vocal technique.

A trained ear is as important to the speaker, reader, or actor as it is to the musician. A deaf person's voice is dull and lifeless because he can't hear himself. Speech scientists have established a correlation between certain hearing disorders and speech problems. Even though your hearing is normal in ability to pick up sounds, there are wide variations in ability to discriminate between sounds. The radio speaker who cannot interpret a sound as being "right" or "wrong" has a great deal of trouble communicating what is "right" for the situation.

TELEVISION

In television, there is a microphone, and one or more cameras. There will be many more cables on the floor and chalked "x" marks to show you where to stand when you're "on camera." There are people setting lights, moving sets, giving directions, putting on make-up, and the thousand and one things it takes to produce a television program.

The popularity of television as an entertainment medium has produced a number of program types. Because of the high cost and demands on station time, local talent can't easily be featured on television programs. But the interview and discussion programs give opportunities for high-school students, particularly on local stations.

484

The most important thing to understand about television is that it is *not* radio with pictures. The two techniques are very different. When people can *see* what is happening they become impatient if they are also *told* what is happening. In the early days of television this mistake was general. It can still be found in many instructional films now being shown.

The ability to see what is going on has made it necessary for television to adopt a kind of *visual grammar* similar to that used in films. It is a way of organizing the pictures much as you organize words.

We communicate with one another through words that we combine into phrases and sentences. Just as the individual word is basic to the language, television's individual picture or shot is the basic and fundamental unit of visual grammar.

In television (and films) a shot consists of one uninterrupted segment of action. The shot ends when a new one takes its place. During the shot the actors may move around, the camera may follow them, and a good deal of action may take place. But when a different camera position is needed to get a new view of the actor or the scene and the director uses a different camera, then a change to a new shot is made. Consider the following succession of shots:

Shot #1   Camera 1   View of house and front yard and a man walking up the front walk.

Shot #2   Camera 2   View of front door as man walks up to it.

Shot #3   Camera 1   Close-up of lock as he unlocks door.

Shot #4   Camera 2   View of front door and man as he opens door to enter.

Shot #5   Camera 3   View from inside the house as the man walks in.

If these five shots were viewed separately they wouldn't mean anything, but when put together a story is told: a man comes home to his own house. What if we just saw the close-up of a key being put in a lock? It might be a burglar. But with the shots put together we have a *visual sentence* that has only one meaning.

A television program is made up of many shots, and each is separated by means of a transition. A transition is a method of getting from one shot to the other.

The most common type of transition is a *cut.* This is a split-second switch from one picture to another. Between each of the five shots of the man entering his house, a cut could be used. In general, when an action takes place at the same time and in the same place, cuts are used between shots. When there is a change of time or place, a *dissolve* is often used. Dissolves are accomplished by fading one picture while strengthening the other picture. By cutting or dissolving from shot to shot, the television director gives movement and rhythm to his program as a speaker or interpreter gives movement and rhythm to his reading by varying his rate of speaking, and by tonal variations in his voice.

There are three basic methods of television presentation. The first, and the one with which you would be involved if you appear on television, is live production. The program goes on the air at the same time it is produced in the studio. The second is a taped broadcast that uses a recording device, *Videotape,* to capture the sound and picture on a plastic tape that can be reproduced through the recorder at any time. A Videotape recorder is like an ordinary tape recorder except that it records the picture as well as the sound, and it is larger and more complicated.

The third uses a film similar to those in a motion-picture theater or a classroom. These films are not produced in the television station over which they are broadcast, but are made by independent companies.

Both live and Videotape productions are produced in television studios, and, whichever is used, the problems of television communication are the same. To appreciate the complicated problems that must be met in television and how the techniques of the medium affect your job, you should know something about the equipment and the people who work with it.

Television Equipment

The most important piece of equipment in the studio is the camera. In a small studio it is mounted on a wheeled pedestal that can be moved smoothly and silently any place in the studio. Large studios have cameras on cranes that can lift the camera above the set.

A television camera has several lenses. If your part of the program involves looking at your unseen audience you should know that it is the top lens in the circle of lenses that is taking your picture. If you look into one of the other lenses the viewing audience will see that you are not looking at them.

There are one or two small red lights on the front of the camera. These are *tally* lights. It is very important that the performer know which

of the two or three cameras pointed at him is actually photographing him. If he is speaking directly to his unseen audience rather than playing a scene with another actor, he faces the camera with the tally light on.

Another piece of equipment is the boom microphone. Television performers move around a great deal and this microphone is on a long, mobile boom that can follow the performers. The boom is operated by a boom man who uses a silent crank to extend or retract the long projectile with the microphone. It is his responsibility to keep it in the right place all the time. In using radio you stay within the microphone range. In television, the microphone follows you and you trust the boom man and speak at your normal volume and avoid dropping your head.

Over the set are the lights that illuminate the scene. Two types of lights are used: spots or Fresnels, and scoops or area lights.

Theater and television lighting are very similar. The difference lies in the fact that television needs more light and that the varying angles from which shots are made makes lighting much more difficult.

Then every studio has a *monitor*. This is mounted on casters for ease in moving and looks much like your television set at home. The monitor has many uses. A good example is the newscaster who must describe what is going on in a film used on his program. He has to see the action, and he watches it on a monitor which shows the same picture going out on the air.

487

If you are on television, firmly resist the temptation to steal a look at yourself on the monitor. This will divert your eyes away from that all-important camera lens, or from the person to whom you are talking. It is almost sure to distract you, break your train of thought, and lessen your effectiveness.

Studio Personnel

All this equipment would be so much glass and metal if it were not for the people who operate it. For each camera there is a cameraman who takes the shots, changes the lenses, and focuses the camera. The boom man follows the performer with his microphone, and the floor men move sets and arrange furniture and properties.

The most important person in the studio is the floor manager. Like all members of the technical crew, he wears earphones and a small microphone, called a *PL*. Through the PL each man on the crew keeps in constant communication with the director in the control room. The radio director is limited to visual signals through the control-room window, but the television director can speak directly to the members of the technical crew.

The Control Room

In television the control room is not always visually connected with the studio. The television studio provides its director with the pictures as they are taken by the cameras. He sees them on control room monitors. He has one monitor for each camera lined up in front of him. Each camera has a number that corresponds to its control room monitor, so the director gives his orders by number to each camera. For example: "Camera 1, get a close-up of the lock on the front door." There is another monitor called the "master." The picture shown by this monitor is the one that goes out over the air. It is the television director's responsibility to select one of these shots to be put on the air. He may have as few as two or as many as six pictures to choose from. In the selection and arrangement of these pictures the director does his work through the use of the visual grammar of television.

Depending on the size of the station, the director may do the actual "punching" of buttons to select the pictures, or he may have a technical director who selects the pictures. Then it is the technical director who punches the correct shots into the monitor and out over the air.

488

There is also an audio engineer in the control room. It is his job to turn the microphone on and off, and adjust the volume of sound coming from the studio, handle musical selections, and even sound effects.

All control-room personnel wear PLs and all are in communication with one another. The floor manager is the director's right-hand man in the studio. People who work in television watch him for all directions that come from the control room.

Television is a complicated medium of communication, and the people who work in it are highly skilled. Amateurs who make a television debut in such studios do a much better job when they know something about the medium before they come into actual contact with it.

Television Performance

When television was first used by politicians in campaigns most of those who appeared before the camera used the same public-speaking techniques they had used on the platform. They thought they were talking to millions of people when they were *really* talking to small groups looking at many individual sets. It took them years to discover that the intimacy of television required them to speak naturally. Gestures and facial expressions that worked well in front of large groups appeared unnatural and exaggerated through television's eye.

If you appear in a television play, remember that the camera may be but a few feet away when it shoots a close-up of your head and shoulders. The slightest gesture, the smallest change in expression, is picked up and transmitted. The best stage actors have had to modify their performances when they appear on television. Expressions and actions which add vitality on the stage become artificial on the television screen. Since the microphone is suspended just out of sight over the actor's head, he does not raise his voice above conversational level.

Television acting is like film acting except that in live television presentation the actor has the advantage of a continuous performance: that is, he develops his part through the whole drama from beginning to end, rather than breaking it into bits and pieces as he must do in making a film.

Finally, as a participant in an interview or discussion program you may never look directly at the camera but carry on the conversation with your interviewer or group. In this case the viewing audience is eavesdropping on your conversation and would feel awkward if someone suddenly looked at them. The moderator of the discussion can and often does communicate directly with the audience.

If you are in doubt, in a given situation, whether or not to look at the camera, ask yourself the question: "If I were in their living room, would I look at them?" When you think about it this way it is clear that if you are acting in a play with other actors you wouldn't look at them. If you were giving an oral reading, you would look at them. If you were making a speech, you would look at them. It is important for the communicator to understand these distinctions.

In conclusion, everything you have learned about good communication applies directly to television. It is a medium that searches out, and finds, the truth in a performer's art. If the performer expresses himself forcefully and honestly, then the audience sees him as alive, and his message will have meaning. He will reach the minds and hearts of his audience as well as their eyes and ears.

ACTIVITIES

1. Write a thirty-second radio commercial. Double space your script to allow room for marking it in some way to guide you in phrasing, stressing important words, and changing pitch. Play up the best features of your product, but do not make ridiculous and exaggerated claims. Time the script carefully—thirty seconds! Record all commercials on your tape recorder and play them back for evaluation as to conversational tone, smoothness, enthusiasm, and salesmanship. Have one member of the class serve as director, to cue in the announcers, and one member serve as timekeeper.

2. Memorize your commercial and present it as a television broadcast, either to a small group or to the whole class. Have one member serve as the cameraman. Focus your attention on him while giving your commercial. Be gracious, friendly, and enthusiastic. If possible, use visual aids.

3. Divide the class into groups of five and develop a series of five-minute newscasts, the first person handles the international news of the day; the second, national, the third, local; the fourth, sports; and the fifth is the announcer, who is master of ceremonies for the entire program. He identifies the newscasters and signs off. To fill exactly five minutes, this fifth member of the team may have a human interest item (or, possibly, a weather story) ready to give at the end of the entire newscast. Rotate the assignment until each student has served in three capacities.

4. Plan a "special events" program as if it would be done "on the spot"; that is, broadcast while the event is actually happening. Boys can prepare a play-by-play account of an imaginary athletic event—a ball game, a track meet, or

a wrestling match. Choose a sport with which you are familiar, work in groups, if you prefer, and take turns announcing. Prepare in advance a script giving the information you will need about the event: the setting; the names, and positions, and other statistics of the participants; the lineup; previous records; titles at stake; and similar facts to make the broadcast exciting and easy to follow. Do not write a complete script but depend on your imagination and knowledge of the game to enable you to ad lib as the imaginary event proceeds. Set your own time limit—say, ten minutes—and stick to it.

Some girls may want to handle a sportscast. Others may prepare a TV style show by selecting and mounting a series of pictures of the latest styles, which an assistant holds for display as you describe them—their cut, their general attractiveness, their versatility, colors available, and approximate price. Write your script on cards, numbering each description so it corresponds with the garment being shown. Memorize your script, so that your voice and manner is gracious, informal, and direct. Again, set your own time limit and stick to it.

5. Working in pairs, plan a radio or television interview with a famous personality, a politician, an athlete, a theater director, a writer, a musician, an artist, or an educator. Write part of your script, the lead-in, the main questions, and some of the answers, using actual facts that, from your research, you know to be true. One person acts as the interviewer and the other as the famous person. Be sure to use ad-lib comments and conversational style. Keep repeating the names of both participants, the interviewer and interviewee.

6. Plan a fifteen-minute simulated broadcast, consisting of dramatized material, such as a conversational commercial and a scene from a play, explained briefly during the lead-in by the narrator to make the story clear. The format might be as follows:

Station break:
Billboard:

Dramatized or conversational commercial:

Lead-in of play:
The play
Signing off

time and station identification
announcement of what the program will be and who the sponsor is
advertisement of sponsor's product
Title, playwright, cast, situation

7. Use your microphone backstage and your public address amplifier out front, or give a demonstration talk on the use of sound effects in radio drama. Do research on the subject, both in the library and at your local radio stations.

8. Plan a fifteen-minute television show for children, using puppets or marionettes, or characters dressed as animals. Dramatize famous stories most children know.

9. Use scripts from your library, available for classroom use, and cast and present an educational show, perhaps one dramatizing the life of a famous person or a great historical event.

BIBLIOGRAPHY

Technical Books

ALBRIGHT, H. D. *Principles of Theatre Art*. Boston: Houghton Mifflin Co., 1955.

*BAILEY, H. *ABC's of Play Production*. New York: David McKay Co., Inc., 1955.

COLE, TOBY, and CHINOY, HELEN KIRCH (eds.). *Directing the Play, A Source Book of Stagecraft*. New York: Bobbs-Merrill Co., Inc., 1953.

*CORNBERG, SOL, and GEBAUER, EMANUEL L. *A Stage Crew Handbook*. New York: Harper & Brothers, 1957.

DIETRICH, JOHN E. *Play Direction*. Englewood Cliffs, N.J.: Prentice-Hall, Inc., 1953.

*GASSNER, JOHN. *Producing the Play*. New York: Henry Holt and Co., Inc., 1953.

*GRUVER, BERT. *The Stage Manager's Handbook*. New York: Harper & Brothers, 1953.

*SOBEL, BERNARD. *The New Theatre Handbook and Digest of Plays*. New York: Crown Publishers, Inc., 1959.

Acting

*BOLESLOVSKY, RICHARD. *Acting: The First Six Lessons*. New York: Theatre Arts Books, 1937.

*COLE, TOBY, and CHINOY, HELEN KIRCH. *Actors on Acting*. New York: Crown Publishers, Inc., 1954.

*FRANKLIN, MIRIAM. *Rehearsal: Principles and Practice of Acting for the Stage* (3rd ed.). Englewood Cliffs, N.J.: Prentice-Hall, Inc., 1950.

*McGAW, CHARLES. *Acting Is Believing*. New York: Rinehart and Co., 1955.

STANISLAVSKY, KONSTANTIN. *Building a Character*. New York: Theatre Arts Books, 1949.

STRICKLAND, F. C. *The Technique of Acting*. New York: McGraw-Hill Book Co., Inc., 1956.

Scenery

*FRIEDERICH, WILLARD J., and FRASER, JOHN H. *Scenery Design for the Amateur Stage*. New York: The Macmillan Co., 1950.

*HEFFNER, HUBERT C., and others. *Modern Theatre Practice* (4th ed.). New York: Appleton-Century-Crofts, Inc., 1958.

PHILIPPI, HERBERT. *Stagecraft and Scene Design*. Boston: Houghton Mifflin Co., 1953.

SELDEN, SAMUEL, and SELMAN, HUNTON D. *Stage Scenery and Lighting* (3rd ed.). New York: Appleton-Century-Crofts, Inc., 1959.

Lighting

*BOWMAN, WAYNE. *Modern Theatre Lighting*. New York: Harper & Brothers, 1957.

*FUCHS, THEODORE. *Home-Built Lighting Equipment*. New York: Samuel French, Inc., 1939.

McCANDLESS, STANLEY. *A Method of Lighting the Stage* (3rd ed.). New York: Theatre Arts Books, 1954.

*RUBIN, JOEL E., and WATSON, LELAND H. *Theatrical Lighting Practice*. New York: Theatre Arts Books, 1954.

WILLIAMS, R. GILLESPIE. *The Technique of Stage Lighting*. London: Sir Isaac Pitman and Sons, 1952.

Costume and Make-up

*BAMFORD, T. W. *Practical Make-up for the Stage*. New York: Pitman Publishing Co., 1952.

*DAVENPORT, MILLIA. *Book of Costume*. New York: Crown Publishers, Inc., 1948.

*EVANS, MARY. *Costume Throughout the Ages*. (3rd ed.). Philadelphia: J. P. Lippincott Co., 1950.

LANE, YOTI. *Stage Makeup*. Minneapolis: T. S. Dennison and Co., 1961.

McJimsey, Harriet T. *Costume Selection*. New York: Burgess Publishing Co., 1956.

*Paterek, Josephine D. *Costuming for the Theatre*. Crown Publishing Co., 1959.

*Particularly suitable and useful as student reference.

DIRECTORY

American Educational Theatre Association, Dr. Robert I. Schneideman, Executive Secretary, 1925 Orrington Avenue, Evanston, Illinois. (Play lists, audio-visual material, reports of research projects in educational theater available to members and nonmembers.)

Antiquarian Bookman, Box 1100, Newark 1, New Jersey. (Will seek and probably find almost any out-of-print theater book ever published here or abroad.)

Ariel Davis Company, Inc., 3687 South State, Salt Lake City, Utah. (Useful catalog available; general lighting equipment; manufacturers of "Davis" dimmers.)

Brooks Costume Company, 3 West 61st Street, New York 23, N.Y. (Free costume plots and estimates available.)

Century Lighting, Inc., 521 West 43rd Street, New York 36, N.Y.—1840 Berkeley Street, Santa Monica, Calif. (Particularly useful catalogs and lighting charts available; custom-installation, free advice.)

Dazian's, Inc., 420 Boylston Street, Boston, Massachusetts. (Manufacturers and distributors of theatrical fabrics. Catalogs available.)

Drama Book Shop, 47 West 52nd Street, New York 19, N.Y. (Specializing in everything in print on and for the theater.)

Eaves Costume Company, Inc., 151 West 46th Street, New York 19, N.Y. (Free costume plots and estimates available.)

Hub Electric Company, 2219 West Grand Avenue, Chicago 12, Illinois. (Control boards, general lighting equipment.)

Kliegl Brothers, 321 West 50th Street, New York 19, N.Y. (Useful catalogs and lighting charts available; control systems and specialized equipment.)

Make-up Center, Inc., 80 Boylston Street, Boston, Massachusetts. (Distributors of "Stein" make-up products; make-up charts, professional equipment and assistance.)

Mutual Hardware Corporation, 141 West 53rd Street, New York 19, N.Y. (Everything in theatrical hardware; catalog available.)

National Thespian Society, College Hill Station, Cincinnati 24, Ohio. (Service organization for secondary school dramatics.)

Package Publicity Service, 247 West 46th Street, New York 36, N.Y. (Publicity materials, posters on most standard plays.)

Paramount Cosmetics and Theatrical Make-up, 431 Fifth Avenue, New York 16, N.Y. (All types of make-up supplies; "Cinabex" color media; special effects.)

Rosco Laboratories, 367 Hudson Avenue, Brooklyn, New York. (Colored gelatins and plastic sheets; color sampler available.)

Theatre Production Service, 52 West 46th Street, New York 19, N.Y. (Properties, scenery, special effects, projection equipment; free catalogs and advice.)

Van Horn and Son, 232 North 11th Street, Philadelphia 7, Penna. (Free costume plots and estimates available.)

ACKNOWLEDGMENTS

The authors and the publisher are grateful to those who contributed materials for the illustration program. The following is a list of sources of illustrative materials.

vi—James Ballard; 4—Peace Corps Photograph by Paul Conklin; Peace Corps Photograph by Rowland Scherman; Peace Corps Photograph by Ray Witlin from Black Star; 6—Wayne Miller, Magnum Photos; Max Tharpe; 7—Wayne Miller, Magnum Photos; 11—Photos by Kosti Ruohomaa from Black Star; 12—Ray Shorr from Black Star; United Press International Photos; Walter Saunders from Black Star; 13—United Press International Photos; 14—United Press International Photos; 15—United Press International Photos; 23—Max Tharpe; 24—Herb Comess; 25—Herb Comess; 27—Wayne Miller, Magnum Photos; 34—Herb Comess; 37—Max Tharpe; Harold J. Finke; 38—Max Tharpe; 41—Herb Comess; 42—Black Star; 43—Black Star; 44—Wayne Miller, Magnum Photos; Herb Comess; 46—Photo Courtesy of Chicago's American; 50—Herb Comess; Wayne Miller, Magnum Photos; 51—Max Tharpe; 52—Herb Comess; W. B. Nickerson; 57—Max Tharpe; 59—Wayne Miller, Magnum Photos; 62—Photos by Hays, Monkmeyer Press Photo Service; Merrim, Monkmeyer Press Photo Service; 65—Hays, Monkmeyer Press Photo Service; 67—Herb Comess; 72—Hays, Monkmeyer Press Photo Service; 77—Harold M. Lambert; 81—Hays, Monkmeyer Press Photo Service; Herb Comess; Sybil Shelton, Monkmeyer Press Photo Service; 94—Hays, Monkmeyer Press Photo Service; Harold M. Lambert; Sybil Shelton, Monkmeyer Press Photo Service; 99—A. Devaney, Inc., New York; 102—Hays, Monkmeyer Press Photo Service; Sybil Shelton, Monkmeyer Press Photo Service; 107—Max Tharpe; 111—Hays, Monkmeyer Press Photo Service; 113—Herb Comess; 115—Hays, Monkmeyer Press Photo Service; 116—Herb Comess; 117—Harold M. Lambert; 126—Herb Comess; 128—Hays, Monkmeyer Press Photo Service; 131—Hays, Monkmeyer Press Photo Service; Sybil Shelton, Monkmeyer Press Photo Service; 134—Wayne Miller, Magnum Photos; 139—A. Devaney, Inc., New York; W. B. Nickerson; 141—Wayne Miller, Magnum Photos; Hays, Monkmeyer Press Photo Service; 144—Herb Comess; Sybil Shelton, Monkmeyer Press Photo Service; 145—Sybil Shelton, Monkmeyer Press Photo Service; United Press International Photo; 152—Hays, Monkmeyer Press Photo Service; 154—Herb Comess; 155—Herb Comess; 156—Harold J. Finke; 158—Max Tharpe; Herb Comess; 169—Wayne Miller, Magnum Photos; 186—H. Armstrong Roberts; 189—Hays, Monkmeyer Press Photo Service; Sybil Shelton, Monkmeyer Press Photo Service; 197—Ross Madden from Black Star; H. Armstrong Roberts; 208—Hays, Monkmeyer Press Photo Service; 209—Herb Comess; 220—W. B. Nickerson; 221—W. B. Nickerson; 230—Herb Comess; 236—Hays, Monkmeyer Press Photo Service; 239—Herb Comess; 246—James Ballard; 250—Herb Comess; 253—Herb Comess; 256—Max Tharpe; 261—The Bettman Archive; 269—The Bettman Archive; 271—The Bettman Archive; 272—Don Ornitz, Globe Photos; 275—Don Ornitz, Globe Photos; 277—The Bettman Archive; Don Ornitz, Globe Photos; 279—Don Ornitz, Globe Photos; 281—Don Ornitz, Globe Photos; The Bettman Archive; 283—Don Ornitz, Globe Photos; The Bettman Archive; 289—Don Ornitz, Globe Photos; 294—Don Ornitz, Globe Photos; The Bettman Archive; 299—Don Ornitz, Globe Photos; 300—Dennis Stock, Magnum Photos; 307—Globe Photos; 316—Dennis Stock, Magnum Photos; 319—The Bettman Archive; 323—Robert L. Campbell; 327—Herb Comess; 332—New York Public Library; 333—New York Public Library; 354—James Ballard; 357—Friedman-Abeles; 362—The Bettman Archive; 372—Friedman-Abeles; 376—Friedman-Abeles; 377—Friedman-Abeles; 381—Friedman-Abeles; 384—Friedman-Abeles; 390—Friedman-Abeles; 391—Friedman-Abeles; 394—Friedman-Abeles; 396—The Bettman Archive; 397—The Bettman Archive; 399—Erich Hartmann, Magnum Photos; Friedman-Abeles; 401—United Press International Photo; 402—James Ballard; 411—James Ballard; Dennis Stock, Magnum Photos; 420—Herb Comess; 428—Friedman-Abeles; 429—Friedman-Abeles; 431—Friedman-Abeles; 433—Herb Comess; 435—The Bettman Archive; 436—William Read Woodfield, Globe Photos; 438—William Read Woodfield, Globe Photos; 439—William Read Woodfield, Globe Photos; 442—Don Ornitz, Globe Photos; Kobrin, Globe Photos; 443—Kobrin, Globe Photos; 449—New York Public Library; 450—James Ballard; 456—James Ballard; 466—Herb Comess; 470—Herb Comess; 471—Herb Comess; 474—Herb Comess; James Ballard; 475—James Ballard; 478—Erich Hartmann, Magnum Photos; 483—Max Tharpe; Wayne Miller, Magnum Photos; 487—Elliott Erwitt, Magnum Photos; Silhouette Photos in Part I, James Ballard.

Cover—Design, James Minnick; Photos, James Ballard.
Design—James Minnick.
Typography—Mary Ann Dorr.

494

INDEX

496

3 4 5 6 7 8 9 10 11 12 13 14 15 16 17 18 19 20 21 22 23 24 25   A   75 74 73 72 71 70 69 68 67 66